Foundations of Customer Service

LOMA (Life Office Management Association, Inc.) is an international association founded in 1924. LOMA is committed to a business partnership with its worldwide members in the insurance and financial services industry to improve their management and operations through quality employee development, research, information sharing, and related products and services. Among LOMA's activities is the sponsorship of the FLMI Education Program—an educational program intended primarily for home office and branch office employees.

The *Associate, Customer Service (ACS) Program* is designed to meet the specific customer service education needs of employees in the financial services industry. To earn the ACS designation, students must complete one of the ACS Program Tracks outlined in LOMA's most current *Education and Training Catalog*. Upon successful completion of the required courses, students receive a diploma awarded by LOMA and are entitled to use the letters ACS after their name.

The *Professional, Customer Service (PCS)* Program builds on the fundamentals in the ACS Program by providing students with a more detailed understanding of customer service within the financial services industry. To earn the PCS designation, students must complete the ACS Program and the required PCS courses outlined in LOMA's most current *Education and Training Catalog*. Upon successful completion of the required courses, students receive a diploma awarded by LOMA and are entitled to use the letters PCS after their name.

Statement of Purpose: LOMA Educational Programs Testing and Designations

Examinations described in the *LOMA Education and Training Catalog* are designed solely to measure whether students have successfully completed the relevant assigned curriculum, and the attainment of the FLMI and other LOMA designations indicates only that all examinations in the given curriculum have been successfully completed. In no way shall a student's completion of a given LOMA course or attainment of the FLMI or other LOMA designation be construed to mean that LOMA in any way certifies that student's competence, training, or ability to perform any given task. LOMA's examinations are to be used solely for general educational purposes, and no other use of the examinations or programs is authorized or intended by LOMA. Furthermore, it is in no way the intention of the LOMA Curriculum and Examinations staff to describe the standard of appropriate conduct in any field of the insurance and financial services industry, and LOMA expressly repudiates any attempt to so use the curriculum and examinations. Any such assessment of student competence or industry standards of conduct should instead be based on independent professional inquiry and the advice of competent professional counsel.

Foundations of Customer Service

Mark Adel, FLMI, PCS, AIRC, PAHM
Barbara Foxenberger Brown, FLMI, ACS, AIAA, AIRC

Information in this text may have been
changed or updated since its publication date.
For current updates, visit www.loma.org.

 LOMA's Associate, Customer Service Program
Atlanta, Georgia
www.loma.org

Information That Works

PROJECT TEAM:

Authors:	Mark Adel, FLMI, PCS, AIRC, PAHM Barbara Foxenberger Brown, FLMI, ACS, AIAA, AIRC
Manuscript Editor:	Gene Stone, FLMI, ACS, CLU
Project Manager:	Jena L. Kennedy, FLMI, ALHC, ACS, PAHM, CLU
Production/Editorial Manager:	Stephen Bollinger
Copyeditor:	Jennifer Burns
Permissions Editor:	Iris F. Hartley, FLMI, ALHC
Index:	Robert D. Land, FLMI, ACS
Print Buyer:	Audrey M. Gregory
Production/Print Coordinator:	Amy Souwan
Cover/Interior Design:	Allison Ayers Stephen Bollinger
Administrative Support:	Aurelia Kennedy-Hemphill

Library of Congress Cataloging-in-Publication Data
Brown, Barbara Foxenberger.
    Foundations of customer service / Barbara Foxenberger Brown, Mark Adel.
      p. cm.
    Includes index.
    ISBN 1-57974-175-4
    1. Customer services. 2. Customer relations. I. Adel, Mark, 1953-II. Title.

HF5415.5 .B762 2003
658.8'12--dc21

2001038961

ISBN 1-57974-175-4
Printed in the United States of America

In memory of our colleague and friend, Caroline W. Sundberg, who coauthored a prior edition of this text. Caroline's courageous and joyful spirit will be with us always.

CONTENTS

PREFACE

To be successful in today's highly competitive financial services market, a company must have an excellent reputation and must offer its customers the products they want at prices they are willing to pay. Although many factors contribute to this formula for success, none is more important than exceptional customer service. Why? Because without customers there is no company. For the most part, a financial services company's reputation is built on day-to-day interactions with its customers, and the quality of its products is determined by the quality of its services. Exceptional customer service is an investment that pays continuous dividends in customer retention and additional business, enabling a company to offer competitive prices and outstanding value. Increasingly, customers decide whether to do business with a company based on their interactions with service providers and on the company's ability to deliver exceptional customer service.

Foundations of Customer Service provides a thorough introduction to the knowledge, skills, and perspective every person in a financial services company needs to work effectively with customers.

In this text, we help you understand the importance of customer service to you, your company, and the financial services industry. We discuss how a company and its service providers work together to ensure that customers are satisfied and delighted by the people who serve them. We explore what motivates your customers, what expectations they have, and how their expectations are based on their perceptions of you and the service you provide. We explain basic communication techniques that can improve your ability to communicate verbally and nonverbally, in person, on the telephone, in writing, and through electronic media. We show you ways to improve your listening skills and your ability to understand customers, and we teach you the basic steps in interacting with customers and dealing with upset customers. We show you how customer service is planned, organized, and implemented at the organizational level, and we examine the processes and technologies that are so important to providing exceptional customer service. Finally, we offer you tools to help you meet the challenges that accompany a job in customer service.

In this text, several features are designed to provide you with a variety of perspectives on customer service.

- **Figures.** We include figures to depict the information provided in the text.

- **Insights.** We include articles about current developments in customer service to illustrate concepts in the text.

- **Exercises.** We provide activities to help you strengthen your understanding of the information provided in the text.

In addition, the interactive CD, *Practicing Your Customer Service Skills*, that accompanies this text is designed to help you strengthen your understanding of the concepts and skills presented in the text. Included on the CD are exercises that allow you to listen to customer service interactions and then respond to questions about those interactions. You may choose to review the CD exercises after you read each chapter, or to review the exercises for all chapters after you have read the entire text. The *Practicing Your Customer Service Skills* CD is a fun, interactive way to enhance and improve your customer service expertise.

This course is designed to prepare students for LOMA's ACS 100 examination. Each chapter includes learning objectives and key terms and concepts designed to help you organize your studies.

- **Learning Objectives.** On the first page of each chapter, you will find a list of learning objectives to help you focus your studies. Before reading each chapter, review these learning objectives. Then, as you read the chapter, look for material that will help you meet the learning objectives.

- **Key Terms and Concepts.** This text assumes that you have a basic knowledge of terms and concepts associated with financial services products. Key terms that relate to our discussion of customer service appear in **boldface italics** when they are first used and defined in the text. For your convenience, a list of the key terms and concepts in each chapter can be found at the end of the chapter. All key terms are defined in the glossary at the end of this text.

In addition, LOMA's *Test Preparation Guide for ACS 100* (TPG) helps students prepare for the ACS 100 examination. Used with the textbook, the TPG will help you master the course material. Included in the TPG are practice exam questions for each chapter, a full-scale sample examination in both paper and electronic format, and answers to all of the questions in the TPG. LOMA recommends that you use all of the study aids available for this course. Studies indicate that students who use LOMA study aids perform significantly better on LOMA examinations than students who do not use study aids.

The TPG may be revised periodically. To ensure that you are studying from the correct text, check the current LOMA Education and Training Catalog for a description of the texts assigned for the examination for which you are preparing.

Foundations of Customer Service is the capstone course required to earn LOMA's Associate, Customer Service (ACS) designation. The ACS is the foundation for earning LOMA's advanced level customer service designation, Professional, Customer Service (PCS).

Acknowledgments

Many people have contributed to the publication of *Foundations of Customer Service*. Here, we would like to offer our thanks to all of them.

This text incorporates and builds on the excellent work of Jo Ann S. Appleton, FLMI, ALHC, HIA, CEBS, Senior Associate, Education and Training, Richard Bailey, FLMI, Kenneth Huggins, FLMI/M, and Dani L. Long, FLMI, ALHC, the authors of *Customer Service in Insurance: Improving Your Skills*, Second Edition. It also incorporates and builds on the excellent work of Kenneth Huggins, Dani L. Long, and Caroline W. Sundberg, FLMI, ACS, AIAA, the authors of *Customer Service in Insurance: Principles and Practices*, Second Edition. We wish to express our appreciation to these authors and to the industry reviewers who contributed their time and expertise to these outstanding textbooks.

Textbook Development Panel

We had the great privilege and pleasure of working with an extremely knowledgeable, reliable, and hard-working group of industry experts who served on our textbook development panel. They guided us in the development of the course outline, provided valuable suggestions for material to be included in the course, and carefully reviewed and made recommendations to improve each chapter of the book. Our sincere thanks and appreciation go to

- Shelby Jean Ayers, ACS, Realtor, Junior Accountant 1, Legacy Marketing Group
- Khong Bee, Chartered Insurer, Head, Customer Service, Great Eastern Life
- Fadi Said Chammas, FLMI, ACS, AIAA, Chief Operating Officer, American Life Insurance Company—Gulf AIG
- Bonnie M. Czarny, ACS, AIAA, Supervisor, Insurance Administration, American Bar Endowment
- Angela T. de Leon, AIAA, ACS, Chairperson—Chief Representative, TANDIKA Foundation, Exclusive Representative—LOMA Indonesia
- Philbert S. Delaney, FLMI, ACS, ALHC, AIAA, Assistant Vice President, Head Office Administrative Services, Barbados Mutual Life Assurance Society
- Sharon P. Douglas, ACS, Direct Service Centre Coach, Manulife Financial
- Kang-chuan Fan, Group Strategy Development Center, Ping An Insurance Company of China
- Elizabeth Fang, Head Of Human Resources, HSBC Insurance (Asia Pacific) Holdings Limited
- Brian Ferrar, Manager, National Sales Support Center, GE Financial Assurance
- Donna L. Harden, FLMI, ALHC, HIA, ACS, AIAA, AIRC, ARA, AAPA, Compliance Coordinator, The Canada Life Assurance Company
- Winston R. Johnson, JP, CLU, FLMI/M, ACS, Training and Development Officer, Barbados Mutual Life Assurance Society
- Zern Der Kang, Associate, Society of Actuary, Manager of Strategy Development Center, Ping An Insurance Company of China
- Timothy Kuraszek, FLMI, ACS, AIRC, HIA, ALHC, Assistant Vice President—Customer Service, Bankers Life and Casualty Company
- Ann McGraw, Manager, Corporate Customer Relationship Management Center, Pan-American Life Insurance
- Paula L. Mango, FLMI, ALHC, CLU, Assistant Vice President,

Customer Services, Jefferson Pilot Financial

- Lon D. Oakley, Jr., FLMI, ACS, Director, Life Employee Engagement & CEO Support, USAA Life Insurance Company
- Sean P. O'Brien, Vice President, Administration, CGU Life of America
- Paula Pellow, FLMI, ACS, ALHC, Business Analyst, AEGON USA—The Credit Group
- Debra A. Raetz, ACS, Life/Health Producer - IL, Manager, Agency/Policy Maintenance, Celtic Insurance Co.
- Orwyn Sandiford, B. Sc., HIA, ALHC, Assistant Vice President, Group Life & Health Division, Barbados Mutual Life Assurance Society
- Michele D. Smith, FLMI, ACS, AIAA, Director, Customer Service, The Baltimore Life Companies
- Diana K. Sorrell, FLMI, ACS, Supervisor, Life Services, Ward Outsourcing Solutions, Inc.
- Connie Sousa, ACS, AIAA, Manager (Team Leader), Desjardins Financial Security
- Tamara White, ACS, Business Analyst, State Farm Mutual Insurance Co.

We'd also like to extend special thanks to the following people, who did a final review of the entire text prior to its publication: Khong Bee, Chartered Insurer, Head, Customer Service, Great Eastern Life; Timothy Kuraszek, FLMI, ACS, AIRC, HIA, ALHC, Assistant Vice President–Customer Service, Bankers Life and Casualty Company; Michele D. Smith, FLMI, ACS, AIAA, Director, Customer Service, The Baltimore Life Companies; and Diana K. Sorrell, FLMI, ACS, Supervisor, Life Services, Ward Outsourcing Solutions, Inc.

We also are grateful to Shelton Chellappah, Regional Training Director & Dean of PRUuniversity, Prudential Corporation Asia; Jeffrey R. Pike, FLMI, ALHC, ACS, Director–West Operations, Transamerica Reinsurance; and Robert C. Krokenberger, Jr., for reviewing the course outline and providing helpful comments in the early stages of text development.

Additional Contributors

To prepare for writing *Foundations of Customer Service*, we met with many industry professionals who had recently completed LOMA's ACS 100 course. Our focus group discussions with these students helped shape the overall content and presentation of the text. For providing us with this valuable information and guidance, we would very much would like to thank

- Nelson A. Acain, FLMI, ACS, Health Underwriter, Bankers Life and Casualty
- Shelby Jean Ayers, ACS, Realtor, Junior Accountant 1, Legacy Marketing Group
- Maria Bouchard, MBA, ACS, AIRC, HIA, Senior Compliance Coordinator, The Canada Life Assurance Company
- Doug Christensen, PCS, Accountant, Allstate Insurance Company
- Vaness C. Clark, FLMI, ACS, PCS, Billing Supervisor, Fort Dearborn Life Insurance Company
- Joy Cotto, ACS
- Maria Embon, ACS, Senior Claims Specialist, Munich American Reassurance Company
- Kimberly D. Flock, ACS, Supervisor, Customer Call Center, AFLAC
- Brenda A. Gregory, ACS, Senior Coordinator, Primerica Financial Services
- Donna L. Harden, FLMI, ALHC, HIA, ACS, AIAA, AIRC, ARA, AAPA, Compliance Coordinator, The Canada Life Assurance Company
- Sheila Jumper, FLMI, ACS, Group Underwriter, Fort Dearborn Life Insurance Company
- Timothy Kuraszek, FLMI, ACS, AIRC, HIA, ALHC, Assistant Vice President—Customer Service, Bankers Life and Casualty Company
- TK Lansdon, Senior Account Enrollment Executive, AFLAC
- Myrna M. Lee, ACS, AIRC, Senior Sales Specialist, AMA Insurance Agency, Inc.
- Mindy Morrison, ACS, Training Specialist, Blue Cross/Blue Shield of Illinois
- Sherrill Nobles, FLMI, ACS, Accounting Tech II, AEGON USA
- Carolyn Parks, ACS
- Nancy Pavlica, FLMI, ACS, Senior Marketing Analyst, United Insurance Company of America
- Jennifer A. Pearson, ACS, Sr. HR Service Center Representative, UnumProvident Corporation
- Paula Pellow, FLMI, ACS, ALHC, Business Analyst, AEGON

USA–The Credit Group

■ Debra A. Raetz, ACS, Life/Health Producer - IL, Manager, Agency/Policy Maintenance, Celtic Insurance Co.

■ James Savaiano, Customer Service Supervisor, AMA Insurance Agency, Inc.

■ Connie Sousa, ACS, AIAA, Manager (Team Leader), Desjardins Financial Security

■ Ellen S. Thomas, ACS, Corporate Licensing Coordinator, Primerica Financial Services

We would also like to thank the more than 1,000 ACS 100 students who, by participating in an online customer survey, helped shape the content and presentation of this text.

In addition, we are grateful to the following industry professionals who responded to our call for "real world" examples that illustrate customer service concepts:

■ Alison Andrews-Benn, Agency Secretary, Colonial Life Insurance Company (Trinidad) Limited

■ Kathy E. Brooks, Conservation Specialist, Legacy Marketing Group

■ Kirsty Edwards, ACS, AIAA, FLMI, Team Leader, Corporate Client Service Centre, London Life Insurance Co.

■ Toni W. Golden, Annuity Services Teams Trainer, AIG Annuity Insurance Co.

■ Karen Hall, AAPA, Operations Trainer, AIG Annuity Insurance Co.

■ Colleen M. LaRochelle, Client Information Center Coordinator, Berkshire Life Insurance Co. of America

■ Wendy LeGresley, Bilingual Senior Client Service Representative, London Life Insurance Co.

■ Veronica Medlin, Manager, Qualified Retirement Plan Administration, Pan-American Life Insurance

■ Ralitsa Morris, Project Analyst, SAFECO Life Insurance Co.

■ Tannis Noble, Client Service Representative, London Life Insurance Co.

■ Julie Parent, Client Service Representative, London Life Insurance Co.

■ Cécile Pelletier, Bilingual Client Service Representative, London Life Insurance Co.

■ Brad M. Phillips, Network/Desktop Manager, AIG Annuity

- Thelma Tyra, ACS, Lead Specialist, Customer Call Center, AFLAC
- Rebecca V. Welchel, Policyholder Services Phone Representative, Legacy Marketing Group

Customer Service Curriculum Committee

We would like to thank the members of LOMA's Customer Service Curriculum Committee who provided feedback about the overall direction for this course and the ACS educational program in general. The Customer Service Curriculum Committee included the following industry professionals:

- Lori Bracken, Associate Director, National Accounts, Principal Financial Group
- Angela T. de Leon, AIAA, ACS, Chairperson—Chief Representative, TANDIKA Foundation, Exclusive Representative—LOMA Indonesia
- Eric Hagerstrom, Vice President, Customer Service, Asia Region, New York Life Insurance Worldwide, Ltd.
- Kathrine Heide, FLMI, ACS, AAPA, Supervisor, Individual Communications, Standard Insurance Company
- Ann McGraw, Manager, Corporate Customer Relationship Management Center, Pan-American Life Insurance
- Michele D. Smith, FLMI, ACS, AIAA, Director, Customer Service, The Baltimore Life Companies
- Mary Suppan, Director, Guardian Life Insurance Company of America

LOMA Staff and Consultants

At LOMA, textbook development is a team project. Many LOMA staff members and consultants provided valuable contributions to this text.

Gene Stone, FLMI, ACS, CLU, Senior Associate, Education and Training, served as manuscript editor and provided valuable advice, suggestions, and assistance throughout the project. Nick Desoutter, FLMI, AAPA, Senior Associate, Education and Training and Miriam A. Orsina, FLMI, PCS, ARA, PAHM, Senior Associate, Education and Training, reviewed several chapters and made many valuable suggestions for enhancing the material. Nick Desoutter also developed the exercises and oversaw development of the interactive CD, *Practicing Your Customer Service Skills*. Gene Stone and Miriam Orsina also played essential roles in organizing and administering the focus groups and online survey that supplied customer feedback about this course and greatly shaped the development of the text.

Martha Parker, FLMI, ACS, ALHC, AIAA, Senior Associate, Education and Training, painstakingly reviewed the manuscript and made many valuable suggestions. Beth Burnett-Balga, FLMI, ALHC, ACS, AIRC, PAHM, Senior Associate, Sean Schaeffer Gilley, FLMI, ALHC, HIA, ACS, CEBS, AIAA, PAHM, MHP, Senior Associate, and David A. Lewis, FLMI, ACS, Senior Associate, also provided many valuable suggestions. Kelly W. Neeley, FLMI, ALHC, ACS, AIAA, PAHM, Senior Associate, Education and Training, Donna Dorris, FLMI, ACS, AIRC, AIAA, Senior Associate, Education and Training, and Melanie R. Green, FLMI, ACS, AIAA, Senior Associate, Education and Training, each provided valuable information and guidance about the content and presentation of the material during the early stages of text development. Susan Conant, FLMI, CEBS, HIA, PAHM, Senior Associate, Education and Training, also reviewed text material and provided valuable input about the financial services industry.

We appreciate the time and effort that Ina Allison, Ph.D., ACS, Employee Assessment Manager, Management Services Division, and Nicole Newberry, ACS, AIAA, Business Development Associate, Management Services Division, contributed to this project by sharing with us their knowledge of other LOMA customer service products and programs.

We also would like to thank Joel V. Basarich, Ph.D., FLMI, ACS, Managing Director, International Division, and other members of LOMA's International Division for the assistance and guidance they provided during the course of this project. The following people helped us recruit textbook reviewers from our member companies around the world: Xianoi Gainey, FLMI, ACS, Senior Regional Associate, Greater China; Allison Middleton, FLMI, PCS, AIAA, AIRC, FAHM, Assistant Vice President, International Division; Laura Perry-Bates, FLMI, PCS, AIAA, PAHM, Senior Regional Associate; Marie F. Prince, FLMI, ACS, Educational Associate; and Ines J. Watson Vallenilla, FLMI, ACS, Senior Education Associate. In addition, the following people reviewed a portion of the text: Kira P. Deck, FLMI, PCS, Administrative Specialist; Li-Min Hu, Chinese Education Assistant; Kasy Khaikham, ACS, FLMI, International Coordinator; Laura Perry-Bates; Marie F. Prince; Stephen Quina, International Coordinator; and Ines J. Watson Vallenilla.

The following people provided information and guidance that led to an extremely successful online survey in the early stages of textbook development: Todd Blandin, Director, Education and Training Marketing; Tom Moormann, Ph.D., FLMI, Director, Management Services Division; Cherie E. Mosley, ACS, AIAA, AIRC, CPS, Coordinator, Management Services Division; Meg Rose, FLMI, ACS, e-Business Manager; Teri L. Smith, Jr., Programmer/Analyst, Management Services Division; and Shannon R. Wortman, FLMI, PCS, AIAA, PAHM, Registrar and Manager.

Olivia Blakemore, ACS, Technical Administrator, Information Center; Mallory Eldridge, Research Analyst/Writer; and Janet Smith, Information Center Researcher, provided a wealth of research material on customer service.

Michelle Stone Weathers, ACS, former Production Manager, oversaw the early stages of the text's production process, and Stephen Bollinger, Manager, Editorial/Production, Education and Training steered the text through typesetting and the final stages of production. Amy Souwan, Production Coordinator II/Scheduling Coordinator, Education and Training, coordinated typesetting and printing of the book, and Allison Ayers, Production Coordinator II, Education and Training, helped create the book's interior design and typeset the text. Heather Adel contributed artwork to the text. Jennifer Burns copyedited the manuscript. Robert D. Land, FLMI, ACS, compiled the index. Iris F. Hartley, FLMI, ALHC, secured the necessary permissions. Audrey H. Gregory, Inventory Manager, served as print buyer. Aurelia Kennedy-Hemphill, Administrative Assistant III, Education and Training, provided support throughout the entire project.

We would also like to thank Jena L. Kennedy, FLMI, ALHC, ACS, PAHM, CLU, Assistant Vice President, Education and Training, for her commitment to developing an exceptional customer service educational program and for the direction, support, and encouragement she provided throughout this project. And, we would like to thank Katherine C. Milligan, FLMI, ACS, ALHC, Second Vice President, Education and Training, and William H. Rabel, Ph.D., FLMI, CLU, Senior Vice President, Education and Training, for their support and dedication to continually improving this course and the ACS and PCS programs.

Finally, we would like to thank you, the student—our valued customer—for reading and studying this text and for having the interest and initiative to seek to improve your customer service skills and knowledge.

Mark Adel, FLMI, PCS, AIRC, PAHM
Barbara Foxenberger Brown, FLMI, ACS, AIAA, AIRC
Atlanta, Georgia
2003

Introduction to Customer Service

After studying this chapter, you should be able to

- Define customer service and distinguish between basic customer service and value-added customer service

- Explain why providing exceptional customer service is a top priority for many financial services companies

- Distinguish between individual and organizational customers, and between external and internal customers

- Discuss intermediaries and business partners as customers of financial services companies

- Identify and describe two general categories of customer service providers

Help Wanted:

Creative thinker with outgoing personality and positive attitude to make a difference in people's everyday lives and contribute to our company's financial success ...

I f you saw this job advertisement in a newspaper, would it catch your attention? Do you think you would like working with fun, energetic professionals to assist other people, while helping a business—and your career—grow and thrive? If so, this may be the perfect job for you.

Welcome to the world of customer service.

"Wait a minute," you may be thinking, "what does creativity have to do with customer service? How do customer service providers help anyone except their own company? And what does customer service have to do with a company's finances?"

The answers are simple. Companies today are making customer service their top priority and looking for new ways to attract, retain, and delight customers. To reach their goals for providing exceptional customer service, these companies need resourceful people who can be creative and flexible when helping customers. As more and more people throughout a company begin thinking creatively and focusing on serving customers, amazing things can happen. For instance, a call from an elderly woman—who wasn't even a current customer—prompted an employee at one U.S. financial services company to contact the Red Cross, whose workers promptly went to the woman's home in upstate New York, where they found her sick, without her medicine, and freezing.[1] The employee's concern and resourcefulness may have saved the woman's life. When people believe that a company truly cares about its customers as people and not just as a source of revenue, they are likely to want to do business with that company. A greater number of customers, especially loyal customers who stay with a company for many years, translates into greater profits and financial stability for the company.

Although the reasons for providing superior customer service may be simple, the actual process of delivering such service can be more complicated. As you will learn in this book, a company must have the right people, processes, and resources to meet and exceed customers' needs and expectations. Unfortunately, because those needs and expectations continually change, providing exceptional service can be like trying to hit a moving target. Few companies, however, can afford not to at least take aim. When choosing to do business with a company, many customers consider the quality of service provided by the company to be as important as, and sometimes even more important than, the cost of the products or services they purchase from the company. Therefore, a company must provide exceptional customer service if it wants to develop and maintain positive, lasting, and profitable relationships with its customers. With determination and practice, many companies can hit the target.

To consistently deliver exceptional service, a financial services company typically relies on the combined efforts of many people from various areas within the organization. Everyone who works for a financial services firm is responsible for ensuring that customers receive high-quality service. Senior managers—who may rarely be involved in day-to-day customer service interactions—greatly affect a company's ability to provide exceptional customer service because they determine and plan the role that customer service will play in the company's overall operations and they budget the necessary resources to support that plan. Middle managers and supervisors influence customer service quality through the policies and procedures they establish to hire, organize, train, and

Everyone who works for a financial services firm is responsible for ensuring that customers receive high-quality service.

> A customer is the most important visitor in our premises. He is not dependent on us, we are dependent on him. He is not an interruption in our work, he is the purpose of it. He is not an outsider to our business, he is part of it. We are not doing him a favor by serving him, he is doing us a favor by giving us an opportunity to do so.
>
> — Mahatma Gandhi[2]

motivate employees. Obviously, front-line employees who interact directly with external customers must act courteously, quickly, and effectively to fulfill customers' needs. But even employees who may never communicate directly with a customer have an impact on the quality of a company's customer service. These employees generally work "behind the scenes" to perform administrative functions, conduct transactions, and ensure that the people who deal directly with customers have the knowledge, information, systems, and technology they need to meet customers' needs. Regardless of your position within a financial services organization, be assured that you play an important role in satisfying customers and contributing to your company's success.

In broad terms, a **customer** is any person or organization that interacts with a company. A customer may be a person, a business, a broker or agent, or even another person or department in your company. While different types of customers have different needs, all customers have the need for timely, reliable, accurate, and professional assistance from the people who serve them. No matter who your customers are or where they are located, sharpening your customer service knowledge and skills will improve your job performance, making you more valuable to your customers and, therefore, to your company.

By reading this book, you will learn the basic concepts and skills that serve as a foundation for providing exceptional customer service. You will learn what "exceptional customer service" means and how your individual contributions can help deliver it. You will understand more about customers and how to communicate and interact with them. You will see the role that customer service plays in a financial services organization, and learn about the processes, practices, and technology underlying customer service operations. Whether you are a new customer service representative dealing with customers for the first time, or an experienced professional wanting to refresh your customer skills, this book can help you improve and strengthen your customer relationships.

What Is Customer Service?

Customer service refers to the broad range of activities that a company and its employees perform to keep customers satisfied so they will continue doing business with the company and speak positively about it to other potential customers. At its most basic level, customer service involves answering customers' questions, providing requested information, and processing transactions. These activities are an integral part of any business because they connect a company to its customers. When customers purchase a product or service, they expect that someone from the company will be available to answer questions or solve problems that might arise during or after the purchase. All financial services companies provide this minimum level of service to avoid losing customers and eventually failing.

Simply performing basic customer service activities, however, does not ensure that a company is meeting its customers' needs and expectations; to effectively serve customers, a company must do these activities *well*. Companies must respond to customer questions and requests quickly, accurately, and in a professional manner. A company that is slow to respond to customers' requests or that responds in a manner that seems unprofessional or careless is not serving its customers well. Rude or uninformed company representatives, sloppy record keeping, failure to follow through on promises, and mishandled transactions are all indications of poor customer service.

Value-Added Customer Service

Companies that consistently exceed their customers' expectations for service usually offer *value-added customer service*, which consists of activities that provide customers with additional benefits that do not routinely come with the product or service

Many financial services companies deliver good basic customer service by generally providing prompt, accurate, and courteous responses to customers. But a few companies seem to excel in serving their customers, earning a reputation among customers and competitors alike as providers of outstanding service. What distinguishes exceptional customer service from ordinary customer service? Companies that consistently exceed their customers' expectations for service usually offer *value-added customer service*, which consists of activities that provide customers with additional benefits that do not routinely come with the product or service they have purchased. Providing value-added customer service involves learning what customers want and making sure they get it, and then taking whatever reasonable steps are required to consistently exceed their expectations. Figure 1-1 illustrates the difference between value-added customer service and basic customer service.

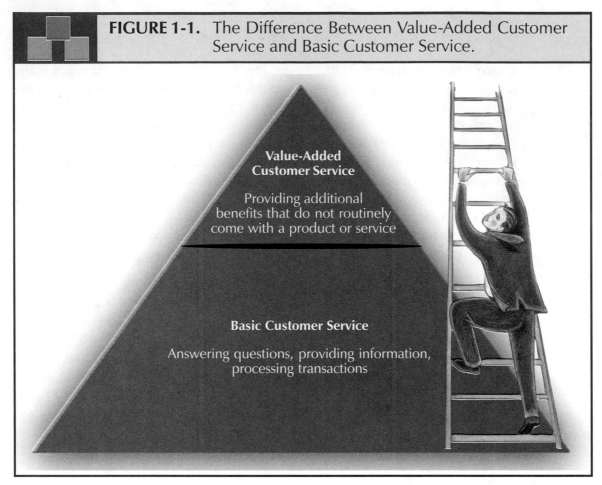

FIGURE 1-1. The Difference Between Value-Added Customer Service and Basic Customer Service.

For example, some managed health care companies enable their members to select participating health care providers via the Internet, rather than by using the traditional method of selecting a physician from a printed directory and mailing in an enrollment form. Because this feature is not offered by all plans and it makes using the plan more convenient, it is likely to be considered a value-added customer service by plan members.

On the other hand, many managed care plans also minimize the paperwork required from their members by having participating health care providers file claims directly with the insurer. Because many plans offer this service, however, customers have come to expect this activity as part of the basic customer service offered by health care plans. Generally, when customers expect a particular service from a company or industry, they will be disappointed when that service is not available, but they will take it for granted when it is available; in other words, they will not consider it to be a value-added service.

As the previous example illustrates, when more companies begin to offer a particular value-added service, customers often begin to expect that service as a matter of course when purchasing a certain product. A service that was a value-added service when first introduced can eventually become part of the basic services that customers expect. Companies committed to providing exceptional customer service continually look for new ways to add value to their service offerings.

In financial services companies, value-added customer service takes many forms. Banks, for example, provide value-added service when they establish offices with non-traditional business hours in grocery stores or other retail outlets. An insurer provides value-added customer service when it pledges to its customers that it will process customers' policy loan requests within two working days of receipt. Many investment companies offer value-added customer service by establishing Web sites through which customers can view their account balances and place buy or sell orders at any time of day or night.

By providing added value, each of these services offers an extra incentive for customers to do business with the company that provides the service. Value-added customer service activities help a company to (1) become more appealing to customers, (2) attract new customers, (3) create loyalty among existing customers, (4) create additional sales opportunities with existing customers, and (5) differentiate itself from its competitors.

The importance of providing value-added customer service cannot be overestimated. The more valuable a company is to its customers, the more likely those customers are to continue doing business with the company. One study shows that 73 percent of financial services customers who are completely satisfied with the service they receive from a company will definitely or probably purchase products from the company again, compared to 17 percent of dissatisfied customers who are likely to repurchase.[3] And, because acquiring a new customer can cost up to 20 times more than retaining an existing customer, cultivating loyalty among its current customers is in a company's best interest.[4] By providing its customers with the kinds and quality of service that they need, a company improves its chances of meeting or exceeding its bottom-line business goals.

Much of what we call "added value" is really emotional value. Include a little more attention, consideration, enthusiasm, patience, and sincerity in your interactions and you'll add your own version of value.

— JoAnna F. Brandi [5]

Through value-added customer service, a company can encourage customer loyalty by building a relationship with a customer and treating her as a person, rather than as just an account number. Many financial services firms train their employees to recognize other needs a customer might have beyond those being dealt with in the immediate transaction, and to anticipate how the firm can help meet those needs. Such attentiveness to customers' needs can help build customer loyalty. Studies show that customers who believe they receive special treatment will continue doing business with a company even if the same product or service is available elsewhere at a lower cost.[6]

In a financial services company, value-added customer service activities can include

■ Having sales representatives such as brokers or agents provide service in a customer's home or office

■ Giving a customer the name of a service representative or the direct telephone number of a customer service team that the customer can contact for any type of product or service offered by the company

■ Using Web technology or automated telephone systems to enable customers to obtain information and conduct transactions at any time of day or night

■ Using customer-focused information management systems that enable customer service providers to access all information on a single customer at one time

■ Providing fast turnaround on transactions and requests for information

■ Establishing a complaint-handling mechanism, such as a department of consumer affairs, through which customers can present their concerns and have them resolved

■ Distributing an informational customer newsletter about financial or other related issues

■ Conducting seminars on topics of interest to customers

■ Providing customers with points of contact at other organizations that can offer assistance, such as government agencies

Each time a company establishes a service like one of those just listed, the company creates an incentive for a customer to do business with the company. Insight 1-1 explains how one bank has added value to its customer service activities.

Many financial services firms train their employees to recognize other needs a customer might have beyond those being dealt with in the immediate transaction.

INSIGHT 1-1. New Information System Adds Value to Bank's Customer Service.

Recently, PNC Bank (a subsidiary of PNC Financial Services Group, Pittsburgh, Pennsylvania) launched a new branding position called, "The Thinking Behind the Money," which relies on PNC's ability to know its customers intimately to offer them insightful advice based on their needs. With this new marketing strategy, PNC recognized the need to have its traditionally separate business units work together in order to serve clients better. Consolidating customer information and allowing employees across the organization to access this information is the key factor in making PNC's market strategy work. "Customers want PNC to know everything about them and be able to see their own information in one place. They don't care about PNC's business units being separately managed," says Marian Dezelan, vice president of corporate marketing and director of e-marketing.

"The Thinking Behind the Money,"

One of the ways that PNC has worked to bridge the gap between the separate business units is with the implementation of a central data warehousing system. This system is intended to be a company-wide data warehouse that can reveal the multiple relationships that PNC has with any one customer. This information then links each of the separate business units so that account relationship managers have access to the critical information they need to serve their clients.

Given that many PNC customers want to use branch offices, making those offices convenient and reliable is important. PNC's objective is to enable all customer touch points across the enterprise to have access to the same data and customer insights. PNC's new telecom network will enable the bank to provide Web access to all customer contact personnel. According to Anuj Dhanda, CIO at PNC, the network will connect people to each other and to customers, and will provide information to all PNC employees.

One of the network's main benefits will be allowing customers to have "conversations" that can begin in one communication channel, continue in a second, and finish in a third without having to repeat or re-key any data. So, for example, if a customer starts a loan application process in a branch office with a bank employee, she can ask more questions of a telephone agent, and complete the application online. What's important is that the client's experience is seamless and convenient. "The client will see a fast, efficient process," Dhanda said. "Relevant information is right there, and this provides insight to the customer contact representative. We can cross-sell [products and services], solve problems, and provide the same level of customer intimacy in all channels."

Source: Adapted from *One to One in Retail Financial Services: New Strategies for Creating Value Through Customer Relationships* by Jonathan Brookner and Julian Beresford (Atlanta: Peppers and Rogers Group and LOMA, © 2001), 147–149. Used with permission; all rights reserved.

Moment of Truth

During a moment of truth, a customer makes a judgment about the company based on the service he has received and determines whether or not he is satisfied with the company.

Every contact between a company and a customer produces a **moment of truth**, an instant when the company has an opportunity to create a good or bad impression in the mind of the customer. During a moment of truth, a customer makes a judgment about the company based on the service he has received and determines whether or not he is satisfied with the company. A moment of truth can have a positive or negative outcome. Any company employee—but particularly those who interact directly with customers—can have a tremendous influence on a customer's moment of truth. One of the keys to providing exceptional customer service is how well employees respond to customers during each moment of truth.

For example, suppose Carlos Torres calls his credit card company and is put on hold by the company's automatic telephone system. After waiting on hold for 10 minutes, Mr. Torres becomes frustrated and begins to wonder if he should continue doing business with a company that can't answer his calls more quickly. His call is finally answered by Amelia Rashad, a customer service representative who is friendly and immediately apologizes for the long wait time, acknowledging Mr. Torres' frustration even before he expresses it. Ms. Rashad then helps Mr. Torres by answering his questions and quickly processing a transaction, and asking if she can help him with anything else. Mr. Torres says no, and Ms. Rashad once again apologizes for how long he had to wait on the phone. Mr. Torres, who had been very angry 15 minutes earlier, hangs up the phone feeling satisfied with the company.

In this scenario, the moment of truth occurred when Ms. Rashad answered Mr. Torres' call—had she seemed uncaring about his long wait and hurriedly rushed him through the call, he might have still been frustrated when the call ended. Ms. Rashad's pleasant demeanor, sincere apologies, and effective service, however, made him feel that the company cared about him as a customer, despite the long wait at the beginning of the call. Ms. Rashad greatly contributed to a positive moment of truth for Mr. Torres, resulting in a satisfied customer who is likely to continue doing business with the company and to speak favorably about it to other people.

To deliver exceptional customer service, a financial services company and its employees should strive to make every moment of truth a positive and beneficial experience for the customer. Some companies refer to a moment of truth that delights a customer as a *moment of magic*. Insight 1-2 provides an example of a moment of magic.

INSIGHT 1-2. A Moment of Magic.

Alan Baker and his wife were on a trip to visit relatives—about 1,300 miles from their home—when their vehicle was struck by a speeding motorist's car. Fortunately, Mr. Baker's car was towed to a repair shop across the street from the office of Sean Dee, an agent for American Family Insurance Company, which was Mr. Baker's insurer.

Although his office was about to close, Mr. Dee and his secretary immediately went to work to help the Bakers. Before leaving the office, Mr. Dee helped the Bakers find a rental car, contacted the Bakers' agent in their home town to obtain the necessary policy information, initiated a claim with the local claim office, authorized towing of the Bakers' vehicle to a local American Family-approved repair shop, and confirmed that the other driver had an in-force policy with another insurer. On the following day, Mr. Dee monitored the progress of the vehicle's tow into the repair shop and made sure the Bakers had a repair shop estimate within two days.

In a letter to American Family, Mr. Baker stated: "Although the unfortunate chain of events surrounding the accident pretty much ruined our trip, it was a pleasure to meet Agent Dee. When traveling, it is certainly reassuring to know caring, capable people like Agent Dee are available to help, thousands of miles away from home. Agent Dee is a very fine representative of your company. His attitude and actions in my time of need certainly have reinforced my decision to do business with American Family Insurance Company."

These efforts by Mr. Dee to help another agent's policyowner provided a positive moment of truth for the Bakers. Mr. Dee had nothing to gain personally from helping the Bakers; another agent will receive any commissions on the Bakers' renewal premiums or future insurance purchases from American Family. Yet, at the moment of truth, he took the time and made the effort to create a *moment of magic* for the Bakers, thereby winning a loyal customer for American Family Insurance.

Source: Adapted from "Would You Help Another Agent's Policyholder?" *All American* (January 1997): 12. Used with permission.

Customer Service in the Financial Services Industry

In this book, we focus on customer service in the *financial services industry*, which is an industry consisting of financial institutions that offer products and services that help individuals, businesses, and governments save, borrow, invest, protect, and otherwise manage assets.[7] A *financial institution* (also called a *financial services company*) is a business that collects funds from the public and owns primarily financial assets, such as stocks and bonds, rather than fixed assets, such as equipment and raw materials. Financial institutions include insurance companies, mutual funds (investment companies), securities brokerages, investment banks, commercial banks, finance companies, credit unions, and pension funds.

The primary goal of a financial institution is to meet the financial needs of its customers and help the customers meet their long-term and short-term goals. Such goals typically include improved lifestyles, financial security, and protection from financial losses due to unexpected events. To fulfill these needs, the financial services industry offers a variety of products and services, which generally fall into four categories: cash management, credit, asset accumulation, and financial protection. Figure 1-2 describes each of these categories and gives examples of products within each category.

Providing exceptional customer service is a top priority for many financial services companies for several reasons. First, because financial institutions generally offer products that are useful but intangible—that is, they cannot be grasped with the senses—customers of financial institutions often cannot separate the company and the product from the people providing the service. Thus, the success of a financial services company depends to a large extent on the behavior of the people who work in that company.

When many companies offer similar products, customers can have difficulty distinguishing one company or product from another.

In addition, the financial services industry has become intensely competitive as financial institutions increasingly expand their product offerings and enter each other's traditional core businesses. For example, many banks, securities firms, and mutual fund companies now distribute life insurance and annuities, and some insurers and banks sell mutual funds. As more companies compete against each other to attract and retain customers, customer service becomes increasingly important. When many companies offer similar products, customers can have difficulty distinguishing one company or product from another. A financial services company that provides exceptional customer service adds value to its products, thereby gaining an advantage over its competitors.

Another reason customer service is important in the financial services industry is the rising expectations of customers, who often demand instantaneous responses and actions from financial institutions. When customers receive exceptional customer service from one company—whether that company is in the financial services industry or some other industry—they begin to expect the same level and quality of service from other organizations. For example, some Internet retailers allow customers to view the status of their order online, so customers can know when their orders have been fulfilled and shipped. A customer accustomed to such service is likely to be impatient if a bank cannot tell her whether her car loan has been approved yet or an insurer cannot tell her the status of her policy loan request. Furthermore, as customers grow accustomed to receiving excellent customer service, they become dissatisfied with companies that fail to provide it.

FIGURE 1-2. Types of Financial Products and Services.

Financial products and services generally can be grouped into the following four categories:

CASH MANAGEMENT

Cash management is the process of using readily available funds for everyday living expenses, as well as for short-term savings and investment purposes. For example, cash management products enable people to pay bills, buy groceries, and save money for periodic expenses, such as a large property tax bill or holiday gift purchases. Debit cards, money orders, cashiers' checks, travelers checks, and interest-bearing checking accounts are examples of common cash management products.

CREDIT

Credit is the ability to purchase now by giving a promise to pay in the future. Using credit, a consumer borrows money from a financial institution to make a purchase, and then pays the financial institution for that purchase. Common forms of credit include credit cards, auto loans, equipment leases, and mortgage loans.

ASSET AND WEALTH ACCUMULATION

Asset and wealth accumlation is the gathering of a substantial amount of money over time. People accumulate funds for many different reasons, such as for large purchases, education, retirement, and emergencies. A variety of asset accumulation products offer investors the opportunity to enlarge, or grow, their investments over a period of time. Such products include savings accounts, certificates of deposits (CDs), stocks, bonds, mutual funds, annuities, and retirement plans.

FINANCIAL PROTECTION

Financial protection is typically known as insurance. People face the risk of financial loss from many sources, such as natural disasters, automobile accidents, illness, or the death of a family member. Many types of insurance, including automobile, homeowner's, liability, health, disability, and life insurance, provide protection against financial loss caused by one of these events.

In short, having high-quality products is not enough to ensure the success of a financial services organization. The company must have exceptional customer service to back up its products or the company will flounder.

Who Is the Customer?

Financial services companies and their employees can have many different types of customers, ranging from individuals to organizations and from external customers to internal customers. As an employee of a financial services firm, you might provide service primarily to one type of customer or you might interact with several different kinds of customers. To provide the best possible customer service in any given situation, you must first identify and understand who your customer is. In this section, we discuss various ways to categorize customers: (1) individual or organizational customers, (2) external or internal customers, and (3) intermediaries and business partners.

Individual Customers and Organizational Customers

An ***individual customer*** is a person who buys or uses a product primarily for his own benefit or the benefit of his family. Individual customers are often referred to as *consumers* or *household customers*, and they typically are the people who purchase and own a financial product or service. For example, an individual customer could be a person who opens a brokerage account, buys an insurance policy, owns a credit card, or takes out a bank loan.

For financial services companies, individual customers also include the people who benefit from the financial products or services purchased by another person or an organization. One example is a life insurance policy beneficiary, the person named by the policyowner to receive the policy proceeds upon the insured person's death. Many other financial products, such as brokerage accounts, pension plans, and mutual funds also require the account holder to designate a beneficiary in the event of the account holder's death. Another example is an individual group member who is covered under a group insurance contract purchased by his employer.

Every company's greatest assets are its customers, because without customers there is no company.

— Michael LeBoeuf [8]

An **organizational customer** is a business or other organization (such as a government, educational institution, or charity) that buys a product or service for its benefit or the benefit of its employees or members. Organizational customers, also known as *business-to-business (B2B) customers* or *institutional customers*, use financial products and services to conduct ongoing business activities and to improve and protect the organization's long-term financial security. For example, a sporting goods retail chain that wants to expand into a different region of the country might borrow money to finance the building of new stores. Some companies acquire corporate credit cards that certain employees can use to pay for travel and other work-related expenses. A large corporation might invest a portion of its profits in securities to accumulate the funds needed for future product development. Many employers and other organizations also use financial products and services to provide benefits, such as health insurance or retirement plans, for their employees or members.

In addition, a financial services firm's organizational customers can include other financial services companies. For instance, a brokerage firm might manage an insurer's investment portfolio. Or, one insurance company might enter into a reinsurance agreement with other insurers to transfer some of the risk on its policies.

External Customers and Internal Customers

An **external customer** is any person or organization in a position to buy or use a company's products. External customers are sometimes referred to as *end customers* to distinguish them from internal customers. Examples of external customers in the financial services industry include

- Holders of bank accounts or credit cards

- People or organizations that borrow money

www.grantland.net

- Owners and beneficiaries of insurance policies and annuity contracts

- People or organizations that file insurance claims

- Investors in securities or mutual funds

- Participants in retirement plans

When we use the term "customer" in this text, we generally are referring to external customers. However, as you read, keep in mind that most of the customer service concepts and skills discussed can be applied when working with internal customers as well.

An **internal customer** is a company employee or department that receives support from another employee or department within the organization. In some financial services companies, fellow employees are referred to as *partners*, *team members*, or *associates* to emphasize that all company employees are working together toward a common goal, rather than in isolation. Other companies believe that the term *internal customer* maintains the emphasis on service both inside and outside the company. Regardless of the terminology used, at any given time, any employee may be the customer of any other employee in the same company.

For example, when a company's marketing managers ask the accounting department to develop a new financial report, those managers become customers of the accounting department. When the accounting department asks the information systems (IS) department to write a computer program to produce the new report, the accounting department becomes a customer of the IS department. Similarly, much of the work that managers do to help other staff members complete their work can be seen as customer service. For example, managers who make sure that their staff members are adequately trained and have enough time and resources to do their work are not just being good managers, they are being good customer service providers. Ultimately, all internal customer service reaches, and has an effect on, external customers. See Figure 1-3 for an example of exceptional internal customer service.

Much of the work that managers do to help other staff members complete their work can be seen as customer service.

Intermediaries and Business Partners

Some customers can have characteristics of both external customers and internal customers. In the financial services industry, intermediaries and business partners are two such groups of customers.

FIGURE 1-3. Example of Exceptional Internal Customer Service.

One morning at 9:00, Debra Paterno, a customer service representative at the Field Financial Services Company, received a call from a customer who wanted to terminate his pension plan and needed the surrender check (which he would receive upon termination of the plan) to reflect that day's date for tax purposes.

Debra, who knew that a surrender usually took two weeks to be processed, faxed the customer the appropriate forms, which he completed and faxed back to her. Debra then called John, one of Field's processors, and explained the situation and asked if the surrender could be processed that day. John assessed his workload and told Debra he could begin processing the surrender that morning.

When John had completed the necessary calculations for the plan surrender, he notified Debra. The next step was to issue a check to the customer, a process which usually takes 24 hours. Because the customer needed the check to reflect that day's date, John told Debra he could wire the funds to an account of the customer's choice that same day and provide a written statement indicating that the plan surrender was completed and the funds were paid out on that date. Debra called the customer to inform him that the surrender was complete and obtain the necessary account information so he could receive the funds that day.

Because John provided excellent internal customer service to Debra, she was able to provide the customer with the service that he had expected and needed.

An ***intermediary*** is a person who links buyers of financial products and services with the companies that sell those products and services. For example, a financial planner is an intermediary because he helps his clients select and apply for products and services that are developed and marketed by financial services companies. Other intermediaries include insurance agents, stockbrokers, mortgage brokers, investment advisers, and accountants.

Note that the term *financial intermediary* is often used to refer to an organization that transfers funds from one person or group to another person or group. Such organizations include banks, investment companies, mutual funds, and insurance companies. However, in this text, we use the term *intermediary* to refer to the people—rather than the organizations—who link buyers and sellers of financial products.

Financial services companies can consider intermediaries to be external customers because they are in a position to influence customers' purchase of financial products and services. Companies can also view intermediaries as internal customers because the intermediaries are typically paid by the company and receive services from other company employees. Regardless of their exact relationship to a company, intermediaries are some of a financial services company's most important customers.

Intermediaries are a critical link in distributing products and providing service to end customers.

Because intermediaries are a critical link in distributing products and providing service to end customers, most financial services companies try to provide intermediaries with the highest possible level of customer service. In fact, some financial services companies consider intermediaries to be the company's primary customers. These companies concentrate on providing service to the intermediary, who in turn is expected to provide service to the end customer, as we discuss in the next section.

In the context of customers, a ***business partner*** is an organization that helps a company develop, distribute, or service its products. For example, an insurer might enter into an agreement with a bank to offer the insurer's products at the bank's branch offices, so the bank becomes the insurer's business partner. Other examples of business partners in the financial services industry include third-party administrators, outsourcing companies, medical providers, and vendors that perform specific functions to help companies serve their customers.

A financial services company can consider a business partner to be an external customer because the partner's actions can influence the way a significant number of a company's customers view the company and its products, and because business partners require service and support from company employees. A financial services company can also consider a business partner to be an internal customer because the two organizations work closely together to meet the needs of the company's end customers.

Whatever the relationship between a company and its business partners, the company must provide effective and professional service and support to its partners to create and maintain a productive and beneficial partnership. A business partner that is not satisfied with the support it receives from a company might choose to end the partnership, thereby hindering the company's ability to effectively meet its customers' needs.

Who Provides Customer Service?

In one way or another, everyone in an organization provides customer service. The purpose of every business activity performed within a company is, ultimately, to satisfy the company's external customers. It's easy to see how activities that touch customers—such as sales and customer service—play an important role in satisfying customers. But even business activities that may seem far removed from customer interactions affect customers. For example, the people who work in a company's mailroom may rarely interact with external customers, but if the mailroom does not operate efficiently to distribute incoming and outgoing mail, communication with customers is slowed down, resulting in poor customer service. Financial services companies that are committed to delivering exceptional customer service encourage all employees, regardless of their specific job responsibilities, to think of themselves as providers of customer service and to think about how any changes they make to their work processes and procedures will affect customers.

Staying focused on providing exceptional customer service while still performing job duties can be a challenge. Some employees, especially those not directly involved with external customers on a regular basis, may develop a **manufacturing mentality**, a state of mind in which employees concentrate so much on the functions and procedures of their day-to-day responsibilities that they forget about the customer. They become so involved in processing, writing, or reviewing all the reports, files, forms, and letters that are such a large part of their daily routine that they start thinking that handling paperwork—not serving customers—is their job.

A service provider performs his required job duties while being mindful of how those duties ultimately affect the company's customers.

This manufacturing mentality occurs because, in many ways, being a manufacturer is easier than being a service provider. In this text, we define a **service provider** as a person whose primary focus is on meeting the needs of customers, regardless of the person's job responsibilities or position within a company. A service provider performs his required job duties while being mindful of how those duties ultimately affect the company's customers. In the financial services industry, examples of service providers include customer service representatives, bank tellers, insurance claims examiners, and employees who process withdrawals from retirement accounts.

Even employees who do not interact directly with customers can be service providers; for example, an office supply clerk who keeps the appropriate office supplies in stock because he knows that company employees need these tools to perform their work and serve customers is also a service provider. Service providers also include senior managers who create a strategy for how the company will provide customer service and then allocate funds to implement that strategy. Anyone in a financial services firm can be a service provider by focusing on how the work he performs affects customers.

One reason it is easier to be a manufacturer than a service provider is that a manufacturer controls most of the variables; there are no outside factors, and there is no customer interference. A manufacturer concentrates on speed, efficiency, and quality control. In contrast, a service provider's actions are dictated by customer requests, and the service provider has limited control over the nature and scope of those requests. A service provider must focus on the customer's need, and then be flexible and resourceful in taking whatever reasonable steps are necessary to fulfill that need.

If the system encourages employees to be outward-looking and focused on the customer, employees will be much more likely to adopt a customer-centered approach.

Employees can have difficulty overcoming a manufacturing mentality if a company's culture and incentives do not promote customer service as a top priority for all of its employees. If management places a great deal of importance on completing paperwork and not on serving the customer, employees will concentrate on paperwork. People tend to do what they are rewarded for doing, and employees learn to function within the system that their company establishes. If the system encourages an inward-looking manufacturing mentality, employees will likely assume that mentality. However, if the system encourages employees to be outward-looking and focused on the customer, employees will be much more likely to adopt a customer-centered approach.

Generally, service providers can be grouped into two categories: those who provide service directly to external customers and those who serve customers indirectly. Every employee in a company is either a direct or indirect service provider. Figure 1-4 illustrates how the two types of service providers work together to serve customers.

Direct Customer Service Providers

Some of the most important people in any financial services company are those who interact directly with the company's customers, because they are in a position to create a positive—or negative—perception of the company in the customer's mind. We define a ***direct customer service provider*** as a person who routinely communicates with his company's external customers and serves as their link to the information, products, or services

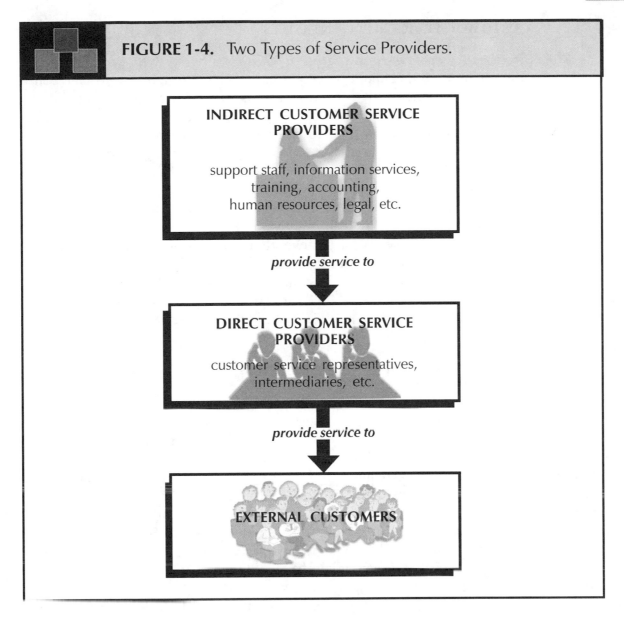

FIGURE 1-4. Two Types of Service Providers.

INDIRECT CUSTOMER SERVICE PROVIDERS

support staff, information services, training, accounting, human resources, legal, etc.

provide service to

DIRECT CUSTOMER SERVICE PROVIDERS

customer service representatives, intermediaries, etc.

provide service to

EXTERNAL CUSTOMERS

that they need. These people represent the company to its customers; they are the "face" and the "voice" of the company. Direct customer service providers include customer service representatives, intermediaries, marketing and sales staff, receptionists, insurance claims examiners, bank tellers, brokers' assistants, and any other employees who regularly come in contact with their company's customers. In this section, we'll discuss two of the most common types of direct customer service providers in the financial services industry: customer service representatives and intermediaries.

CUSTOMER SERVICE REPRESENTATIVES

A *customer service representative (CSR)* is a person whose primary job responsibility is to support external customers through face-to-face communications or through communications media, such as the telephone, fax, electronic mail (e-mail), or Internet chat sessions. Some financial services companies also refer to CSRs as *service representatives*, *service associates*, *service agents*, *contact center agents*, or *call center representatives*. In many financial services companies, CSRs are employed in specific departments designed to help external customers. These departments are often organized as call centers or customer contact centers and they can have a variety of names, including customer service, client services, member services, policyowner services, financial services, or administrative services. In customer service, a *call center* is an organizational unit that receives and/or places telephone calls to customers. A *customer contact center* is an organizational unit that provides customers with a variety of channels—such as telephone, fax, and e-mail—for communicating with a company.

In the past, the nature of their work frequently required CSRs to concentrate primarily on administrative tasks, such as processing paperwork. Because administrative services are part of what customers purchase when they buy financial products, performing such tasks will always be an important part of what CSRs do. However, many financial services companies now ask their CSRs to go a step further—to think not only of the customer's specific request, but also to consider the array of customer needs that the company can fill. Customer service representatives are being trained to understand the full range of a company's products and activities and to recognize marketing opportunities. For example, some insurers encourage CSRs to go beyond the customer's current request and identify life events—such as a birth, marriage, or retirement—that would suggest the need for an insurance program review. Typically, however, CSRs in financial services companies do not actually sell products unless they are appropriately licensed and trained to do so.

Customer service representatives also receive more intensive training in interpersonal skills and learn how to process a wide variety of customer requests. They are being given authority to make customer service decisions and are encouraged to develop creative solutions to customers' problems. In particular, *dedicated customer service representatives*, or *account managers*, who are service providers assigned to assist specific customers or groups of customers, have wider latitude to solve problems. Dedicated CSRs are usually experienced and highly skilled customer service professionals who often work in teams to serve their designated customers. Many financial services companies use dedicated CSRs as a

> Customer service representatives are being trained to understand the full range of a company's products and activities and to recognize marketing opportunities.

means of providing consistent, reliable, high-quality service to customers who have special needs (such as organizational customers), who purchase certain products (such as "gold" credit cards), or who represent a significant source of revenue for the company (such as high-producing insurance agents). A company might also assign a dedicated CSR to preserve the business of an organizational customer that has been dissatisfied with the company's service in the past and is at risk for taking its business elsewhere.

As part of the customer service department, all CSRs perform a valuable function. Many companies use the customer service department as a central point for providing seamless or "one-stop" customer service. In these companies, CSRs are expected to handle all of a customer's requests, bringing in expertise from other areas of the company as needed. As we will discuss later in this book, some companies provide interdepartmental training that helps CSRs become more knowledgeable about other company operations, such as accounting or marketing. Such knowledge can enable CSRs to handle a wider range of customer inquiries without assistance from other areas, which allows the CSRs to serve customers more quickly and efficiently.

Some companies provide inter-departmental training that helps CSRs become more knowledgeable about other company operations, such as accounting or marketing.

Because CSRs interact directly with customers, they gain valuable information about what customers like and dislike about the company's products and services. A customer service department should convey customers' problems, opinions, and concerns to the areas of the company that can provide a solution. For example, if CSRs receive a multitude of calls from customers who are confused by information they received in a marketing brochure, the customer service department should notify the marketing department of the customers' confusion so that future brochures can be modified. In Chapter 10, we will discuss further the role the CSRs play in providing information about a company's customers.

INTERMEDIARIES

Many external customers consider the person who helps them purchase a financial product or service to be their primary, or only, connection to a financial services company. Generally, these customers have developed a relationship with the person who sold them the product, and they expect that person to be able to answer their questions, resolve any problems they have with the product or service, and generally represent their interests to the financial services company. Therefore, the intermediaries who sell financial products and services play a vital role in providing customer service.

The number of customer service activities that an intermediary and her staff perform varies according to the type of products being marketed and the type of agreement that exists between the intermediary and the financial institution. Some companies rely heavily on intermediaries to meet customers' service needs and maintain relationships with them, while other companies handle most customer service activities internally. Usually, however, a financial services company and its intermediaries share responsibility for identifying and fulfilling customers' wants and needs, working together to ensure that customers remain satisfied.

Indirect Customer Service Providers

Although the people who interact directly with customers tend to be the most visible providers of customer service, they would have difficulty performing their jobs without the support of the many indirect customer service providers who work alongside them. An **indirect customer service provider** is a person who does not routinely interact with external customers, but who performs activities that facilitate customers' receipt of the information, products, and services that they need. In other words, these people keep the company operating and able to help its customers. Indirect customer service providers include administrative and support staff in the customer service area, as well as people from other areas or departments in the company, including information services, training, accounting, human resources, and legal. Generally, indirect customer service providers include anyone in a company who is *not* a direct customer service provider.

Because they do not routinely interact directly with external customers, indirect customer service providers usually serve internal customers. For example, an information services technician who troubleshoots and repairs a problem with a CSR's desktop computer is providing a service for the CSR, who, at that moment, is the technician's internal customer. However, the technician's work also benefits the company's external customers, because the CSR can only provide efficient and effective customer service if her desktop computer, which allows her to access customer records and other information, is functioning properly.

At other times, an indirect customer service provider performs activities for the sole benefit of an external customer.

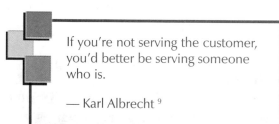

If you're not serving the customer, you'd better be serving someone who is.

— Karl Albrecht [9]

For example, an accounting staff member who processes and mails a check to a customer is performing an activity that serves the external customer, even though this employee does not typically interact directly with customers.

Regardless of whether they are serving internal or external customers, indirect customer service providers play a vital role in a company's ability to provide exceptional customer service. Without the work of these people, a company would be unable to meet the needs of its customers. Therefore, indirect customer service providers must perform their jobs quickly, accurately, and thoroughly while staying focused on the ultimate goal of providing superior customer service.

As you have learned in this chapter, customer service in a financial services company is multifaceted, with many different people providing several types of customers with a variety of services. Achieving exceptional customer service on all these levels requires a commitment by the company and each of its employees to provide the best possible service to any and all customers. In the next chapter, we will describe in more detail the ingredients of exceptional customer service.

To practice and review the skills and information you learned in this chapter, see the interactive CD, *Practicing Your Customer Service Skills*, included with this book.

Key Terms and Concepts

customer
customer service
value added customer
  service
moment of truth
financial services industry
financial institution
cash management
credit
asset and wealth
  accumulation
financial protection
individual customer
organizational customer
external customer

internal customer
intermediary
business partner
manufacturing mentality
service provider
direct customer service
  provider
customer service
  representative (CSR)
call center
customer contact center
dedicated customer service
  representative
indirect customer service
  provider

Endnotes

1. Lucy McCauley, "How May I Help You?" *Fast Company*, March 2000, http://www.fastcompany.com/online/32/one.html (18 December 2001).

2. *National Consumer Policy, Final Draft*, adopted New Delhi, 3 March 1998, http://www.cuts.org/NCP.htm (8 January 2002).

3. John Goodman, Pat O'Brien, and Eden Segal, "Selling Quality to the CFO," *Quality Progress*, March 2000, http://www.tarp.com/pdf/sellingtocfo.pdf (9 October 2002).

4. John Goodman, "Basic Facts on Customer Complaint Behavior and the Impact of Service on the Bottom Line," *Competitive Advantage*, June 1999, http://www.e-satisfy.com/pdf/basicfacts.pdf (9 October 2002).

5. JoAnna F. Brandi, *Building Company Loyalty: The 21 Essential Elements...IN ACTION* (Dallas: Walk the Talk Company, 2001), 17.

6. Steven E. Prokesch, "Competing on Customer Service: An Interview with British Airways' Sir Colin Marshall," *Harvard Business Review* (November–December 1995): 102–103.

7. Portions of this section are adapted from Mary C. Bickley and David F. Johnson, *Intro to Financial Services* (Atlanta: LOMA, © 2001). Used with permission; all rights reserved.

8. The People's Cyber Nation, "Great Quotations to Inspire and Motivate You!" http://www.cybernation.com/victory/quotations/subjects/quotes_customers.html (15 October 2002).

9. Karl Albrecht and Ron Zemke, *Service America!: Doing Business in the New Economy* (New York: Warner Books, 1990).

CHAPTER 2

Exceptional Customer Service

After studying this chapter, you should be able to

- Identify several characteristics of exceptional customer service, including the three organizational components that affect customer service

- Describe the knowledge and skills that service providers should possess to provide exceptional customer service

- Describe some of the customer service challenges faced by financial services companies and the people who provide customer service

- Explain the importance of customer loyalty and retention

- Discuss the benefits that financial services companies can gain by providing exceptional customer service

Some people say that customer service is largely a matter of common sense. Listen to your customers, treat them courteously, and give them what they want—within reason, of course. Most of us believe we deliver satisfactory, if not exceptional, customer service in our jobs, and most senior executives state that superior customer service is essential to a company's success. Given these factors, we would expect that the majority of customers would be completely satisfied with the service they receive.

Yet, as customers ourselves, we know that exceptional customer service is the exception rather than the rule. Some people say, "I may not be an expert, but I know good customer service when I see it—and I seldom see it." So where is the "common sense" in customer service? What actions and attitudes lead to outstanding customer service, and what circumstances prevent it? Why do so many companies tout the importance of customer service, while more and more customers lament its absence? In this chapter, we will explore exceptional customer service—what it is, how it is attained, and what makes it worth the effort.

> To hold on to customers in today's marketplace of intense and fast-paced competition, companies have to make a giant leap from lip service to real service.
>
> — Laura A. Liswood[1]

Characteristics of Exceptional Customer Service

Companies that provide exceptional customer service are those that effectively meet customer needs and consistently exceed customer expectations. These companies deliver on their promises to customers, and they help customers feel appreciated by delivering value-added service. Exceptional customer service comes from two sources, each of which relies heavily on the other: (1) the organization and (2) individual service providers. Without the commitment and abilities of the organization and its representatives, customer service efforts are not likely to succeed.

Organizational Components

As Figure 2-1 highlights, three organizational components greatly affect customer service: (1) a company's business philosophy, (2) its strategic planning process, and (3) its business systems. In this section, we briefly

FIGURE 2-1. What Makes Customer Service Exceptional?

- [−] Characteristics of exceptional customer service
  - [−] Organizational components
    - [+] 📁 Business philosophy
    - [+] 📁 Strategic planning
    - [+] 📁 Business systems
  - [−] Individual service providers
    - [+] 📁 Motivation
    - [+] 📁 Knowledge of products and services
    - [+] 📁 Knowledge of procedures and technology
    - [+] 📁 Effective interpersonal skills

examine customer service in terms of each of these components, which we will discuss in more detail in Chapters 10 through 13.

BUSINESS PHILOSOPHY

A company that has a business philosophy focused on the needs of customers and how to fill those needs is said to have a ***customer-centric philosophy***. A customer-centric organization develops strategies and business systems with the customer in mind, and virtually every employee understands the importance of customer service. A customer-centric company explores customer needs first and then designs products and services to meet those needs. On the other hand, a ***product-centric philosophy*** focuses on product features. A product-centric organization designs products it believes customers will want and then tries to persuade customers to buy those products.

Being customer-centric does not mean that a company is willing to do anything and everything for its customers without regard to business realities. Instead, a customer-centric company recognizes the importance of thinking about customers in ways that cut across product lines to produce outcomes that are mutually beneficial to the company and its customers.

STRATEGIC PLANNING

Strategic planning is the process of determining an organization's long-term corporate objectives and deciding the overall course of action the company will take to achieve those objectives. To provide exceptional customer service, a financial services firm must develop a strategic plan that makes customer service a central part of the company's entire planning process.

Recognizing the critical importance of customer service, many financial services companies also develop a **customer service strategic plan** that establishes corporate objectives specifically tied to customer service and determines an overall course of action the company and its employees will follow to achieve those objectives. A customer service strategic plan is coordinated with and becomes a part of the company's corporate strategic plan. Some companies also undertake organization-wide initiatives, such as customer access strategies and customer relationship management (discussed later in this text), to maximize their interactions and relationships with customers.

To determine if they are meeting their objectives and to examine the results of their strategic plans, companies rely on performance measurement processes, which we will discuss in Chapter 12. Then, after analyzing performance results, they revise existing plans and develop new plans, as needed, to continually improve performance.

BUSINESS SYSTEMS

The customer service system transcends functional and organizational lines.

A **business system** is a set of processes and other elements designed to work together to meet a company's performance requirements. Within a company's overall business system, many subsystems help a company operate. One such subsystem is a company's customer service system. Although customer service may be a separate department in some organizations, the customer service system transcends functional and organizational lines and requires the participation and cooperation of various departments throughout the organization. A customer service system, like any type of business system, is made up of (1) processes and procedures, (2) financial and physical resources, and (3) people.

For the many activities performed in a business system to work in a well-coordinated manner, they typically follow established processes. A *process* (also called a *workflow*, *work practice*, or *procedure*) is a series of steps involved in performing a recurring activity designed to produce a specific outcome. For example, when an insurance company receives a completed claim form, all the activities involved in recording, verifying, and authorizing payment of the claim are steps in a process. Processes are designed to ensure that activities are done correctly, consistently, and in a timely manner—as customers expect when they do business with a company.

Business systems also include a variety of organizational resources that support both the people and the processes involved in customer service. For example, written procedural guidelines outline the steps that employees follow to perform certain functions. The organizational resources in a customer service system include a broad array of items, from buildings to individual workstations, telephone systems to telephone headsets, and computer networks to computer monitors.

A significant resource in many financial services firms is technology. Technological advancements make it possible for customers to help themselves by performing self-service functions—such as obtaining account balances, reporting address changes, and checking the status of financial transactions—on a company's Web site or automated telephone system. In addition, through information technology, service providers can obtain electronic access to information resources, which at one time were available only on paper, to handle customer requests quickly and accurately.

If a financial services firm combines effective processes and resources with a customer-centric philosophy and customer-focused strategic planning, then it is well on its way to providing exceptional customer service. However, as you will see in the following section, these organizational factors alone do not produce exceptional customer service.

> If a financial services firm combines effective processes and resources with a customer-centric philosophy and customer-focused strategic planning, then it is well on its way to providing exceptional customer service.

Individual Service Providers

People are the most important component of a customer service system because they work directly with and provide "behind the scenes" support to customers. Each interaction that a service provider has with a customer contributes to the customer's overall opinion of the company. Service providers who work directly with customers are more effective if they have a people-oriented personality and outlook. In addition, to deliver exceptional customer service, employees must be highly motivated and they must possess the knowledge and skills highlighted in Figure 2-2.

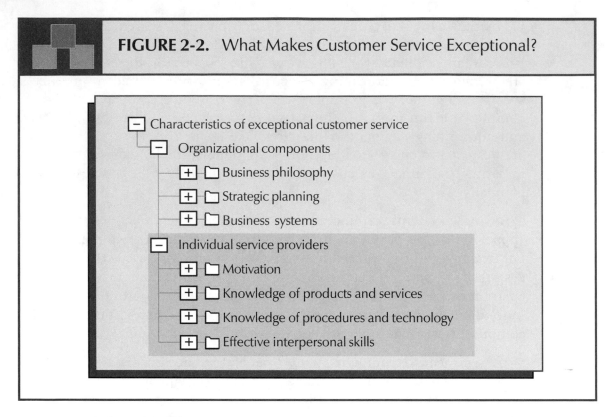

FIGURE 2-2. What Makes Customer Service Exceptional?

- Characteristics of exceptional customer service
  - Organizational components
    - Business philosophy
    - Strategic planning
    - Business systems
  - Individual service providers
    - Motivation
    - Knowledge of products and services
    - Knowledge of procedures and technology
    - Effective interpersonal skills

MOTIVATION

As you will see in Chapter 4, a company and its managers can encourage commitment and a desire to excel, but ultimately motivation comes from the individual service provider. For example, suppose you are a client services employee in a life insurance company and you receive a telephone call from an insurance agent at 8:10 a.m. The agent asks you to send him two in-force illustrations by 9:30 a.m. for a meeting with a prospect at 9:45 a.m. You immediately get to work to meet this request, but soon encounter a problem obtaining the necessary data. At this point, some employees would simply give up and call the agent to deliver the bad news. But you call the actuarial department to request that the illustrations be prepared in that department and faxed directly to the agent. And so, with your commitment to exceptional customer service and with the help of a motivated employee in another department, you meet the needs of your customer.

A service provider's ability to deliver exceptional customer service begins with a desire to excel. However, as important as such motivation is, service providers must also possess or develop the necessary knowledge and skills to meet the needs of their customers.

A service provider's ability to deliver exceptional customer service begins with a desire to excel.

KNOWLEDGE OF PRODUCTS AND SERVICES

To provide exceptional customer service, service providers must know the products and services their company offers. The more knowledgeable they are, the better they can communicate with and support their customers, as the examples in Figure 2-3 illustrate.

KNOWLEDGE OF PROCEDURES AND TECHNOLOGY

Ideally, every procedure in a financial services organization has a readily understood purpose. Life insurance companies have procedures to handle beneficiary changes, claim processing, or policy loans. Banks and credit

FIGURE 2-3. Examples of How Service Providers Use Product Knowledge.

Marty Hulkower, a health care policyholder, calls for help in completing a claim form for the wheelchair and medical supplies his wife will need when she comes home from the hospital. Amir Naderi is the service provider who receives the call. Because Mr. Naderi is familiar with the applicable policy provisions, he informs Mr. Hulkower that the supplies will be covered only if they are provided by a licensed home health care agency. Then Mr. Naderi refers to a computer data base of licensed home health care agencies and he provides the names, addresses, and telephone numbers of the agencies located within a 10-mile radius of Mr. Hulkower's home address.

David Wickersham calls to surrender his endowment life insurance policy because he needs the money to pay some debts. The net surrender amount will be $56,000. When the service provider, Celeste DeNucci, reviews the policy information, she realizes that the policy is going to mature in six months and the net maturity amount will be $62,000. Ms. DeNucci suggests that Mr. Wickersham consider taking out a policy loan for the amount he needs to pay his debts. After some discussion, they determine that the interest on the loan will be significantly less than the $6,000 Mr. Wickersham would have forfeited by surrendering his policy before its maturity date.

unions have procedures to handle deposits and withdrawals, stop payment orders, or fund transfers. Brokerage firms have procedures for opening investment accounts, transacting buy and sell orders, and so on. One of the most important responsibilities of a service provider is to be familiar with appropriate procedures and technology, as Figure 2-4 illustrates.

Not every customer service function requires step-by-step procedures. Unnecessary procedures can stifle employee initiative and irritate customers. Also, employees must have the flexibility to deal creatively with unique customer service situations. However, initiative and creativity come easier when service providers don't have to spend time deciding how to perform common tasks. By becoming familiar with available procedures and technology, service providers are better able to provide timely, consistent, and high quality customer service.

EFFECTIVE INTERPERSONAL SKILLS

Motivation, knowledge of company products and services, and familiarity with procedures and technology are key to providing quality customer service. However, if service providers lack interpersonal skills, then their interactions with customers will seldom result in exceptional customer service. *Interpersonal skills* (sometimes called *soft skills*) are the skills used to understand and interact with internal and external customers.

> Employees must have the flexibility to deal creatively with unique customer service situations.

FIGURE 2-4. Examples of How Service Providers Use Knowledge of Procedures and Technology.

Wei Chen calls her insurance company's policyowner service (POS) department to obtain information about the cash value of her life insurance policy and to obtain information about buying an annuity. She mentions that she is calling this number because she no longer has the number of the agent who sold her the policy several years ago. One way to handle this request would be to furnish Ms. Chen with the cash value information, inform her that another department handles annuities, and transfer her call, thereby providing adequate but unexceptional customer service. But because the service provider, Peter Nye, is familiar with his company's technology and procedures, he is able to provide the cash value information and then give the customer several options for learning more about annuities. He quickly checks his company's computerized agent database, and provides Ms. Chen with the agent's telephone number and e-mail address. He also offers to transfer Ms. Chen directly to the agent or to arrange for the agent to call or e-mail her. In addition, he informs Ms. Chen of the company's Web site where she can find information about annuity products.

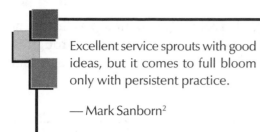

Excellent service sprouts with good ideas, but it comes to full bloom only with persistent practice.

— Mark Sanborn[2]

Interpersonal skills include the ability to listen well, use appropriate words and tone of voice, express empathy, and effectively handle conflict. The first step in improving interpersonal skills is to identify areas in which additional training may be needed. Exercise 2-1 provides a method for assessing your interpersonal skills.

Through training, employees can improve their interpersonal skills, product knowledge, and familiarity with resources, procedures, and technology. Most companies provide newly hired employees with training in their basic job duties. Companies also offer or arrange for additional training when products, systems, or other factors change or when an employee's responsibilities expand. As we will see in Chapter 3, companies utilize a

Exercise 2-1.   An Interpersonal Skills Inventory.

Read each statement and place a check mark in the box that best describes your behavior.

	Almost Always	Some-times	Almost Never
I answer the telephone with a "smile in my voice."			
I listen actively to customers.			
I listen and apologize when customers complain.			
I show empathy by trying to understand the customer's situation.			
I am polite and courteous to all customers, even angry customers.			
I address customers by name.			
I know how to phrase answers to customers' questions, and use simple language without financial jargon.			
I thank customers and let them know that I appreciate their business.			

If you answered every question *Almost Always*, congratulations. Your interpersonal skills are most likely very effective for customer service. If you answered any of these questions *Sometimes* or *Almost Never*, then you might want to consider additional training in the applicable skills.

variety of training techniques. One such technique, which you are benefiting from as you read this text, is self-study. In Chapters 5 through 9, we will discuss ways you can increase your interpersonal and customer service skills.

Challenges of Customer Service

Sometimes, the sheer volume of transactions can create an environment in which the customer is seen as just another number.

Like any important business activity, customer service presents certain challenges. Sometimes, the sheer volume of transactions can create an environment in which the customer is seen as just another number. Other times, customers behave in ways that test the patience of even the most experienced service providers. Several factors contribute to the challenge of providing customer service in the financial services industry. Some of these factors apply to customer service in general, while others pertain primarily to financial services companies. These factors are shown in Figure 2-5.

Challenge No. 1: Customer Service as an Experience

Often, customer service is inextricably bound to the people who provide service. But no matter how skillful or well-intentioned these people may be, they do not always perform consistently. People sometimes forget details, procrastinate, or treat customers discourteously. Periodic bursts of

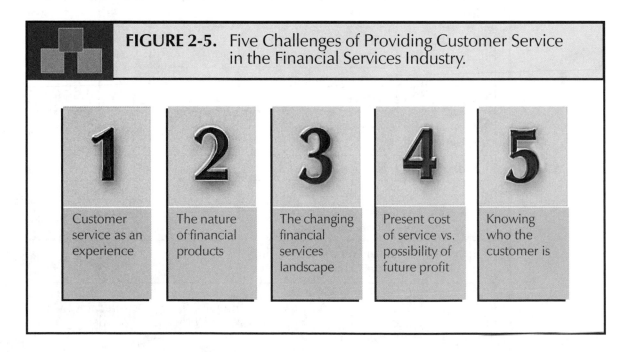

FIGURE 2-5. Five Challenges of Providing Customer Service in the Financial Services Industry.

1	2	3	4	5
Customer service as an experience	The nature of financial products	The changing financial services landscape	Present cost of service vs. possibility of future profit	Knowing who the customer is

exceptional customer service may be attainable, but providing a consistently high level of service is a challenge.

Customer service, compared to most "goods" or "products," is relatively intangible. Customers and companies have few concrete factors on which to judge the value or quality of service. If the color on a television set is washed out, a customer can point to the screen and say the quality is poor. Customer service, on the other hand, is seldom this black and white. Assessing the quality of customer service is usually more subjective.

Furthermore, no inventory exists for customer service. Service providers have only a limited number of hours each day in which they can provide customer service, and unused hours from one day cannot be carried forward to another day. Financial services companies cannot stockpile large quantities of services—such as address changes, claim payments, and fund transfers—and supply these services when customers need them. Instead, companies must be able to forecast accurately the number and timing of customer requests and allocate the resources needed to perform the necessary services.

Finally, customer service is consumed at the same time it is produced, through a process called **simultaneous production and consumption**. The quality of the service is created and determined during the interaction between service providers and customers. After service has been completed, nothing is left but the customers' perceptions of whether the service met their expectations, and, as you saw in Chapter 1, *exceptional* customer service today often becomes *expected* customer service tomorrow.

Challenge No. 2: The Nature of Financial Products

The intangibility of financial arrangements and promises can cause anxiety, suspicion, or frustration in some customers, which can make the work of service providers especially difficult.

Financial products have certain characteristics that present customer service challenges. These characteristics include intangibility, complexity, and situational factors.

THE INTANGIBILITY OF FINANCIAL PRODUCTS

As we saw in Chapter 1, financial products are useful but intangible. For instance, although a brokerage account may generate periodic statements, the actual "product" is an *arrangement* for buying and selling securities. Similarly, insurance coverage is described in a written contract, but the "product" is a *promise* to pay a benefit if a specified loss occurs. The intangibility of financial arrangements and promises can cause anxiety, suspicion, or frustration in some customers, which can make the work of service providers especially difficult.

THE COMPLEXITY OF FINANCIAL PRODUCTS

Partly because they are intangible, financial products are sometimes difficult to grasp. A variety of terms and conditions add to the complexity of financial products. Customers don't always have the time or the inclination to carefully read and understand insurance and loan contracts, banking agreements, or other documents associated with financial services. Because many customers don't fully understand these products, the role of customer service is one of providing education, as well as assistance, to customers.

The complexity of financial products also can challenge service providers. Many positions require extensive training to develop the expertise needed to administer products and provide support to customers. Further complicating matters is the extent to which some financial products are regulated. For example, in the United States, laws apply to a variety of product features, and service providers must be careful to furnish information that reflects these requirements. Insurance products are regulated by each state and, as a result, a policy in one state may have provisions that differ from the same type of policy in another state. Service providers must be aware of the different requirements and handle customer requests accordingly. In addition, service providers must be careful to comply with all regulatory requirements that pertain to privacy and the confidentiality of personal information.

Many positions require extensive training to develop the expertise needed to provide support to customers.

SITUATIONAL FACTORS

Certain types of financial products present challenges because of the situational factors surrounding their use. For example, because insurance often involves sickness, injury, accident, disability, or death, when insurance customers make a claim, they frequently do so under unpleasant circumstances. Emotional or financial stress also occurs in other situations, for instance, when customers have difficulty making loan payments, when they incur high credit card debt, or when they worry about the performance of their investments.

Because so much is at stake, customers expect their financial matters to be handled professionally, and if problems arise, customers are likely to become upset. Financial services employees must be prepared to deal with more than just products and services. They must be prepared to handle a full range of emotions.

Challenge No. 3: The Changing Financial Services Landscape

In recent years, the financial services landscape has changed dramatically, with corporations restructuring in a variety of ways. These corporate changes invariably affect how companies provide services. For example, when two companies merge, the "new" organization must often determine which computer systems to use and how to organize functions like customer service that were formerly performed by both companies. Employees sometimes have to become familiar with additional types of customers, products, regulatory requirements, procedures, and resources. Similarly, the company and its employees must address the concerns that many customers have about the impact of corporate changes on existing products, services, and relationships.

Challenge No. 4: Present Cost of Service vs. Possibility of Future Profit

Some companies are willing to invest in customer service resources now to increase revenue and profits later.

Typically, the financial rewards of providing exceptional customer service are not realized at the time of service, and they can be difficult to quantify at any time. Such rewards come later and may not appear to be connected to customer service activities. For example, a company might not realize that a customer purchased additional products and referred several friends to the company because of exceptional customer service she received several months ago. However, some companies are willing to invest in customer service resources *now* to increase revenue and profits *later*. These companies spend time and money on customer service by hiring, training, and rewarding the right employees, developing

"I'm sorry, sir, but unless you are referring to term, permanent, or endowment policies, I'm afraid I won't be able to help you with the meaning of life."

and implementing the right processes, and acquiring and using the right technology.

Other companies take a shorter view of the bottom line, and devote the bulk of their resources to generating sales rather than providing services that may retain business and foster sales in the future. However, an organization that acquires customers without the means to support them invariably establishes a "revolving door" through which customers are constantly coming and going. Eventually, as former customers spread the news about the organization's inadequate service, the volume of incoming customers declines.

Challenge No. 5: Knowing Who the Customer Is

Financial services companies must avoid confusion about who their customers are and how those customers will be supported.

Some financial services companies provide customer service primarily through intermediaries, such as agents or brokers. Other companies provide the bulk of their post-sales customer service through home office operations, such as call centers or service centers. Some companies use a combined approach, providing customer service through home office operations and intermediaries at the discretion of the customer or according to the type of product or service provided. Regardless of which approach they use, financial services companies must avoid confusion about who their customers are and how those customers will be supported.

In a company where intermediaries are the primary customers, the company focuses its customer service efforts on supporting intermediaries who in turn support external customers. However, because many intermediaries are not company employees, the company does not directly manage the customer service activities that are provided to its external customers. Therefore, a major challenge for this company is to effectively support its primary customers, the intermediaries, without losing sight of its "paying" customers, the external customers who are supported by the intermediaries. When uncertainty arises about whether the intermediary or the external customer is the actual customer, the company is said to be suffering from the ***who's-the-customer syndrome***.

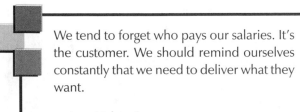

We tend to forget who pays our salaries. It's the customer. We should remind ourselves constantly that we need to deliver what they want.

— Lars Nyberg[3]

Similarly, when external customers have the option of obtaining service from more than one source in a company, responsibilities must be clearly assigned and communicated. For instance, consider a customer who calls his automobile insurance agent to point out a problem on his premium statement. The agent calls the home office for assistance. To avoid confusion, the agent and the home office should clearly establish who will be responsible for resolving this issue and for communicating the answer to the customer. From the customer's perspective, job responsibilities are meaningless; the only thing that matters is that someone takes ownership of the problem and solves it, as Figure 2-6 illustrates.

Why Provide Exceptional Customer Service?

Financial services companies provide exceptional customer service to retain their customers—a task that has grown increasingly complex over the years. Some customers, who are inexperienced with certain types of financial products and services, require special attention; while others, who are well informed and financially sophisticated, demand a different kind of care. Most customers have a variety of financial options to choose from, so if they are not happy with the service they receive from one company, they can take their business elsewhere. Frequently, a company must *delight* or *dazzle* its most valued customers to earn their loyalty, retain their business, and remain financially viable.

FIGURE 2-6. Taking Ownership of a Customer's Problem.

David Bernard, a CSR at Glenforest Insurance, was having difficulty obtaining medical records from a physician's office. These records were needed to complete the underwriting of a customer's life insurance application. The doctor's administrative assistant was not responding to repeated requests from the third party paramedic company that represented Glenforest Insurance, and the paramedic company was not responding to Mr. Bernard's follow-up requests. Mr. Bernard solved the problem by calling the physician's office and explaining to the administrative assistant that the patient would not be able to obtain life insurance coverage if his medical records were not furnished in a timely manner. When the administrative assistant understood the significance of the request, she sent the records.

Customer Retention and Loyalty

Companies typically spend large sums of money obtaining new customers. However, **customer retention**—the act of keeping the business of existing customers—is also essential if a company is to profit and grow. In the insurance industry, for instance, a policy must remain in force several years to offset acquisition and set-up costs.

Exceptional customer service significantly improves retention because it helps foster customer loyalty. **Customer loyalty** represents a customer's feeling of attachment to or preference for a company's people, products, or services.[4] As we saw in Chapter 1, a company typically earns customer loyalty by cultivating a relationship with the customer and being responsive to what the customer needs and wants. A loyal customer is less likely to defect to another company. Thus, as customer loyalty increases, so does customer retention.[5]

BEYOND CUSTOMER SATISFACTION TO CUSTOMER LOYALTY

A highly satisfied customer is more likely to remain loyal to a company in spite of enticements offered by other companies.

Providing basic satisfaction of a customer's needs does not automatically guarantee customer loyalty. Customers who claim to be satisfied with the service they have received may be willing to defect to another company if they are offered lower prices or more value for the money. Some studies have shown that 65 to 85 percent of customers who switch companies had previously responded that they were satisfied with the first company. However, the degree of customer satisfaction has an impact on loyalty. A study by Xerox Corporation revealed that the company's *totally* satisfied customers were six times more likely than its *merely* satisfied customers to buy from Xerox again during the next 18 months.[6] These results support the idea that a highly satisfied customer is more likely to remain loyal to a company in spite of enticements offered by other companies selling the same product or service.

To attain a high degree of customer *satisfaction*, a company's performance must significantly exceed the customer's expectations. To attain customer *loyalty*, a company must foster the same high degree of satisfaction, while also developing a strong ongoing relationship with the customer, typically through value-added service. The following formulas illustrate the factors involved in creating customer satisfaction and customer loyalty:[7]

$$\text{Satisfaction} = \text{Performance} - \text{Expectations} \ (S = P - E)$$
$$\text{Loyalty} = \text{Satisfaction} + \text{Relationship Strength} \ (L = S + RS)$$

A financial services company can improve its profits by 100 percent by retaining 5 percent more of its customers for an additional year.

Source: CRM-Forum.com[8]

Typically, people, not organizations, build relationships with customers, by listening, empathizing, thinking creatively, and taking appropriate action. Companies help build such relationships by empowering and supporting service providers. **_Empowerment_** is a management approach that gives service providers the authority to make decisions on behalf of the company in the course of performing their regular job functions. For example, a CSR at a bank might have the authority to refund overdraft charges applied to customer accounts, or a CSR at a credit card company might have the authority to waive late payment charges. As part of empowerment, a company furnishes its service providers with the training and resources they need to support customers; furthermore, the company provides assistance in situations where service providers do not themselves have the time or the expertise needed to help customers.

Although there is no single method that will tell you how to turn a satisfied customer into a loyal customer, Figure 2-7 provides a few examples.

SERVICE RECOVERY

No matter how much effort a company and its employees put into providing exceptional customer service, things can go wrong. Some problems have more to do with a customer's perception of a situation than with the situation itself. However, if the customer perceives a problem, then a problem exists, and the company must act to correct it.

If the customer perceives a problem, then a problem exists and the company must act to correct it.

Far from being catastrophes, such breakdowns (so long as they don't happen all the time) can give a company a second chance, and can result in service recovery. **_Service recovery_** occurs when a problem that causes customer dissatisfaction and a possible loss of business is fully resolved to the customer's satisfaction. Research has shown that customers who experience problems or make complaints and then receive exceptional customer service tend to be more loyal than customers who never had a problem. In addition, service recovery provides an organization and its employees with an opportunity to learn from the experience and make changes to improve service. Insight 2-1 presents an example of a missed opportunity for service recovery.

If a company succeeds in its efforts at service recovery and in providing exceptional service, its customers often become that company's **_advocates_**—people who are so convinced of the company's merit that they share

FIGURE 2-7. Examples of Providing Exceptional Customer Service to Create Customer Loyalty.

During the course of a telephone conversation with a service provider at Green Valley Insurance Company, an elderly customer, Naomi Albert, remarks that she is worried about her health because the heat is oppressive, and she can't afford to buy an air conditioner. Recalling a local news report about free air conditioning units for those in need, the service provider, Mishra Easwaran, suggests that Ms. Albert contact her local utility company to see if it offers a similar service. Now, whenever Ms. Albert calls Green Valley with a question, she asks to speak to Ms. Easwaran because she feels this service provider cares about her as a person as well as a customer.

Several minutes after a bank's branch office closes, one of the tellers, Soloman Mokogi, sees someone peering in through the glass door. Mr. Mokogi unlocks the door to find out why. The customer, Abby Durham, is very disappointed because she thought the bank was open later and she rushed to arrive on time, taking a taxi from work. When Mr. Mokogi cheerfully invites her inside to complete the transaction, Ms. Durham is elated.

A customer, Peter Ruth, calls his insurance company because his last premium payment was not credited to his account, although he mailed it several days ago. The CSR, Khaleelah Burnam, politely explains that the process can sometimes take several days. Hearing the concern in Mr. Ruth's voice, Ms. Burnam promises to check his account each day and notify him as soon as the payment is posted. Mr. Ruth feels confident that Ms. Burnam will follow through on her commitment. Two days later, he receives confirmation from Ms. Burnam that his account has been credited, and because of the special attention he has received, he recommends the company to several friends.

Paula Manchester calls her mutual fund company to make an emergency withdrawal from her account. "I know I should have made this request sooner," she says. "But I need the money to close on a house in two days. I'd really appreciate it if you could help me out." The CSR, Arie Shwartz, works with Ms. Manchester to have the necessary paperwork completed via fax and then he arranges for a wire fund transfer to deposit the money into Ms. Manchester's bank account the next day. Because of Mr. Shwartz's extra effort, Ms. Manchester is able to close on her new home.

their strong feelings with family, friends, and acquaintances. In the financial services industry, where referrals account for a large amount of new business, advocates are extremely valuable. Conversely, customers whose complaints are not satisfactorily resolved can become that company's *detractors*—people who have had one or more unpleasant experiences with a company and freely share their stories and disparaging remarks with others.

INSIGHT 2-1. A Missed Opportunity.

by Mark Sanborn

I used to buy my homeowner's and automobile insurance through an insurance brokerage. I'd been doing business with this brokerage for nearly a decade when I finally got fed up with its increasingly poor service. The service representative assigned to me was immature and incompetent, and when my wife called for a quote on a new vehicle, this person took a week to call back. By then we'd taken our insurance business elsewhere.

I figured I owed the CEO of the business an explanation of why we'd left. So I called, presented my list of the problems we'd experienced, and informed him that we'd taken our business elsewhere. His response?

"Mr. Sanborn, it sounds like there is nothing I can do to bring back your business. I'm sorry you decided to leave."

The fact is he might have recovered my business— if only he had tried. Even the most jaded and upset customers might reconsider going elsewhere if the provider makes a sincere effort to regain their loyalty.

Given the cost of acquiring a new customer, to give up on saving a current customer's loyalty is a costly proposition. Even the best service providers aren't perfect. But when they make a mistake, they recover remarkably.

Figure 2-8 lists eight key factors that help build a company's relationship with customers, leading to increased customer loyalty and retention.

Benefits of Exceptional Customer Service

Exceptional customer service helps a company reap many benefits that build on customer retention and loyalty. These benefits include

- **New customers.** Exceptional customer service results in "word-of-mouth advertising," which helps attract new customers and makes the selling process easier for sales representatives.

- **Improved recruiting.** Prospective employees and intermediaries are more likely to want to work for an organization with a reputation for exceptional customer service than for a less renowned company.

FIGURE 2-8. Eight Keys to Building Customer Loyalty.

Retaining customers starts when a prospect first hears about your company. Manage service expectations right from the start.

At every single point of contact you have with a customer, reinforce the customer's decision to buy from your company. Help customers continue to feel comfortable about that decision.

Do what you said you would do (keep your promises).

Stay in touch with your customers. Ask for feedback. Bring in new ideas.

Pay immediate attention to service problems.

Maintain some degree of price stability, if possible. Price increases often prompt people to see if a better deal is available.

Enhance your company's value to your existing customers by offering them additional benefits. For example, you could offer them preferential pricing if they purchase additional products.

Be graceful when customers decide to take their business elsewhere. Keep the doors open to future relationships.

Source: Adapted from Lynn C. Kelly, "Winning, Losing, and Loyalty," *Journal of the Society of Insurance Research* (Winter 1995): 55–56. Used with permission.

■ **Enhanced company image.** In the eyes of many customers, financial products and prices look the same from one company to the next. The company that provides exceptional customer service stands out from its competitors, and may find that customers are even willing to pay more for such service.

■ **Increased productivity and reduced expenses.** As a company's customer service improves, its employees become more productive because they spend less time and money trying to correct problems caused by poor service.

■ **Greater profitability.** By attracting and retaining the most desirable customers, a financial services firm can generate more profits.

As you have seen, exceptional customer service demands commitment, resources, and skills, but it is well worth the effort. In this chapter, we have described the characteristics, challenges, and benefits of exceptional customer service. In the next two chapters, we will examine in more detail one of the most important factors in providing exceptional customer service: the people who deliver it.

To practice and review the skills and information you learned in this chapter, see the interactive CD, *Practicing Your Customer Service Skills*, included with this book.

Key Terms and Concepts

customer-centric philosophy
product-centric philosophy
strategic planning
customer service strategic
    plan
business system
process
interpersonal skills
simultaneous production and
    consumption
intangibility of financial
    products

complexity of financial
    products
situational factors
who's-the-customer
    syndrome
customer retention
customer loyalty
empowerment
service recovery
advocates
detractors

Endnotes

1. Laura A. Liswood, *Serving Them Right* (New York: Harper Business, 1990).

2. Mark Sanborn, "The Ten Practices of Exceptional Service," *Best Practices in Customer Service*, ed. Ron Zemke and John A. Woods (New York: HRD Press, 1998), 206.

3. "Fast Talk: The Old Economy Meets the New Economy," *Fast Company* (October 2001): 80.

4. Thomas O. Jones and W. Earl Sasser, Jr., "Why Satisfied Customers Defect," *Harvard Business Review* (November–December 1995): 94.

5. Joseph Pine II, Don Peppers, and Martha Rogers, "Do You Want to Keep Your Customers Forever?" *Harvard Business Review* (March–April 1995): 103–114.

6 Jones and Sasser, 91.

7. Lynn C. Kelly, "Winning, Losing, and Loyalty," *Journal of the Society of Insurance Research* (Winter 1995): 49.

8. Chris Saunders and Michael Meltzer, *Driving Customer Retention, Development and Acquisition for Profit in the Insurance Business*, white paper supplied by CRM-Forum, Ó Chris Saunders and Michael Meltzer, 2000, http://www.crm-forum.com/library/art/art-013/brandframe.html (11 October 2002.

CHAPTER 3

The People Who Drive Customer Service: Selection and Training

After studying this chapter, you should be able to

- Identify several core competencies for customer service jobs

- Summarize the steps of the employee selection process

- Explain the importance of employee training

- Describe two types of training programs and five methods of training

People are central to customer service. Long before advanced technology and elaborate customer service processes came along, businesses relied on people to take care of customers. A century ago, customers with a question or a problem took it directly to the person who could help them—the bank officer who assessed loan requests, the insurance agent who sold policies, the general store manager who arranged credit plans. The customer would explain his needs or wants and the business owner or representative would present possible solutions. Based on this personal exchange, the customer would form opinions about the business and how much it valued its customers.

Today, exchanges between a customer and a business are less likely to happen in person and are more likely to occur over the phone, fax, or Internet. Nonetheless, the nature of the exchanges hasn't changed much: two people—a customer and a service provider—discussing needs, wants, and possible solutions. The effect of this exchange, whether positive or negative, can make a lasting impression on the customer. In addition, many employees contribute to a company's ability to provide exceptional customer service by performing administrative or "back office" functions to support customers and other employees who interact with customers. Regardless of the customer service technology and processes a financial services company uses, if a customer service exchange fails to satisfy or impress a customer, the company risks losing that customer. Therefore, the people who interact with and support customers are one of a financial services company's most valuable assets.

A financial services company acknowledges the importance of service providers by hiring the right people, developing their existing and potential skills through effective training and education, compensating them fairly, and inspiring them to perform to the best of their abilities. A service provider acknowledges the importance of her job by continually evaluating her personal and professional strengths and weaknesses, working to enhance skills and improve shortcomings, and letting managers know which tools, training, and other resources she needs to better serve customers.

In this chapter and the next, we will discuss how a company and its service providers can work together to ensure that customers are

> Motivate them, train them, care about them and make winners out of them … we know that if we treat our employees correctly, they'll treat the customers right. And if customers are treated right, they'll come back.
>
> — J. Marriot Jr.[1]

satisfied and delighted by the people who serve them. We will begin in this chapter by exploring the importance of identifying and selecting the right people for customer service jobs and discussing various types and methods of training available to ensure they can do those jobs well. We will continue in the next chapter by discussing the purpose of and strategies for evaluating and motivating service providers.

Note that when discussing service providers in these two chapters, we will be referring primarily to direct service providers such as customer service representatives and others who routinely interact with external customers, as these positions have unique demands and challenges. Most of the concepts we will discuss, however, are also relevant and applicable to anyone who serves customers in some way.

Identifying Potential Customer Service Professionals

The people who interact with and support customers are one of a financial services company's most valuable assets.

Before beginning the process of selecting customer service providers, most financial services organizations develop a *job description*, a document that identifies the duties, responsibilities, and accountabilities of a job. A job description usually specifies (1) the name or title of the job, (2) the actual work done on the job, (3) the position within the organization that supervises the job, (4) how the job relates to other jobs in the company, and (5) the required level of education, amount of experience, type of training, and personal characteristics that a person must have to be considered a qualified candidate for the job.

In developing job descriptions, many financial services companies establish core competencies for specific jobs or classes of jobs. A *core competency* is an ability, skill, or characteristic that has been shown to cause or predict outstanding performance in a given job. Core competencies include traits, motives, values, attitudes, knowledge, and skills.[2] Well-defined job descriptions and core competencies not only help a financial services organization identify the kinds of people it needs to provide outstanding customer service, but they also give job applicants an understanding of the kind of work and type of behavior that the organization expects. Figure 3-1 shows an example of a job description and core competencies for a customer service position.

Qualifications of Customer Service Professionals

At one time, many companies considered customer service a necessary business function and not much more. Customer service areas were often seen as revenue-draining complaint departments that did not require highly skilled or experienced employees. As a result, candidates for customer service jobs were not expected to have very extensive qualifications. Typically, a high school education, with little or no experience working in customer service, was sufficient.

Now, as financial services companies increasingly focus on outstanding service as a way to attract and retain customers and increase profits, candidates for customer service jobs are expected to have a greater number of qualifications. For example, many companies require customer service job candidates to have a college degree or a combination of education and customer service work experience. In addition, today's customer service providers are expected to possess a broad range of traits, attitudes, knowledge, and skills.

Although every financial services organization must decide which attributes it considers most important in its customer service providers, experts have identified the following core competencies usually found in successful customer service professionals:

- **Effective communication skills**. Service providers must be able to express themselves clearly and concisely when writing and speaking. Effective communication includes using proper grammar, syntax, and enunciation as well as presenting ideas in a logical, organized manner. Active listening, such as paraphrasing and asking questions to clarify information, is also an important part of effective communication. Service providers must be able to listen carefully to identify a customer's real need or concern before they can offer a solution.

Today's customer service providers are expected to possess a broad range of traits, attitudes, knowledge, and skills.

FIGURE 3-1. Sample Job Description and Core Competencies.

Position Title: Customer Service Representative
Department: Customer Service Center
Reports to: Manager, Customer Service Center

Job Requirements:
- One to three years of customer service experience
- An associate's or bachelor's degree preferred
- Proficient in Microsoft Office and Excel
- Strong organizational skills
- Ability to learn all current company operating systems needed to perform the job
- Ability and willingness to master system and software upgrades

Job Responsibilities:
- Receive, prioritize, process, and resolve inquiries and problems via incoming telephone calls and correspondence. Fulfill requests that require transaction processing or sending forms and/or additional information to customers.
- Give careful attention to details to detect, correct, and prevent problems. Handle problems in a timely, confidential, professional, and thorough manner.
- Enter required information into the database, in a timely manner, for the accurate printing of both standard and requested reports. Provide adequate follow-up on files with outstanding items.
- Stay current and proficient with information technology including computer systems, workflow, latest forms, and departmental goals.
- Process financial information as necessary, including balancing departmental accounts. Prepare, collect, input and reconcile billing information.

Core Competencies:
Customer Focus
- Looks for ways to meet or exceed customer expectations and service quality on a consistent basis
- Considers customers' needs as the primary guide in decision-making
- Regularly follows up to make sure customer needs are met
- Displays confidence and a willingness to take ownership of a request or problem
- Does not promise more to customers than can be delivered

Team Work
- Develops and maintains effective working relationships with supervisor, peers, and internal and external customers
- Participates actively in development of team goals and plans; ultimately supports team decisions though they may differ from own opinions
- Works diligently to achieve team goals
- Understands how team and personal goals support business unit and company goals overall
- Keeps team members abreast of individual progress and shares information
- Ensures own efforts on team are also in support of other teams'/business units' goals

continued on next page

FIGURE 3-1. Sample Job Description and Core Competencies (*continued*).

Leadership
- Deals openly and honestly with others; accepts responsibility for personal decisions and actions
- Encourages coworkers to work together toward a common goal
- Supports team members by encouraging participation and listening to others' ideas
- Lives up to individual, team, and customer commitments; actions are in line with stated intentions

Communication
- Demonstrates strong verbal and written communication skills
- Participates in group meetings and provides thoughtful and appropriate comments
- Practices good listening skills by seeking clarification and checking for understanding
- Uses vocabulary and terminology appropriate to the audience
- Demonstrates respect, courtesy, tact, and cooperation in interaction with others
- Uses appropriate interpersonal skills when meeting with people at different levels, positions, and backgrounds

Planning, Organizing and Implementing
- Sets appropriate priorities
- Organizes materials and resources within own work area
- Analyzes appropriate data and makes decisions in reasonable time frames
- Creates confidence in others that assignments will be successfully completed
- Sets clear goals and measures performance against personal plan

Initiative, Flexibility and Innovation
- Seeks alternative solutions to problems and searches for ways to improve work processes
- Exhibits openness to ideas and operates efficiently in a changing environment
- Encourages diverse views and solicits ideas that are different from own
- Volunteers to serve on committees, task forces, and to provide help to other associates
- Demonstrates ability to keep end results in sight while responding to changing conditions

Professional Self Development
- Understands scope and responsibility of own job and how the position interacts with others
- Demonstrates a comfort level with giving and receiving feedback
- Takes responsibility to seek out resources to enhance industry and job specific knowledge
- Actively participates in the performance development process
- Supports change by continuously developing new skills

- **Professionalism**. Having a positive attitude and treating others with courtesy and respect help a service provider act professionally even when faced with a challenging situation or unhappy customer. Professional people also tend to have high self-esteem, which enables them to deal with customer complaints without being offended. Professional behavior includes representing the company in a positive light to customers and working as part of a team to achieve departmental or company goals.

- **Interpersonal sensitivity**. Being aware of other people's circumstances and feelings enables a service provider to respond to customers with empathy. *Empathy* is the process of understanding another person's emotional state and imagining how you would feel in a similar situation. When customers believe that a company and its service providers sincerely care about customers' needs and concerns, they feel more comfortable and confident in dealing with the company. Interpersonal sensitivity also includes accepting and valuing differences among people, which helps build relationships with both customers and coworkers.

- **Problem-solving skills**. Not only must service providers have the ability to analyze and resolve problems, they must also know when to probe further, asking questions that identify the customer's real need or concern. An important part of effective problem solving is the ability to prioritize tasks and recognize situations that require immediate attention or resolution.

- **Flexibility and resourcefulness**. Responding to customers' needs often requires service providers to take unexpected courses of action and adapt company procedures. A flexible, resourceful person can be empowered to handle unanticipated situations and turn them into positive experiences. Resourcefulness includes being familiar with company resources—such as other departments or subject matter experts—and knowing when to involve them to help meet a customer's needs.

- **Conflict management skills**. Discord can arise when customers become upset about a company's products, policies, or actions. Knowing how and when to suggest alternative solutions or compromises is critical to successful conflict resolution. Being able to deal with contentious situations is as important as knowing when to involve a supervisor or manager in the conflict.

- **Customer focus**. Employees who understand how valuable customers are to a company's financial success are likely to make customer satisfaction their first priority. By staying focused on customers, service providers learn to think creatively and to be flexible in meeting customer needs. Focusing on customers also helps service providers identify trends in customer inquiries or complaints, which can be shared with other areas of the company so that problems with products, sales and marketing materials, or procedures can be corrected.

■ **Aptitude for technology.** Service providers who are comfortable and familiar with advanced technology (such as operating various computer applications and finding information on the Internet) require less training and become proficient users more quickly than those who are unfamiliar with or uneasy using technology. Increasingly, financial services firms expect service providers to be able to use various technologies to provide fast and accurate customer service. Service providers who lack technological aptitude can compensate with a willingness to learn about and practice using new technologies as needed.

■ **Ability and willingness to learn.** To deliver the best possible service to customers, service providers must be eager and able to learn about new people and new or modified products, processes, and technology. Regardless of how much training and education a financial services company provides to its employees, much of the knowledge and skills that service providers acquire ultimately comes from their own ability and willingness to learn through training and on-the-job experiences. A willingness to learn also can help service providers adapt to the many changes that they might encounter in their jobs and in the financial services industry.

■ **Knowledge of financial products**. Understanding financial products not only helps a service provider to answer customer questions, but also to recommend other products that can meet changing needs. In addition, staying informed about new or evolving products and services helps ensure that service providers deliver accurate information to customers.

Many financial services firms seek these core competencies (summarized in Figure 3-2) as well as any others related to a specific job, in candidates applying for customer service positions. Identifying core competencies is useful to companies not only during the employee selection process, but also when developing training programs and establishing performance evaluation systems, as we'll see later in this chapter and the next.

Financial services firms expect service providers to be able to use various technologies to provide fast and accurate customer service.

FIGURE 3-2. Core Competencies for Customer Service Jobs.

When both the company and its employees know the skills and attributes that are important in a particular job, they can work together to ensure that service providers have the resources and support they need to achieve excellence in their jobs. Service providers wishing to improve their job performance can use these competencies as a basis for improving their skills, as Exercise 3-1 illustrates. In addition, throughout this book, we will discuss ways that service providers can develop and improve skills related to these core competencies.

Selecting Customer Service Professionals

A company is known by the people it keeps.

— Harry Klinger, Industrialist[3]

After a financial services company develops a job description and identifies core competencies for its customer service positions, it recruits job applicants and begins the selection process. The employee selection process typically includes pre-employment screening tests, personal interviews, and background checks. Ultimately,

Exercise 3-1.   Developing Exceptional Customer Service Skills.

As a service provider, you can improve your chances of job and career success by working to master the skills, or competencies, that your company considers important. Listed below are tips for improving skills related to the customer service core competencies discussed in this chapter. After studying these tips, try to incorporate them into your daily work routine.

Communication

The next time you speak with someone, give your undivided attention to the speaker, listen without judging, and be sure you understand what is being communicated by paraphrasing what you believe you heard.

Professionalism

Find a coworker who is effective at always giving the customer a positive impression of the company. Role-play a situation in which a customer has developed a poor opinion of the company, with your coworker playing the part of the unsatisfied customer. Ask him to critique your ability to present a positive image of the company to the customer.

Interpersonal Sensitivity

List phrases you hear coworkers use to show that they empathize with the customer's problem, such as "I know it must be frustrating to have difficulty reaching the correct person…" Refer to these notes on a regular basis, and use a few of these phrases in your interactions with customers.

Problem Solving

Before asking your supervisor for help in solving a problem, make your own evaluation. Identify the consequences of the problem, then identify and evaluate several options for solving the problem. Based on this information, try to arrive at a solution on your own. Then present the options and your recommended solution to your supervisor.

Flexibility and Resourcefulness

Look back on the way you have dealt with customers' problems. Do you have a tendency to hold on to a procedure or solution because you've "always done it this way?" Try to consider other reasonable alternatives. Work with your supervisor to develop new, more effective ways of handling specific customer problems.

Conflict Management

Make sure you understand the reasons for company policies. This understanding will help you to enforce policies and negotiate appropriate compromises with your customers. Talk with your supervisor or a knowledgeable coworker if you have questions about the feasibility of a particular compromise.

Customer Focus

Always fulfill commitments you have made to customers. Provide customers with information to contact you directly if they are not satisfied, and communicate to them your plans for follow-up. Put a reminder on your calendar to ensure that you will carry out the commitment and follow up.

Exercise 3-1.   Developing Exceptional Customer Service Skills (*continued*).

Aptitude for Technology

Learning more about the technology you use can help you overcome your fears of using it. If you're uncomfortable using a system or process, practice using it as often as possible. During training sessions, take detailed notes that you can refer to later to clarify your understanding.

Ability and Willingness to Learn

Be proactive about learning. Find out what kind of training and education programs are available within or outside your company and ask your supervisor or manager for permission to attend those that would help you in your job. Pursue learning opportunities in areas that interest you, such as technology or interpersonal skills.

Knowledge of Financial Products

Take time to learn more about the products your company offers. Review marketing materials and ask questions about products or features that you don't understand.

Source: Adapted from LOMA, *ASK On-the-Job Activities* (Atlanta: LOMA, © 1993) Used with permission; all rights reserved.

the selection of a suitable candidate for a customer service position should be based on a number of factors, including how well the candidate meets the core competencies, the candidate's score on pre-employment testing, the quality of the candidate's experience and references, and the impression the candidate makes on the interviewers.

Pre-Employment Screening Tests

To determine whether a job candidate has the right competencies, as well as the appropriate education, training, and work experience for a job, most financial services companies use pre-employment screening tests. Such tests attempt to assess a candidate's mental abilities, specific job skills, and behavioral tendencies. A ***mental abilities test***, also known as a *cognitive abilities test* or an *aptitude test*, attempts to determine a candidate's general level of intelligence and reasoning ability by evaluating abilities such as remembering details, solving problems, and understanding and using words accurately. A ***specific job skills test*** attempts to evaluate how well the applicant has mastered specific skills needed to perform well in the position—for example, typing (keyboarding), using word processing or spreadsheet applications, and writing business letters. A ***behavioral tendencies test***, also known as a *personality test*, attempts to discover the candidate's typical job behaviors, such as whether the person is a team player, is honest, follows rules and procedures, and remains calm under pressure.

In most jurisdictions, regulatory requirements specify how pre-employment screening tests can be used. For example, many jurisdictions mandate that such tests can be used only if they accurately assess the candidate's ability to perform specific tasks related to the position to be filled. To ensure that screening tests meet applicable requirements, many financial services firms use testing systems developed, validated, and verified to be compliant with regulatory requirements by outside vendors. Figure 3-3 describes two such systems.

Personal Interviews

A job applicant who successfully completes required screening tests is usually asked to participate in a personal interview. The interview process is particularly important for potential customer service providers because it presents an opportunity for the job candidate to demonstrate effective communication skills and professionalism, two significant core competencies for customer service positions. Generally, human resources personnel conduct the testing and initial interviews to eliminate obviously unsuitable candidates, then customer service managers and employees interview the remaining candidates to determine whether they are a good fit for the job, work group, and department. In some companies, team members interview a potential new member so both parties get a feel for whether the candidate might be easily assimilated into the team. Also, team members or peers who participate in interviewing and selecting a new employee have an investment in helping that person succeed.

Background Checks

The final step in the employee selection process typically involves verifying the background information and references provided by the applicant. Although information about a person's performance and behavior on a previous job can be very valuable in helping a company select the right candidate, privacy laws and concerns about potential lawsuits have made companies in most jurisdictions wary about revealing negative information about a former or current employee. Many companies will only confirm dates of employment, salary levels, or job titles that the applicant has given the hiring company. Because personal references, such as letters of recommendation, usually provide only favorable information about a job applicant, greater weight is usually given to more objective information when considering a candidate's suitability for a job.

FIGURE 3-3. Examples of Pre-Employment Testing Systems.

The Thomas PPA System
(Also known as the "DISC" system)

Developed by Thomas International, this system is designed to help companies select the right person for a job, as well as identify strengths and weaknesses, build teams, and identify leadership potential among current employees.

This system requires a job candidate to complete a questionnaire called the Personal Profile Analysis (PPA), which is designed to assess the person's communication style and techniques, leadership qualities, self-image, dependability, competitiveness, attitude, and response to stress. The DISC system is based on Dr. William Marston's 1928 theory that all human behavior traits are based upon four key characteristics: **D**ominance, **I**nfluence, **S**teadiness, and **C**ompliance. Although most people show all four of these characteristics at various times, usually one is more dominant.

A trained analyst evaluates a candidate's responses to the PPA questionnaire to help determine which of the four characteristics the candidate exhibits most strongly. Such information can provide insight into how the person is likely to behave in the work situation. For example, a person who shows a tendency toward compliance (referred to as a "High C") is likely to be diplomatic, careful, compliant, precise, logical, a perfectionist, systematic, and accurate. A person who tends toward dominance (a "High D") is likely to be driving, competitive, forceful, inquisitive, direct, self-starting, and assertive.

Source: TG & Associates, "DISC Summary," http://www.tgassociates.com/disc.asp (12 March 2002), and Thomas International, "THOMAS DiSC," http://www.nbogroup.com/thomas/introd.asp (12 March 2002).

LOMASelect™

This series of selection tools developed by LOMA is designed to assess candidates for entry-level, supervisory, and customer service positions and to help companies choose the most qualified candidate for a job.

Tests for entry-level candidates assess their cognitive and personal attributes, including skills and competencies such as reading, math, adaptability, and willingness to learn. Tests for supervisory candidates measure 11 areas considered key to supervisory positions, including leadership, interpersonal skills, and handling employee problems.

The selection tool for customer service candidates is a 30-minute, Web-delivered simulation system that requires candidates to assume the role of the customer service representative. The system allows companies to determine how well candidates interact with customers using live text messages and telephone conversations. Candidates face several different scenarios, including angry and confused customers, technical support issues, and general account inquiries. The system measures a candidate's skills in key customer service competencies—including accuracy, efficiency, empathy, listening, problem solving, multitasking, and rapport—and then calculates results and generates reports.

*"Allen is an incredible, wonderful, fun, generous,
exciting, kind, loving, brilliant, very special human being.
This personal reference from your dog is quite impressive."*

Customer Service Training, Education, and Career Development

Job enrichment is the process of increasing the authority and complexity of a job to make the job more rewarding to the employee.

Even a service provider with many or all of the core competencies we discussed earlier cannot perform his job well without the proper training and development. New employees need to learn about company-specific systems and procedures, and all employees need additional training and education throughout their careers to keep up with changes within the company, the financial services industry, and customer service in general. Whenever possible, training and educational opportunities should correspond to the core competencies for a position, to ensure that employees advance in areas that are critical to their job performance. In addition, many financial services companies offer service providers the opportunity to increase their job responsibilities and authority through job enrichment and promotions. *Job enrichment* is the process of increasing the authority and complexity of a job to make the job more rewarding to the employee.

In the American Society for Training & Development's *2001 State of the Industry Report*, the top 10 percent of companies surveyed spent an average of $1,665 on training per eligible employee, compared to $677 for the average survey respondent.

Source: American Society for Training & Development (ASTD)[4]

Learning about new products, processes, and technology as well as acquiring communication and interpersonal skills help service providers become more proficient in their jobs and contribute to a company's intellectual capital. **Intellectual capital** is the sum of all employee knowledge in a company that gives it a competitive edge in the marketplace.[5]

Companies can increase their stores of intellectual capital by hiring people who bring a strong base of knowledge to the company.

Many businesses have found that their long-term profitability depends less on what employees produce in the short-term than on what employees know and can apply over time. Generally, as a company's intellectual capital grows, its profitability also grows. Companies can increase their stores of intellectual capital by hiring people who bring a strong base of knowledge to the company and by helping service providers continually increase their knowledge and skills through training and job experience.

Types of Training Programs

Training programs can generally be classified as (1) job orientation or (2) continuous training.

JOB ORIENTATION

The training typically given to all new employees is *job orientation*, which introduces them to the company they are joining and to the work they will perform. Two kinds of orientation are particularly important for people entering a customer service role: (1) company-specific orientation and (2) department-specific orientation.

Company-specific orientation introduces new employees to the company's organizational structure, shows how the employee's department fits into that structure, and explains how employees benefit from their employment with the company. During this orientation, employees usually learn about the company's business philosophy and goals, policies and procedures, and benefits such as group insurance and vacation.

Department-specific orientation introduces new employees to the basic operations of the work group to which they are assigned and to the other employees in that work group. In this orientation, employees learn what is expected of them and how their work benefits the organization and its customers. For customer service employees, department-specific orientation usually focuses on basic rules of customer service and on the economic importance of customer service to the company and the employee.

Many companies provide a customer service training program for employees who are new to the customer service department. These programs—which employees attend for several days or weeks—are designed to introduce employees to the basic concepts of customer service and to the company's approach to providing customer service. Such a training program might explain, for example, the company's preferred way of answering telephone calls or any privacy guidelines that must be followed when giving out customer information. Often, new employees also learn about the company's products and processes and the systems that support them during department-specific orientation. Customer service training activities usually include having service providers respond to sample customer calls and use the company's customer service technology. Customer service training programs for new employees can be very comprehensive; however, most service providers require continuous training to become and remain proficient in their jobs.

CONTINUOUS TRAINING

As we mentioned earlier, training must continue throughout a service provider's career. As people advance in their jobs or move into new jobs, they must acquire new skills and different levels of knowledge. Even when a person keeps the same job, existing skills and knowledge must be reinforced and updated so as not to become stale. For customer service providers in the financial services industry, several kinds of continuous training are important.

Technology

Service providers must be proficient in using the hardware, software, databases, and networks required to perform their jobs. Continuous training is needed to enhance employees' use of existing technology, as well as to introduce them to new or modified technology. We will discuss technology in more detail in Chapter 13.

Products and Processes

To answer customer questions, service providers must be knowledgeable about all of a company's products and understand the processes used to support those products. Because a financial services firm's product offerings and processes can change frequently, continuous training in these areas is needed to ensure that service providers give accurate information to customers. Sometimes, subject matter experts from other departments are brought into the customer service area to share their knowledge with service providers. Other times, service providers attend training sessions conducted by other functional areas, such as billing or marketing.

Customer-Focused Service and Sales

As we mentioned earlier, newly hired service providers usually receive some customer service training during department-specific job orientation.

> Even when a person keeps the same job, existing skills and knowledge must be reinforced and updated so as not to become stale.

INSIGHT 3-1. The Principal Gets Focused on The *Customer*®.

The Principal Financial Group replaced a variety of facilitator-led and computer-based customer service training programs with a single, company-wide approach for customer service training that instills the fundamental values, attitudes, and skills of a customer-focused organization. The Principal uses *The Customer*®, a program developed by Integrity Systems®, to develop customer service behaviors that are consistent with the company's core competencies.

The Customer is a hands-on, comprehensive 16-hour program that is presented in nine sessions over a nine-week period. Its primary objective is to help employees and their leaders understand and support the company's commitment to outstanding service. Instead of simply teaching employees how to react to customer questions or problems, the program establishes and enhances the customer-focused behaviors that demonstrate the "care more, know more, do more" approach to customer service that The Principal is committed to providing.

By combining self-study reading, classroom presentations, and on-the-job application activities, *The Customer* helps employees of The Principal:

- Understand the mission and overall purpose of the company
- Gain a clear understanding of who their customers are and what their needs are
- Develop a sincere interest in serving their customers
- Apply customer service behaviors successfully in any situation
- Assume full responsibility for carrying out their service roles to the best of their abilities

Comments from employees who have completed the program include:

"The Customer is a wonderful, refreshing program which allows all participants to learn more about themselves and their own perspective of service."

"I am more than ever aware of the fact that my actions all have end results…that affect everyone down the line, from internal to our external customers. The majority of my time is helping my internal customers. What I do for that person eventually affects our external customer."

"It has…given me an easy-to-follow guide to customer satisfaction."

Mike Obal, SPHR
Assistant Director—HR Employee Development
The Principal Financial Group

In addition, ongoing training in the concepts and practices of customer service is important to ensure that customer service providers maintain a focus on providing exceptional service. For example, such training might include sessions on how to gain customers' respect and cooperation or how to deal with demanding or angry customers. Insight 3-1 describes how one company's customer service training program encourages all employees to focus on providing outstanding service. Also, financial services companies that encourage customer service providers to promote or sell products and services must train those employees in effective sales techniques.

Communication and Interpersonal Skills

One of the most important types of continuous training focuses on the skills needed to effectively interact with customers. Ongoing training in communication and interpersonal skills can help a service provider deliver better service to external and internal customers.

Conflict management training focuses on techniques that service providers can use to effectively handle customer complaints, especially in situations in which the customer is angry.

Two specific types of communication and interpersonal skills training that are especially beneficial to customer service providers are conflict management training and diversity training. ***Conflict management training*** focuses on techniques that service providers can use to effectively handle customer complaints, especially in situations in which the customer is angry. For example, service providers need to know how to respond to customers who exhibit hostile or abusive behavior, such as name-calling and swearing. ***Diversity training*** focuses on first recognizing gaps caused by cultural or other differences and then developing the skills needed to bridge those gaps. Such gaps may exist with coworkers or with customers.

Diversity training can help service providers learn how to communicate more effectively with customers from various backgrounds. For example, Joseph Essel, a service provider at the Olympic Life Insurance Company, received a telephone call from Thomas Cho, who wanted information about the premium payment owed on his mother's life insurance policy. Mr. Essel explained that, due to confidentiality guidelines, he could only release the requested information to Mr. Cho's mother, the policyowner. Mr. Cho, who spoke broken English, said that his mother spoke very little English. Speaking slowly and precisely, Mr. Essel explained that he needed to speak to the mother briefly and have her answer a few security questions. Because Mr. Essel understood that a communication barrier existed and took time to modify his behavior by speaking more slowly and precisely than he normally would have, Mr. Cho was able to understand his request. His mother came on the phone and, by once again speaking carefully and clearly, Mr. Essel was able to obtain the necessary security information and then fulfill Mr. Cho's original request.

Training Methods

A financial services company can use various methods to provide the types of training we have just discussed. Generally, training methods can be categorized as self-study, classroom, on-the-job, simulation, or computer-based training.

SELF-STUDY TRAINING

Self-study training is a training method in which the trainee works independently to complete a training course or program. Self-study training materials are available in various formats including textbooks (such as this one), guidebooks, computer software programs, or Web-based programs. Typically, the trainee is responsible for learning the material and taking any examinations or quizzes required to complete the training course or program.

The advantage of self-study training is that it allows material to be presented systematically at a pace and schedule that is convenient for the trainee. The disadvantages of this training method are that it does not provide interactive, situation-based training or personalized attention for each trainee. To minimize these disadvantages, many financial services companies offer classroom training to provide support for employees taking certain self-study courses or programs.

The advantage
of self-study
training is that it
allows material
to be presented
systematically at
a pace and
schedule that is
convenient for
the trainee.

CLASSROOM TRAINING

Classroom training is a training method in which an instructor typically lectures to the group, leads the group in discussion, or directs the group as they do various exercises, such as role-playing. Usually, classroom training is conducted by a person whose primary job is to train a company's employees, although it can also be conducted by a supervisor or an employee.

The advantage of classroom training is that it removes trainees from the pressure of the work environment and allows them to concentrate completely on the skills and knowledge they are learning. In addition, because professional trainers—people whose primary responsibility and expertise are to teach employees how to work more effectively—usually supervise and lead classroom training, the quality of the training is typically high and consistent among all employees.

The fact that classroom training occurs away from the actual work environment also can be a disadvantage of using this method. Because the training occurs away from the work unit and is provided by trainers who might not be aware of a job's actual working conditions, the training might not be completely applicable on the job.

ON-THE-JOB TRAINING

During **on-the-job training**, an employee learns by performing real work in the actual work environment. In on-the-job training, a coworker or supervisor explains the step-by-step operations of a job, watches while the new employee does the job, and provides immediate feedback on the employee's performance.

The advantages of on-the-job training are that new employees learn by performing the actual work they will be doing on a daily basis in their job, and they become productive from their first day on the job. Also, on-the-job training offers job variety for the person who provides the training, which may increase that person's job knowledge and satisfaction.

One disadvantage of on-the-job training is that the people providing the training become less productive because they must take time away from their jobs to instruct someone else. Another significant disadvantage of on-the-job training is that, because the training is done in the actual work situation, errors made during training are errors in real work that may have repercussions for the company. In addition, the informal structure of on-the-job training can lead to gaps or inconsistencies in training.

To minimize these disadvantages, many customer service departments allocate staff and other resources accordingly when experienced service providers are busy providing on-the-job training, to ensure that enough people are available to serve customers effectively. Also, many companies formalize the on-the-job training process as much as possible by developing training guidelines and checklists, which can be used during training to ensure that all new service providers receive the same learning experiences. Figure 3-4 shows a sample checklist for training a new employee in the policyowner services area of a life insurance company.

The on-the-job training we have just discussed is basic training that many new employees receive when they first begin their jobs. In some companies, employees also may participate in other types of job-related training, including *job rotation* and *mentoring*. In **job rotation**, employees move periodically from one job to another, staying in each job just long enough to learn how the job is done and how it relates to other jobs in the company. For example, a customer service representative might spend time in a transaction-processing job to learn how various activities are performed.

FIGURE 3-4. Sample On-the-Job Training Checklist.

The following partial checklist is an example of the guidelines used for on-the-job training of a new employee in the policyowner service area of a life insurance company.

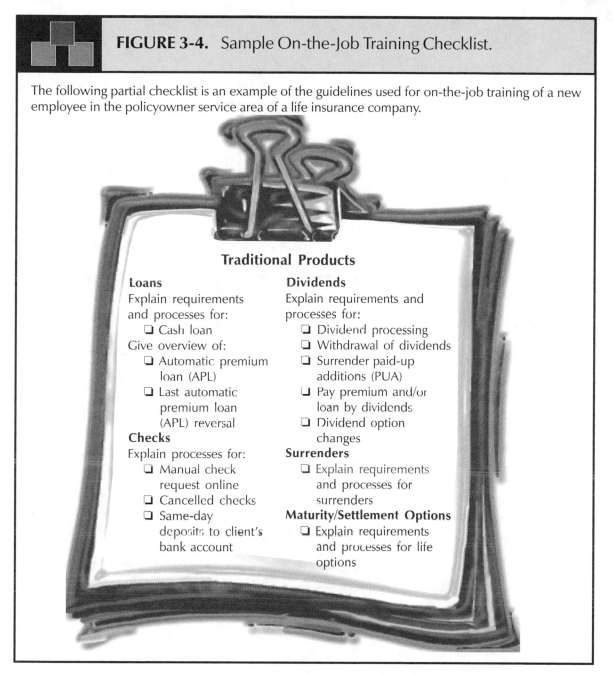

Traditional Products

Loans
Explain requirements and processes for:
- ❏ Cash loan

Give overview of:
- ❏ Automatic premium loan (APL)
- ❏ Last automatic premium loan (APL) reversal

Checks
Explain processes for:
- ❏ Manual check request online
- ❏ Cancelled checks
- ❏ Same-day deposits to client's bank account

Dividends
Explain requirements and processes for:
- ❏ Dividend processing
- ❏ Withdrawal of dividends
- ❏ Surrender paid-up additions (PUA)
- ❏ Pay premium and/or loan by dividends
- ❏ Dividend option changes

Surrenders
- ❏ Explain requirements and processes for surrenders

Maturity/Settlement Options
- ❏ Explain requirements and processes for life options

One advantage of job rotation is that it helps employees understand other company operations, which can benefit an employee when he returns to his job. For instance, in an insurance company, a customer service representative who works in the claims department for a few days or weeks gains a better understanding of how claims are handled. This knowledge can help him when he returns to his job and fields questions from customers about their claims. Job rotation also can provide an employee

with versatile job skills, which can result in more opportunities for advancement.

One possible disadvantage of job rotation is that employees typically stay in each job just long enough to learn the basics but not long enough to become really proficient in the position. In addition, job rotation requires a company to commit the resources necessary to train employees in each job they rotate through.

In **mentoring**, a less experienced employee is assigned to work with a more experienced employee, or *mentor*. A mentor answers questions, offers advice, and provides general guidance to the less experienced employee. Mentoring may be a short-term situation used only during an employee's training period, or it may be a long-term relationship that nurtures the

---

INSIGHT 3-2. Mentoring Program Fosters Partnerships, Friendships.

The mission of the Mentoring Program at the Woodmen of the World Life Insurance Society is to foster partnerships by promoting job satisfaction, loyalty, personal growth, fraternal awareness, fraternal involvement, and diversity. Woodmen has a formal guided mentoring program intended to enhance on-the-job learning and growth by matching a new employee (the protégé) with an experienced associate in a nonsupervisory relationship.

Mentoring provides the protégé with an alternative channel of communication, which serves as an additional source of guidance and counsel in a supportive, nonjudgmental environment. Mentoring is intended to complement and not to replace or interfere with the normal interaction between an employee and his supervisor. The program is not specifically designed to develop employees for higher level positions, nor is there a promise of promotion as a result of program participation.

Mentors and new employees become acquainted through workshops and the new employees submit their top three choices for mentors. Based

on this information, Woodmen's Advisory Board on mentoring matches mentors with protégés. The matches are effective for one year, although the mentor and protégé may dissolve the partnership at any time.

The mentor and the protégé choose how often to meet and determine their own goals for program participation. They complete a career development plan that assists them in achieving those goals. Various activities and discussion groups are conducted through the mentoring program, including training on insurance terms and products, goal setting, teamwork, problem solving, leadership skills, listening skills, and coaching skills.

The program has grown each year, both in terms of numbers of participants and in how it is administered. Through the enhanced knowledge, personal growth, and friendships gained, the Mentoring Program has helped provide Woodmen with a motivated, productive, and customer service-oriented workforce.

Source: Adapted from Deanne Adams et al., Woodmen of the World Life Insurance Society, *Mentoring,* report to LOMA Policyowner Service Seminar, Miami (May 2000). Used with permission.

employee's career development over many years. For mentoring to be effective, a company must (1) make mentoring duties an official part of the mentor's job responsibilities so the mentor has the time and motivation to perform the mentor role, and (2) carefully match mentors with employees to ensure the relationship is a positive one for both people. Insight 3-2 describes the success of one company's mentoring program.

SIMULATION TRAINING

Simulation training is a training method that gives trainees an opportunity to experience a job's working conditions without the pressure of actually being on the job.

To combine the benefits of on-the-job training with the benefits of classroom training, some financial services companies try to create training conditions that are as much like actual working conditions as possible. *Simulation training* is a training method that gives trainees an opportunity to experience a job's working conditions without the pressure of actually being on the job. In simulation training, employees can practice the procedures and techniques they have learned in classroom situations and learn from whatever errors they make without worrying that their mistakes have negatively affected the company.

Simulations vary greatly in their attempts to match working conditions. Some are highly sophisticated and replicate working conditions almost exactly, such as the flight-simulation cockpits used by pilots and astronauts. Others are less sophisticated and imitate only certain aspects of a job's working conditions. For example, a financial services company with a large call center might train new CSRs by placing them in a room with telephone equipment and having them answer calls placed by trainers playing the role of customers. Such simulation training allows trainees to practice answering customer calls and dealing with problems that often occur on the job.

A significant advantage of simulation training is that trainees experience working conditions similar to those they will experience on the job. They deal with situations that strongly resemble real problems. Employees who have completed simulation training can almost feel like seasoned veterans before they even get on the job. The disadvantage of simulation training programs that replicate working conditions to a high degree is that they can be expensive to create and maintain. To avoid this expense, financial services companies create less exact replicas or use computer software to simulate working conditions.

> If you think training employees and having them leave is expensive, try not training them and having them stay!
>
> — Telephone Doctor[6]

COMPUTER-BASED TRAINING

Computer-based training (CBT) is a training method that uses computer hardware, software, and, in some cases, networks, to deliver training. Computer-based training includes software programs on CD-ROMs and disks as well as Web-based programs available via the Internet. In addition, some financial services companies offer CBT programs on their internal computer networks.

Computer-based training programs vary widely in complexity and effectiveness. Some programs simply present information and questions that students can read and answer on-screen. Others are more interactive and, as mentioned above, attempt to simulate actual working conditions. ***Interactive video training (IVT)*** is a type of computer-based training that uses video to create a more interesting and realistic training situation than standard CBT. An IVT program requires the trainee to respond to information presented (usually in video format) by choosing various responses and courses of action. The program then indicates where the trainee made errors and suggests ways to correct them.

A great advantage of computer-based training programs is their convenience, because employees can access the training according to their schedules and without having to leave their workstations. CBT also benefits companies with employees in many different cities or countries, where it is impractical to send instructors to each location. A disadvantage of CBT programs is that they generally do not provide the structure, motivation, and assistance provided by classroom training. Also, some CBT programs—such as interactive video training—can be quite expensive.

Because each of the training methods we have just discussed has advantages and disadvantages, many financial services companies combine one or more methods to create a "blended" approach to training. For example, a company might offer classroom instruction to supplement a Web-based, self-study training program. The advantage of blended training programs is that they provide trainees with various ways to learn.

Education

As we discussed earlier, employees who have a wide range of knowledge about various subjects contribute to a company's intellectual capital. While employees who are trained to perform specific jobs are essential to a company's operations, employees who also have a broad education provide the company with a reservoir of talent and wisdom that can help the company adapt to internal and external changes. Because of their expansive backgrounds and knowledge, such employees may be able to respond more quickly and imaginatively to unexpected situations.

Financial services companies that understand the value of intellectual capital usually encourage employees to pursue educational development activities, such as attending industry seminars and conferences and completing independent study programs (such as LOMA's Professional, Customer Service Program) and university courses. Many businesses pay for all or part of the fees associated with educational development activities, and many provide financial or other rewards to employees who complete certain courses.

Financial services companies that understand the value of intellectual capital usually encourage employees to pursue educational development activities.

Career Development

As customer service providers participate in training and education programs, they will naturally want to use their new or enhanced skills and knowledge in their work. Because many customer service jobs enable employees to use a broad range of skills in varying degrees, some service providers may be satisfied with finding ways to apply new skills in their current jobs. Generally, however, as service providers acquire additional experience and knowledge, they tend to want more challenges and opportunities in their work. In addition, most people want to earn higher pay as they become more knowledgeable and proficient in their jobs.

Financial services companies that recognize employees' need for growth and development in their jobs and salaries typically develop career paths for employees. A *career path* is an outline of the types of advancement available to an employee within a particular department and within the company. A career path provides a logical progression through positions that offer increasing responsibility and pay. This progression can be through promotion or lateral job rotation, or through salary increases based on increased job skills. At many financial services companies, the customer service career path can lead to supervisory or management positions. For an example of a customer service career path, see Figure 3-5.

A career path offers advantages for both employees and the company. Knowing that a customer service job can eventually lead to increased responsibility and authority can inspire many employees to work hard to progress along the path. Also, following a career path provides the job

FIGURE 3-5. A Customer Service Career Path.

Senior Customer Service Representative

Individuals have a minimum of three years of service with the company and have received training on all of the duties performed by CSRs. In addition to CSR duties, Senior CSRs are responsible for contacting new customers to promote loyalty and answer questions. They also serve as mentors for new Associates.

Customer Service Representative

Individuals have 18 months of service with the company, in addition to meeting accuracy, phone monitoring, and attendance standards. CSRs perform all the functions of Associates and also answer customer calls.

Customer Service Associate

Individuals are hired into this entry-level position based on typing speed performance and pre-employment test scores. Associates train to handle customer phone requests for all of the company's products and to conduct various service transactions.

Source: Adapted from LOMA, *Career Paths for Service Representatives*, Information Center Brief (August 2000).

variety that many people need and value. A career path benefits the company by encouraging good employees to stay in customer service rather than transfer to other departments or leave the company altogether.

In this chapter, you have learned about the importance of identifying and selecting the right people for customer service jobs, as well as about the many types and methods of training available to provide them with the appropriate skills and knowledge to succeed in those jobs. In the next chapter, we will continue our discussion of the people who drive customer service by explaining the purpose and methods of performance evaluations and effective ways to motivate customer service professionals.

To practice and review the skills and information you learned in this chapter, see the interactive CD, *Practicing Your Customer Service Skills*, included with this book.

Key Terms and Concepts

job description

core competency

empathy

mental abilities test

specific job skills test

behavioral tendencies test

job enrichment

intellectual capital

job orientation

company-specific orientation

department specific
  orientation

conflict management
  training

diversity training

self-study training

classroom training

on-the-job training

job rotation

mentoring

simulation training

computer-based training
  (CBT)

interactive video training
  (IVT)

career path

Endnotes

1. The People's Cyber Nation, "Great Quotations to Inspire and Motivate You!" http://www.cybernation.com/victory/quotations/subjects/quotes_customers.html (15 October 2002).

2. LOMA, *Service Skills and Competencies*, Information Center Brief (May 2000).

3. Jim Clemmer with Brian Sheehy, *Firing on All Cylinders: The Service/Quality System for High-Powered Corporate Performance* (New York: Irwin Professional Publishing, 1992), 148.

4. American Society for Training & Development, "ASTD Releases Its 2001 State of the Industry Report," 26 March 2001, http://www.astd.org/ (1 August 2001).

5. Debra Bailey Helwig, "Intellectual Capital: Key to Profitability," *Resource* (July 1996): 7.

6. Telephone Doctor® Customer Service Training, *Thought for the Day* in an e-mail from Staff of Telephone Doctor Customer Service Training, info@telephonedoctor.com (20 May 2002).

CHAPTER 4

The People Who Drive Customer Service: Evaluation and Motivation

After studying this chapter, you should be able to

- Discuss the purpose and several methods of performance evaluations

- Identify several guidelines for performance evaluations

- Explain how monitoring is used to gather performance information and distinguish between real-time and recorded monitoring

- Describe several types of financial and nonfinancial rewards that financial services companies use to motivate customer service providers

A s you learned in Chapter 3, service providers can succeed in delivering exceptional customer service only when they have the right job qualifications and the appropriate training to perform their work. In addition, service providers need constructive feedback about their strengths and weaknesses and positive reinforcement and encouragement to continue performing well over time. In this chapter, we will look at two more areas in which a company and its service providers can work together to ensure their customers are receiving the best possible care from the people serving them: performance evaluations and motivational rewards.

Customer Service Evaluations

As employees, most of us enjoy being praised for the work we do. On the other hand, most of us do *not* enjoy being told that we have done something incorrectly or that our work needs to be improved. Receiving both praise and constructive criticism, however, are necessary for all of us to learn and grow in our jobs. To ensure that employees receive positive feedback as well as suggestions for improving their work, most companies use performance evaluations. A ***performance evaluation*** (also called *performance appraisal)* is a formal process of reviewing and documenting an employee's job performance with the primary goal of continually improving performance. Ideally, performance evaluations are linked to a job's core competencies, so employees receive feedback and suggestions for improvement in areas that are important to job and career success. Because performance evaluations also are used to support decisions related to compensation, promotion, or termination, they have significant meaning to both employees and managers.

Performance Evaluation Methods

Understanding the purpose and structure of the performance evaluation system used by a company can help service providers better meet their performance goals. In this section, we discuss the most commonly used performance evaluation methods, including

- Management by objectives (MBO)

- Graphic rating scale appraisal

- Essay appraisal

- Critical incident appraisal

- 360-degree feedback

Note that a company's human resources department usually plays a pivotal role in selecting and administering performance evaluation systems. As Figure 4-1 explains, this role provides an excellent opportunity for human resources personnel to deliver exceptional service to internal customers such as managers and employees.

FIGURE 4-1. How Human Resources Staff Can Deliver Exceptional Internal Customer Service.

Choosing and administering performance evaluation systems provide a company's human resources personnel with many opportunities to deliver superior service to internal customers, including managers, supervisors, and employees. To effectively serve their internal customers, human resources staff can

- Select a performance evaluation method that is appropriate for measuring the type of work employees perform

- Ensure managers are trained in how to use performance evaluations to appraise employees' job performance objectively and fairly

- Initiate the performance evaluation process in a timely manner and ensure that managers complete evaluations on schedule

- Help employees understand the purpose and benefit of performance evaluations by clearly explaining the system to new employees and being available to answer employee questions

MANAGEMENT BY OBJECTIVES (MBO)

Management by objectives (MBO) is a performance evaluation method in which the employee and his supervisor work together to set clear and attainable goals or objectives that the employee should achieve in the upcoming evaluation period and develop a plan for achieving the objectives. During the evaluation period, the employee and his supervisor discuss the employee's progress toward the objectives and, if necessary, agree on ways to improve the employee's performance. At the end of the evaluation period—which could be a month, a quarter, or a year—the supervisor and the employee together evaluate the employee's success or failure in achieving the goals, discuss any problems that occurred and how they can be prevented in the future, and agree upon goals for the next evaluation period. Financial services companies reward employees based on how well they achieved the objectives agreed upon at the beginning of the period. When an employee has long-range objectives—for example, goals that span more than one year—the supervisor should conduct periodic reviews to monitor the employee's progress toward those goals.

To be effective, the specified objectives must be (1) meaningful, (2) valid, (3) realistic, (4) understandable, and (5) accepted. These traits will be defined and discussed in more detail when we discuss organizational performance standards in Chapter 12. For purposes of this discussion, the following examples can help you understand the difference between an ineffective and an effective objective.

For instance, "Complete 99 percent of service requests quickly" is *not* an effective objective because it does not specify what "quickly" means and is therefore not understandable. On the other hand, "Complete 99 percent of service requests within three calendar days" is an effective objective because it clearly states what will be measured—whether or not most service requests were completed in three days—and therefore is understandable. Figure 4-2 lists examples of performance objectives for customer service providers.

GRAPHIC RATING SCALE APPRAISAL

Graphic rating scale appraisal is a performance evaluation method in which the supervisor grades an employee's work during the evaluation period based on a number of factors identified at the beginning of the period. The factors used in the scale identify the core competencies required for a specific job. As Figure 4-3 illustrates, this method requires the supervisor to rate the employee from below average to exceptional on each factor on the scale.

Management by objectives (MBO) is a performance evaluation method in which the employee and his supervisor work together to set clear and attainable goals that the employee should achieve in the upcoming evaluation period.

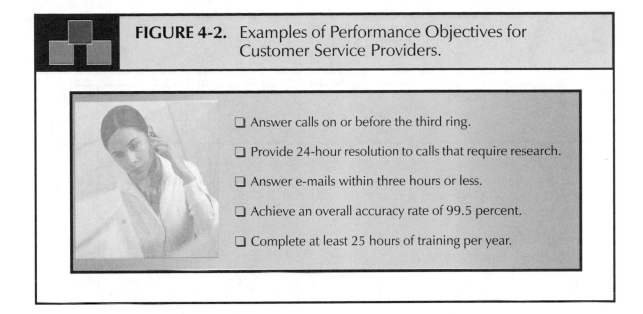

FIGURE 4-2. Examples of Performance Objectives for Customer Service Providers.

❑ Answer calls on or before the third ring.

❑ Provide 24-hour resolution to calls that require research.

❑ Answer e-mails within three hours or less.

❑ Achieve an overall accuracy rate of 99.5 percent.

❑ Complete at least 25 hours of training per year.

The advantages of the graphic rating scale are that it (1) provides the supervisor with an objective, structured format on which to base evaluations, and (2) the employee knows in advance what factors will be considered in the evaluation. A drawback of the graphic rating scale is the possibility that the rating factors might not reflect the most important components of an employee's job. To avoid this possibility, supervisors and employees should work together to develop rating factors that reflect the employee's actual job activities.

ESSAY APPRAISAL

Supervisors and employees should work together to develop rating factors that reflect the employee's actual job activities.

Essay appraisal is a performance evaluation method in which, at the end of the evaluation period, the supervisor writes a description of an employee's performance during that period. The essay appraisal method is much less structured than the MBO or graphic rating scale methods and therefore has some disadvantages. For instance, an essay appraisal can be

- Subjective, because no objectives or other criteria for judging performance are established and the supervisor's personal bias can easily influence the evaluation.

- Inconsistent, because a supervisor's ability to express himself in writing has an enormous impact on the evaluation and not all supervisors have the same writing ability.

FIGURE 4-3. Example of a Graphic Rating Scale.

	Below Average (Rating=75)	Average (Rating=100)	Above Average (Rating=120)	Exceptional (Rating=150)	Rating
Work Volume	❐ Work volume below average	❐ Average work volume	❐ Above average work volume	❐ Exceptional work volume (continually exceeds expectations)	
Quality of Work	❐ Careless/greater than usual number of errors	❐ Acceptable number of errors	❐ Few errors/ above average quality	❐ Almost no errors/ consistently meticulous	
Meeting Deadlines	❐ Difficulty meeting deadlines	❐ Usually meets deadlines	❐ Occasionally finishes job ahead of schedule	❐ Regularly finishes job ahead of schedule	
Setting Priorities	❐ Difficulty determining order of importance and changing tasks when emergencies arise	❐ Completes most important tasks first and stops one task to focus on emergencies	❐ Sometimes optimizes time to perform most important tasks and to concentrate on emergencies	❐ Consistently optimizes time to perform the most important tasks and to focus on emergencies	
Making the Customer a Priority	❐ Difficulty establishing customer needs; makes little effort to gain customer confidence and loyalty	❐ Analyzes customer needs; gains customer confidence and ensures customer loyalty	❐ Helps customers define needs and is proactive; gains customer confidence and ensures customer loyalty	❐ Consistently provides excellent customer service through proactive measures; systematically gains customer confidence and ensures customer loyalty	

FIGURE 4-3. Example of a Graphic Rating Scale (*continued*).

	Below Average (Rating=75)	Average (Rating=100)	Above Average (Rating=120)	Exceptional (Rating=150)	Rating
Respect for Others	❏ Shows little respect in discussions with others and lack of sensitivity in written and verbal communications	❏ Respectful in discussions with others and adapts communications to their specific needs and situations	❏ Respectful in interpersonal relationships and helps create a supportive work environment; often adjusts communications to the specific needs of others	❏ Consistently respectful in interpersonal relationships and greatly contributes to a supportive work environment; constantly adjusts communications to the specific needs of others	
Openness and Innovation	❏ Perceives change as an obstacle to be overcome; rarely questions work methods	❏ Open to change; occasionally rethinks work methods to bring fresh, constructive ideas	❏ Very open to change and perceives it as a stimulating chance to learn, often rethinks work methods to bring fresh, constructive ideas	❏ Perceives change as a springboard for optimizing potential; constantly questions work methods to bring fresh, constructive ideas	
Group Success	❏ Little concern for team success; rarely consults or provides support	❏ Contributes to team success; consults and provides support when needed	❏ Contributes actively to team success; consults frequently and cooperates easily	❏ Contributes greatly to team success; frequently consults and systematically supports team members	

Overall Performance Rating = Total of Ratings/
Total of Selected
Indicators

Interpretation of Overall Performance Rating

87.5 or less = Requires improvement   **87.6 to 112.5 = Meets expectations**

112.6 to 137.5 = Exceeds expectations   **137.6 or higher = Greatly exceeds expectations**

■ Incomplete, because strict record keeping during the evaluation period is not required, so many important examples of good and bad work may be left out of the evaluation.

Despite its drawbacks, the essay appraisal is often used in conjunction with other performance evaluation methods—for example, with a graphic rating scale—because essays allow supervisors to expand on specific measurements and provide examples of outstanding performance and suggestions for improvement. In addition, some companies ask employees to use the essay appraisal approach and write their own description of their job performance during the review period. This form of self-evaluation allows an employee to highlight her successes and explain any shortcomings, which can help provide a more thorough review of the employee's performance.

CRITICAL INCIDENT APPRAISAL

Critical incident appraisal is a performance evaluation method in which the supervisor records examples of an employee's accomplishments as well as any errors or problems that occurred during the evaluation period. Any incident that seems significant to the supervisor is written down and discussed when the supervisor evaluates the employee. Examples of critical incidents include, "Trained two new employees while still completing all of her work on time," and "Was chronically late for work during the month of April." Ideally, the supervisor discusses each critical incident with the employee soon after it happens, so there are no surprises at the end of the evaluation period.

The advantage of the critical incident appraisal method is that it requires the supervisor to keep accurate records of an employee's specific activities, so the evaluation is based on particular incidences and not on the supervisor's general recollection. On the other hand, the supervisor's record keeping may not be accurate, and her interpretation of what is and is not critical might differ from the employee's interpretation or may reflect the supervisor's personal bias.

360-DEGREE FEEDBACK

Some companies use *360-degree feedback*, which is a performance evaluation method in which feedback about the employee's performance is solicited from many sources, including the employee's superiors and peers, any people the employee supervises, and the internal and external customers the employee serves. The employee also assesses her own

---

Critical incident appraisal is a performance evaluation method in which the supervisor records examples of an employee's accomplishments as well as any errors or problems that occurred during the evaluation period.

performance as part of the evaluation. Each evaluator completes a questionnaire that asks for feedback about specific areas of the employee's performance. Responses, which are kept confidential and anonymous so that the evaluators feel free to be candid and honest, are compiled and shared with the employee by her supervisor or, in some companies, by human resources personnel.

A performance evaluation prepared using the 360-degree feedback method is more likely to be accurate and balanced than an evaluation prepared by only one person because it includes feedback from people who regularly interact with the employee. Gathering information from several sources helps avoid the bias that can occur when only one person evaluates an employee's performance. Employees also have an opportunity to view their performance from a variety of perspectives and to compare these observations with their own perceptions.

Disadvantages of the 360-degree feedback method include the time and cost required to design the program and to gather, compile, and interpret data from multiple sources. This method requires a considerable investment by the company and a significant time commitment on the part of the people who prepare and conduct the evaluations. In addition, peer evaluations sometimes include personal biases; to prepare a fair and balanced evaluation, supervisors or other managers who receive the feedback results must be trained to detect such biases. Because of these disadvantages, some companies only use the 360-degree feedback method to evaluate senior-level staff, such as managers and executives.

Although each of the performance evaluation methods we have just discussed—MBO, graphic rating scale appraisal, essay appraisal, critical incident appraisal, and 360-degree feedback—can be used independently, many financial services companies combine one or more methods when evaluating employees. For example, the MBO method and the graphic rating scale appraisal can be used together to allow managers to grade an employee's performance on meeting specific objectives. Also, managers might use the essay appraisal and/or the critical incident appraisal method to record job performance information, which is then used to evaluate an employee's progress toward meeting goals established using the MBO method.

Many financial services companies combine one or more methods when evaluating employees.

Guidelines for Performance Evaluations

No matter which performance evaluation method a financial services company uses, the company should take steps to ensure the method is effective for both employees and managers. The following guidelines can help ensure that performance evaluations are planned and conducted appropriately:

- Managers should be trained to conduct performance evaluations effectively.

- Employees should be trained to accept and learn from the feedback offered in performance evaluations.

- Performance evaluations should be used to recognize the employee's strengths as well as areas that need improvement.

- During performance evaluations, managers should offer specific suggestions for improvement and growth.

- Performance evaluations should be based on work done, not on personal feelings about the person doing the work.

- Performance evaluations should be a two-way conversation: managers should ask employees to evaluate their own performance as well as the manager's performance.

- To gain a more complete picture of an employee's performance, managers should solicit input for the performance evaluation from people the employee interacts with in doing his job.

- Employees should understand the performance evaluation method being used, to ensure that both the employee and the manager have similar expectations during the evaluation period.

- If possible, performance evaluations should be conducted frequently—even on an informal basis—so employees are aware of their progress and are not surprised by what they hear at their annual performance evaluation. Ongoing feedback gives employees the opportunity to make adjustments and improve their performance, which benefits both the employees and the company.

Monitoring

All performance evaluation methods require information about an employee's job performance. In customer service, one of the most effective ways to gather such information is through **monitoring**, a process used to review and evaluate the quality of customer service interactions either as they happen or after the fact. Monitoring can be used with various types of customer service interactions, including telephone calls, e-mail messages, Web chats, and videoconferencing. Monitoring is considered one of the most effective ways to

- Evaluate a service provider's customer service skills.

- Identify any problems a service provider or group of service providers is having in using these skills.

- Gather information needed to develop new or modified employee training programs.

- Determine whether a company's customer service system is achieving its objectives and meeting specified standards.

The information acquired through monitoring can be used in performance evaluations. For example, a customer service representative and her supervisor can review recorded telephone conversations to assess the CSR's strengths and opportunities for improvement. At some companies, service providers monitor each other's customer interactions and provide constructive feedback, as Figure 4-4 explains. Typically, the person doing the monitoring completes an evaluation form, such as the example shown in Figure 4-5.

FIGURE 4-4. Monitoring by Peers.

Peer monitoring can be an effective way for service providers to improve their customer service skills. At one financial services company, customer service representatives evaluate each other's performance by monitoring telephone calls on a weekly and monthly basis. For the weekly evaluation, one CSR listens to another CSR's telephone call, then completes a call evaluation form to provide constructive feedback and suggestions for improvement. Once a month, the entire work team listens to and evaluates a call chosen by the CSR being evaluated. Team members provide the CSR with feedback, which usually leads to a team discussion about customer service skills. Such peer evaluations help improve the skills of both the person being evaluated as well as the people who perform the evaluations.

FIGURE 4-5. Sample Call Evaluation Form.

CALL EVALUATION FORM

CSR/Evaluator: Date: Time: Call #:

Account #: Caller:

Details of Inquiry:

1. Telephone Etiquette - 25%	Yes	No	N/A
CALL OPENING			
Uses proper greetings and introductions (name of company, department, and CSR) and offers to help			
DEMEANOR			
Displays a friendly, courteous, and professional attitude			
LANGUAGE AND TONE			
Uses appropriate tone of voice and phrasing, avoids jargon, and speaks clearly			
CONTACT SKILLS			
Uses appropriate contact handling procedures (use of the customer's name)			
TRANSFER AND HOLD COMPLIANCE			
Demonstrates proper transfer/hold procedures (if required)			

Comments

2. Customer Interaction and Relationship - 35%			
LISTENING SKILLS			
Listens attentively; empathizes and acknowledges customer concerns			
PROBLEM SOLVING			
Gathers information to determine customer's root concerns and needs; applies problem-solving skills and resolves the inquiry effectively			
COMMUNICATION SKILLS			
Communicates information about the resolution of the inquiry to the customer clearly and completely			
CALL APPROACH			
Controls pace and flow of the conversation, minimizes dead-air			

Comments

3. Information Handling and Knowledge - 30%			
EXPERTISE			
Demonstrates expert knowledge regarding products and services; instills confidence in customer's perception of company's products and services			
ACCURACY OF INFORMATION			
Provides accurate and complete information to the customer			
SYSTEM USE AND ADHERENCE TO SCRIPTS AND GUIDELINES			
Adheres to scripts and guidelines; effectively utilizes systems and tools			

Comments

4. Call Closing - 10%			
Uses appropriate closing; confirms understanding of information and actions taken; thanks the customer for calling and CSR gives name at end of call			
Section 1 number of "yes" answers divided by 5 × 25%	Section 1		
Section 2 number of "yes" answers divided by 4 × 35%	Section 2		
Section 3 number of "yes" answers divided by 3 × 30%	Section 3		
Section 4 number of "yes" answers × 10%	Section 4		
Total Score			%

Although monitoring can be quite valuable, companies must ensure that all monitoring activities comply with applicable legal requirements regarding notification to callers about the company's monitoring practices.

Generally, companies can monitor customer service interactions in two ways: in real-time and by recording. **Real-time monitoring**, also known as *live coaching*, is a process in which the evaluator observes and/or listens to a customer service interaction as it is taking place. Real-time monitoring allows the supervisor to provide immediate feedback to the service provider.

Real-time monitoring can be side-by-side or remote. Side-by-side monitoring occurs when the evaluator sits in view of the service provider being monitored. As Figure 4-6 indicates, side-by-side monitoring is commonly used to evaluate customer service telephone calls. The advantage of side-by-side monitoring is that the evaluator can experience everything that is going on during the customer service interaction, such as the noise level in the room and other distractions, as well as any problems caused by processes or technology. On the other hand, service providers may feel self-conscious about being observed and may not behave as they normally would when interacting with customers.

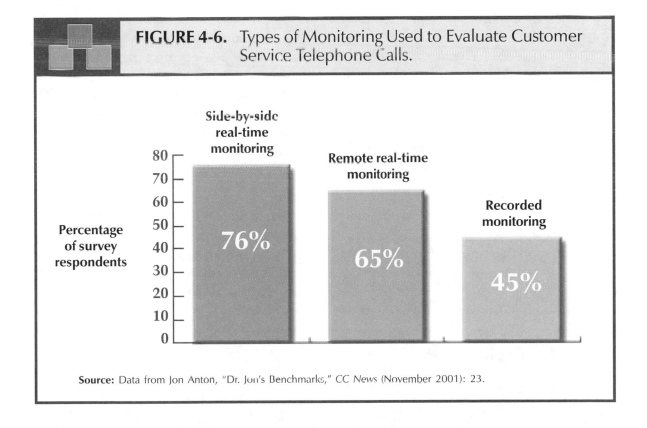

FIGURE 4-6. Types of Monitoring Used to Evaluate Customer Service Telephone Calls.

Source: Data from Jon Anton, "Dr. Jon's Benchmarks," *CC News* (November 2001): 23.

For remote monitoring, the evaluator is electronically linked to the customer service interaction, but is located away from the service provider's workstation. For instance, a supervisor might listen in on a telephone call or view an e-mail exchange from her office, without the service provider's knowledge. Compared with side-by-side monitoring, remote monitoring can provide a more accurate picture of service providers' performance because the service providers are unaware that they are being monitored and therefore behave as they usually would when interacting with customers.

Recorded monitoring is a process in which customer service interactions, such as telephone calls, e-mails, Web chats, or videoconferences are recorded for later review. The advantage of recorded monitoring is that it allows service providers and their supervisors to observe or listen together to the service provider's performance to identify strengths and opportunities for improvement. A company might record only some customer service interactions for review, or it may record all customer service interactions and later select random samples for review. Some companies allow service providers to record a certain number of their customer service interactions to be reviewed by their supervisor.

The advantage of recorded monitoring is that it allows service providers and their supervisors to observe or listen together to the service provider's performance to identify strengths and opportunities for improvement.

Some service providers dislike or feel uncomfortable having their work monitored, possibly because they equate monitoring with snooping and worry that their privacy is being violated. These feelings are understandable, especially in countries where a citizen's right to privacy is highly regarded. To alleviate employee concerns about monitoring, companies should be honest and forthright about how and when monitoring will be used, and ask service providers to help determine how monitoring will be carried out and for what purposes. To ensure personal privacy, companies that use telephone monitoring should provide a separate, non-monitored telephone line—at the service provider's desk or in a break area—that employees can use to make private calls.

Service providers also are likely to feel less anxious about the monitoring process when they know in advance what aspects of their performance will be evaluated. As shown in Figure 4-7, customer service managers can consider many factors during monitoring and should share these factors with service providers. In addition, service providers should receive proper education and training so that they have the knowledge and skills needed to perform well on the factors to be evaluated.

Finally, service providers should keep in mind that monitoring is designed to identify areas of strength and weakness and improve their job

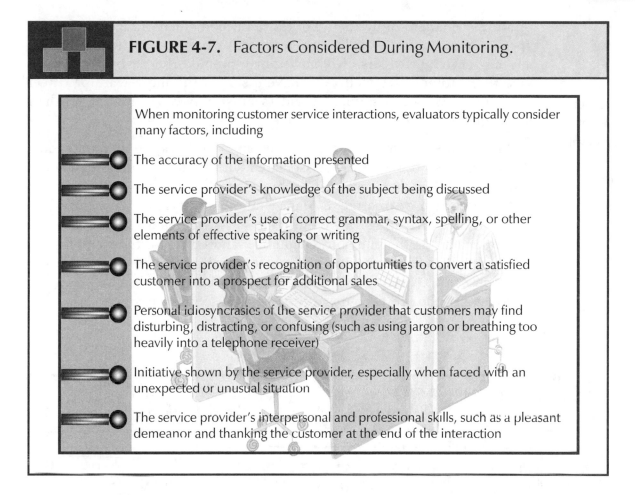

FIGURE 4-7. Factors Considered During Monitoring.

When monitoring customer service interactions, evaluators typically consider many factors, including

The accuracy of the information presented

The service provider's knowledge of the subject being discussed

The service provider's use of correct grammar, syntax, spelling, or other elements of effective speaking or writing

The service provider's recognition of opportunities to convert a satisfied customer into a prospect for additional sales

Personal idiosyncrasies of the service provider that customers may find disturbing, distracting, or confusing (such as using jargon or breathing too heavily into a telephone receiver)

Initiative shown by the service provider, especially when faced with an unexpected or unusual situation

The service provider's interpersonal and professional skills, such as a pleasant demeanor and thanking the customer at the end of the interaction

performance—not to punish them. The purpose of monitoring is not to "catch" employees on every little error they make, but to detect recurring or serious problems that hinder a company's ability to provide exceptional customer service.

Motivating Customer Service Professionals

Because of the emphasis that many financial services firms now place on customer service, working as a service provider can be an exciting, challenging, and rewarding job. It can also be a demanding job that puts tremendous pressure on the people who perform the work. Dealing with customers, especially those who are hostile or rude, all day, every day can sometimes discourage even the most cheerful service providers. In addition, service providers who feel unappreciated, see no future in their jobs, or are not challenged by their work often become demoralized. A lack of appropriate training or sufficient resources can also lead to frustration among service providers. To consistently provide the best possible service to customers—as well as to have a successful and rewarding career in customer service—service providers must stay motivated to do their jobs well.

Managers and supervisors play an important role in motivating service providers.

While some people are self-motivated and find a way to do outstanding work regardless of the rewards associated with their jobs, most of us need some external encouragement to achieve excellence, especially when we feel discouraged or frustrated. Managers and supervisors play an important role in motivating service providers. When managers and supervisors take actions that support, encourage, and motivate their employees, they are providing superior internal customer service, as Figure 4-8 explains. As we discuss in this section, financial services firms can use many approaches to encourage, or motivate, service providers.

FIGURE 4-8. How Managers and Supervisors Can Provide Superior Internal Customer Service.

Generally, managers can directly influence the attitudes and behaviors of their employees. By responding to employee requests for support and assistance in an effective and timely manner, managers not only help encourage and motivate employees, but they also provide exceptional internal customer service to those employees. Actions that managers can take to motivate and serve the customer service providers who work for them include

● Offering rewards and incentives for superior customer service results

● Allowing routine breaks and job variety

● Providing daily or frequent feedback on employees' performance

● When appropriate, assisting with challenging or difficult customer requests or complaints

● Fostering creativity and individuality, and empowering employees to make decisions

● Supporting training, education, and development activities

Rewards as Performance Motivators

In Chapter 1, we noted that people tend to do what they are rewarded for doing. For example, if a company rewards speed in completing telephone transactions, service providers are likely to focus on keeping telephone transactions short rather than on making them complete or accurate. Similarly, if companies reward outstanding customer service, service providers are likely to focus on providing the best possible service to customers.

To be effective, rewards must relate directly to the desired behaviors; if this relationship does not exist, then the rewards are unlikely to achieve their primary goal. In addition, the relationship between rewards and performances should be clear and well publicized to employees. Service providers who know what they must do to earn rewards usually are motivated to achieve the desired performance levels. For example, a financial services call center might offer gift certificates for dining, entertainment, or shopping to customer service representatives who achieve an adherence rate of 95–100 percent. (An *adherence rate* is the degree to which a CSR follows the staffing schedule developed to handle calls.)

Developing appropriate reward systems for a group of employees can be challenging because people value rewards differently. What is a reward to one person may seem like an inconvenience to another. For example, some service providers enjoy attending company parties, while others feel uncomfortable socializing with coworkers. To create an effective reward program, a company and its employees should work together to identify meaningful rewards. Insight 4-1 describes the employee-developed reward system used at one financial services company.

Celebrate what you want to see more of.

— Tom Peters[1]

FINANCIAL REWARDS

Financial rewards include salary increases, bonuses and commissions, and educational expense benefits.

Salary Increases

Almost all financial services companies establish a salary, or base pay, for similar types of jobs. Although salary amounts are often set to attract and retain employees, generally, neither employees nor companies think of salaries as rewards; rather, salaries are considered to be payment made in return for the time, knowledge, and work employees contribute to a company. Usually, as long as employees meet acceptable performance

---

INSIGHT 4-1. An Employee-Developed Reward System.

Customer Service Employee Reward and Recognition Program

Definition

Developed by a focus group of 10 volunteer staff members, this program enables peer recognition and achievement. Awards can be given to an individual or a team (two or more staff members). Nominations will be validated on the basis of excellent performance in handling a service transaction that is deemed above and beyond normal job responsibilities and expectations.

Requirements

Winning nominations will be validated by consensus of the focus group. Selection criteria for both individual and team awards are as follows:

- Taking ownership of the successful completion of a service transaction that results in delighting the client

- Leading by example in the areas of positive attitude and consistent, quality service

- Receiving a letter or e-mail from a client, intermediary, or member of another department acknowledging excellence in a service transaction above and beyond normal job responsibilities and expectations

- Exhibiting leadership on an ongoing basis

- Volunteering for work on a special assignment or project

Presentation

- A certificate of recognition will be presented to the winner(s) by a member of the Focus Group, on the last Friday of every month at 2 P.M.

- The reward recipients will be entered into a quarterly drawing for a gift certificate.

- The reward recipients will also be entered into an annual drawing for a bonus.

---

standards they will continue to receive their salary and, in many cases, a ***cost-of-living pay raise***, which allows salaries to rise at a rate similar to the rate of inflation.

Other types of salary increases, however, are considered rewards for superior work. For example, a ***merit pay raise*** rewards an employee or a work team whose performance exceeds minimum performance standards. A merit pay raise is added to an employee's prior base salary to determine the new base salary, which represents the employee's total compensation. In general, the frequency and amount of merit pay raises increase as job performance increases. Merit pay raises are effective motivational tools because the reward is tied directly to each employee's performance. To be equitable and valued by employees, merit pay raises must be based on timely and accurate performance evaluations.

A *skills-based pay raise* is a variation of a merit pay raise that rewards employees for developing and improving job skills. Employees typically receive a skills-based pay raise when they achieve a specified level of proficiency in a specific skill. For example, a service provider who is assigned to review a new product line and help develop training material for his coworkers might receive a pay raise based on his acquisition of significant knowledge about products and the training process. As this example shows, skills-based pay encourages *lateral skill development*, which is growth within an employee's current job. Skills-based pay also can help motivate an employee to progress along a career path.

To motivate employees to achieve company-wide goals, some financial services companies use a *variable compensation system*, in which a portion of an employee's annual salary is based on the profits the company earned during the preceding year. Each employee receives a predetermined base salary and, depending upon the company's performance during the previous year, an additional amount that represents the employee's contributions toward the company's profits. The additional amount varies from year to year—and may even be nonexistent some years—depending on how well both the employee and the company perform. Note that, unlike a merit pay raise, variable compensation does *not* increase an employee's base salary. The variable portion of an employee's salary is paid as "installments" in each paycheck throughout the year, rather than as a lump-sum payment.

Compared to a merit pay raise system, the variable compensation system presents more risk to the employee, because her total compensation could decrease from one year to the next if an excellent performance one year is followed by a lackluster performance the next year. In addition, while a merit pay raise is directly tied to an employee's job performance, variable compensation is only indirectly related to individual performance.

One advantage of variable compensation systems is that they can allow employees to earn more if they help the company to be more successful.[2] On the other hand, employees who are unfamiliar with variable compensation and whose performance has no directly quantifiable correlation to the company's success or failure may be uncomfortable with such plans. To help alleviate employee concerns, variable compensation should be tied to measurable goals that employees can directly influence and understand. The goals and measurement techniques for variable compensation should be clearly and frequently communicated to employees. In addition, employees should realize that variable compensation is not a given benefit; it must be earned through outstanding performance by all areas of the company.

Bonuses and Commissions

A *bonus* is a lump-sum amount awarded to an employee to recognize outstanding achievement by either the employee or a work group. A bonus, which can be given at any time, is in addition to an employee's normal pay and does not affect the employee's base salary. Some bonuses, such as annual bonuses, are given on a regular basis. An example of an annual bonus is one awarded under a profit-sharing plan. Under a *profit-sharing plan*, a financial services company establishes a pool of money—based on some percentage of profits or the total compensation pool—and pays a lump sum bonus to each employee based on the employee's performance, his work group's performance, or a combination of the two. A profit-sharing bonus is similar to a variable compensation plan in that both allow employees to earn more money by contributing to the company's success. Unlike variable pay, however, profit-sharing bonuses are typically paid in a lump sum, rather than distributed throughout the year.

A *commission* is an amount of money, usually a percentage of the sale amount, that is paid to an employee or intermediary for selling a product or service. Generally, people who sell financial products and services must be specifically trained and licensed in the jurisdictions in which they sell products; therefore, commissions are most often used as rewards for intermediaries such as insurance agents and securities brokers.

Commissions are effective motivators for many people because the payment amount is directly related to job performance—the more products sold, the more commission earned. Some people, however, are uncomfortable with the uncertainty of commission payments and prefer the reliability of a salary.

Educational Expense Benefits

Some financial services companies offer an *educational expense benefit*, which is an amount that helps pay the cost of an employee's education. Typically, this benefit reimburses an employee for course tuition or fees only if the course relates to the employee's job and the employee earns at least a specified minimum grade in the course. Companies may reimburse costs for high school equivalency education, college and university education, professional designation and certification programs, and skills-related training programs and seminars.

To be effective, a company's system for giving financial rewards must be based on criteria that are fair and well publicized to employees. If employees feel that financial rewards are not given often enough, are not

To be effective, a company's system for giving financial rewards must be based on criteria that are fair and well publicized to employees.

large enough, or that some people have more opportunity to earn rewards than other people do, the system can discourage employees rather than motivate them.

NONFINANCIAL REWARDS

Nonfinancial rewards include alternate work arrangements, recognition, and others.

Alternate Work Arrangements

Some financial services firms use alternate work arrangements, such as flexible work hours or telecommuting, to attract potential employees or to reward or motivate staff. By offering flexible schedules, allowing service providers to work from home (telecommute) on an occasional or a regular basis, or establishing part-time schedules, a company offers the flexibility and independence that many employees desire and value. Knowing that alternate work arrangements are available can motivate service providers to work hard to prove they're capable of being productive in a nontraditional work arrangement. In addition, alternate work arrangements meet the business needs of companies that provide customer service during nontraditional hours, such as nights and weekends.

Alternate work arrangements also present many challenges, such as ensuring that telecommuting employees are readily available to customers and coworkers and that employees who work nontraditional hours have access to the same team-building and support activities as their colleagues who work during normal business hours. Financial services firms that use such arrangements must ensure that managers, work groups, and individual employees are prepared for these challenges. In addition, the company must be willing to invest in the technical infrastructure needed to support alternate work arrangements. Insight 4-2 describes how implementing an alternate work arrangement helped one financial services call center cut costs and boost productivity.

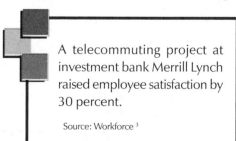

A telecommuting project at investment bank Merrill Lynch raised employee satisfaction by 30 percent.

Source: Workforce [3]

Employee Recognition

Recognizing employee accomplishments is one of the most important ways for a company to reward and motivate service providers. People who work hard in their jobs are usually proud of their achievements and want to know that their supervisors and

INSIGHT 4-2.   Telecommuting CSRs Boost Call Center's Productivity.

When Ric Decker saw a job listing in the *Kansas City (Missouri) Star* newspaper advertising "Work @ Home," he decided to inquire. The company looking for help, ARO Call Center, handled customer service for insurers such as Citigroup and AIG, among others. He'd need two phone lines and a quiet home office, ARO told him. For Decker, the decision was simple. Now, instead of commuting to Kansas City from his home in the suburbs, he just walks down one flight of stairs to go to work.

ARO instituted telecommuting four years ago as it sought ways to reduce its astonishing annual employee turnover rate of 60 percent. The company had been attracting mainly young workers with little, if any, experience and consequently was spending far too much on recruiting and training. ARO had to either hike its wages or find another way to appeal to prospective employees. So the company spent about $900,000 on a telecommute-friendly call center system using technology from eOn Communications and Avaya.

Today, 85 of ARO's 100 representatives work from home. Annual turnover has plummeted to just 5 percent, and ARO's employees tend to be older and have more significant workplace experience. "The candidates have changed drastically," says Michael Amigoni, ARO's COO. "I don't believe we'd be able to recruit most of these people to work in a [traditional] call center."

The software that makes this possible is an eOn "switch" that acts like an operator. When, for example, a Citibank insurance customer calls the company's toll-free number, the switch recognizes the number and routes the call to a CSR qualified to handle Citibank callers. Then the CSR—sitting in a home office—helps the caller with his request.

Even with most of its agents working from home, ARO supervisors still watch over them. The computers at the main office let managers view the telecommuting CSR's screen during a customer interaction and listen in on the conversation. "The only thing we can't see is the back of their head," Amigoni says. "We're seeing better than [if we were] looking over their shoulder." The managers also can send instant messages to CSRs if they need to give them directions.

Because of these changes, ARO says, CSRs are handling about 20 percent more calls than they used to. (Amigoni suspects that workers are simply more productive when they're not in a conventional office setting.) The company's operating costs have dropped by about 30 percent, saving it almost $400,000 a year. In part this is because ARO hasn't had to lease more office space, despite the fact that it employs three times more people than it did just five years ago.

Ric Decker, however, *has* invested in real estate. He and his family have moved even farther from Kansas City, into a home with a ready-made home office, where he spends as many as 10 hours a day helping customers with his Jack Russell terrier in his lap and his prize Doberman pacing outside.

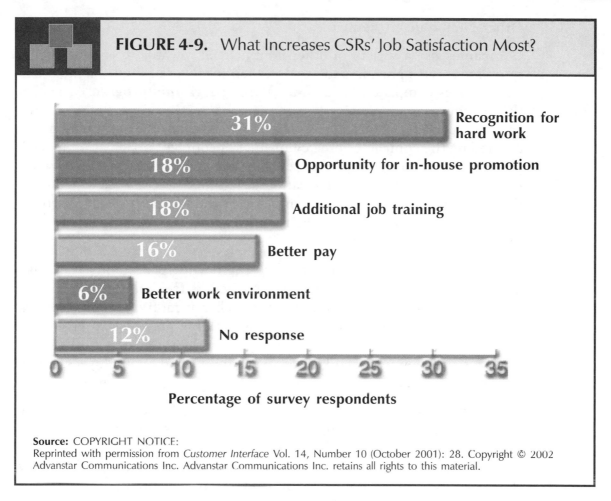

FIGURE 4-9. What Increases CSRs' Job Satisfaction Most?

- 31% Recognition for hard work
- 18% Opportunity for in-house promotion
- 18% Additional job training
- 16% Better pay
- 6% Better work environment
- 12% No response

Percentage of survey respondents

managers recognize those achievements as well. Many customer service representatives consider recognition for a job well done to be the most important factor in increasing their job satisfaction, as Figure 4-9 shows.

Companies can use formal and/or informal programs to recognize employees' special achievements. For example, a formal recognition program might encourage employees to nominate coworkers who provide outstanding service to external or internal customers; those nominees are then eligible to win a prize, such as an extra vacation day. Informal recognition efforts include posting complimentary letters from customers in a prominent place or by publishing success stories in the company newsletter. Holding celebratory parties when a work group meets or exceeds an important goal or deadline can also make service providers feel appreciated and rewarded for their efforts.

Other Nonfinancial Rewards

Companies use a variety of other nonfinancial rewards to encourage and motivate service providers to excel in their jobs. For example, some financial services companies have an ***employee suggestion program***, a system that encourages employees to submit constructive suggestions, which are promptly and seriously reviewed and—when appropriate—implemented by the company. Some companies encourage participation in such programs by offering a tangible reward—such as gift certificates to local restaurants or shops or extra vacation days—for implemented suggestions that improve processes and save money for the company. Service providers who have input into how their work is done will be motivated to see that the work is done well.

Allowing employees to personalize their workspaces and wear business casual clothing can make service providers feel comfortable and enjoy being in their work environment, which can motivate them to work harder. Organizing picnics or luncheons, holding drawings to give away tickets to sporting or cultural events, or awarding extra days off can inspire positive feelings toward the company on the part of employees, which can motivate service providers to perform at their highest levels.

Perhaps most importantly, people are motivated to do their best when they enjoy their jobs and find their work interesting and stimulating. Job enjoyment is only possible when companies hire the right people, give them the proper training and career development opportunities, evaluate them fairly, encourage improvement, and reward outstanding performance. But it's not just the financial services company's responsibility to help employees enjoy their jobs—employees must do their part, as well. Service providers must make sure they are well suited for customer service work, pursue growth and learning opportunities, strive for continuous improvement, and pursue excellence by taking pride and ownership in their work.

As you have learned in this chapter and the previous chapter, developing and fostering the people who drive customer service is a key factor in a financial services company's ability to deliver exceptional service to its customers. In the next chapter, we take a closer look at the people who directly benefit from these efforts—the customers.

To practice and review the skills and information you learned in this chapter, see the interactive CD, *Practicing Your Customer Service Skills*, included with this book.

Key Terms and Concepts

performance evaluation

management by objectives (MBO)

graphic rating scale appraisal

essay appraisal

critical incident appraisal

360-degree feedback

monitoring

real-time monitoring

recorded monitoring

cost-of-living pay raise

merit pay raise

skills-based pay raise

lateral skill development

variable compensation system

bonus

profit-sharing plan

commission

educational expense benefit

employee suggestion program

Endnotes

1. JoAnna F. Brandi, *Building Company Loyalty: The 21 Essential Elements...IN ACTION* (Dallas: Walk the Talk Company, 2001), 42.

2. LOMA Research Division, *Managing Pay for Performance in the Life Insurance Industry* (Atlanta: LOMA, 1995), 15.

3. Shari Caudron, "Workers' Ideas for Improving Alternative Work Situations," *Workforce*, 1 December 1998, http://www.workforce.com/archive/article/21/96/53.php (7 February 2002).

Understanding Customer Expectations, Perceptions, and Behavior

After studying this chapter, you should be able to

- Distinguish between the needs and wants that motivate customers

- Define *expectation* and explain how customers develop expectations about customer service

- Define *perception* and describe the service dimensions that influence customer perceptions

- Describe proactive service and distinguish it from reactive service

- Explain the service gap and other gaps in customer service and how financial services companies and service providers manage customer expectations to reduce or overcome these gaps

- Describe the Myers-Briggs Type Indicator as a tool for identifying and classifying personality traits

- Discuss the transactional analysis approach to analyzing behavior patterns

- Identify the following four general behavior patterns: passive, aggressive, passive-aggressive, and assertive

- Distinguish between secondary and primary data, and describe qualitative and quantitative research methods

Providing exceptional customer service requires financial services companies to anticipate, and then fulfill, their customers' needs and wants. A *need* is a requirement to improve an unsatisfactory condition—for example, food to satisfy hunger, shelter to stay warm and dry, and transportation to travel to work. A *want* is a desire to have more than is absolutely necessary to improve an unsatisfactory condition—for example, gourmet food, a large house, or a sports car.[1] Financial services customers have both needs and wants. For instance, most banking customers *need* checking accounts to manage their daily cash transactions; many of these customers *want* checking accounts with certain features, such as the ability to earn interest, free checks, and debit cards. Customer-focused financial services companies attempt to determine and satisfy both the needs and wants of their customers.

Learning about customers' perceptions, expectations, and behavior is the primary way to identify customers' needs and wants. Understanding the importance of customer expectations and perceptions can help companies and their service providers detect where their service efforts fail to satisfy customers' wants and needs. Also, knowing why customers sometimes behave a certain way—and developing the knowledge to effectively deal with those behaviors—helps a company and its service providers influence customers' expectations and perceptions.

We will begin this chapter by discussing the significance of customer expectations and perceptions and ways that financial services companies can minimize the gap between the two. Then we'll examine various behavior patterns and explain how recognizing and influencing customer behavior helps service providers deliver outstanding customer service. Finally, we will discuss how to use research to gather information about customer perceptions, expectations, and behaviors.

Customer Expectations

An *expectation* is what a person believes is likely or certain to happen. Most customers have expectations of how they will be treated when they contact a financial services company. One of the most important ways that customers develop their expectations is by experiencing similar or related events. For example, if one insurer treats customers well and provides them with good service, they will expect the same treatment from other insurers until something happens to change their expectations. Other ways that customers develop expectations are by observing, listening to, or reading about other people's customer service experiences and by being exposed to promotional materials, such as advertisements, that tell customers what to expect. Figure 5-1 illustrates how customers develop expectations.

Because customers develop their expectations largely through experience, every contact with a service provider can be either a positive or negative learning experience for the customer. Therefore, service providers who consistently deliver efficient, effective, and accurate service help create more positive customer

FIGURE 5-1. How Customers Develop Expectations.

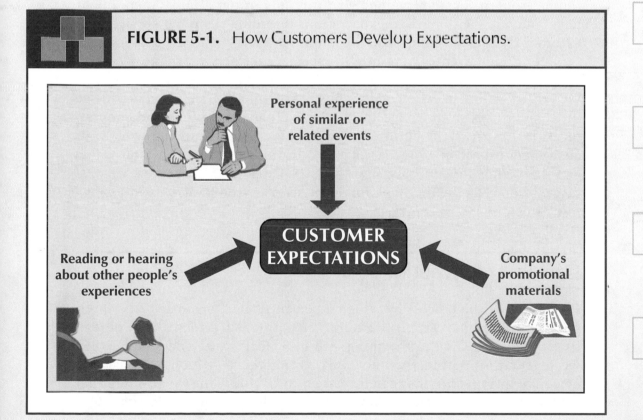

expectations, which, in turn, make the service providers' jobs easier. When customers have positive expectations—that is, when they expect a company to be able to fulfill their requests—they are likely to be more patient and willing to answer questions and provide information, making the service provider's job easier. (Keep in mind that, although their jobs might be easier, service providers must continue to deliver the high-quality service that customers expect.) In contrast, when customers have negative expectations—that is, when they expect a company to botch their requests—they are likely to be impatient and irritable, making the service provider's job more difficult.

As other companies provide higher levels of service, your company must also provide higher levels of service, just to meet the customers' rising expectations.

Customers' expectations tend to increase as the level of service they receive increases. As customers receive better service, they expect to continue receiving better and better service. These rising expectations result not only from experiences with you and your company, but also from experiences with other companies as well. As other companies provide higher levels of service, your company must also provide higher levels of service, just to meet the customers' rising expectations.

Expectations for service vary from customer to customer and from customer group to customer group. For example, internal customers might have much higher (or lower) expectations regarding customer service than external customers. Intermediaries often have very high expectations for service. Younger customers might expect faster service than older customers do, and Internet customers usually expect more immediate service than customers who conduct business by mail. Also, as you will see in Chapter 6, customer expectations (as well as perceptions and communications) can vary by culture or geographic region. Knowing what your customers expect is an essential part of fulfilling their needs and wants and delivering superior customer service. Later in this chapter, we will discuss some of the methods financial services companies use to determine customer expectations.

Customer Perceptions

Perception is the process by which a person selects, organizes, and interprets information to give it meaning. Perception is a person's view of reality; it gives meaning to the things we hear, feel, taste, and smell. When we perceive something, we not only notice *facts*—which are pieces of objective information that can be proven to be true—but we also interpret what we notice by making *inferences*, which are conclusions based on facts as well as other information, such as our personal knowledge or past experiences. Exercise 5-1 presents several examples to help you distinguish between facts and inferences.

Exercise 5-1.   Distinguishing Between Facts and Inferences.

When Tom Salley returns to his desk after lunch, he finds the following phone messages:

- Your children's babysitter called. Call her back immediately.
- Howard Smyth called to get an application form. His address is…
- Janet [Tom's boss] called about the response-time report that you left on her desk.
- The office manager for the Syracuse office called. They ran out of marketing brochures. He wants you to call him as soon as possible. His phone number is…
- Someone from LOMA called about next year's Customer Service Conference.

Based on the information in the phone messages, Tom concludes that…

1. … one of his children is sick.
2. … Mr. Smyth is a customer who wants to open a new account.
3. … Janet has some concerns about his report.
4. … the office manager in Syracuse expects him to call.
5. … he is going to be asked to speak at LOMA's next Customer Service Conference.

Is each of Tom's conclusions a fact or an inference? Decide for yourself, then read our answers below.

1. *Inference.* Although one of his children could be sick, this information is not given in the message. The sitter could have called for any number of reasons.
2. *Inference.* Mr. Smyth might be an intermediary or someone else who needs the form for another person. Tom must call Mr. Smyth to find out exactly what his needs are.
3. *Inference.* Janet may be calling to thank Tom for a job well done, or she may simply have some questions about the report.
4. *Fact.* The message clearly states that the office manager wants a return call.
5. *Inference.* The caller may be letting Tom know about a change in the date of the meeting or asking if he plans to attend. Of course, LOMA may be calling to ask Tom to be a speaker, but that information is not known based on the phone message alone.

Being aware of the difference between facts and inferences can improve your perception in customer service situations.

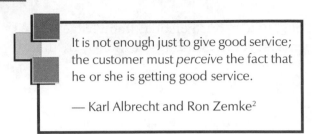

It is not enough just to give good service; the customer must *perceive* the fact that he or she is getting good service.

— Karl Albrecht and Ron Zemke[2]

As a result of inferences, each person's perception of reality can be somewhat different. For example, if two people saw the same person driving the same expensive car, one might perceive the driver to be hardworking and successful, while the other might perceive the driver to be pretentious and extravagant.

To understand their customers, financial services companies must identify and understand their perceptions, because customers base decisions on their perceptions. Even if a company believes it is doing everything possible to satisfy or delight its customers, those customers might have a different perception. For example, if customers perceive a financial services company's service response times to be slow—even though they meet industry standards—the company must address this perception. Perhaps customers are comparing the financial services company's service to the service provided by a company in an entirely different industry. Whatever the reason, the company will need to change the perceptions of its service (or change the service) if it wants to keep those customers.

In this section, we discuss factors that influence customers' perceptions of service and explain how financial services companies can use these factors to create positive perceptions.

Factors That Affect Perceptions of Service

In their model of service quality, researchers A. Parasuraman, Valarie A. Zeithaml, and Leonard L. Berry identified five criteria—called *service dimensions*—that customers typically use to judge the quality of service they receive. These criteria, which influence customers' perceptions of service, are (1) reliability, (2) assurance, (3) empathy, (4) responsiveness, and (5) tangible factors.[3] Figure 5-2 illustrates the relationship between the five service dimensions and customers' perceptions.

RELIABILITY

Reliability means performing the promised service consistently and accurately. Customers do not want to conduct business with an unreliable company, especially when their financial well being is involved. Rather, customers want a level and quality of service that they know they can

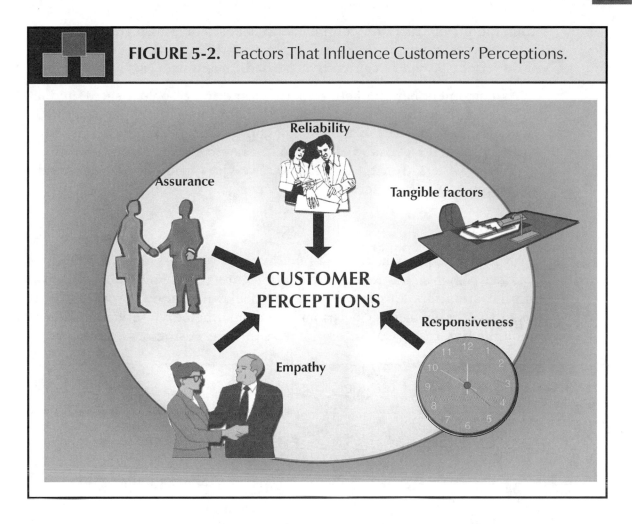

FIGURE 5-2. Factors That Influence Customers' Perceptions.

expect time after time. Financial services companies can enhance the perception of their reliability by consistently maintaining accurate records, processing transactions quickly and correctly, and billing customers accurately.

ASSURANCE

Assurance refers to the competence and credibility of service providers, their ability to convey trust and confidence, and the courtesy and respect they show to customers. Service providers must have the necessary knowledge, skills, and systems to perform required services, and they must be empowered to handle a variety of customer situations. Service providers must also treat customers in a polite, considerate, and friendly manner. The level of assurance displayed by service providers strongly affects the amount of trust and confidence that customers develop in a financial services company. Insight 5-1 explains the importance of trust and how service providers can cultivate it with customers.

As customers become better educated and more sophisticated, and as the level and quality of service required to support various financial products increases, the degree and level of competence needed by service providers also increases. As we discussed in Chapter 3, educated, well-trained service providers are vital to a financial services firm's ability to provide exceptional customer service.

EMPATHY

As you learned in Chapter 3, *empathy* is the process of understanding another person's emotional state and imagining how you would feel in a similar situation. Customers prefer to deal with service providers who seem to care about their needs and concerns; therefore, service providers should strive to have a sincere interest in their customers.

INSIGHT 5-1.   Do Your Customers Trust You?

When it comes to buying products, consumers around the world consider trust to be one of the most important factors in doing business with a company. A study by Harris Interactive found that more than 80 percent of consumers stopped using a company's product or service when they felt that their trust in the company had been broken.

Trusting a company is especially important to financial services customers. According to LIMRA research, some customers realize that they are not knowledgeable about financial products, so, if they are to make an informed purchase decision, they need to trust someone who is more knowledgeable. Many times that  "someone" is an intermediary who sells the financial product or service, but it can just as easily be a service provider who answers customers' questions and helps resolve problems.

Creating a trusting relationship with customers has many benefits for you as a service provider, including less job stress because customers who trust you tend to treat you with respect. They also are more likely to accept your recommendations, share more information with you, involve you sooner (which prevents "crisis" situations from arising), and be more forgiving of your mistakes. Customers who trust you and your company have fewer complaints, refer more people to your company, and are more loyal—all of which results in more business growth and success.

Source: Adapted from James O Mitchel, "What Women Want—And Men, Too," *LIMRA's MarketFacts Quarterly* (Fall 2001): 17, and Ann C. Gersie, "You Gotta Have Trust: Developing Client Trust and Enhancing It with Every Client Transaction," LOMA's Customer Service Conference, The Walt Disney World Resort, Orlando, Florida, February 2002.

Empathy is especially important in dealing with an unhappy or emotionally distraught customer. A service provider who can empathize with a dissatisfied customer has made an important step in recovering that customer's confidence and loyalty. The service provider might simply state, "I'm so sorry you're having a problem. Let me see what I can do to resolve it." Acknowledging the customer's perception of a problem and showing a willingness to help can set the stage for service recovery, which we discussed in Chapter 2.

Empathy also entails a strong commitment to customer communication. Empathetic companies listen to their customers and keep customers informed about products and services in language they can understand. For example, a financial services company that is committed to customer service trains its service providers not to use jargon or technical language that could confuse customers. And if the company has a significant number of customers who speak a foreign language, the company hires at least some service providers who are fluent in that language. For example, a company that has customers who live in the province of Quebec, Canada, might hire a customer service provider who speaks not only French, but also French Canadian, to assist those customers.

RESPONSIVENESS

Responsiveness implies a willingness to help customers and an ability to provide them with prompt service. Customers want fast, appropriate service. Responsiveness requires a positive attitude from the service provider and a level of support from the company (in staffing, training, procedures, and technology) that allows service providers to be responsive.

Responsiveness is also essential in providing proactive, rather than reactive, service to customers. **Proactive service** is a type of customer service that looks beyond what the customer asks in an effort to anticipate and fulfill the customer's unexpressed needs. A truly proactive company doesn't wait for a problem or a question to occur, but recognizes potential opportunities for providing service and acts on them. In contrast, **reactive service** is a type of customer service that responds only to a customer's specific request or problem—that is, answering the question or fulfilling a specific request, but no more. Many financial services companies have found that delivering proactive service helps them improve the responsiveness of customer service and gather information about customers' needs and wants, which enables them to develop products and provide services that customers truly value.

A service provider who can empathize with a dissatisfied customer has made an important step in recovering that customer's confidence and loyalty.

Proactive service providers go beyond simply answering customers' questions; they also use listening and questioning skills (discussed in Chapter 8) to help identify a customer's unspoken question or concern and determine the best possible solution. For example, if a customer calls a financial services company and asks questions about one of the company's products, a service provider could just provide the appropriate information and then move on to the next customer. To provide proactive service, however, the service provider should provide the requested information *and* also ask questions to find out why the customer is interested in the product. The customer might have a particular financial need that, if identified by the service provider, could be satisfied more effectively by a different product or service than the one the customer has inquired about. Figure 5-3 describes other examples of proactive service.

When a knowledgeable service provider listens carefully and probes further into the reasons or motivations behind customers' questions and concerns, she can help them better identify their true needs.

Keep in mind that customers do not always completely understand financial products and services or the terminology surrounding them. When a knowledgeable service provider listens carefully and probes further into the reasons or motivations behind customers' questions and concerns, she can help them better identify their true needs and find solutions to meet those needs.

Being responsive and delivering proactive customer service also requires service providers to be flexible and have the authority to take action. Customers expect a company's service providers to be able to handle the customers' problems. To do this, service providers must be able to think for themselves and to have the flexibility and authority to deal with problems that the company's procedures manual might not address. When properly trained service providers have the flexibility and authority to make instantaneous decisions, they can improve the quality and speed of customer service.

Providing responsive service requires financial services companies to hire a sufficient number of staff and to support their service providers with appropriate training, procedures, and technology. For example, using a customer-oriented database allows a service provider to quickly view all the pertinent information available about a particular customer—such as which products the customer owns and how often he has contacted the company for various services—which enables the service provider to understand the customer's needs more quickly. Other ways in which financial services companies can improve their responsiveness include

- Providing external customers and intermediaries with easy access to product and account information through automated telephone systems or Web sites

FIGURE 5-3. Examples of Proactive Service.

An investment company keeps records of how many forms an organizational customer—such as a business—uses for employee enrollment and participation in its retirement program. By tracking the business's form usage during a certain period, the investment company can determine when supplies might be running low and offer to send additional forms. By anticipating the customer's needs, the investment company saves the business from having to request forms every time they run low.

A customer called her life insurance company to request a change of beneficiary form. By asking additional questions, the service provider learned that the customer had gotten married and bought a new home. The service provider then offered to change the woman's name and address on her policy, and forwarded the call to the customer's agent, who made an appointment to discuss additional coverage with her. Through questioning, the service provider identified additional service needs that could be met immediately, saving the customer time and the effort of contacting her agent directly.

When an elderly customer called her bank and asked a service provider to send her forms that the service provider knew could be somewhat complicated, the service provider sent the forms *and* also called the customer a few days later to ask if she needed help completing them. By recognizing that the customer might have difficulty with the forms, the service provider was able to offer assistance without the customer having to specifically request it.

A customer called the downtown office of his auto insurance company to ask what the office's business hours were. The service provider answered the question, then politely inquired about the purpose of the customer's visit. When the customer explained that he wanted to pay his premium, the service provider told him that he could pay the premium using an automated teller machine located near his suburban home. By probing for more information, the service provider was able to tell the customer about a convenience that saved him valuable time.

- Making customer services available for longer hours

- Placing company listings in telephone books in areas in which the company still has customers but no longer maintains an office

- Allowing customers to conduct as many transactions as necessary during a single telephone call, rather than requiring them to make multiple telephone calls or spend additional time writing the company

TANGIBLE FACTORS

Tangible factors are the physical aspects of a financial services company and its employees. Tangible factors include

- The appearance of buildings, offices, and other physical facilities

- The appearance of company personnel

- The quality and appearance of any supplies, equipment, or other items used to provide service, such as the company's Web site, forms and contracts, and marketing brochures

Physical appearance is frequently a critical factor when customers judge the service they receive. Customers notice whether (1) offices are clean and well organized, (2) employees are well groomed and well spoken, (3) letters are neat and well written, and (4) forms are easy to read and fill out. Most financial services organizations try to give their marketing materials and products a consistent look and feel so customers can instantly recognize the company's information. Although tangible factors may seem superficial, they help influence customers' perceptions of a company.

The service-producer, unlike the product-producer, carries the burden of *being* what is bought. If a front-line service [provider] is poorly trained, dressed sloppily, unmotivated, or using antiquated equipment, then the service is bad.

—Laura Liswood [4]

The Service Gap: When Expectations and Perceptions Differ

The most meaningful measure of customer service quality is how well a service matches customer expectations. Delivering outstanding service requires a company to consistently meet or exceed customer expectations. A service provider's primary goal is to reduce any gap between customers' expectations and their perceptions.

When customers evaluate the quality of the service they have received, they compare the **expected service**, which is the quality of the service they think they will receive, with the **perceived service**, which is the quality of the service they believe they actually received.[5] A **service gap** exists when the perceived quality of a company's service is lower than the customers' expectations regarding the service, as illustrated by the following equation:

> **Expected Service – Perceived Service = Service Gap**
>
> **If Expected Service = Perceived Service, then Service Gap = 0**

For a more detailed discussion of other kinds of gaps that can lead to inadequate customer service, see Figure 5-4. Reducing or eliminating a service gap involves not only continually improving customer service activities, but also managing customers' expectations.

Managing Customers' Expectations

Customers with positive expectations tend to be more cooperative with service providers, which results in more positive customer service experiences.

Managing customers' expectations occurs at many different levels within a financial services company. Senior management helps establish customer expectations by (1) determining the types and levels of service that the company will provide, (2) advertising and promoting those services to customers, and (3) empowering and enabling service providers to deliver exceptional service so that customers develop positive expectations about interacting with the company. As we mentioned earlier, customers with positive expectations tend to be more cooperative with service providers, which typically results in more positive customer service experiences.

Individual service providers also influence customer expectations. As we discussed earlier, every interaction between a service provider and a customer helps set that customer's expectations for future interactions. When a company's service providers consistently meet or exceed customers' expectations, those customers will expect the same or even better service every time they contact the company. Therefore, exceptional service providers help raise customer expectations for the quality of service they will receive from the company. On the other hand, when service providers regularly fail to meet customers' expectations, those customers will lower their expectations of the service provided by the company (if they don't leave the company first). Having low expectations for service can cause customers to become unsatisfied and stop doing business with the company.

FIGURE 5-4. Understanding and Managing Gaps in Customer Service.

In their book *Delivering Quality Service: Balancing Customer Perceptions and Expectations*, A. Parasuraman, Valarie A. Zeithaml, and Leonard Berry present a comprehensive model for examining service quality, in which they identify five gaps that can prevent businesses from providing exceptional customer service. Analyzing the first four gaps can help a company determine the reasons for differences between expected service and perceived service and take steps toward eliminating the gap that is always most apparent to the customer: Gap 5, the service gap.

Businesses that understand the five gaps in customer service are more prepared to avoid or overcome the problems encountered in areas where service typically breaks down.

Gap 1

Customer Expectations vs. Management Perceptions—the difference between what customers want and what the company thinks they want. Gap 1 usually occurs because the people responsible for establishing service levels neither talk nor listen to their customers. The most effective way to prevent this gap is to ask customers what they want by using customer research tools, which we discuss later in this chapter.

Gap 2

Management Perceptions vs. Service Specifications—the difference between what a company's management believes that customers want and the service specifications that management sets for the work its employees do. Gap 2 usually occurs because (1) the company is unable to provide the service that customers want or (2) the company's top management does not recognize the importance of quality customer service. Companies can close Gap 2 by learning what kind of service customers expect and setting job and performance specifications that allow service providers to deliver the expected service.

Gap 3

Service Specifications vs. Service Delivery—the difference between the service specifications set by the company and the service that employees actually deliver. Employee performance can fall short of company specifications for several reasons, including a lack of the right employees, lack of employee training, lack of resources, lack of well-defined jobs and standards, and lack of motivation. To close Gap 3, a company must determine why the gap exists and then take steps to correct the deficiencies.

FIGURE 5-4.   Understanding and Managing Gaps in Customer Service (*continued*).

Gap 4

Actual Service Levels vs. Advertised Service Levels—the difference between the service a company advertises that it will provide and the actual service levels that it does provide. Gap 4 occurs when a company promises its customers a higher-quality service than it can provide. To close this gap, a company must either raise its service to the level of its promises, or it must promise less.

Gap 5

(The Service Gap) Expected Service vs. Perceived Service—the difference between the service that customers expect to get and the service that they believe they actually receive. The service gap is the culmination of the four preceding gaps; by reducing or eliminating Gaps 1 through 4, a financial services company can reduce or eliminate the service gap. Another way to reduce Gap 5 is to change customer expectations by educating customers about the company's products and levels of service it provides, as well as by continually improving service.

Source: A. Parasuraman, Valarie A. Zeithaml, and Leonard L. Berry, *A Conceptual Model of Service Quality and Its Implications for Future Research* (Cambridge, MA: Marketing Science Institute, 1984), 3, 11; Leonard L. Berry, David R. Bennett, and Carter W. Brown, *Service Quality: A Profit Strategy for Financial Institutions* (Homewood, IL: Dow Jones-Irwin, 1989); Jan Carlson, *Customer Focus Research: Building Customer Loyalty as a Strategic Weapon* (Atlanta: TouchStone Marketing Research, 1989).

Service providers also play an important role in managing customers' unrealistic or misguided expectations. For example, if a customer has had a difficult experience with one financial services company, he might expect to have a similarly unpleasant experience with another financial services company. When dealing with customers who seem to expect the worst from a company, service providers should keep in mind that the customers' expectations might be based on factors beyond the service provider's control—such as a negative experience with another company, another service provider, or an intermediary. By responding in a calm, understanding, and informative manner, the service provider can create a positive service experience for the customer, raising his expectations—and, in the process, his opinion of the company. Figure 5-5 explains how one customer service representative managed a customer's negative expectations about an annuity product.

FIGURE 5-5. Managing Customers' Negative Expectations.

When Mary Smith, a customer service representative at Rainbow Financial Services Company, answered a call from Stuart Tompkins, she immediately noticed his angry tone of voice. Mr. Tompkins had recently purchased a Rainbow annuity from an intermediary, but now he was having doubts about his decision and was concerned about his investments. In an agitated manner, he asked for information about the annuity's 10-day free look period, during which he could cancel the contract for a full refund of premiums paid.

Ms. Smith, who realized that Mr. Tompkins was not angry with her but with his situation, knew she needed to remain calm and reassure Mr. Tompkins that his investment was sound. She began by giving him a brief history of Rainbow, emphasizing its solid reputation. Then she explained that the intermediary who sold him the annuity was properly licensed and well respected in the industry.

Ms. Smith also reviewed Mr. Tompkins' annuity contract with him in great detail, explaining the many benefits it provided. She assured him that Rainbow was here to help him meet his financial needs and that he could call for assistance when it was time to complete any required forms or to help with any other aspect of his annuity. By the end of the conversation, Mr. Tompkins was no longer angry and seemed much more satisfied with his purchase decision.

The following day, Ms. Smith received a call from the intermediary who had sold the annuity to Mr. Tompkins, thanking her for saving Mr. Tompkins' business. The intermediary also told her that Mr. Tompkins had come back to his office and purchased another annuity.

Mr. Tompkins' uncertainty about his annuity purchase led him to develop such negative expectations about Rainbow Financial Services that he was ready to cancel his contract. Although Ms. Smith did not know why Mr. Tompkins had such negative expectations, she knew it was her job to reassure him and help him develop more positive and accurate expectations for Rainbow and its products. Not only did her efforts to manage his negative expectations make Mr. Tompkins feel better about his purchase decision, but they also resulted in additional business for Rainbow.

Sometimes, customers have unreasonable expectations. For example, suppose a customer demands that her credit card company increase the credit limit on her credit card by $10,000, but her credit history does not meet the company's requirements for such an increase. In situations in which a customer has expectations that cannot be fulfilled, the service provider's job is to modify the customer's expectations through explanation, persuasion, and negotiation. Service providers must communicate, in the most positive manner possible, what *can* be done and work with the customer to reach a mutually satisfying conclusion. We'll discuss explanation, persuasion, and negotiation in more detail in Chapter 9.

A company engages in customer education when it provides information through its Web site, customer newsletters, advertisements, or other types of marketing communications.

One way that both a financial services company and its service providers can manage customers' expectations is through **customer education**, which is the activity of educating existing or potential customers about a company's products and the level of service it provides. Such education influences customer expectations and reduces the gap between customers' perceptions and expectations. At the corporate level, a company engages in customer education when it provides information through its Web site, customer newsletters, advertisements, or other types of marketing communications. This information can include, for example, procedures for making inquiries, registering complaints, or exercising various rights and options. Such information helps ensure that customers have realistic expectations and an accurate perception of the services that the company can provide.

Generally, service providers deliver customer education in more informal ways than those used at the corporate level. Any time a service provider shares information about the company's products, services, or procedures with customers, she is providing customer education. By explaining as clearly and as positively as possible the product features and kinds of services that the company offers, service providers can help align the customer's expectations with what the company can deliver, as we saw Mary Smith do in Figure 5-5. In addition to educating customers about company-specific products and services, a service provider may also need to explain broader concepts, such as basic financial concepts (e.g., compound interest) or regulatory changes regarding certain financial products. To sufficiently and accurately educate customers, service providers must stay well informed about their company's products, services, and procedures, as well as about the financial services industry in general.

In the financial services industry, intermediaries are also an important source of customer education. Many customers rely on intermediaries for information and advice; as a result, intermediaries play an important role in helping customers develop appropriate and realistic expectations for products and services. Figure 5-6 describes one way that intermediaries influence customers' expectations.

FIGURE 5-6. How Intermediaries Help Set Customer Expectations.

One way that intermediaries—such as attorneys, accountants, insurance agents, tax advisors, trust advisors, bankers, and fee-based financial planners—influence customers' expectations for financial products and services is through financial planning. *Financial planning* is a coordinated process for identifying, planning for, and meeting goals related to financial needs. Financial planning includes gathering information about a person's or a family's financial position, setting financial objectives, and specifying intervals or events that would signal a need to review and revise the overall financial plan.

By helping customers identify their financial needs and explaining various ways to meet those needs, intermediaries educate customers. When intermediaries provide clear, accurate information about financial services products and companies, they help customers develop realistic expectations about how those products or companies can meet their needs. When a customer has practical expectations about what a product or company can do to help her accomplish her financial goals, she is likely to be satisfied with that product's or company's performance. If, however, a customer has unrealistic expectations for a product or a company, she is likely to be disappointed.

To ensure that intermediaries help customers develop realistic expectations, a financial services company must communicate effectively and honestly with intermediaries about the products and services it provides. In this way, a company helps intermediaries provide an accurate view of a product's or company's capabilities, thereby setting accurate customer expectations. (Note that in many sectors of the financial services industry, regulatory requirements also prohibit intermediaries or salespeople from providing misleading or inaccurate information about a product or company to a customer.)

Customer Behavior

A service provider in a financial services company might interact with dozens of different customers every day. Thus, service providers know from experience that each customer is unique and has his own ***personality***, which refers to a person's consistent, repeated patterns of behavior.[6] When we refer to people as thrifty or extravagant, outgoing or reserved, or aggressive or timid, we are referring to their personalities.

Note that a behavior must be *consistent* and *repeated* to be considered part of someone's personality. For example, if a customer is argumentative during one phone conversation with a service provider, we cannot assume that the customer has an aggressive personality, based on this one observation. However, a customer who contacts a company often and is excessively argumentative every time she calls is exhibiting the same behavior over and over, so we can assume that aggressive behavior is part of her personality. Psychologists have created different systems, theories, and categories to explain personality types; one well-known system, the Myers-Briggs Type Indicator® system, is highlighted in Figure 5-7.

Identifying Patterns of Behavior

Although people with certain personalities tend to exhibit certain behavior patterns, anyone is capable of using any behavior pattern, depending on the circumstances. Knowing how to identify and manage behavior patterns can help service providers respond to customers in an effective and productive way, enabling them to meet their ultimate goal of satisfying customers' needs quickly and accurately. In this section, we first discuss one method of analyzing behavior patterns, then we explain four general patterns of behavior.

TRANSACTIONAL ANALYSIS

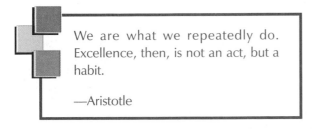

We are what we repeatedly do. Excellence, then, is not an act, but a habit.

—Aristotle

Transactional analysis is an approach to analyzing behavior patterns which suggests that, at any given moment, a person exhibits one of three behavior patterns or ego states: parent, adult, or child.[7] Each behavior pattern is described as follows:

FIGURE 5-7. The Myers-Briggs Type Indicator® System.

Personality models can help service providers understand the many personalities—including their own—that they deal with every day. Learning to recognize and analyze different personalities enables a service provider to adapt his behavior to suit the needs of different customers. One well-known system for identifying and classifying personality traits is the Myers-Briggs Type Indicator® system, a tool that analyzes people according to their preferences for one of two opposite characteristics in the following areas:

Introverted/Extraverted (I/E).

An *introverted* person prefers quiet and enjoys doing things alone. An *extraverted* person is outgoing and enjoys doing things with other people.

Sensing/Intuitive (S/N).

A *sensing* person trusts only what he can see or hear or touch when making decisions. An *intuitive* person is willing to make decisions based on what feels right and to rely on hunches.

Thinking/Feeling (T/F).

A *thinking* person takes actions and makes decisions based on logical thought processes. A *feeling* person relies more on emotional responses to make decisions and take actions.

Judging/Perceiving (J/P).

A *judging* person desires a fairly high level of certainty in day-to-day activities; she is not comfortable with ambiguous situations. (Note that, in this model, judging does not indicate the need to pass judgment on others.) A *perceiving* person is comfortable with variety and change, likes a wide range of possibilities, and has a high tolerance for ambiguity.

To use the Myers-Briggs™ model, the participant completes a questionnaire, which is then "scored" to determine her personality preferences—for example, she might be introverted, intuitive, feeling, and judging. Another person might be extraverted, sensing, thinking, and perceiving. Under the Myers-Briggs™ model, 16 different combinations of preferences are possible; we've reprinted four of the combinations here as an example.

ISTJ	INTJ	ESTJ	ENTJ
Quiet, serious, earn success by thoroughness and dependability. Practical, matter-of-fact, realistic, and responsible. Decide logically what should be done and work toward it steadily, regardless of distractions. Take pleasure in making everything orderly and organized—their work, their home, their life. Value traditions and loyalty.	Have original minds and great drive for implementing their ideas and achieving their goals. Quickly see patterns in external events and develop long-range explanatory perspectives. When committed, organize a job and carry it through. Skeptical and independent, have high standards of competence and performance for themselves and others.	Practical, realistic, matter-of-fact. Decisive, quickly move to implement decisions. Organize projects and people to get things done, focus on getting results in the most efficient way possible. Take care of routine details. Have a clear set of logical standards, systematically follow them and want others to also. Forceful in implementing their plans.	Frank, decisive, assume leadership readily. Quickly see illogical and inefficient procedures and policies, develop and implement comprehensive systems to solve organizational problems. Enjoy long-term planning and goal setting. Usually well informed, well read, enjoy expanding their knowledge and passing it on to others. Forceful in presenting their ideas.

- *Parent ego state (P).* An ego state in which a person responds to others as a parent might, as if he knows everything and wants to tell everyone else what to do.

- *Adult ego state (A).* An ego state in which a person objectively analyzes data and makes decisions based on this analysis.

- *Child ego state (C).* An ego state in which a person responds to others in the helpless, complaining tone of an unhappy child.

According to transactional analysis, communication problems are less likely to occur between two people in the adult ego state. When both a service provider and a customer are in the adult ego state, they conduct themselves in a mature, businesslike manner without interpersonal difficulty. Figure 5-8 illustrates an adult-to-adult interaction between a customer and a service provider.

Many problems occur, however, between people who are in different or conflicting ego states—for example, parent to adult. When a customer speaks from a parent ego state, he talks down to the service provider as though the service provider is a child. When the service provider responds

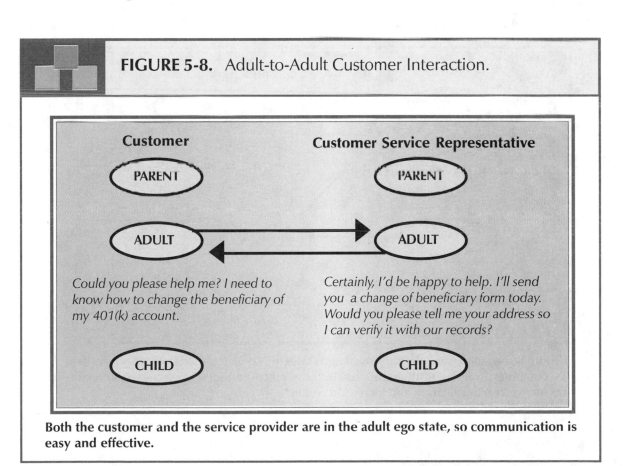

FIGURE 5-8. Adult-to-Adult Customer Interaction.

Customer

PARENT

ADULT

Could you please help me? I need to know how to change the beneficiary of my 401(k) account.

CHILD

Customer Service Representative

PARENT

ADULT

Certainly, I'd be happy to help. I'll send you a change of beneficiary form today. Would you please tell me your address so I can verify it with our records?

CHILD

Both the customer and the service provider are in the adult ego state, so communication is easy and effective.

as an adult to another adult, a crossed communication transaction occurs, as Figure 5-9 shows. If the service provider continues to respond as an adult to an *adult* when a customer is in the *parent* ego state, conflict is likely.

In such a situation, the service provider's goal is to help the customer move to an adult ego state so that they can participate in an adult-to-adult interaction. However, before the customer's adult ego state can take control, the feelings or emotions that have caused the parent ego state to surface must be addressed. Having his feelings acknowledged will make the customer more likely to continue the conversation from an adult ego state, resulting in an adult-to-adult interaction, as Figure 5-10 illustrates.

A similar approach could be used with a customer in a child ego state. For example, suppose a customer calls and states in a whining voice that she is confused about the company's beneficiary change form. To help her reach an adult ego state, the service provider could respond, "That's one

FIGURE 5-9. Crossed Communication Transaction.

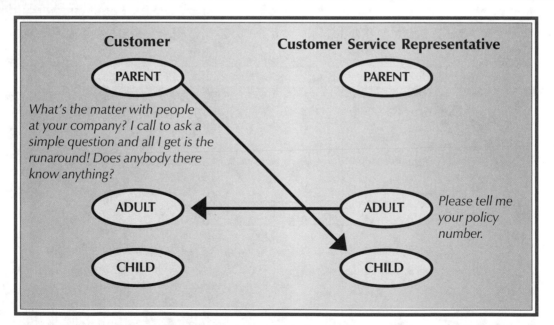

Although the customer is in the parent ego state, the service provider responds as though the customer is in the adult ego state. This crossed communication transaction results in ineffective communication and increased conflict.

FIGURE 5-10. Helping the Customer Move to an Adult Ego State.

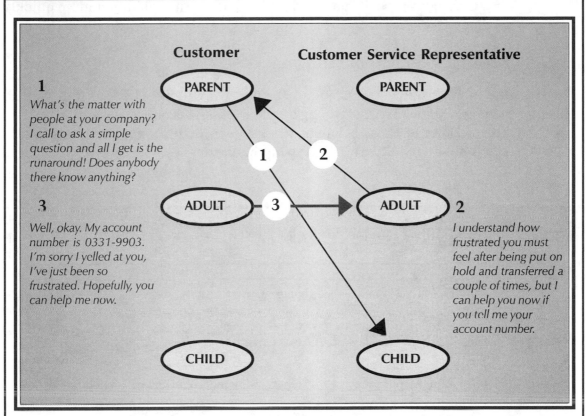

Customer

1

What's the matter with people at your company? I call to ask a simple question and all I get is the runaround! Does anybody there know anything?

3

Well, okay. My account number is 0331-9903. I'm sorry I yelled at you, I've just been so frustrated. Hopefully, you can help me now.

Customer Service Representative

2

I understand how frustrated you must feel after being put on hold and transferred a couple of times, but I can help you now if you tell me your account number.

PARENT — PARENT
ADULT — ADULT
CHILD — CHILD

The service provider recognizes the customer's parent ego state and knows he must acknowledge the customer's feelings before they can communicate effectively. After the service provider's empathetic response, the customer's adult ego state takes over, enabling an adult-to-adult interaction to take place. Although in this example the customer transitions quickly to the adult ego state, it can sometimes take several attempts to change a customer's ego state.

of our most confusing forms. If you'd like, we can go through it together and I'd be happy to answer any questions you may have."

When any customer interaction seems negative, try to identify whether the customer is in a parent or child ego state. Then, gently help the person reach the adult ego state by following the "feelings first, facts second" model we have just illustrated, in which you acknowledge the customer's feelings before asking for information. Sometimes, you might have to make several empathetic responses before you can diffuse a customer's anger. If you are busy and a customer is being difficult, you might be inclined to react to the customer's sarcastic or critical remark from your own parent or child ego state; however, doing so will only escalate the conflict. Instead, stay in your adult ego state and use the "feelings first, facts second" approach to bring the situation much more quickly to a positive, productive resolution.

GENERAL PATTERNS OF BEHAVIOR

For more insight into people's behavior, we will now look at four general behavior patterns: passive, aggressive, passive-aggressive, and assertive. Learning about these behavior patterns can help service providers understand how to deal with each type of behavior.

FIGURE 5-11. Dealing with Passive Behavior.

Patricia Jakarta, a customer service representative for the Eastern Mortgage Company, is just finishing a telephone conversation with customer Caroline Tresolini. Ms. Jakarta has just explained the use of the electronic funds transfer method to pay the monthly mortgage on Ms. Tresolini's house.

Ms. Jakarta: (voice friendly, self-assured) Does this method of payment suit your needs, Ms. Tresolini?

Customer: (voice hesitant) Well, I guess so. I mean, well, I suppose that's all right.

Ms. Jakarta: Are you sure, Ms. Tresolini? It sounds like you still have some concerns.

Customer: Oh, no, it's fine. I think it's all fine.

Ms. Jakarta: Are you sure? I could go over the payment schedule again if you like.

Customer: Well…

Ms. Jakarta: Really, it's no problem. I'd be happy to.

Customer: Well, you know, I understand the payment schedule, but I don't feel comfortable with your company making withdrawals from my bank account each month.

Because Ms. Jakarta sensed that the customer still had some concerns, she continued probing in a courteous, caring manner. She continued to reassure Ms. Tresolini that she was willing to take time to explain the matter further, until eventually Ms. Tresolini felt comfortable enough to express her real concern. Using this approach, Ms. Jakarta effectively drew out this passive customer and identified her real need.

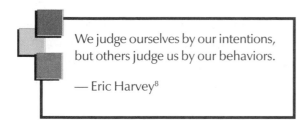

We judge ourselves by our intentions, but others judge us by our behaviors.

— Eric Harvey[8]

Passive Behavior

Passive behavior occurs when a person does not try to influence the behavior of other people. Generally, passive people are unwilling to express their feelings or state their position on an issue. They might not believe that their opinions matter to anyone else, or they might be afraid of the consequences of acting more assertively. Passive people may fear that another person will be angry if they assert themselves.

Passive customers generally are hesitant to state what they really want, so a service provider must draw them out by asking questions to determine their actual needs. Letting such customers know that their concerns are important and that someone is willing to take the time to listen to them provides the reassurance they need, as Figure 5-11 illustrates.

Taking time to help these customers is important, even though they seem unwilling to ask for what they want or need. Passive customers are the customers who are least likely to complain when they aren't satisfied, and studies indicate that dissatisfied customers who don't complain are more likely to stop doing business with a company than are customers who complain and then have their problems resolved in a satisfactory way. Most customers who do not complain—silent, passive customers— punish service providers and their companies by taking their business elsewhere and advising their friends to do likewise. Therefore, probing to determine the unstated needs of passive customers is essential.

Aggressive Behavior

The opposite of passive behavior is *aggressive behavior*, which occurs when a person lashes out at others with little regard for their feelings. Aggressive behavior is emotional, judgmental, fault-finding, and attacking. Yelling, swearing, and finger-pointing are all examples of aggressive behavior.

When some customers get angry, they direct their aggressive behavior toward service providers even though the service providers may not be the real cause of the anger. A customer might be upset about a letter she received from the company, about a company policy or procedure, or about something completely unrelated to the company or its products and services. To the customer, service providers represent the company and, therefore, are often the target of the customer's frustration and aggressive behavior. Although being the target of aggressive behavior can be offensive and upsetting, service providers should not take the behavior personally.

To deal with aggressive customers, a service provider must address the customers' emotional concerns before attempting to work with them in a reasonable manner. By letting such customers express themselves and release some of the pent-up emotions and energy that cause aggressive behavior, the service provider can help reduce the aggressive behavior. A service provider can encourage customers to express their emotions by assuring them that she sympathizes with their situations, is interested in helping them, and is willing to take the time to listen, and ultimately, find a solution. Active listening, which we will discuss in Chapter 8, is a good way to help customers release aggressive energy.

If a customer's aggressive behavior continues beyond a reasonable time or becomes abusive, the service provider must take steps to stop the behavior. We will discuss several ways of dealing with extremely aggressive or abusive customers in Chapter 9.

Passive-Aggressive Behavior

An apparently contradictory combination of passive behavior and aggressive behavior, *passive-aggressive behavior* occurs when a person feels hostile about something but is afraid or unwilling to be openly aggressive and show hostility.

For example, suppose that customer Pamela Koch calls the Rock Solid Investment Company to request a withdrawal from her retirement account. Rock Solid service provider Mario Fuentes informs Ms. Koch that because she is not of retirement age yet she will have to pay a penalty for such a withdrawal. Ms. Koch was not aware of the penalty and is disappointed and angry when she hears this, although she does not express her feelings to Mr. Fuentes. Although Mr. Fuentes senses Ms. Koch's disappointment and courteously attempts to further explain the situation and offer alternate solutions to meet her financial needs, Ms. Koch thanks him and hangs up. When, however, Ms. Koch receives a routine customer survey asking her to rate the quality of service she received during her most recent call to Rock Solid, she responds negatively, indicating she received poor service from Mr. Fuentes, despite the fact that he performed his job well. Ms. Koch's action is an example of passive-aggressive behavior. She has committed a hostile act, but camouflaged it to avoid a directly aggressive confrontation.

When a service provider senses that more intense feelings lie beneath a customer's passive words or behavior, the service provider must encourage the customer to express those emotions. Then the service provider must be prepared to deal with the hostile behavior that surfaces. Without taking these two steps, the service provider will find that working effectively with such customers is difficult because their underlying emotional concerns will keep getting in the way.

Assertive Behavior

In some regions of the world, such as North America and Europe, many people consider the ideal demeanor to be **assertive behavior**, which occurs when a person states his positions clearly and firmly, but in a *constructive* rather than *destructive* manner. People who are assertive describe their feelings fully and clearly; give good, objective reasons for the position they are taking; suggest behavior that they think is fair; avoid exaggerating for dramatic effect; and don't resort to personal attacks.

An assertive person will say what needs to be said in a courteous and appropriate manner. However, many factors can interfere with our ability to act in such a composed, forthright manner—for example, some people worry that assertive behavior will be interpreted as rudeness. And, unfortunately, the boundary between assertive and aggressive behaviors can be hard to define. What seems like aggressiveness to you might seem like healthy assertiveness to someone else. When trying to distinguish between assertive and aggressive behaviors, remember that assertive behavior tends to be constructive, looking for a positive outcome for everyone involved in a situation, while aggressive behavior tends to be destructive, looking for an opportunity to "win" a confrontation.

An assertive person will say what needs to be said in a courteous and appropriate manner.

Note also that in certain regions of the world, such as Asia, assertive behavior is *not* considered the ideal behavior. In many cultures, assertive people are often seen as abrasive and rude. These cultures value traits such as humility and politeness more than they value assertiveness. When interacting with customers, being aware of cultural differences in behavior can help you adjust your own behavior to make customers feel comfortable and confident that you care about their needs and concerns.

In Figure 5-12, we compare passive, assertive, and aggressive behaviors (recall that passive-aggressive behavior combines the characteristics of both passive and aggressive behaviors).

FIGURE 5-12. Comparison of Passive, Assertive, and Aggressive Behavior Patterns.

	Passive Behavior	Assertive Behavior	Aggressive Behavior
Trait	Failing to stand up for one's self or standing up for one's self in such an ineffectual manner that one's rights are easily violated	Standing up for one's self in a way that does not violate the basic rights of another person	Standing up for one's self in a way that violates the rights of another person
Goal	Typically, to avoid conflict or to gain approval from others	To communicate honestly and openly	To dominate or win, not simply to honestly express your own feelings
Motive	A lack of respect for one's self (or one's position), or to follow cultural norms that value humility over assertiveness	Respect, not deference, both for one's self and for another person	A lack of respect for another person

Customer Service Research

As we mentioned earlier in this chapter, a financial services company must conduct research to accurately determine its customers' expectations and whether its customers perceive that their expectations are being met. Being familiar with customer research techniques can help service providers to better understand the origin of the information that is used to establish a company's service levels and processes. Understanding research purposes and methods can also help a service provider be better prepared to participate in customer service research if called upon to do so.

A financial services company typically gets research information from a combination of secondary data and primary data. **Secondary data** is research information that already has been collected for some other purpose, either by the company doing the research or by some other organization. Examples of secondary data include information obtained from the company's accounting and sales records and customer files, government sources, industry and trade associations, and commercial research firms (such as Gallup or A. C. Nielsen). Secondary data is usually less expensive and less time-consuming to obtain than is primary data.

Primary data is research information that has not been collected previously and that is observed and collected to provide information on a specific problem.[9] Compared to secondary data, primary data is usually more timely and relevant to the problem being studied; however, it is also usually more expensive and time-consuming to collect. Primary data is obtained using two types of research methods: qualitative and quantitative.

Qualitative Research

Qualitative research is designed to assess people's attitudes, opinions, and behaviors about or toward a particular subject.[10] Qualitative research, which is often referred to as *exploratory research*, is not intended to provide conclusions; rather, it is used to investigate a situation and provide direction for further research. For example, financial services companies often see the symptoms of a problem (such as increasing customer complaints) rather than the problem itself. When companies can only identify symptoms and are not sure how to define a problem, they often conduct qualitative research, which frequently leads to more specific research.

Typically, qualitative research is highly flexible and unstructured. It is usually conducted using a relatively small number of people in group sessions, although it can be conducted using in-depth interviews with individuals. Some common forms of qualitative research that are most useful in customer service research include the following:

- **Focus group interviews.** A *focus group interview* is an unstructured, informal session during which six to ten participants are asked to discuss their opinions about a certain topic. Led by a professional group moderator, focus groups help financial services companies understand customers' general perceptions, expectations, attitudes, and opinions about specific topics. Financial services companies also use focus groups to help them generate ideas for new services and modifications to current services. In addition to external customers, focus groups also can consist of employees or intermediaries.

■ **Advisory panels.** An *advisory panel* is a standing group that meets on a regular basis to provide a company with qualitative information about the company's services and to suggest ways to improve those services. Unlike focus groups, which usually meet only once, advisory panels provide companies with a continuous flow of qualitative information. In exchange, companies typically report back to the advisory panel regarding its suggestions. An advisory panel can consist of a financial services company's external customers, intermediaries, or employees.

■ **In-depth interviews.** In the context of qualitative research, an *in-depth interview* is a loosely structured conversation during which a few respondents, usually customers, are interviewed individually and asked to provide detailed information on a specific topic. In-depth interviews can be extremely useful for providing complex and technical customer information. In customer service, in-depth interviews are most commonly used in business-to-business situations, such as when an insurer provides services to commercial clients with large group policies.

Complaint monitoring can help a company identify service problems that customers commonly encounter.

■ **Complaint monitoring.** Monitoring complaints that come from customers, intermediaries, employees, regulatory agencies, and consumer groups is an important method of gathering qualitative research. Complaint monitoring can help a company identify service problems that customers commonly encounter and instances where service gaps and service breakdowns occur. A financial services organization can use the information obtained from complaints to improve its processes and its communication with customers, with the goal of improving customer service and increasing customer satisfaction and loyalty. To monitor complaints, many companies use a *complaint management system*, which consists of the processes and procedures for recording, evaluating, and taking action on complaints. Computer-based complaint management systems allow for quick recording and retrieval of detailed information.

Quantitative Research

Quantitative research is designed to generate concrete information about a group's characteristics and behavior. Quantitative research attempts to quantify, or assign a numerical value to, customers' needs, preferences, and attitudes. For example, an investment company could use quantitative

FIGURE 5-13. What Is Sampling?

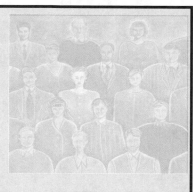

Quantitative research helps a financial services company determine the proportion of customers who have specified needs, preferences, or attitudes. To accurately represent customer views, researchers use a technique called *sampling*, in which they examine a portion of a group to develop conclusions about the entire group. The entire group is called the *population*, and the portion, or subset, of the population that is studied to develop conclusions about the total population is called the *sample*. The sample is generally chosen using statistical methods that help ensure that the sample is representative of the entire population. Properly used sampling ensures that a company will include the right kinds of customers in its research base and, consequently, reduce its chances of gathering misleading or inaccurate information.

research to learn what percentage of its customers is satisfied with its investor services activities. To gather information that best represents the overall views of a company's customers, quantitative research uses a technique called sampling, which is explained in Figure 5-13.

Typically, researchers survey a representative sample of a total population, analyze the data, and then develop conclusions about the population as a whole.

Compared to qualitative research, quantitative research uses more structured data collection methods and a larger number of respondents, and results in data that can be quantified or summarized in numerical form. Surveys are the most frequently used method for conducting quantitative research about customer service.

SURVEYS

A *survey* is a data-collection method that uses structured data-collection forms, such as questionnaires, to gather data directly from the group, or population, being studied. Typically, researchers survey a representative sample of a total population, analyze the data, and then develop conclusions about the population as a whole; although a company sometimes surveys all its customers. The three major survey methods include

- *Personal interview*, in which the interviewer meets face-to-face with each survey participant to ask the survey questions and record the responses

FIGURE 5-14. Strengths and Weaknesses of the Three Major Survey Methods.

	Personal Interview	Mail Survey	Telephone Survey
Versatility of questioning	**High**, because interviewer can adapt questions based on what transpires during the interview	**Low**, because the highly standardized format is limited to simple, clearly worded questions	**Moderate**, because this method is more versatile than mail surveys but less versatile than personal interview surveys
Amount of data that can be collected from each respondent	**Large**	**Small, moderate or large**	**Moderate**
Time required	**Moderate amount**, depending on the size of the sample	**Can be slow**, because mailing time can be long	**Quite fast**
Cost	**Usually most expensive**, because the interviewer's time and travel can be costly	**Usually least expensive**, if response rate is adequate	**Inexpensive**
Accuracy	**Varies, least accurate on sensitive questions**	**Varies, most accurate on sensitive questions**	**Varies, moderate on sensitive questions**
Potential for misunderstood questions	**Low**, because interviewer can clarify questions	**High**	**Moderate**
Potential for interviewer to influence answers	**High**	**None**, although phrasing of questions can influence answers	**Moderate**

■ *Written survey*, in which survey participants respond to questions that are sent to them via mail or e-mail, or that can be accessed online through a specified Web site

■ *Telephone survey*, in which the interviewer calls survey participants on the telephone to ask the survey questions and record the answers

Figure 5-14 describes the relative strengths and weaknesses of each survey method.

Customer service surveys help a financial services company measure, among other things, how satisfied customers are with the service they receive and how likely they are to do business with the company again. When conducted on a regular basis, such as annually, customer service surveys can help companies and service providers understand customers' expectations and perceptions and develop strategies to better meet customers' needs and wants.

In addition to gathering information from external customers, financial services companies use surveys to solicit feedback from internal customers, as Insight 5-2 explains.

Conducting research is a crucial part of a successful financial services company's customer service activities. Only by regularly communicating with people whose behavior, attitudes, perceptions, and expectations are representative of its customers, can a company be reasonably assured that it is capable of satisfying its customers' service needs. Although most customer service research is conducted at the corporate level, service providers by the nature of their jobs are in an excellent position to communicate with customers as well. By asking customers questions such as "What else could I have done to make your experience today more pleasant?" service providers can learn a great deal about customer expectations, perceptions, and behavior. Such knowledge enables service providers to better anticipate and meet customer needs and wants.[11] In addition, by reporting trends in customer inquiries and requests, service providers can alert managers to the need for changes in customer materials or procedures. This ongoing feedback is a valuable addition to a company's more formal customer service research.

As we stated at the beginning of this chapter, predicting and then meeting customers' needs and wants is essential to providing exceptional customer service. Understanding customers' behavior is key to uncovering their needs and wants. Knowing what customers expect from you and your company and being aware of how they perceive the service you provide can help you interpret their behavior and then respond appropriately to meet their needs, delivering the kind of superior service that results in satisfied, loyal customers. Understanding customers' behavior ultimately helps service providers improve their communication skills, which is the focus of the next two chapters.

INSIGHT 5-2.   Customer Surveys Improve IS Department's Service.

The Information Services (IS) department of the Victorious Financial Services Company has instituted a Customer Satisfaction Survey that it sends to every fifth person for whom a service ticket is opened. It sends the survey after closing the service ticket (that is, after completing the service).

The survey asks respondents (other employees in the company) to select one of five responses—from "Completely Unsatisfactory" to "Met Expectations" to "Superior"—for questions such as

- Was the technician knowledgeable about this issue?
- Was the technician courteous?
- Was the response timely?

Respondents also can write additional comments in a special section.

The survey allows the IS manager to evaluate technicians' abilities and attitudes and indicates whether the department is responding to service requests quickly enough and performing follow-up calls. The goal is to make users happy and allow them to vent frustrations or praise excellent service.

The IS manager forwards negative and positive comments to the technicians and, if necessary, holds a meeting to discuss ways to fix recurring problems or lack of responsiveness. Occasionally, the manager contacts the survey respondent to obtain additional feedback on how the department could have handled the problem more effectively.

Victorious publishes the survey results on its Intranet monthly and annually so that all employees can see how the IS department is performing. The survey has about a 60 percent response rate, and the department's year-to-date rating is 3.15 out of a possible 4, which equates to an overall rating of "Exceeds Expectations." As evidenced by the response rate and overall rating, the IS staff and its customers take the survey seriously, which results in improved internal customer service.

To practice and review the skills and information you learned in this chapter, see the interactive CD, *Practicing Your Customer Service Skills*, included with this book.

Key Terms and Concepts

need
want
expectation
perception
facts
inferences
service dimensions
reliability
assurance
responsiveness
proactive service
reactive service
tangible factors
expected service
perceived service
service gap
customer education
financial planning
personality
transactional analysis

parent ego state
adult ego state
child ego state
passive behavior
aggressive behavior
passive-aggressive behavior
assertive behavior
secondary data
primary data
qualitative research
focus group interview
advisory panel
in-depth interview
complaint management
  system
quantitative research
sampling
population
sample
survey

Endnotes

1. Jagdish N. Sheth, Banwari Mittal, Bruce I. Newman, *Customer Behavior: Consumer Behavior and Beyond*, LOMA ed. (Fort Worth: Dryden Press, 2001), 41.

2. Karl Albrecht and Ron Zemke, *Service America!: Doing Business in the New Economy* (New York: Warner Books, 1990).

3. A. Parasuraman, Valarie A. Zeithaml, and Leonard L. Berry, *A Conceptual Model of Service Quality and Its Implications for Future Research* (Cambridge, MA: Marketing Science Institute, 1984), 3, 11. The researchers originally identified 10 criteria (called *dimensions*) that customers typically use to judge the quality of the service they receive. Because some overlap existed among the original 10 dimensions, the researchers later condensed them to five.

4. Laura A. Liswood, *Serving Them Right* (New York: Harper Business, 1990), xxix.

5. Valarie A. Zeithaml, A. Parasuraman, and Leonard L. Berry, *Delivering Quality Service: Balancing Customer Perceptions and Expectations* (New York: The Free Press, 1990), 19.

6. Sheth, Mittal, and Newman, 129.

7. Eric Berne, M.D., *Games People Play* (New York: Ballantine Books, 1992), Chapter 2; Edwin G. Davis, *Customer Relations for Technicians* (Westerville, OH: Glencoe/McGraw-Hill, 1991), 13–16.

8. JoAnna F. Brandi, *Building Company Loyalty: The 21 Essential Elements...IN ACTION* (Dallas: Walk the Talk Company, 2001), 23.

9. Sheth, Mittal, and Newman, FS-54.

10. Ibid., FS-55.

11. Brandi, 6.

CHAPTER 6

Customer Service and Communication

After studying this chapter, you should be able to

- Describe the communication process and discuss the importance of communication in customer service

- Explain the difference between the denotative and connotative meanings of words

- Describe how the right choice of words can improve verbal communication by setting a positive tone and achieving clarity

- Discuss the various forms of nonverbal communication, including body language and the use of voice, space, touch, and time

- Discuss the importance of nonverbal communication and the common problems associated with nonverbal communication

- Describe how cultural differences can affect communication and how you can improve communication with customers from other cultures

As you have seen, service providers must understand their customers and various job-related products, services, processes, and resources. In addition, they must make use of interpersonal skills. One such skill is communication. Through communication, service providers interact with customers to learn about and satisfy their needs. Whether working with external customers, internal customers, or coworkers, service providers must communicate effectively to provide exceptional customer service.

Like most skills, communication can be improved through learning and practice. In this chapter, we will discuss the communication process, verbal and nonverbal communication, and various ways to enhance communication in a customer service environment.

The Communication Process

Communication is the process of transferring information and understanding from one person to another. Because virtually all customer service interactions involve communication, the level of skill with which service providers communicate has a major impact on how well they perform in a customer service setting.

In Chapter 5, we discussed how people differ in their perceptions, personalities, and behavioral patterns, and how these differences affect customer service interactions. As you will learn in this section, factors related to communication also create challenges in customer service interactions. A better understanding of the elements in the communication process can help you overcome many of these challenges.

Elements of the Communication Process

The main components of any type of communication are the message, sender, receiver, channel, noise, and feedback. A *message* is the information that is transmitted during communication. When you speak with a customer, write a letter, or even expresses your feelings by smiling or changing your tone of voice, you are sending a message. The person who transmits the message is the *sender*.

When you listen to a customer's questions or concerns, read a customer's letter, or notice a customer's tone of voice or facial expression, you are receiving a message. The person who obtains the message from the sender is the **receiver**.

A **channel**, also called a *communication channel*, is the medium used to transmit or deliver a message. Channels include face-to-face communication, letters, the Internet, e-mail, fax, and the telephone.

Anything that interferes with communication is called **noise**. A few examples of noise include sounds that make hearing difficult, strong emotions or attitudes that hinder speaking or listening, negative expectations, technical jargon, regional accents, bad reception on telephones, and daydreaming. For example, suppose you receive a telephone call from a customer who is so upset that he has difficulty speaking calmly or listening objectively. In this situation, noise—in the form of the customer's strong emotions—is interfering with communication.

Anything that interferes with communication is called **noise**.

Feedback is a return message that a receiver sends in response to a sender's message. Feedback can be in words or through other means of expression. A customer might respond to something you say by asking a question, nodding, yawning, smiling, complaining, or expressing thanks for the information received. When someone receives a message and then replies with feedback, the receiver becomes the sender.

Figure 6-1 shows how the elements of the communication process fit together.

What Can Go Wrong in the Communication Process?

The communication process sounds simple, but many things can go wrong. One problem might be the sender's failure to express the message clearly. Suppose, for example, that when a customer calls to find out why he hasn't received his check for a retirement fund withdrawal, the service provider discovers the problem and promises to "take care of it right away."

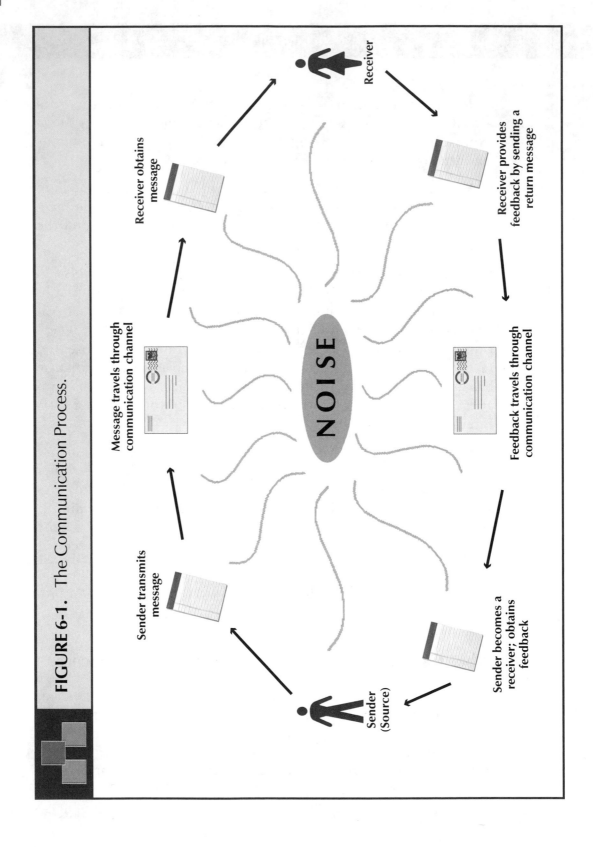

FIGURE 6-1. The Communication Process.

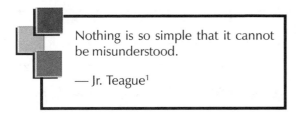

Nothing is so simple that it cannot be misunderstood.

— Jr. Teague[1]

Does this mean that the service provider will correct the error as soon as she hangs up the telephone, and then simply allow the withdrawal process to move forward according to the usual timeframe? Or will she also make sure the check is mailed to the customer that same day? If so, will she send the check via regular mail or overnight mail?

Suppose the service provider tells the customer that the check will arrive within three days. Although this message is less ambiguous than "right away," it still may not prevent a misunderstanding. Will the check arrive in three calendar days or three business days—not counting Saturdays, Sundays, or holidays?

Sometimes, even when the sender expresses the message clearly and completely, the receiver fails to understand. For example, if you are explaining to a customer how to complete a form, and the customer's attention wanders for just a moment, he may miss an important part of the message.

Culture refers to the customary beliefs, attitudes, practices, and behaviors that are learned and shared by a group.

Other times, problems arise in the communication process because of cultural differences between the sender and receiver. *Culture* refers to the customary beliefs, attitudes, practices, and behaviors that are learned and shared by a group. Although the most obvious cultural differences are in language and dialect, many other differences exist. For example, people from Western cultures typically prefer direct, simple communication ("get to the point" and answer the question with a simple "yes" or "no"). People from Eastern cultures typically place a high value on relationship building and harmony in communication. People from Middle Eastern and Mediterranean cultures often have an intense, animated style of communication. To an individual from another culture, any of these communication styles might cause uneasiness or lead to misunderstanding.

Problems also arise in the communication process because of the sender's choice of communication channel. For example, as Figure 6-2 illustrates, a long or complex message is often more easily understood if it is expressed in writing, while a short message or a message that requires an immediate response is usually more effective if delivered in person or by telephone.

As you have seen, many things can go wrong in the communication process. Some problems are associated with verbal communication and

FIGURE 6-2. Communicating a Complex Message.

Linda Hisle calls her insurance company for information about annuity products. The service provider, who is an annuity expert, launches into a long, detailed description of the various features of deferred and immediate annuity contracts. When the service provider starts explaining the tax advantages of annuity products, Ms. Hisle excuses herself and says she has to go.

What happened? Maybe because of the complexity of the message, the telephone was an ineffective communication channel. Another service provider, Mitsuhisa Katsuno, takes a different approach. Instead of immediately launching into a detailed explanation of annuities, Mr. Katsuno begins by offering Ms. Hisle a choice of channels.

He mentions that annuities can be somewhat complex, and he asks Ms. Hisle if she would like him to send her a brochure that describes the company's annuity products. If Ms. Hisle chooses the brochure, Mr. Katsuno could offer to speak with her at a later date to answer any questions she might have. On the other hand, if Ms. Hisle chooses to receive the information over the telephone, then Mr. Katsuno could improve the communication process by avoiding technical terms (a type of noise) and by periodically asking questions to check Ms. Hisle's understanding (encouraging feedback). At the end of the discussion, Mr. Katsuno could again politely offer to send the brochure.

other problems are associated with nonverbal communication. ***Verbal communication*** is the use of language (spoken or written) to send and receive messages. ***Nonverbal communication*** is a type of communication that conveys messages in ways that do not rely on the meaning of words. In the following sections, we will explore the use of verbal and nonverbal communication in customer service. Figure 6-3 provides a list of some potential pitfalls of the communication process.

Verbal Communication

Most intentional efforts to communicate rely on verbal communication. Choosing words carefully is an important part of the verbal communication process, but it presents challenges. Glance through a dictionary and you will notice that most words have more than one meaning. Language is neither exact nor static. As the world changes and generations come and go, new words are coined and existing words take on additional meanings.

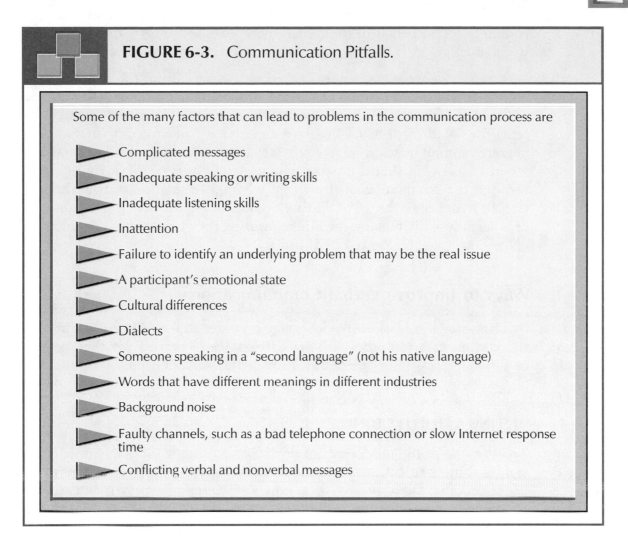

FIGURE 6-3. Communication Pitfalls.

Some of the many factors that can lead to problems in the communication process are

- Complicated messages
- Inadequate speaking or writing skills
- Inadequate listening skills
- Inattention
- Failure to identify an underlying problem that may be the real issue
- A participant's emotional state
- Cultural differences
- Dialects
- Someone speaking in a "second language" (not his native language)
- Words that have different meanings in different industries
- Background noise
- Faulty channels, such as a bad telephone connection or slow Internet response time
- Conflicting verbal and nonverbal messages

Furthermore, many words have both a denotative meaning and a connotative meaning. A ***denotative meaning*** is the direct, literal meaning of the word. A ***connotative meaning*** is the word's suggested or implied meaning. Connotative meanings are far more subjective than denotative meanings because they vary from one person to another, depending on a person's background and experience. An awareness of the different meanings of words can help you avoid communication problems.

For example, in *Merriam-Webster's Collegiate® Dictionary*, the word *form* has twenty-one separate definitions, one of which is "a printed or typed document with blank spaces for insertion of required or requested information."[2] Forms facilitate the work of many service providers in the financial services industry. Correct and complete information provided on the appropriate form makes it easier for service providers to conduct transactions on behalf of their customers. In this context, the word *form* has a slightly positive or at least a neutral connotative meaning.

However, when a customer is asked to fill out a form, the request often conveys images of a time-consuming process consisting of bureaucratic red tape, tedious questions, delays, and an invasion of privacy. In this context, the word *form* has a negative connotative meaning. To reduce the negative connotations, a service provider could take the following approach when requesting that a customer complete a form: "May I guide you through the completion of this form, which will give us your authorization to make the change?" Offering assistance makes the completion process seem less intimidating, while requesting the customer's authorization gives him a greater sense of control.

Ways to Improve Verbal Communication

By choosing words carefully, a service provider can significantly improve the communication process. The right choice of words, whether spoken or written, facilitates communication by (1) setting a positive tone and (2) achieving clarity.

SETTING A POSITIVE TONE

One way to set a positive tone is to use language that avoids placing blame.

Because one of the main goals of providing customer service is to encourage customers to continue doing business with your company, you must use words that set a positive tone. One way to set a positive tone is to use language that avoids placing blame. For instance, assume that a customer, Josephine Fry, calls her credit card company to question a late charge on her monthly statement. "I mailed last month's payment on the 4th," she says. "And the due date was the 6th. I don't understand why I'm being assessed a late charge." Consider the following two responses to this statement:

> − "That's why our billing statement tells customers to mail their payments at least five business days prior to the due date."
>
> + "I'm sorry to hear that your payment didn't arrive on time, Ms. Fry."

Both responses are true and accurate. The first leaves the customer feeling like she did something wrong. The second, while acknowledging that something has gone wrong, avoids confrontation by not assigning blame. A better time for the service provider to gently remind the customer to mail her payments earlier would be after the issue has been resolved.

Another way service providers can use words to set a positive tone is by phrasing statements in a positive manner. For example, rather than say, "I *can't help* you until you send me the request form," you could say, "I'd be *happy to help* you as soon as I receive the form that gives your consent to this change." Both statements have the same meaning, but the first stresses what *can't* be done for the customer, while the second stresses what *can* be done. To create an even more positive impression, you could add, "And if you'd like, I can help you complete the form now." Figure 6-4 provides additional examples that illustrate how negative or positive phrasing can affect customer perception.

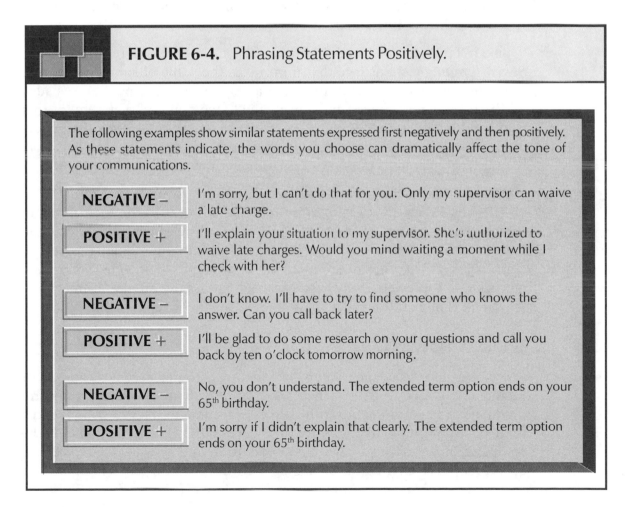

FIGURE 6-4. Phrasing Statements Positively.

The following examples show similar statements expressed first negatively and then positively. As these statements indicate, the words you choose can dramatically affect the tone of your communications.

NEGATIVE –	I'm sorry, but I can't do that for you. Only my supervisor can waive a late charge.
POSITIVE +	I'll explain your situation to my supervisor. She's authorized to waive late charges. Would you mind waiting a moment while I check with her?
NEGATIVE –	I don't know. I'll have to try to find someone who knows the answer. Can you call back later?
POSITIVE +	I'll be glad to do some research on your questions and call you back by ten o'clock tomorrow morning.
NEGATIVE –	No, you don't understand. The extended term option ends on your 65th birthday.
POSITIVE +	I'm sorry if I didn't explain that clearly. The extended term option ends on your 65th birthday.

Earlier, we introduced the concept of noise. Certain words and phrases qualify as noise because they act as barriers to communication. For instance, red-flag words can quickly undermine any attempts to set a positive tone in customer communications. **Red-flag words** are words that carry strong emotional overtones and are likely to trigger negative feelings in listeners. Red-flag words or phrases include strong political or religious statements, profanity, derogatory terms, sexist language, and racial slurs. A red-flag word interferes with the communication process because the receiver reacts emotionally to the word and stops paying attention to the rest of the message.

Under no circumstances is it appropriate for a service provider to use profanity (curse words, cussing, or swearing) or derogatory terms (words or phrases that belittle or show disrespect). On the other hand, if you find yourself in a situation that deteriorates to the point where a customer uses profanity or derogatory terms, you should act to stop the abusive behavior. In Chapter 9, we will discuss some techniques you can use for dealing with this type of situation.

Sexist language and racial slurs are specific types of red-flag words. **Sexist language** is language that minimizes the value of someone because of his or her gender, usually implying a negative stereotype. Phrases such as "little lady" or "baby" can be insulting to women, and a statement that begins with "Real men don't..." can be offensive to men. **Racial slurs** are derogatory words or statements pertaining to a person's race or, more broadly, to a person's ethnic or religious heritage.

Try to be aware of the effect your words can have on others.

Although service providers are not likely to use red-flag words in an openly hostile way, they sometimes use these words without realizing it. For this reason, you should try to be aware of the effect your words can have on others. You should also be wary of discussing religious, political, controversial, or other potentially offensive topics with customers and coworkers. Topics such as these can lead to disagreements or emotional reactions that could damage customer or business relationships.

ACHIEVING CLARITY

Most customers say they want "excellent customer service," and most financial services firms say they want to deliver it. However, if a company and its customers interpret excellent customer service differently, then customers are likely to feel frustrated. If, on the other hand, the company uses surveys to ask customers to define and describe excellent customer service, then the company will have a much better chance of

Service providers should make their communications specific and concrete, and they should try to clarify meaning and expectations whenever necessary.

understanding and meeting customer expectations. Similarly, service providers should make their communications specific and concrete, and they should try to clarify meaning and expectations whenever necessary.

People often use words or phrases that do not have clear meanings, as we saw in our earlier example of the service provider who promised to "take care of it right away." Such inexact language frequently occurs when relative words are used. A **relative word**, such as *soon*, *later*, *long*, *short*, and *frequently*, is a word that implies some type of measurement, but can vary widely in meaning according to the interpretations of the sender and receiver.

For instance, what exactly does *soon* mean? *Soon* could be in five minutes or in five days, depending on the subject and the perspectives of the people involved. For a customer calling to report a lost debit card, soon is five minutes, but certainly not five days or even five hours. For a customer calling to request a change of address form in anticipation of a possible move, five days may be soon enough. Be aware of the words you choose. Use *exact language* and avoid relative words—saying, for example, "in 15 minutes" or "before noon Friday," rather than "soon."

If a customer uses relative words, you can try to clarify the message by using feedback. Ask questions to probe for specific information. Use paraphrasing, which we will discuss in more detail in Chapter 8, to help ensure that the message you received is the message the sender intended to send. By asking questions and paraphrasing, you will have a much better chance of understanding the customer.

Another way to achieve clarity is to use familiar, everyday words whenever possible. When using technical words, make sure the customer understands the meaning of those words. To avoid confusing customers, some service providers compile a vocabulary list of the many different terms they use in the course of doing business, and they write simple, easy-to-understand definitions for use in conversations with customers.

A major barrier to clear communication is jargon. **Jargon** is a specialized language of technical terms and acronyms that only a specific group of people is familiar with and understands. Jargon is used in most companies, including financial services firms. In the proper circumstances, jargon can be an excellent way to communicate. It is verbal shorthand that allows more efficient communication among people familiar with the terminology. Unfortunately, some service providers become so accustomed to using jargon that they forget that customers don't always understand it. Use of jargon offends some customers. They might feel they are being excluded from the "in-group" or they might feel embarrassed for not knowing the meaning of these terms. Figure 6-5 lists a few of the many examples of jargon used in the financial services industry.

Nonverbal Communication

In some jobs—where interaction with external customers is primarily through remote communication such as telephone, mail, fax, and e-mail—the use of nonverbal communication may seem unimportant. However, nonverbal cues such as tone of voice can greatly influence the effectiveness of remote communication. Furthermore, many jobs require interaction with internal and/or external customers, which are frequently face-to-face and involve additional types of nonverbal communication, such as facial expressions, body posture, and the distance maintained between sender and receiver.

According to some studies, as much as 80 percent of a message's meaning can come from nonverbal sources. Often, as the saying goes, "it's not what you say, but how you say it." People usually put more faith in nonverbal signals than in the actual words of a message. For example, suppose you have just spent 15 minutes explaining a variety of investment

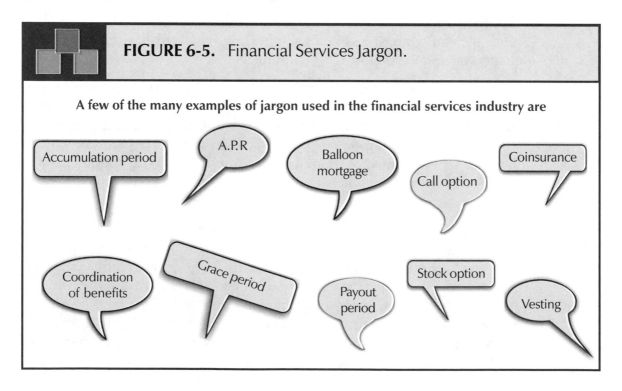

FIGURE 6-5. Financial Services Jargon.

A few of the many examples of jargon used in the financial services industry are

Accumulation period

A.P.R

Balloon mortgage

Call option

Coinsurance

Coordination of benefits

Grace period

Payout period

Stock option

Vesting

options to a new mutual fund customer who then says in a sarcastic tone of voice, "Now I understand perfectly." Interpreting the meaning conveyed by the customer's tone of voice, you might determine that despite his words, the customer really doesn't understand.

Often, nonverbal communication accurately conveys a person's true emotional state. People might say they feel fine, while appearing to be unhappy or disturbed. In such situations, you can rely on nonverbal communication to learn how a person feels.

The friendliness, irritability, or lack of interest expressed in your tone of voice will influence a customer's perception of you and the company you represent.

Similarly, customers often make judgments based on nonverbal signals from service providers. For instance, the friendliness, irritability, or lack of interest expressed in your tone of voice will influence a customer's perception of you and the company you represent.

In addition, nonverbal communication regulates the flow of conversation. Often, a speaker will use facial expressions, gestures, eye contact, and vocal tones to let the listener know when to talk or when the speaker wants to continue. One reason telephone communication can pose more of a challenge than face-to-face communication is that it depends solely on vocal signals, such as a rising or falling tone of voice, to regulate conversation flow.

By interpreting the nonverbal signals customers send, you can improve your understanding of what customers really want. Also, by being aware of the nonverbal signals that you send, you can improve your ability to effectively communicate your message to customers.

Problems Associated with Nonverbal Communication

Nonverbal communication is seldom effective in communicating factual information, which is best conveyed verbally. Because nonverbal communication is an inexact method of communicating, it is often difficult to interpret. No official dictionary of nonverbal communication exists to provide "definitions" for service providers. Consider our earlier example involving the explanation of investment options to a new mutual fund customer who said, "Now I understand perfectly." We assumed from the customer's sarcastic tone of voice that he did not understand the information. But maybe he *did* understand, and he was using sarcasm to indicate that he didn't like what he heard or didn't appreciate what he perceived as a condescending explanation.

Often, you can identify the exact meaning of nonverbal signals by providing feedback. Like relative words, nonverbal signals can be clarified through questions and paraphrasing. For example, in the case of the mutual fund customer, you could say, "Is there a specific topic or investment option you would like to discuss?" The customer's response to this question is likely to give you additional information about the intended message.

Verbal and nonverbal communications often take place at the same time, sometimes, as in the preceding example, contradicting each other and other times complementing one another. When nonverbal signals complement the verbal message, they reinforce that message. If you answer the telephone by saying, "How may I help you?" in a pleasant tone of voice, the nonverbal signal reinforces the verbal message. However, if you answer the telephone by saying, "How may I help you?" in a lazy monotone voice, the nonverbal signal contradicts the verbal message. Customers might think that you would rather be doing anything other than helping them. Figure 6-6 shows the elements of verbal communication discussed earlier in this chapter and the elements of nonverbal communication we will describe in the following pages.

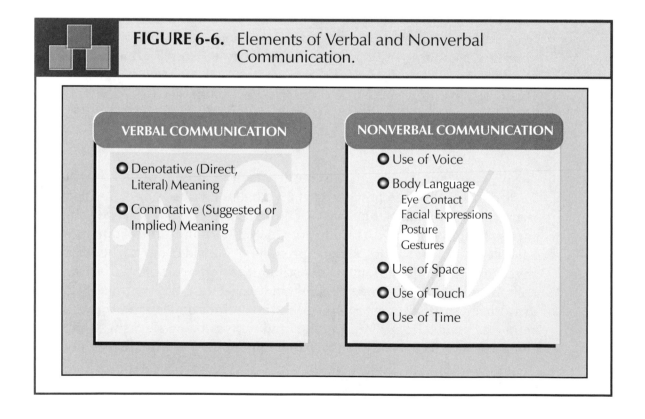

FIGURE 6-6. Elements of Verbal and Nonverbal Communication.

VERBAL COMMUNICATION

- Denotative (Direct, Literal) Meaning
- Connotative (Suggested or Implied) Meaning

NONVERBAL COMMUNICATION

- Use of Voice
- Body Language
  Eye Contact
  Facial Expressions
  Posture
  Gestures
- Use of Space
- Use of Touch
- Use of Time

Use of Voice

When people speak, their voices carry a great deal of information that isn't included in the words. *Paralanguage* is a term used to describe the information obtained from vocal quality, volume, rate of speech, pitch, enunciation, and pauses. Each of these elements conveys information about the person speaking and the meaning of the message. Paralanguage is especially important in telephone communication, where other forms of nonverbal communication are absent.

You can listen to a customer's rate of speech and pitch (how high or low the voice goes) to obtain information about that customer's state of mind. In general, when people become nervous, upset, or excited they speak more rapidly and their pitch rises. Also, you should be aware of how you use your own voice. A high-pitched voice is often associated with youth, enthusiasm, and a lack of control, while a low-pitched voice is considered authoritative.

A high-pitched voice is often associated with youth, enthusiasm, and a lack of control, while a low-pitched voice is considered authoritative.

Suppose you are a CSR at a bank and you receive a telephone call from a customer, John Fancher, about a recent automated telephone banking transaction. In an agitated tone of voice, Mr. Fancher explains that he requested a transfer of $500 from his savings account to his checking account, but instead the funds were moved from checking to savings. Speaking slowly and with a slightly lowered pitch, you say, "I'm sorry there was a problem with this transfer, Mr. Fancher, and I'll do everything I can to resolve it for you. Can you please tell me one of your account numbers?" By adjusting your rate of speech and tone of voice to fit the circumstances, you convey a message of control and professionalism.

Under normal circumstances, you should try to adjust your rate of speech to match your customer's rate of speech. Otherwise, the customer might misinterpret your message or your handling of the conversation. For example, if the customer talks slowly and you talk too quickly, he might become confused or miss important information. He might think you are rushing him or that you just don't have the time or the inclination to provide attentive service. Conversely, if the customer speaks rapidly and you speak too slowly or you pause too often, the customer might become bored or impatient and miss important information. He might think his time is being wasted or that you are incompetent. One way to keep your listeners interested is by varying your pitch and rate of speech.

Speakers can pay attention to verbal and nonverbal cues from listeners to determine an appropriate rate of speech. For instance, if a customer is sighing, tapping his fingers, or fidgeting impatiently as you speak, this might indicate that you are speaking too slowly. Although normal speech rates vary considerably from one region or culture to another, a rate of speech between 135 and 175 words per minute is generally considered most effective. To get an idea of your normal speech rate, try Exercise 6-1.

Another important part of communication is ***enunciation***, which refers to the articulation of sounds and the pronunciation of words. Poor enunciation makes speech difficult to understand and it creates a bad impression of the speaker. To be easily understood and create a good impression, you should be aware of your enunciation, as Exercise 6-2 demonstrates.

Exercise 6-1.   What Is Your Normal Speech Rate?

First, familiarize yourself with a standard presentation from your job, or use the one shown below.

> Good morning, Mr. Jones. This is [your name] from ABC Financial. I am calling to inform you that your term life insurance policy has lapsed due to non-payment of premium, and I would like to offer you the opportunity to reinstate your policy. If you would like, I can fax or mail you a form, which needs to be signed, dated, and returned to our office with your premium payment in the amount of $100. This will pay your policy to the next quarterly billing date. Also, with this extended reinstatement offer, you have the opportunity to increase your coverage. If you would like, I can fax or mail you the reinstatement form and the application for an increase in coverage. Would you be interested in either of these options?

After familiarizing yourself with the material, record yourself reading it aloud as if you were talking to a customer. Also, use a clock or watch to time your presentation.

Next, use this formula to find out your rate of speech:

$$\text{RATE OF SPEECH} = \frac{60 \text{ seconds}}{\text{\# of seconds to read message}} \times \text{\# of words in message}$$

For example, there are 130 words in the message shown above. If you complete your reading in 50 seconds, then your rate of speech is 156 words per minute (60 seconds ÷ 50 seconds = 1.2 × 130 words = 156 words per minute). Because the normal speech rate ranges from 135 to 175 words per minute, you are probably speaking at an appropriate rate.

Next, play back the recording and listen to yourself as if you were a customer. Do you sound too hurried? Do you sound too leisurely? Would you be able to improve your ability to hold the listener's attention by varying your rate of speech or pitch?

Exercise 6-2.   Improving Enunciation.

Can you identify your own style of enunciation? If your voice is very nasal or harsh, practice the way you articulate the letters *a, e, i, o,* and *u.* Vowel sounds help determine your voice quality. If people frequently say they can't hear you, you may be mumbling. Instead of raising your voice, take more care in articulating consonants. In particular, many English speakers skip over the consonants *t, g, l,* and *d.* Also, many English speakers drop consonants at the end of words. For example, they might say "goin" instead of "going." Often, regional dialects affect the way people enunciate. By noticing and consciously practicing the way you enunciate, you can communicate more effectively.

Body Language

Body language, also known as *kinesics,* refers to the way people use their bodies to communicate. The major forms of body language are eye contact, facial expressions, posture, and gestures. People use each form separately or in combination to communicate thoughts and emotions.

EYE CONTACT

During face-to-face discussions, people use eye contact to make sure they are communicating effectively. A speaker tends to look into a listener's eyes to make sure the person is listening, understanding, and interested in what is being said. In turn, the listener tends to make frequent eye contact with the speaker to convey interest and understanding. Studies have shown that, on average, speakers look at listeners about 40 percent of the time and listeners look at speakers about 70 percent of the time.

However, the acceptable amount and duration of eye contact differs among individuals and cultures. In North American culture, for example, people's eyes generally meet for no more than a few seconds at a time. North Americans usually trust and like people who can maintain eye contact for a few seconds, but they tend to distrust people who avoid eye contact or who meet their eyes for one second or less. North Americans also are uncomfortable with people who stare (generally defined as maintaining eye contact for 10 seconds or more), especially in close proximity. In some cultures, direct eye contact, regardless of duration, is seen as issuing a challenge. In Asian cultures, looking someone directly in the eye is considered rude.

The use of eye contact also depends on additional types of communication. For example, if you are speaking in a meeting and a person makes eye contact with you and smiles, the message is completely different than if shc makes eye contact and folds her arms. Most people use eye contact to get someone's attention, much like students raise their hands in class. For example, instead of interrupting the speaker in a meeting, a person tries to catch the speaker's eye to indicate that she has something to say.

FACIAL EXPRESSIONS

The facial expressions that people use to show emotion are sometimes called **affect displays**. For example, if you stub your toe, you will probably make some sort of facial expression, an affect display, that shows you are in pain. As Figure 6-7 illustrates, people's faces tend to express six basic emotions: happiness, sadness, fear, anger, disgust, and surprise. These six facial expressions are generally recognized throughout the world.

FIGURE 6-7. Facial Expressions and Six Basic Emotions.

HAPPINESS SADNESS FEAR

ANGER DISGUST SURPRISE

Nam

Location:

Other:

Telephone: 610-992-1380

Sun Code: 7120

Course: ACS 100-Foundations of Customer

I am:

Taking an exam at a site other than Wellesley or a paper exam (
form to order Study Materials only. (LOMA/ICA paper exams are n

Comments:

However, interpreting emotions through facial expressions is not as simple or direct as it might seem. The human face produces many distinct expressions that typically remain on the face for only a brief moment, and are easily overlooked. Also, most people can mask their expressions at least to some extent and sometimes very effectively.

Only the most basic human emotions are expressed universally through facial expressions. More complex emotions, such as regret, embarrassment, sincerity, and respect are expressed in ways that vary from person to person and from culture to culture. Like other types of nonverbal communication, facial expressions between people who know each other well can sometimes be revealing. However, in a business setting, facial expressions are usually interpreted best in conjunction with other forms of communication.

In a business setting, facial expressions are usually interpreted best in conjunction with other forms of communication.

POSTURE

Posture tells a lot about people and their outlook. Sometimes this form of nonverbal communication is intentional; sometimes it is not. People tend to lean forward when someone has their full attention. They turn their backs to someone who doesn't interest them. People slump back when they are bored or they disagree. They withdraw when they feel nervous or uncomfortable. Often, people who stand with their shoulders back and their heads raised feel self-confident, while people who stand with their shoulders slumped and their heads lowered may feel insecure.

Posture and facial expressions play an important role in face-to-face communication. However, even in telephone calls, your body language affects your tone of voice, which in turn affects your message. Therefore, when using the telephone you should use posture and facial expressions to enhance your words and the attitude you want to convey. If you want to sound friendly, then take a deep breath, sit in a straight but relaxed position, and remember to smile. Some service providers place a mirror near the telephone to make sure they are smiling during telephone conversations. If you want to sound authoritative, you should sit or stand as straight as possible and plant your feet firmly on the floor. Keep your mouth relaxed but neutral and keep your eyes intense and focused.[3]

GESTURES

Gestures are another form of body language. For example, *stop, go, yes, no,* and *hello* are expressed through common gestures that most North Americans recognize. Gestures such as these, which take the place of words, are called **emblems**. Although used all over the world, emblems have different meanings in different places. For example, shaking your head from side to side means "no" in some parts of the world, but in others, it means "yes" or has no meaning. Besides emblems, most people use a variety of other gestures to communicate, including illustrators, regulators, and adaptors, as described in Figure 6-8.

Use of Space

The study of the way people use space while communicating is called **proxemics**. In face-to-face communication, people have different comfort zones, which vary depending on the individuals involved, the situation, and cultural norms. Service providers must be aware of these comfort zones to avoid misunderstandings. For example, the acceptable speaking distance for business conversations tends to be closer in South American

FIGURE 6-8. Types of Gestures.

Illustrators

Illustrators are gestures that complement words to enhance or clarify verbal messages. Pointing at an object, drawing pictures in the air while talking, and using the hands to indicate size or shape are common illustrators.

Regulators

Regulators are the gestures people use to control the flow of conversation. For example, people commonly use an extended index finger to indicate that they aren't finished speaking.

Adaptors

Adaptors are generally unconscious movements that release some form of tension or emotion. Finger tapping, crossing and uncrossing legs, and other restless motions are adaptors that people use when tense or bored. By watching for a customer's adaptors, you can better assess the person's mood or emotional state. You can also find clues in adaptors to determine when to call a break in a discussion or when to change the subject.

than North American cultures. In North America, the distances that people generally maintain between themselves can be broken into four zones, as described in Figure 6-9.

Use of Touch

Often, touch (or tactile communication) is used to communicate in a social or personal setting. In business, where touch is used sparingly, a firm handshake when greeting or leaving someone is usually acceptable. However, even a handshake may present a problem. In some cultures, shaking hands is not common. A service provider should not force a customer to shake hands if the person seems uncomfortable doing so.

Occasionally, a pat on the back or a light touch at the shoulder or elbow may be appropriate. However, such forms of touching communicate a certain amount of familiarity, which might be misinterpreted. For example,

FIGURE 6-9. Proxemics in North American Culture.

In North America, the distances that people generally maintain between themselves can be classified as intimate distance, personal distance, social distance, and public distance.

Intimate distance ranges from touching to about 18 inches. North Americans typically use intimate distance when communicating with someone with whom they have a close relationship, such as a spouse, child, or parent. Sometimes this distance is unavoidable—in a crowded elevator, for instance—but such forced intimacy generally produces discomfort.

Personal distance ranges from 18 inches to 4 feet. North Americans typically use personal distance when talking with friends and business acquaintances.

Social distance ranges from about 4 to 7 feet. North Americans typically maintain social distance when conducting impersonal business. Social distance and personal distance are usually the most appropriate distances for providing face-to-face customer service.

Public distance is generally about 12 feet or more. In North American culture, speakers use public distance in a formal setting when addressing an audience.

patting a coworker on the shoulder might be interpreted as a sign of friendship. But to another coworker, the same touch might be interpreted as sexual harassment. Also, some customers might consider a hand on the shoulder as an attempt to intimidate or persuade. Be aware of the possibility of unintended messages that touch might send.

Use of Time

Chronemics are the nonverbal messages conveyed by the way people use time. As with the use of space and touch, the use of time varies by individual, situation, and cultural norms. The importance placed on time and maintaining schedules is not universal. To keep someone waiting for 20 minutes would be considered rude in most business situations in North America, where businesses tend to follow rigid schedules. In many other cultures, an appointed time is merely a guideline, and a 20-minute wait is considered reasonable. In these cultures, delays are expected and they do not offend people.

However, even allowing for cultural differences, few people like to be kept waiting, and some people view tardiness as a sign of carelessness, arrogance, or disrespect. To maintain a good impression, you should give customers and business associates realistic time expectations and then follow through on your promises. On the other hand, you may need to make allowances for and show understanding to customers and business associates who keep you waiting.

Cross-Cultural Communication

As you have seen, cultural differences can present challenges in the communication process. You can minimize problems by observing some general communication guidelines and by learning about other cultures.

If a customer or business associate is not fluent in your language, speak slowly, pay close attention to enunciation, and use simple words and sentence structure.

For example, if a customer or business associate is not fluent in your language, speak slowly, pay close attention to enunciation, and use simple words and sentence structure. Avoid using *idioms*, which are phrases with a meaning that cannot be determined from the words in the phrase (such as "on a roll" or "ballpark figure" in American English). Don't speak louder in an effort to make yourself understood—an increase in volume does not make your words easier to understand. Give the customer time to comprehend what you are saying, but avoid checking comprehension by asking, "Do you understand?" because people will often answer "yes," even if they don't understand.

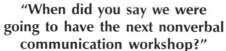

If you can see your listener, look for nonverbal signals and adaptors—such as nervousness, repetitive nodding, smiling, or an absence of questions—that might indicate a lack of comprehension. When a customer appears to misunderstand what you are saying, try saying it another way. If possible, use written communication, because many people are better able to comprehend another language when it is written rather than spoken.

When you are listening to someone from another culture or country, give the speaker enough time to express himself. Don't interrupt or finish sentences. Ask the person to repeat or spell words you have difficulty understanding.[4]

You can improve cross-cultural communication by paying careful attention to how the other person is communicating nonverbally. Be attuned to the customer's pace, tone, and style. If the customer wants to spend extra time getting acquainted, try to allow the time. If the customer's style seems excessively formal, be aware that in many cultures formality denotes respect.

Avoid saying no, because in many cultures no is considered very harsh. While you may not be able to accommodate every customer's request, you can present a negative response in a respectful, positive way. As we saw earlier, this suggestion proves valuable, regardless of cultural norms.

Read and learn about other cultures. If you support a significant number of customers from a cultural background that differs from yours, you can provide better customer service by learning more about that culture.[5]

INSIGHT 6-1. Cultural Differences in Communication.

Although each person is unique, people within the same cultural group or country usually follow certain customs when they communicate, and these customs vary from one culture or country to another.

Greetings Throughout the world, a variety of gestures are used for greetings, such as a handshake, an embrace, a bow, cheek-kissing, and palms pressed together. For example, in Brazil, greetings are expressive and may involve hand-shaking, embracing, and kissing the air next to the cheeks. In China, traditional greetings include a bow to show respect, and more recently, a handshake in formal situations. In India, the traditional greeting is a slight bow with palms together, although the handshake is common in interactions with Westerners.

Handshake The handshake varies in many ways, including duration and firmness of grip. For example, in France, a handshake is a light grip with a single shake. In Canada, the United Kingdom, and the United States, a firm handshake for a couple of seconds is common, but in some Asian and Middle Eastern countries, a firm handshake may suggest unnecessary aggressiveness. In Japan, a handshake is sometimes accompanied by a bow, avoiding eye contact.

Use of Names and Titles In most Western countries, the first and last names are used for initial greetings. In China, titles are usually used when introducing guests, and names begin with the family name, typically followed by one or two given names. Traditionally, the Japanese use only their last name when introducing themselves, and people are called by their last name followed by "san." In Japan, people pay strict attention to titles and job status. In Nigeria, the terms "Sir" and "Madam" are often used when speaking to business associates, officials, or elders; also, titles are important. In Germany and the United Kingdom, proper titles in greetings are important, but in Australia, academic and job-related titles do not command as much respect as they do in many other countries.

Conversation Style, "Yes and No," and Use of Language Australians value directness and brevity in speaking; they prefer straightforward and concise communication. The British do not hesitate to say "no" and can be very direct in their responses. In Japan and South Korea, the word "yes" may indicate understanding rather than agreement and "no" is seldom used, but may be demonstrated by verbal and nonverbal cues. In many cultures, criticizing others (people or competitors) is considered rude.

Smiling and Laughing Not all cultures use a smile as a symbol of welcome and warmth. In some cultures, smiling, especially when first meeting, can arouse suspicion; loud laughing is sometimes considered rude. In South Korea, laughter may indicate amusement, but it may also be used to cover hurt, shock, or embarrassment.

Hand Gestures Hand gestures have different meanings in different cultures. For example, forming a circle with the thumb and index finger while extending the other three fingers upward means "OK" in the United States, "money" in Japan, and "zero" or "worthless" in France, while it is an obscene gesture in Brazil. Different cultures use different gestures to indicate "no." For example,

INSIGHT 6-1. Cultural Differences in Communication (*continued*).

no is signified by waving the index finger with the palm outward in Mexico and brushing the hand quickly back and forth in front of the face in Japan.

Pointing Pointing with the index finger is considered impolite or rude in Middle Eastern countries and in Japan. In India and Australia, pointing with an open hand is preferred to pointing with the index finger. In the United Kingdom, gesturing with the head is preferred to pointing with the index finger.

Crossing Legs Crossing legs by resting the ankle on the knee is considered impolite in the United Kingdom and Germany. Showing the sole of the shoe is considered rude in Russia, Germany, and some African, Middle Eastern, and Asian countries.

Source: Rahe Hospitality Services, *World Bridge: Bridging the Communication Gap Among Cultures* (© 1997 Rahe Hospitality Services) and "Culture Maps," http://www.css.edu/users/dswenson/web/CULTURE/CULTMAPS.HTM (23 May 2002).

Finally, when interacting with a person from another culture or country, be conscious of your responsibility as a service provider to help bridge cultural differences. Don't think "foreign," think "global" or "international." And remember, each person is unique. Just as everyone within your culture is not identical, people from other cultures are not all alike and do not all behave and communicate the same way.[6]

Although it would be impossible to present every meaning of every type of verbal and nonverbal communication used throughout the world, Insight 6-1 provides some examples that illustrate the variety of cultural differences in the communication process.

In this chapter, we have explored the basic components of the communication process and how they affect customer service. In Chapter 7, we will continue this discussion by examining specific types of communication.

To practice and review the skills and information you learned in this chapter, see the interactive CD, *Practicing Your Customer Service Skills*, included with this book.

Key Terms and Concepts

communication	culture
message	verbal communication
sender	nonverbal communication
receiver	denotative meaning
channel	connotative meaning
noise	red-flag words
feedback	sexist language

Key Terms and Concepts (*continued*).

racial slurs
relative word
jargon
paralanguage
enunciation
body language
affect displays
emblems
proxemics

illustrators
regulators
adaptors
intimate distance
personal distance
social distance
public distance
chronemics
idioms

Endnotes

1. JoAnna F. Brandi, *Building Company Loyalty: The 21 Essential Elements...IN ACTION* (Dallas: Walk the Talk Company, 2001), 14.

2. *Merriam-Webster's Collegiate® Dictionary*, 10th ed. (Springfield, MA: Merriam-Webster, 1997), 458.

3. Susan Berkley, "How to Play Your Voice Like a Finely Tuned Instrument (and Skyrocket Your Sales!)," Berkley Productions, Inc., http://www.greatvoice.com/report2.html (28 May 2002).

4. Rahe Hospitality Services, *World Bridge: Bridging the Communication Gap Among Cultures* (© 1997 Rahe Hospitality Services), 10–11.

5. Leslie Aguilar and Linda Stokes, *Multicultural Customer Service* (Chicago: Irwin Professional Publishing, 1996), 83–84.

6. Rahe Hospitality Services, 4, 26.

CHAPTER 7

Types of Communication

After studying this chapter, you should be able to

- Discuss how preparation, professional appearance, and proper business etiquette can improve face-to-face communication

- Apply various techniques to handle telephone calls effectively

- Perform telephone activities—including answering calls for others, placing callers on hold, taking messages, transferring calls, and using voicemail—in a professional manner

- Apply techniques to write effective business letters and memos

- Discuss various forms of electronic communication, including e-mail and Internet-based communication

In this chapter, we will build on our previous discussion of verbal and nonverbal communication to examine four types of communication commonly used to provide customer service in the financial services industry. We will describe face-to-face communication, telephone communication, written communication, and electronic communication, and we will present various techniques you can use to improve each type of communication.

Face-to-Face Communication

Despite advances in communication technology, face-to-face communication remains an important part of customer service in the financial services industry.[1] Most intermediaries and many service providers rely heavily on face-to-face communication to perform their jobs. Furthermore, most employees meet with internal customers and coworkers on a daily basis. Virtually all jobs in a financial services company depend at least in part on face-to-face communication. In this section, we discuss how preparation, a professional appearance, and proper business etiquette improve face-to-face communication.

Preparation

Effective face-to-face communication requires preparation and organization. Before hosting a meeting with a customer, for example, try to reserve a private location (such as a conference room or an office) and review the customer's file and any other pertinent material. Make sure necessary documents and supplies (such as pens, paper, calculator, and computer) are on hand for the meeting. In some cases, you might call the customer a day or two before a scheduled meeting to confirm the appointment and to find out if the customer has any special needs or requests that you might address. By making this extra effort, you are showing that you are a customer service professional who genuinely cares about meeting your customer's needs.

Also, keep your work area neat and clean. A disorderly workspace creates an impression of carelessness and disorganization, and it may give

FIGURE 7-1. Appearance and Customer Perceptions.

Imagine you are a customer meeting face-to-face with a financial services employee. What would you think in each of the following situations?

The service provider wears an old suit that is wrinkled and has food stains on the lapel.

The service provider's perfume is so powerful that you can't concentrate on the conversation.

The service provider wears a dark business suit (freshly dry-cleaned and pressed) and a simple gold watch.

In each situation, would you consider this person to be a financial services professional? Would you feel confident that your financial concerns would be handled in a competent and professional manner?

The first rule of business etiquette is to treat all customers, coworkers, and business associates with courtesy and respect, realizing that what is considered appropriate in one situation may be inappropriate in another. For example, if you have lunch with a *coworker*, you might speak informally on a first-name basis, but if you have lunch with a *customer*, the conversation might be more formal, and as a sign of respect you might refer to the customer as "Mr." or "Ms."

To determine proper business etiquette in different situations, you need to be aware of industry standards for professional conduct and be familiar with the expectations of the people you meet. Also, as we saw in Chapter 6, you should consider the cultural, religious, ethnic, or national backgrounds of your customers, business associates, and coworkers.

Telephone Communication

In most customer service jobs, the telephone plays an important role, and in many jobs it is the primary means of communication with customers. When used effectively, the telephone enhances customer service, but when used ineffectively, it hampers communication, wastes time, and frustrates customers. Effective use of the telephone requires preparation, focus, and the ability to make a good impression. It also requires skill in several telephone-specific functions. For service providers who handle a high volume of calls, using the telephone requires the ability to deliver quality customer service as quickly as possible.

Preparation

Preparation and organization are as important in telephone communication as they are in face-to-face meetings. When providing customer service over the telephone, you should clear your desk of clutter and keep necessary forms, notepads, pens, reference material, and other resources within reach.

Many companies provide resources called scripts or talking points that CSRs can use when handling certain types of customer inquiries or requests. A *script* is a written dialogue or set of systematic instructions that employees usually follow word-for-word. *Talking points* are a list of important items that employees refer to using their own words. Scripts and talking points are often provided to support new products and services and in situations that do not occur often enough to remain fresh in the minds of CSRs. They also are used to help answer sensitive questions on company polices or procedures that may concern customers. In general, scripts work best for subjects that require complete and accurate information, such as legal explanations.

> Preparation and organization are as important in telephone communication as they are in face-to-face meetings.

It doesn't matter whether you're on the phone with your customer 30 seconds or 30 minutes. You own that portion of the customer relationship.

— Now Hear This, Inc.[2]

Staying Focused

In face-to-face communication, you can rely on eye contact to help stay focused on what a customer is saying. However, on the telephone, you do not have this luxury. If you are distracted by communication noise, you may have trouble giving customers the attention they deserve. You can minimize distractions in your work environment by placing a "Do Not Disturb" sign outside your work area, or by turning your chair away from the aisle before answering a telephone call. On the other hand, you can minimize distractions for your coworkers by not speaking too loudly and by not holding conversations near their workstations.

Sometimes communication noise comes from within. For example, suppose during a telephone call you start thinking of errands you have to run after work. Or perhaps you have a headache. To avoid distractions such as these, you can make a list—before you start answering calls—of the things you have to do after work, and you can keep pain reliever at your desk in case you get a headache. By taking care of these personal needs, you can better focus on your customers' needs.

Making a Positive Impression

Most people know how to use a telephone, but not everyone knows how to do so in ways that enhance customer service. Because your customers cannot see your facial expressions and posture, verbal communication and use of voice are especially important in telephone communication. Exercise 7-1 describes two techniques you can use to improve your ability to make a positive impression over the telephone.

Exercise 7-1.   Using the Telephone to Make a Positive Impression.

The next time you find yourself in the role of a customer, using the telephone to conduct personal business, study the interaction. No doubt, you will form an impression of the person who handles your call. Try to determine what contributes to this impression by keeping the following questions in mind:

- What is your impression of the person's greeting, choice of words, tone of voice, enunciation, and rate of speech?

- What do you think the person is doing while talking to you?

- What do you learn about the person during the conversation?

Next, make a recording of yourself handling either an actual customer service telephone call or a "practice call" from a friend or coworker. Then listen to the recording and answer these questions:

- Does the tone of your telephone voice sound friendly?

- Does your rate of speech match your customer's?

> **Exercise 7-1.   Using the Telephone to Make a Positive Impression (*continued*).**
>
> - Do you use simple, straightforward language?
>
> - Do you think the customer formed a good impression of you? Why or why not?
>
> If you answer "no" to any of these questions, consider changing your telephone style. For instance, if you dislike the sound of your voice, try speaking at a lower pitch or at a slower, more relaxed pace. Another idea, as you saw in Chapter 6, is to align your facial expressions and posture with the impression you are trying to make. For example, smile to help convey a friendly and helpful attitude.
>
> **Source:** LOMA, *ASR On-the-Job Activities* (Atlanta: LOMA, © 1993).

Handling Inbound Telephone Calls

Now that we have covered the basics—being prepared, staying focused, and making a positive impression—let's take a step-by-step look at ways to improve your handling of inbound telephone calls. ***Inbound telephone calls*** are calls initiated by customers to request information, products, services, or transactions.

THE GREETING

Your telephone greeting creates an immediate impression in the mind of a customer.

Your telephone greeting creates an immediate impression in the mind of a customer. For example, if you answer in a monotone voice, the customer may feel you aren't interested in helping her. If you answer with a simple "hello," you may sound unprofessional or you may lead a customer to believe that she has mistakenly reached a residence, rather than a place of business. At a minimum, your telephone greeting should identify the name of your company or department. The standard greeting at many companies provides additional information, as the following sample illustrates:

> "Welcome to ABC Auto Insurance. Monique Bravant speaking. How may I help you?"

This greeting welcomes the customer, gives the name of the company and the service provider, and offers assistance. Some companies have a standard greeting that all service providers are expected to use. Other companies provide general guidelines for employees to follow, but do not dictate the exact wording. When choosing a greeting, select one that is appropriate and natural, and use it consistently.

If you answer the telephone many times a day, your greeting may sound uninspired at times. At some companies, service providers use **auto-greeting** technology to record their "best" greeting, which automatically plays each time a call arrives. If your company does not have auto-greeting, you might want to imagine you are making an auto-greeting recording each time you answer the telephone, reminding yourself that you are not just saying the words, but offering to help a customer.

IDENTIFYING THE CUSTOMER, GATHERING INFORMATION, AND PROVIDING SERVICE

Most customers begin a call by introducing themselves or stating the reason for the call:

> "Hi. My name is Les Randolph and I'd like to make a change to my auto insurance policy."

If the customer doesn't provide the basic information for handling the call—such as name and account number—you must ask for it. In addition, at most financial services companies, CSRs request information such as the customer's address, telephone number, social security number, or mother's maiden name to verify the customer's identity. We will discuss this verification process in more detail in Chapter 12.

Once you learn the customer's name, you typically refer to the customer by last name, preceded by Mr. or Ms., to show respect and to establish rapport with the customer. For example, you might say

> "I'd be happy to help you with this change, Mr. Randolph. May I please have your policy number?"

If the customer responds by saying, "You can call me Les, and my account number is 12345," then you can call the customer by his first name. If, on the other hand, the customer simply provides his policy number, then you should continue to refer to him by his last name.

After verifying the customer's identity and obtaining the necessary account information, the next step is to find the customer's file, if applicable. During the course of the conversation, listen carefully, taking notes if necessary, to fully understand the customer's request. Once you have gathered all the applicable information, work with the customer to address the reason for the call. Sometimes, you can provide the information or service during the course of the telephone call. Other times, you will need additional time or resources, or you will have to refer the customer's request to someone else.

SUMMARIZING THE COURSE OF ACTION

After the service has been provided, arranged, or promised, summarize the result for the customer. In doing so, you can take the opportunity to confirm that the customer is satisfied with the course of action. For example, if additional service will be required, you might say

> "As you requested, Mr. Randolph, I will cancel the emergency road service coverage under your policy at the end of this coverage period. The amount of your six-month premium will decrease by $7.60, and we will send you a revised policy declarations page. We also will send you a new premium statement, which you can use to mail your renewal payment, which is due on May 30th."

If you are unable to accommodate a customer's request, you should say so clearly and politely. Informing the customer exactly what *can* and *cannot* be done helps promote trust and avoid future misunderstandings.

ENDING THE CALL

The end of a telephone call gives you an opportunity to leave the customer with a favorable impression. If the call concludes the transaction, you can extend a sincere offer to provide future assistance. If additional service or a follow-up discussion will be needed, then you and the customer can agree on a time for completion or further communication.

Sometimes service providers give the caller their name, carefully spelled, along with their telephone number. This information helps reassure the customer that someone at the company is responsible for taking care of the request. For example, the service provider might say

"If you don't receive your revised declarations page and premium statement by May 15th, please call me. You can use the same customer service number you dialed for today's transaction. Again, my name is Monique Bravant—B-R-A-V-A-N-T—and my extension is 401. Have a pleasant day, Mr. Randolph, and thank you for doing business with ABC Auto Insurance."

In many high-volume call centers, CSRs typically do not give out their telephone extensions because the CSR will most likely be helping someone else when the customer places a follow-up call. In most instances, with the use of computer-based information sharing systems (which we will discuss in Chapter 13), any CSR, regardless of who took the original call, would be able to quickly review the case specifics and handle a subsequent call.

Making Outbound Telephone Calls

Outbound telephone calls are calls initiated by company representatives to customers. Before you place an outbound telephone call, you should have your notes, script, or talking points in front of you and any other resources organized and within reach. Also, each time you make a call, you should be prepared to leave a message. When the other party answers, your greeting should be friendly and to the point, stating who you are and what company you represent, as this example illustrates:

"Good morning, Mr. Martin. This is Dwayne Washington from Hedgerow Mortgage."

State the purpose of the call and—especially if it is likely to take more than a minute or two—ask if this is a good time to talk. At the beginning of the conversation, it is best to follow the customer's lead. Some customers will want to chat for a while about the weather or similar topics, while others will want to get right to the discussion. At the end of the conversation, summarize the important points and confirm any agreed upon actions. Then, thank the customer for his time.

If you are going to place several calls in a day, try making a list, starting with the most important or urgent call and listing the others in descending order of importance. If you are placing calls to other time zones, consider the time of day in each location.

Other Telephone Activities

In addition to handling inbound and outbound telephone calls, service providers perform other telephone activities, such as answering the telephone for coworkers, taking telephone messages, placing callers on hold, transferring calls, and using voicemail.

ANSWERING THE TELEPHONE FOR COWORKERS

When answering the telephone for a coworker, you should first identify whose telephone is being answered (if possible) and then identify yourself. This approach lets callers know that they have dialed the correct number. For example, an employee might answer a coworker's telephone by saying:

> "This is ABC Bank. Ginger Leinweber's office. Daisy Triantos speaking. How may I help you?"

If your coworker is unavailable, you should say so, and ask if you can be of assistance. You should not ask for the caller's name before saying that the coworker is unavailable, nor should you provide personal information about a coworker's absence. For example, if Ms. Triantos asks for the caller's name and then says that Ms. Leinweber is away from her desk, the caller might think that Ms. Triantos is screening Ms. Leinweber's calls—and that he (the caller) wasn't important enough to get through. Or, if Ms. Triantos tells the caller that Ms. Leinweber is out of the office having cosmetic surgery for varicose veins, the caller might consider this a breach of business etiquette or an invasion of Ms. Leinweber's privacy. An appropriate response would be

> "I'm sorry, but Ms. Leinweber is out of the office today. Is there something I can help you with?"

If your coworker will not be available for several days, then you should inform the caller of this and provide the name and telephone number of the person who has been assigned to handle your coworker's calls. Next, you can offer to take a message or transfer the call.

TAKING TELEPHONE MESSAGES

Generally, when you take a message for a coworker, you should provide the following information:

- An accurate spelling of the caller's name

- The caller's company, if appropriate

- The caller's title, if one is given

- The caller's telephone number

- The message given by the caller

- A good time for the coworker to return the call

- Any other pertinent information (for example, the caller's tone of voice might indicate that the caller is angry, frustrated, or agitated)

- The date and time of the call

- Your name, in case your coworker has any questions

At the end of the call, repeat the caller's name and telephone number to make sure this information is correct.

Although some of the information shown above will not apply in all situations, you should keep each of these items in mind. By taking the caller's message, for instance, you are giving your coworker an opportunity to gather pertinent information before returning the call. By identifying a time for a return call, you might save both parties the time and frustration of repeatedly calling and missing each other. You can request this type of information by asking questions such as:

"May I tell her the reason for your call?" "What would be a good time for Ms. Leinweber to return your call?"

PLACING CALLERS ON HOLD

Generally, when customers call a business, they expect to receive prompt attention. Placing callers on hold puts them in a position of helplessness.

According to one study, customers on hold 2 minutes perceive the wait as 3 minutes, customers on hold 3 minutes perceive the wait as 5 minutes, and customer on hold 5 minutes perceive the wait as 15 minutes.

Source: Wake Up Your Call Center[3]

Often, their only choices are to wait or to hang up without receiving the information or service they need. The longer customers wait, the greater their frustration. If circumstances require you to place a caller on hold, you might be able to reduce these feelings of helplessness and frustration by following some simple guidelines:

- Tell the customer why putting him on hold is necessary.

- Inform the caller of the expected hold time.

- Ask the caller whether he would prefer to wait or be called back.

- If at all possible, limit the hold time to 90 seconds or less.

- If a caller must be kept on hold longer than originally anticipated, check in and briefly explain the delay. Ask if he would like to continue waiting or if he would prefer to be called back.

- Upon returning, greet the caller by name, apologize for the delay, and thank him for waiting.

TRANSFERRING CALLS

Sometimes circumstances require transferring a call to another employee. Because poorly handled telephone transfers can be just as frustrating to customers as being put on hold, you should take steps to avoid problems by following these guidelines:

- Ask the caller for permission to transfer the call.

- Get the name and number of the caller, so you or someone else can call back if necessary—for example, if the caller is disconnected.

- Give the caller your name and telephone number.

- Give the caller the name and telephone number of the coworker to whom the call is being transferred.

- Tell your coworker the name and telephone number of the person who is calling and briefly explain the purpose of the call before completing the transfer.

Most companies discourage blind transfers and encourage conference transfers. A **blind transfer**, or *cold transfer*, is when one employee transfers a call to another employee without introducing the caller or explaining the nature of the call. A **conference transfer**, or *warm transfer*, is when the employee who transfers the call states the name of the caller and the nature of the inquiry or request before putting the call through, thus preparing the other employee and saving the customer from having to repeat this information.

If a caller does not want to be transferred, you should offer to arrange for the appropriate person to call back. Never transfer a call if you are not sure who should be receiving it. Instead, find out what the caller needs, and let him know that someone will return the call. If you subsequently learn that the return call will be delayed, call the customer back, and let him know the name of the person who will be calling and when to expect the call.

USING VOICEMAIL

Voicemail is a computerized answering service that provides a personalized greeting and allows one person to leave a recorded message for another.

Often, the purpose of a telephone call is simply to relay information. For instance, a customer may call a bank employee to provide her child's social security number for a new custodial account, or an employee may call a coworker to provide an answer to an earlier question. In situations like these, voicemail works well. *Voicemail* is a computerized answering service that provides a personalized greeting and allows one person to leave a recorded message for another. With voicemail, even if the receiving party is unavailable, the customer can leave the information and avoid unnecessary return calls. Unlike written messages, voicemail gives the recipient an opportunity to interpret the caller's tone of voice and respond accordingly.

If your voicemail system allows you to record your own message, you should consider recording two types of greetings: one for when you are in the office but temporarily unavailable and the other for when you will be out of the office or unavailable all day. When recording your greeting, make it professional and friendly, use simple sentences, and speak clearly at an appropriate rate of speech. Also, include the following information:

- Your department and/or company name

- Your first and last name

- The date

- Whether you are in the office, and if not, when you will return

- Whether you will be checking messages and returning calls, and if so, when

- Instructions for callers who need immediate help

Voicemail, like any technology, can be misused. For example, some employees use voicemail to avoid being disturbed. Other employees don't check their messages regularly. If you are tempted to use voicemail to screen calls, think of the times you needed to speak to someone and were greeted by a recording. Think of the times you left messages and didn't receive timely return calls. Figure 7-2 offers some suggestions for using voicemail effectively.

Written Communication

Written communication in customer service takes a variety of forms, such as telephone messages, handwritten notes, notes to a file, business letters, memos, e-mail messages, and Web chat sessions. Although certain guidelines pertain to specific types of written communication, many universal guidelines also apply. In this section, we provide an overview of general writing techniques as well as formats for business letters and memos. In the next section, we will discuss electronic communication, which includes, among other things, e-mail and Web chat.

FIGURE 7-2. Voicemail Tips.

 Check for messages frequently, at least as often as your greeting implies, and every time you come back to your desk. If you are out of the office, check your messages regularly.

 Act on messages promptly by taking one of the following steps:

- Reply to the message

- Forward the message to someone else for action

- Save the message for later action (if you need to spend more time on an item, let the caller know)

- Delete the message, if appropriate

Source: Queensland University of Technology, "Voice Mail Etiquette," http://www.its.qut.edu.au/cqs/voicemail/etiquett.shtml (5 April 2002).

Written communication differs from many other types of communication in two ways: (1) it seldom provides a real-time exchange of information that participants can rely on to quickly clarify a message, and (2) it provides documentation of the message.

For example, in a telephone call, if you are unsure of the message, you can ask for clarification, but unless the call is recorded, there is no irrefutable documentation of what was said. In a business letter, you cannot immediately obtain clarification, but you and the customer can refer to the letter in the future. Therefore, a letter does not provide the writer with instant feedback, and it is more likely than an unrecorded conversation to legally obligate a company. For these reasons, clarity and accuracy, which are important in all types of communication, are especially important in written communication.

> A letter does not provide the writer with instant feedback, and it is more likely than an unrecorded conversation to legally obligate a company.

Regardless of what you are writing, you can communicate more effectively if you think about your purpose, strive for clarity, and proofread your work.

Prewriting

All written communication has a purpose—for example, to ask a question, request an action, or provide information—but sometimes the purpose is not clear because the writer was not well prepared. To make sure of your purpose, you should begin by prewriting. **Prewriting** is the part of the writing process that occurs before you produce a first draft, when you determine why and what you are writing, for whom the message is intended, and the best way to present it. Depending on the circumstances, prewriting can include anything from spending a few seconds thinking or jotting down notes to conducting extensive research and preparing a structured outline.[4]

An important function of prewriting is to decide the appropriate style and content of your communication. You do this by considering the reader, the impression you want to make, how much the reader knows, and what the reader needs to know. For example, when communicating with an external customer or an insurance regulator, you might choose to write a formal business letter. However, the content and presentation of these two letters would probably differ, because of the background of each reader and because of the different impression you want to make. On the other hand, when communicating with a coworker, you might decide to write an informal handwritten note.

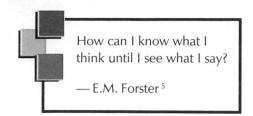

How can I know what I
think until I see what I say?

— E.M. Forster [5]

Prewriting does not necessarily mean that you plan everything you are going to say before you write the first word. Some people write this way, while others find that the act of writing helps shape their thoughts. However, without paying at least some attention to your purpose for writing and your intended audience, you are likely to confuse or mislead your readers.

TEMPLATES

Many financial services companies provide templates as a resource for their employees. Similar to scripts and talking points, **templates** are sample documents that employees use as a model when writing specific types of correspondence. Some templates, called *form letters*, provide pre-printed text for everything but "fill-in-the-blank" items. Other templates provide important information, but require employees to do more original writing, based on the specifics of the customer inquiry or request. Some companies maintain a listing or database of *form paragraphs* that employees can insert into letters as needed to respond to frequently asked questions.

When using templates, you must be careful to select the appropriate template and make all necessary adjustments. Also, whether you are using a template (for correspondence) or a script or talking points (for

FIGURE 7-3. Use Simple Words.

Instead of Writing...	Write...
cognizant	aware
commence	start, begin
concur	agree
endeavor	try
exigency	need
optimum	best
requisite	necessary, needed

telephone calls), you should always keep your customer in mind. Although templates, scripts, and talking points are valuable resources, they cannot take the place of a service provider who adds a personal touch by responding to each customer's unique situation and needs.

Clarity

Some people think long words and complex sentences are a sign of intelligence or professionalism, but actually this writing style confuses and annoys many readers. The goal of written communication is to be understood. Everyday words and a conversational tone make writing easier to understand. A friendly, straightforward writing style is more effective than a cold, formal, complicated style. One way to improve your writing is to use simple words instead of long or technical words, as Figure 7-3 illustrates.

Another way to write clearly is to use only those words needed to communicate your message. By eliminating unnecessary words and phrases, you can save readers' time and you can help them focus on the message. Figure 7-4 shows concise alternatives to wordy phrases and sentences.

In general, effective business writing uses sentences that are short and direct. Some writers are tempted to use words like *and*, *but*, *which*, and *because* to develop rambling sentences full of dependent clauses. These sentences may sound scholarly, but they are difficult to follow. Examine your sentences for unnecessary words and phrases. Try breaking long sentences into two or three sentences.

Another way to shorten sentences and add clarity is to use bulleted lists. For example, instead of writing

> Please complete and return to me in the enclosed self-addressed stamped envelope the Change of Beneficiary form, the Change of Address form, and the Preauthorized Check form.

you could write

> Please complete and return to me in the enclosed self-addressed stamped envelope, the following forms:
>
> - Change of Beneficiary
> - Change of Address
> - Preauthorized Check

One way to improve your writing is to use simple words instead of long or technical words.

FIGURE 7-4. Avoid Wordiness.

Instead of Writing...	Write...
in the event that	if
during the time that	while
conducted an investigation concerning	investigated
please forward to the undersigned	please send me
it goes without saying that	[*If it goes without saying, why say it?*]

Notice how the first example buries the requested forms within the text, while the second example draws the reader's attention to the name of each form.

When writing paragraphs, try to include only one main idea per paragraph, along with supporting information. When that idea is complete, begin a new paragraph.

Remember that short paragraphs are easier to understand than long paragraphs. If you write a very long paragraph, try to cut unnecessary words, phrases, and sentences, or try to find a logical break in thought, and begin a new paragraph.

Also, remember that in a well-written letter or memo, the sections or paragraphs appear in logical order, with each paragraph building on the preceding paragraph.

Clear and concise writing seldom happens on the first try. Usually, you can make improvements with rewrites. The next time you write a letter or memo, try reviewing it with the goal of using simple words, omitting needless words, and shortening complex sentences and paragraphs.

The next time you write a letter or memo, try reviewing it with the goal of using simple words, omitting needless words, and shortening complex sentences and paragraph.

Proofreading

Proofreading is the process of reading through and making corrections to a document. Proofreading gives you a chance to make sure your writing accomplishes its purpose. If you use a word-processing program, you should run the spell-check function, but remember that spell-check is not a substitute for careful proofreading. Spell checkers will not always identify missing words or words that are *spelled* correctly but *used* incorrectly, such as "than" and "then," "there" and "their," and "won" and "one."

Try to put yourself in the readers' place.

When you proofread, make sure your writing provides accurate information, covers all the essential points, and gives readers all the information they need. Try to put yourself in the readers' place. Is the purpose clear? Does the writing address the readers' needs and answer their questions? Does it leave a positive impression?

Finally, when you proofread, make sure the writing is grammatically correct. Are the commas in the right places? Are pronouns used properly? Do subjects and verbs agree? A document with grammatical errors is confusing, and gives the impression that the writer and the company are sloppy and unprofessional.

If you have the opportunity, you could ask a coworker to read what you have written. A second pair of eyes almost always helps uncover problems and errors. For practice, try proofreading the letter in Exercise 7-2.

Choosing a Format for Written Communication

Sometimes a short handwritten note is an effective way to communicate. For example, if a coworker leaves a document on your desk and asks you to comment, you might jot down your thoughts in the margin, make a photocopy for yourself, and return the original. However, other situations might require you to write a business letter or a memo.

BUSINESS LETTERS

Business letters, because they indicate professionalism, are a common way to communicate with external customers and people outside your organization. Typically, a business letter follows a standard format. Figure 7-5 illustrates one such format. Please refer to this figure when reading the explanation that follows.

Exercise 7-2. Proofreading Practice.

Proofread this letter, and see if you can find the errors.

August 7, 2002

Jane Doe
123 Main Street
Anywhere, Nevada 89414

Dear Ms. Doe:

Thank you for you're telephone call regarding account number 87-   (1)
654-321. We were able to locate the error and we has credited your   (2)
account accordingly as of the date of the error. A reports to this effect   (3)
has been sent to are credit reporting company. As of this date, your   (4)
account balance is $2,378. You are valued customer and we apolo-   (5)
gize for any convenience this incident may have caused. If we maybe   (6)
of further assistance, please contact this office.   (7)

Sincerely,

Donald Smithers

Errors: line 1, *you're* should be *your*; line 2, *has* should be *have*; line 3, *reports* should be *report*; line 4, *are* should be *our*; line 5, *You are valued customer* should be *You are **a** valued customer*; line 6, *convenience* should be *inconvenience*; line 6, *maybe* should be *may be*.

Date, Name, and Address. The date includes the day, month, and year the letter is sent. The addressee's name is shown in full—exactly as it appears in that person's business correspondence. The person's business title (such as Vice President or Customer Service Representative) appears on the line beneath the name. The address includes the company, street number and street (or post office box), city, state or province, ZIP code or postal code, and country, if necessary.

Salutation. Most business letters begin with a **salutation**—a greeting that includes the name of the person who is to receive the letter—followed by a colon. Typically, the salutation shows the recipient's last name, preceded by Mr. or Ms. If the writer and recipient know each other, the writer might use the recipient's first name.

FIGURE 7-5. Sample Format of a Business Letter.

[Date]	January 24, 2003
[Name] *[Address]*	Bernice Kilpatrick 222 Plain Street Anywhere, Idaho 40562
[Salutation]	Dear Ms. Kilpatrick:
[Opening]	Thank you for your letter requesting information about your individual life insurance policy's dividend options. I appreciate this opportunity to explain these options to you.
[Body]	Five different policy dividend options are available:

       (1) The cash dividend option

       (2) The premium reduction option

       (3) The accumulation at interest option

       (4) The paid-up additional insurance option

       (5) The additional term insurance option

I have enclosed a pamphlet that describes each of these options in detail.

In your policy application, you chose the premium reduction option. For the past five years, we have applied your policy dividends toward the payment of your renewal premiums. Each year on your annual renewal premium notice, we have subtracted the amount paid for policy dividends and billed you for the difference.

You have the right to change your dividend option at any time. If, after reviewing the enclosed material, you decide you would like to change to the additional term insurance dividend option, please call me at 1-800-555-4444 so that I may send you an evidence of insurability form. As the pamphlet states, changing to the additional term insurance dividend option requires you to submit evidence that you are still an insurable risk.

[Closing]	I hope this information answers all your questions. If you require any further assistance, please call me.
[Complimentary Close]	Sincerely, Noah Kintu Senior Representative

When the recipient's name is not known, a common practice is to use "Dear Sir or Madam" as the salutation. Or, to avoid this impersonal salutation, another practice is to send the letter without a salutation. Neither approach is ideal. People tend to pay more attention to personalized letters than to letters with generalized salutations or no salutation at all. If reasonably possible, you should obtain the recipient's name.

Content. Most business letters have an opening, a body, and a closing. The *opening of a letter* is typically the first paragraph or two, and it attracts the reader's attention, establishes the tone of the message, and states the purpose of the letter. In the sample letter shown in Figure 7-5, notice how the first paragraph sets a helpful tone and lets the customer know the reason for writing. The *body of a letter* is the part of the letter that follows the opening and provides the information that accomplishes the letter's purpose. In the sample in Figure 7-5, the second, third, and fourth paragraphs make up the body of the letter. The *closing of a letter* is typically the last paragraph or two, and it performs one or more of the following functions:

> The *body of a letter* is the part of the letter that follows the opening and provides the information that accomplishes the letter's purpose.

- Summarizes all important points from the body of the letter

- Indicates any steps the writer will be taking

- Asks for any response needed from the reader

- Gives specific information about how and when the reader's response should be communicated

- Concludes on a positive note

Complimentary Close. The formal wording used to end a letter, followed by the writer's full name and title, if applicable, is called the *complimentary close*. A variety of words and phrases are generally considered appropriate complimentary closes, such as *sincerely, sincerely yours, regards, best regards, cordially, cordially yours*, and *best wishes*.

MEMOS

A *memo* (from the word *memorandum*) is a written communication that contains directions, guidelines, or information and is typically sent within an organization. Although memos are most often internal communications, they are sometimes sent to people outside an organization. For instance, a memo might be addressed to intermediaries to announce a new product.

Some memos are brief, informal one-to-one messages. Others, which typically follow a standard format, facilitate communication within an organization and are used to send an identical message to many people. As the sample in Figure 7-6 illustrates, a standard memo heading usually includes the name of the person or people who will receive the memo, the sender's name, the date the memo is sent, and the subject (sometimes introduced by "RE," meaning "regarding").

Because information about the topic is presented in the subject line, the opening of a memo is sometimes more direct than the opening of a business letter. However, you can still use the opening to capture the reader's attention, establish the appropriate tone, and state the memo's purpose. As in a letter, the body of the memo contains the message, while the closing describes what actions, if any, should occur. If the memo is long, the closing briefly summarizes the important points. Occasionally, a memo includes an *executive summary* to highlight the most important points; the executiev summary appears after the heading and before the body of the memo.

Electronic Communication

Electronic communication, or *e-communication*, is communication made possible by the transmission of electronic signals to produce sounds, images, or text. Although this definition is broad enough to include the telephone, many observers refer to newer technologies such as fax, e-mail, Internet/Web-based communications, and videoconferencing when they

FIGURE 7-6. Sample of a Standard Memo Heading.

MEMORANDUM

TO: All Employees   **DATE:** May 24, 2002

FROM: Alexandria G. Bell   **ACTION:** Immediate
Director, Customer Care

RE: Misdirected Telephone Calls

use the term electronic communication. In this text, we use the term electronic communication to refer to these newer technologies.

Fax

A *fax* (from the word *facsimile*) is a paper document that contains text and/or images printed from signals electronically transmitted over a telephone line from one device to another. Faxing allows service providers, intermediaries, and customers to send documents back and forth quickly and efficiently. For example, faxing can provide insurers with the information they need to promptly take action to begin processing applications or claims. Similarly, faxing can provide mortgage lenders with much of the documentation they need to begin processing loans.

The most common way to send a fax is to insert a document in a fax machine, enter the fax number of the receiving machine, and press the transmit button, after which the receiving fax machine receives and prints the document. Some offices use a type of electronic communication called *desktop faxing* that enables users to fax documents from applications available on their personal computers.

You should never fax confidential information without the recipient's permission.

As is the case with any type of communication, you should consider each customer's comfort level before using fax. Also, you should never fax confidential information without the recipient's permission. Office fax machines are typically used by more than one person, and a customer's right to privacy could be jeopardized if a fax arrives without his knowledge.

E-Mail

E-mail (from the term *electronic mail*) is a form of electronic communication that enables a user to type a message into a computer and then send the message to other computers connected to a network.[6] We will discuss computer networks in more detail in Chapter 13. In many companies, e-mail is the preferred way to communicate because it is fast, easy to use, and inexpensive. E-mail demands the same attention to purpose, clarity, and accuracy as other forms of writing.

Although e-mail involves reading and writing, it is more immediate than traditional correspondence and in some ways resembles spontaneous types of communication, such as face-to-face meetings or telephone conversations. Because delivery time is minimal, many customers expect a rapid reply after sending an e-mail message.

When the volume of incoming e-mail messages grows, service providers sometimes feel pressured to read and reply quickly. Consequently, they may not give the same careful attention to e-mail messages that they give to other types of writing. With the slip of a finger, service providers might inadvertently send an e-mail message before it is ready to be sent. Or, they might overlook an inappropriate comment buried in a series of forwarded messages. As you can see, e-mail presents several unique challenges.

WHEN TO USE E-MAIL

E-mail is an excellent form of communication for sending short or informal messages. It also works well when you need to send attached documents and when you need to communicate with many people at the same time. However, e-mail is not always the most effective type of communication.

Before you send an e-mail message, consider if another communication channel might be better suited to your purpose.

Before you send an e-mail message, consider if another communication channel might be better suited to your purpose. Some people use e-mail when the telephone or face-to-face communication would work better. Have you ever sent or received an e-mail message that raised a number of questions and resulted in a flurry of additional e-mails that eventually prompted a telephone call or a meeting to clarify the confusion? In situations like these, a telephone call at the outset (perhaps followed by an e-mail message to confirm the telephone conversation) can save time and avoid frustration. Use e-mail to improve communication, not to avoid discussion.

PREPARING AN E-MAIL

The main sections of an e-mail are the header, the message, and the complimentary close, as shown in Figure 7-7.

Header

The header is the formatted section of an e-mail that indicates the date and time the e-mail was sent, and includes the *from*, *to*, *cc*, and *subject* lines. When preparing an e-mail, take a moment to consider your audience and to make sure that all the recipients actually need to receive this message. Because people often rely on subject lines to screen their e-mails, choose a subject line that attracts the recipient's attention and that accurately reflects the content of the message. Never leave the subject line blank. Also, make sure the subject line is concise, no more than 35 characters, if possible. When the message is truly urgent, you should say so in the subject line; for example, you could type, "Please reply by 4/15."

Message

When writing an e-mail message, use the same care you would use when writing a letter. Most of the techniques of business writing apply to e-mail messages. Be clear. Provide the important information immediately, and then support it with relevant details. End by summarizing or asking for action. Be concise: if possible, limit your message to one screen.

Don't use abbreviations, acronyms, or jargon unless you know the reader will understand them. Although electronic jargon has become popular in personal e-mail messages, you should avoid using it in business. Terms like BTW (by the way), FYI (for your information), and THX (thanks) might annoy some readers.

FIGURE 7-7. Sample E-Mail Message.

| **From:** | Abra@ABC.com (Abraham, Jerry) | **Sent:** | Wed 7/24/02 11:09 |

To: Mapple@Tome.com (Applebee, Maria)

CC: Ban@Tome.com (Banner, Tom)

Subject: TOME Agency Leads Sales Contest

Hi Maria—

Just wanted you and Tom to know that your agency is the leader in the quarterly sales contest. Your nearest competition is the Scafidi Agency in Topeka. I've attached the May sales figures for your information.

Keep up the good work!

Jerry

Make sure your message is complete and accurate, so you can avoid having to send follow-up messages to clarify your original e-mail. Proof-read carefully. If a message is particularly important, you might want to print it and proofread a paper version. Many people find they can proof-read more effectively on paper than on a computer monitor.

Complimentary Close

When sending an e-mail outside your organization, you should use the end of the message to identify yourself, your position, your organization, and your contact information—address, telephone number, and fax. Many e-mail programs have an *auto-signature* feature, which is an option that automatically includes the user's complimentary close at the end of each e-mail message the user sends. Some companies and service providers use auto-signature to add a short message; for instance, to promote a new product or invite recipients to visit the company's Web site.

Most e-mail messages, once sent, cannot be retrieved. If you are not sure whether a message should be sent, discuss it with your supervisor.

ADDITIONAL E-MAIL CONSIDERATIONS

In a business setting, e-mail is a corporate tool and should be used as such. Your approach to e-mail should be the same as if you were writing on company letterhead. Because of the spontaneous nature of e-mail, some employees are tempted to include gossip, jokes, or personal comments in e-mail messages. However, you should avoid these types of topics. With-out the benefit of nonverbal signals, such comments might be interpreted the wrong way. Also, keep in mind that most e-mail messages, once sent, cannot be retrieved. If you are not sure whether a message should be sent, discuss it with your supervisor.

If you send an e-mail attachment, make sure the recipient has the same or compatible software; otherwise, he will not be able to open the attachment.

Reply promptly to every e-mail that requires a response, but if a message does not require a response, don't feel obligated to reply. If you send an e-mail that provides no meaningful information, you are merely wast-ing time that you and your recipient(s) could be using more productively.

Here are some other e-mail practices and guidelines:

- Clean out your mailbox on a regular basis to save system space and to maintain a better-organized "work area." Retain e-mail communications (either in electronic storage or hard copy) the same amount of time you keep other types of written communications.

- The owner of a company e-mail account is not the employee but the organization. In many companies, occasional personal use of e-mail is acceptable. However, some companies only allow their employees to use e-mail within the organization. Others forbid the use of e-mail for personal reasons, whether within or outside the organization.

- There is no guarantee of the privacy of your e-mail messages; once you send a message, the receiver may forward it to someone else. Assume that every message you send will be made public.

- Before you forward an e-mail you received from someone else, review it to see if it contains any information that might be inappropriate. Don't assume that the person who sent it intended for you to share it with others.

- As an employee, you have a responsibility to protect confidential organizational information; you should approach your e-mail communications as if they were public announcements.

- Rules of ethical conduct, nondiscriminatory behavior, and appropriate language apply to the use of e-mail as they do to any other type of business communication.

LEGAL ISSUES ASSOCIATED WITH E-MAIL

In some countries, the widespread use of e-mail has given rise to several legal issues that service providers should be aware of. For example, United States federal law allows companies to conduct electronic surveillance of employee e-mail accounts. In addition, an organization can be held liable for inappropriate e-mail messages sent by its employees, and messages stored on back-up disks or on paper can be subpoenaed in court. In some cases, an e-mail message can be used in a lawsuit or to document a regulatory violation.

An organization can be held liable for inappropriate e-mail messages sent by its employees, and messages stored on back-up disks or on paper can be subpoenaed in court.

Company Web Sites

Most financial services firms maintain a Web site. In Chapter 13, we will discuss how Web sites work; here we examine how they are used to communicate with customers. A well-designed Web site provides a company's customers with a convenient entryway to a variety of services, starting with self-service. By continually monitoring Web-based customer inquiries, a company can determine the information customers are seeking and then make this information readily available. On some Web sites, customers can find what they are looking for 70 to 90 percent of the time.[7]

However, even the most effective self-service Web sites cannot automatically deliver 100 percent of the information and services customers seek. Therefore, a Web site must also provide customers with access to human assistance. For example, a Web site can automatically monitor the amount of time an applicant spends filling out a form, and after a specified amount of time it can display a "click here for help" button to offer the customer assistance.

At the most basic level, a Web site can provide customers with a list of telephone numbers to call for help. Other, more sophisticated options include e-mail, which we discussed earlier, as well as Web chat, Web callback, voice over Internet protocol, and Web collaboration.

Web chat, also called *text chat* or *instant messaging*, is a technology that enables text-based "conversations" over the Internet. When a customer chooses to communicate via Web chat, the customer types a question, which then appears on the service provider's computer monitor. When the service provider types a response, the response appears on the customer's computer monitor, beneath the original question.

Some Web sites have communication mechanisms that allow customers to request additional support via telephone. For instance, using ***Web callback*** (sometimes referred to as *call me back*), the customer clicks on an icon at the Web site, and this sends a request for a company representative to call the customer.

If customers are using their only telephone line to connect to the Internet, then they must log off to receive the telephone call. Therefore, some Web sites allow customers to complete an online form to request a date and time for the Web callback. Typically, the company sends an automated e-mail message to acknowledge receipt of the request.

Customers who have a separate telephone line or a computer configuration that enables voice over Internet protocol can remain connected to the Internet and still receive a call from a company representative. ***Voice over Internet protocol*** (VoIP) is a technology that transmits voice over an Internet connection. With a separate telephone line or VoIP, customers can call for "voice-based" assistance at the same time that they move about on the Web site. Another feature, similar to Web callback, is click-to-call. ***Click-to-call*** is a communication mechanism that enables Web site visitors to initiate a conversation with a company representative by

A Web site must also provide customers with access to human assistance.

clicking on an icon, which then automatically places a call, using VoIP, to a company representative.

Using VoIP or a separate telephone line, a customer and a service provider can discuss information they view together on the Web site. With Web collaboration, they can take the interaction one step farther. **Web collaboration**, or *collaborative browsing*, is a technology that enables participants to "meet" at a Web site, synchronize their browsers, and explore the Web site together, communicating with each other in real time. Web collaboration allows participants to perform a variety of tasks. They can transfer files or transmit pages back and forth (sometimes called *pushing pages*). They also can highlight, underline, circle, or point to items on a page, a process sometimes referred to as *whiteboarding*. With Web collaboration, a service provider can even help a customer complete a form online.

The skills that service providers must develop to work effectively with Web-based communications depend on the particular type of communications they handle. Some of these skills are similar to more traditional communication skills, while others are unique to Internet communications. For example, VoIP in conjunction with Web collaboration requires effective telephone communication skills, the ability to navigate a Web site quickly and effectively, and subject matter expertise to explain Web site content. Web chat requires traditional writing skills plus familiarity with various Web conventions and terms.

Videoconferencing

Videoconferencing is a method of electronic communication in which participants can see and hear one another. Typically, videoconferencing is used for business-to-business contacts, such as meetings between a group insurer and its group clients. It is also used by individual customers in video kiosks located in public places, such as banks or even department stores. Video communication is also available through video cameras and desktop computers connected to the Internet.

Service providers who communicate with customers via videoconferencing must draw upon many of the skills needed for effective face-to-face communication. In addition, they must have a working knowledge of how to operate videoconferencing equipment.

In this chapter, you have learned about the major types of communication used to provide customer service in the financial services industry. As you have seen, effective communication, regardless of the type of communication, requires preparation, focus, and practice. If you believe you would benefit from a more thorough study of a particular type of communication, you can choose from a variety of books and courses on these subjects. For example, through its Workplace Skills Program, LOMA offers *Effective Written Communication*, a self-study program in which students submit writing exercises for review. In the next chapter, we turn our attention to one of the most important communication skills in customer service: the ability to listen to and understand customers.

To practice and review the skills and information you learned in this chapter, see the interactive CD, *Practicing Your Customer Service Skills*, included with this book.

Key Terms and Concepts

corporate culture	body of a letter
etiquette	closing of a letter
business etiquette	complimentary close
script	memo
talking points	executive summary
inbound telephone calls	electronic communication
auto-greeting	fax
outbound telephone calls	desktop faxing
blind transfer	e-mail
conference transfer	auto-signature
voicemail	Web chat
prewriting	Web callback
templates	voice over Internet protocol
proofreading	click-to-call
salutation	Web collaboration
opening of a letter	Videoconferencing

Endnotes

1. Portions of this section are adapted from Barbara Foxenberger Brown and John P. Burger, *Agency Administration Course Manual*, 2nd ed. (Atlanta: LOMA, © 2000), 166–174. Used with permission; all rights reserved.

2. Now Hear This, Inc., "Phone Tip," http://www.phoneskills.com/freearticles.cfm (24 May 2002).

3. Rosanne D'Ausilio, *Wake Up Your Call Center* (West Lafayette, IN: Purdue University Press, 1999), 24.

4. Wilma R. Ebbitt and David R. Ebbitt, *Writer's Guide and Index to English*, 6th ed. (Glenview, IL: Scott, Foresman and Company, 1978), 5.

5. Ibid.

6. Portions of this section are adapted from LOMA, *Effective Written Communication*, (Atlanta: LOMA, © 1997), 175–179. Used with permission; all rights reserved.

7. Greg Gianforte, "Insider's Guide to Delighting the Internet Age Customer," *RightNow Technologies*, 2000, http://www.rightnow.com/resource/whitepaper.html (24 October 2001).7.   Greg Gianforte, "Insider's Guide to Delighting the Internet Age Customer," *RightNow Technologies White Papers*, 2000.

CHAPTER 8

Listening to and Understanding Customers

After studying this chapter, you should be able to

- Explain three reasons why people are ineffective listeners

- Identify four kinds of perceptual errors that cause misunderstandings

- Describe the importance of active listening in providing exceptional customer service

- Identify and describe the steps in the CARESS model of active listening

- Discuss additional guidelines designed to help you be a more effective listener

- Describe the process of paraphrasing

- Distinguish between open and closed questions and explain how the funnel technique and the inverted funnel technique can be used as questioning strategies

- Distinguish between neutral and leading questions

"Y ou're not listening to me!" Think about a time when you have said these words to someone, whether it was a co-worker, a friend, a family member, or a customer service representative. Recall your feelings at the time—were you angry, disappointed, exasperated? Most of us have experienced the frustration of talking to someone who didn't seem to be listening to or understanding what we were saying. Customers experience the same feelings when they believe that you are not listening to or understanding them.

As you'll see in this chapter, listening and understanding are closely related. *Listening* is the effort we make to hear what a person is saying; *understanding* is our ability to grasp the meaning and significance of those words. If you don't listen carefully to a person's entire message, you are likely to miss some part of it, which prevents you from thoroughly understanding the message. Conversely, when you devote your full attention to a speaker and use active listening skills (which we'll discuss later in this chapter), you increase your ability to understand the speaker's message. Effective listening, therefore, leads to more complete understanding, just as complete understanding requires effective listening. Together, effective listening and complete understanding improve your ability to solve customers' problems and manage conflicts.

Service providers can develop and improve their listening and understanding skills through practice. In this chapter, we will provide guidelines and tools that can help you become better at listening to and understanding customers. First we will explain some common causes of misunderstandings. Then we will describe ways to sharpen your active listening skills. Finally, we will present techniques to improve your understanding.

What Causes Misunderstandings?

Some misunderstandings occur because speakers don't express a message clearly, as we have learned in previous chapters. But in many instances, poor listening skills are the root of communication problems. The fact is most people don't listen effectively (for reasons why, see Figure 8-1). Studies show that people understand and retain only about half of what is said

FIGURE 8-1.   Reasons for Ineffective Listening.

If listening is such an important part of effective communication, why don't we listen well all the time? Here are three reasons:

1. **We can listen at a faster rate than we can speak.** The average person *speaks* at about 135–175 words per minute, while the average person can *listen* to 400–500 words per minute. So, the average listener must pay attention to actual words only about 30 percent of the time; if he isn't actively listening the remaining 70 percent of the time, he will become distracted.

2. **Communication barriers interfere with listening.** Barriers such as other people talking or walking nearby can distract someone from thoroughly listening to a speaker. As you learned in Chapter 6, such barriers are also referred to as *noise*.

3. **Listening is hard work.** Studies show effective listening requires a demanding physical effort that increases the listener's heart and pulse rates. Because of these physiological factors, many people find that listening halfway is easier than concentrating on what a speaker is saying.

to them. This fact is troubling for financial services organizations, as ineffective listening can lead to sloppy service, dissatisfied customers, and lost revenue.

A ***perceptual error*** is a mistake that occurs when a person bases his perception on limited information and/ or incorrect assumptions.

Misunderstandings frequently occur because the listener makes a perceptual error. Recall from Chapter 5 that perception is the process by which a person selects, organizes, and interprets information. A ***perceptual error*** is a mistake that occurs when a person bases his perception on limited information and/or incorrect assumptions, resulting in a flawed or limited view of reality. Some of the most common perceptual errors are selective perception, fundamental attribution error, projection, and stereotyping, as summarized in Figure 8-2. Perceptual errors interfere with a person's ability to understand a speaker's message.

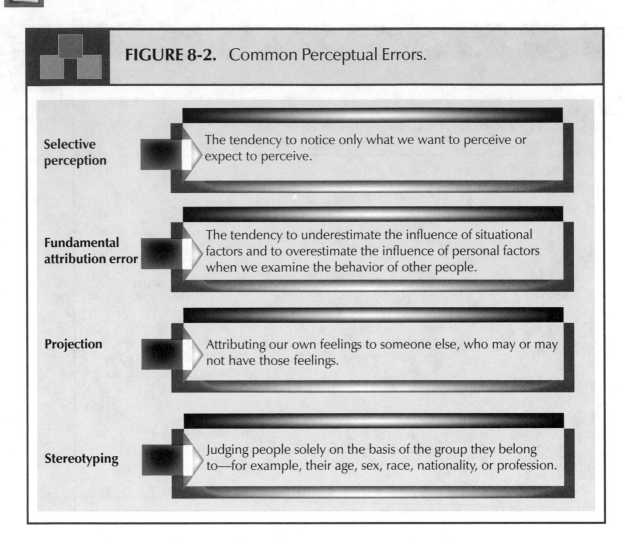

FIGURE 8-2. Common Perceptual Errors.

Selective perception — The tendency to notice only what we want to perceive or expect to perceive.

Fundamental attribution error — The tendency to underestimate the influence of situational factors and to overestimate the influence of personal factors when we examine the behavior of other people.

Projection — Attributing our own feelings to someone else, who may or may not have those feelings.

Stereotyping — Judging people solely on the basis of the group they belong to—for example, their age, sex, race, nationality, or profession.

A perceptual error hinders a service provider's ability to effectively identify and satisfy customers' needs. Recognizing when these errors occur and taking steps to avoid or correct them can help service providers better communicate with and serve their customers.

Selective Perception

Selective perception is the tendency to perceive only what we want to or expect to perceive. For example, if a customer is speaking to you in what you perceive to be a harsh voice, you might pay more attention to his tone than to his words. However, after talking with the customer, you may realize that he is simply in a hurry. Your first impression was incorrect because it was based on your selective perception of his "harsh" tone.

As another example of selective perception, suppose the owner of a variable universal life insurance policy calls her insurance company to inquire about the current value of her account and the process for taking out a policy loan. Upon hearing the customer's questions, the CSR immediately begins the loan process for the customer because, in the CSR's experience, most customers who call with similar questions want to take out a loan that day. This customer, however, simply wanted to know the cash value of her policy and what steps were involved in the loan process; she did *not* want to take out a loan immediately. The CSR incorrectly assumed that he knew what this customer wanted based on his selective perception of her questions.

To reduce selective perception errors, get the facts straight before you make inferences or assumptions about a situation. Avoid jumping to conclusions, and be sure to listen to a customer's whole message, as we will discuss later in this chapter.

Fundamental Attribution Error

Attribution is the perceptual process of assigning reasons for a person's behavior in order to explain his actions. People might behave a certain way because of the situation they're in or because of their personality traits. Typically, both the situation and a person's personality affect her behavior. Trying to understand not only what people do but also why they do it is normal. However, the perceptual error of *attributional bias* occurs when we assign generalized, poorly thought-out reasons for the behavior of others.

The perceptual error of *attributional bias* occurs when we assign generalized, poorly thought-out reasons for the behavior of others.

One common attributional bias, called the *fundamental attribution error*, is the tendency to underestimate the influence of situational factors and to overestimate the influence of personal factors when we examine the behavior of other people. In other words, we tend to assume that a person acts a certain way because of her personality, not because she is affected by situational factors.

For example, suppose Drew Zehnder, a customer service representative for a health maintenance organization, has a customer, Wilma Cooper, who is often rude and angry when she calls to ask questions about her plan's benefits. In Mr. Zehnder's mind—and possibly in his conversations with coworkers—he has classified Ms. Cooper as difficult, and he often stops listening to her when she becomes upset. Might Mr. Zehnder perceive Ms. Cooper differently if he knew that she bears the full responsibility of caring for a dying parent and often gets little or no sleep? If so, he might listen more carefully and begin to realize that what Ms. Cooper really wants is sympathy and understanding.

An attributional bias can make service providers unsympathetic to customers. To avoid this error, think about how situational factors sometimes affect your own mood. For example, how do you feel when you have a sick child or financial worries? Now, imagine that such situational factors might be affecting your customers. By viewing your customers in such a sympathetic way, you can avoid attributional biases.

Projection

Projection is a perceptual error that occurs when we attribute our own feelings to someone else, who may or may not have those same feelings. Although we can project positive feelings, projection usually refers to the negative feelings we attribute to other people because we don't want to admit that we have those feelings ourselves. For example, an angry or stubborn person tends to believe that other people have those traits but that he himself does not. In this sense, projection is used as a defense mechanism that helps us protect our image of ourselves.

Projection can interfere with a service provider's ability to listen to and understand customers. For example, suppose customer Trey Lopez questions the accuracy of information provided by Penelope Roberts, a customer service representative at the Cypress Mutual Fund Company. Ms. Roberts reacts to his questions by immediately assuming that Mr. Lopez doubts her ability to do her job. The truth is that Ms. Roberts feels insecure and anxious when customers question her. Instead of addressing her own feelings, she projects them onto Mr. Lopez by assuming that he is challenging her knowledge and skills. In fact, Mr. Lopez simply did not understand the information provided and needs further explanation. Because she has projected her own feelings onto her customer, Ms. Roberts fails to understand what Mr. Lopez needs from her.

Recognizing situations when we are projecting negative feelings inappropriately can help us deal with such situations thoughtfully, professionally, and unemotionally.

Recognizing situations when we are projecting negative feelings inappropriately can help us deal with such situations thoughtfully, professionally, and unemotionally.

Stereotyping

Stereotyping is a perceptual error that occurs when we judge people solely on the basis of a group they belong to—for example, their age, sex, race, nationality, or profession. Stereotyping denies the individuality of each person. It encourages us to be lazy in our thinking and to pass judgment on large groups of people. Stereotyping encourages us not to perceive the individual people in a group but, instead, to perceive general traits that are usually inaccurate.

We all engage in stereotyping. For example, you might believe that people who use poor grammar or who originate from certain countries will behave in a particular way, or you might make judgments about certain races or religions. A service provider who classifies customers according to stereotypes and does not view customers as individual people is likely to be distracted or judgmental when listening to customers, which prevents her from really understanding their needs and wants.

The next time you find yourself making a judgment about a person based on a group he belongs to, stop and think of that person as an individual. Does the stereotype really do him justice? Being aware of your own stereotypes and recognizing common values, interests, and feelings that you share with people in the stereotyped group will be your best defense against such a perceptual error.

A service provider who classifies customers according to stereotypes and does not view customers as individual people is likely to be distracted or judgmental when listening to customers.

Improving Your Active Listening Skills

Active listening is the process of concentrating entirely on a speaker's verbal and nonverbal communication. An active listener is genuinely interested in what the speaker has to say and uses verbal and nonverbal feedback to indicate that she really understands and feels that what the speaker is saying is important. Active listening makes the speaker feel valuable and facilitates the transfer of information, resulting in fewer misunderstandings and errors. Recall from Chapter 3 that active listening is an important part of effective communication skills, which is a core competency for successful customer service professionals. Active listening, therefore, is an essential skill for anyone who wants to excel as a service provider.

Active listening skills are especially important in providing proactive service, which, as we explained in Chapter 5, looks beyond what the customer asks in an effort to anticipate and fulfill the customer's unexpressed needs. Active listening is essential to proactive service because active listening requires service providers to concentrate not only on the customer's words, but also on the questions, inferences, and assumptions behind his words. A lazy listener—that is, someone who does not devote

> Really listening to the customer is the one competitive advantage that has lasting value. The desire to be heard and understood is universal; and a person who gives a buyer this satisfaction has laid the groundwork for a solid business relationship.
>
> — Kevin Daley[1]

her full attention to a speaker—is likely to overlook the clues that point to a customer's unspoken concerns and, therefore, fail to deliver proactive service and possibly miss an opportunity to strengthen the company's relationship with the customer. As more financial services firms strive to provide proactive service to their customers, service providers must develop their active listening skills to meet the challenge.

Many approaches and tools exist to help service providers become active listeners. In this section, we present one model for improving active listening skills as well as several additional guidelines for effective listening.

The CARESS Model

† Reprinted with the permission of Simon & Schuster Adult Publishing Group, from *Communicating at Work* by Anthony J. Alessandra and Philip L. Hunsaker. Copyright © 1993 by Anthony J. Alessandra and Philip L. Hunsaker.

The CARESS model presents six steps to help develop active listening skills.† We will briefly discuss each of these steps, which are summarized in Figure 8-3.

CONCENTRATE

People do a great deal of casual listening—for example, while watching television or chatting socially. When interacting with customers, however, service providers need to listen actively, which requires concentration and an active effort to hear the customers and to understand what they

www.grantland.net

FIGURE 8-3. Becoming an Active Listener Using the CARESS Model.

The CARESS model presents the following six steps to help you become an active listener:

C oncentrate—focus your attention entirely on the speaker.

A cknowledge—demonstrate to the speaker that you are listening.

R esearch—ask questions that will clarify or expand upon what the speaker is saying.

E xercise emotional control—deal with highly charged emotional messages in a thoughtful and poised manner.

S ense the nonverbal message—pay specific attention to the speaker's nonverbal message.

S tructure—organize the information as you receive it from the speaker.

Source: Reprinted with the permission of Simon & Schuster Adult Publishing Group, from *Communicating at Work* by Anthony J. Alessandra and Philip L. Hunsaker. Copyright © 1993 by Anthony J. Alessandra and Philip L. Hunsaker.

are saying. Your ability to concentrate will vary significantly depending on the presence of communication barriers. For example, extraneous factors such as the speaker's mannerisms or speech patterns can interfere with listening. Your personal opinion of the speaker (whether favorable or unfavorable) also can affect your ability to listen. If you cannot eliminate communication barriers, minimize them by making a conscious decision to focus on the customer's message.

ACKNOWLEDGE

Customers measure a service provider's attentiveness to the conversation by the outward signs the service provider gives that she is paying attention. When you acknowledge a customer, you let him know that you hear and understand what he is saying. For example, over the telephone, make appropriate verbal responses such as "Hmm," "Really," "Go on," and "I understand." In person, nod your head, lean forward, and maintain eye contact.

RESEARCH

In the context of listening, *research* involves asking questions and making clarifying statements to facilitate two-way communication between you and the customer. In two-way communication, the speaker and the listener constantly exchange roles. While one person talks, the other person listens. Then, the listener responds with a question or clarifying statement. Asking thoughtful questions makes customers feel that you are truly listening to what they are saying and encourages them to reveal inner motives, needs, and desires, which can help you deliver proactive service, as we discussed earlier.

EXERCISE EMOTIONAL CONTROL

Exercising emotional control allows you to understand a customer's message even if the customer is using words or a tone of voice that causes an uncomfortable emotional response in you. To exercise emotional control, you first must recognize that what you are hearing is making you feel uncomfortable. Sometimes your heart may beat faster or your face may become flushed, or you may feel a strong urge to interrupt the speaker. Once you have recognized these feelings, you can then take steps to control your response to the speaker.

Start by politely telling the speaker that you need to put her on hold or step away for just a moment. Then take a deep breath, count to 10, and imagine you are in a peaceful, relaxing place. Then return to the customer and respond without emotion in a calm, deliberate manner. Avoid taking an adversarial role, becoming defensive, or looking for a weakness to attack. Remember that your goal is not to win an argument with the customer, but to try to understand what she needs or wants from your company.

Remember that your goal is not to win an argument with the customer, but to try to understand what she needs or wants from your company.

SENSE THE NONVERBAL MESSAGE

Recall from Chapter 6 that nonverbal communication—such as tone of voice or rate of speech—can account for as much as 80 percent of a message's meaning. Take time to listen to the nonverbal signals in a customer's message—does the nonverbal message support or contradict the verbal message? By analyzing a customer's tone of voice or hesitancy in speaking, you can better understand the verbal message.

STRUCTURE

Taking mental or written notes can help service providers organize the information they receive as they actively listen. For example, when talking to a customer, jot down the main ideas, key points, and supporting points as they are presented. Then try to determine what is fact and what is assumption. You may want to clarify some information with the customer to ensure that you heard it correctly and that it is consistent with what the customer communicated. Again, ask questions if you are confused about any point.

Using the steps of the CARESS model can help you improve your listening skills and better serve your customers. To test your understanding of the CARESS concepts, complete Exercise 8-1.

Additional Guidelines for Active Listening

In addition to practicing the six steps of the CARESS model, use the following guidelines to help you focus entirely on customers' verbal and nonverbal messages.

BE A LISTENER, NOT A SPEAKER

Don't assume that you know what customers want; let them tell you.

Many people prefer to talk instead of listen, which prevents them from being active listeners. For example, most of us know someone who always finishes other people's sentences or monopolizes conversations with his own thoughts and assumptions—such a person is a speaker, not a listener. When interacting with customers, allow them to speak. Don't assume that you know what customers want; let them tell you. If you are planning how you will respond to the customer while he is still speaking, you will probably misunderstand what he is saying. If you are thinking like a *speaker* while you are listening, you can't be listening actively and completely.

AVOID INTERRUPTING WITHOUT A GOOD REASON

When customers launch into long explanations, it can be tempting to interrupt them if you think you already know what they want. After all, you might think, I can save both of us a lot of time by getting right to the point. When this temptation occurs, remember that interrupting a speaker is the same as saying, "What you're saying is not important." Actively listening to what a customer says will provide more information, cause fewer mistakes and misunderstandings, and, ultimately, save you time. It also will make customers feel that you are taking their concerns seriously.

Politely interrupting customers, however, is appropriate in certain situations. For example, if you have difficulty hearing a customer because of interference such as background noise or because her voice is too quiet or unclear, you should politely inform her of the problem as soon as possible,

Exercise 8-1.   How Well Do You Understand CARESS?

To test your understanding of the steps in the CARESS model, read the case below and answer the questions that follow.

Melissa Bradley is a customer service representative at the Do Rite Health Insurance Company. She shares an office with 11 other CSRs, each of whom works in a cubicle. In one hour, Ms. Bradley's shift will be over. She has had a long day, handling more than the usual number of customer calls. Ms. Bradley is listening to another CSR's conversation in the next cubicle when her telephone rings.

Ms. Bradley: *(voice pleasant)* This is Melissa Bradley, customer service. How may I help you?

Customer: This is Don Quintano. I have a question about a payment I received for a health claim. The claim number is 232324.

Ms. Bradley: Well, let's see. We paid you $50 for that claim. I'm looking over the calculations, and, yes, we paid you the correct amount.

Customer: *(voice becoming somewhat agitated)* How can that be the correct amount?

Ms. Bradley: *(voice still pleasant)* You see, you could receive only $50 on your claim because you hadn't fulfilled all of your deductible. Plus, the coverage for that particular procedure is based on the reasonable and customary costs in your area, which are about $150. So you see, you couldn't get any more for your claim. It's very clearly stated in your policy.

Customer: *(voice hesitant)* Oh, well, I see.

Ms. Bradley: Well, I'm glad I could explain it to you. Thank you Mr. Quintano. Call me again if you have any questions.

Questions

1. Identify some communication barriers, or *noise*, in this situation that might prevent Ms. Bradley from focusing entirely on her customer.

2. Identify some nonverbal cues that the customer used that should have made Ms. Bradley aware that she was not actively listening to her customer.

3. Think about the six steps in the CARESS model. On a piece of paper, rewrite the conversation to show how Ms. Bradley could have used active listening.

Answers

1. Hearing conversations in other cubicles; being tired from a long day
2. At various times during the conversation, Mr. Quintano spoke in an agitated and hesitant tone of voice
3. Possible rewrite of conversation (see next page):

Exercise 8-1. How Well Do You Understand CARESS (*continued*)?

Ms. Bradley: *(voice pleasant)* This is Melissa Bradley, customer service. How may I help you?

Customer: This is Don Quintano. I have a question about a payment I received for a health claim. The claim number is 232324.

Ms. Bradley: I'm looking at your claim file right now. What questions may I answer for you?

Notice how Ms. Bradley uses the research *step of the CARESS model to clarify the information that the customer needs. In the previous example, Ms. Bradley assumed that she knew what the customer needed, and, instead of asking a question, she made a statement that caused the customer to become agitated. Also, by concentrating on her telephone conversation rather than on the conversation in the next cubicle, Ms. Bradley is better able to focus on the customer.*

Customer: *(voice hesitant)* Well…I don't understand why I received only $50 when I paid the doctor $200.

Ms. Bradley: *(voice pleasant, reassuring)* Okay, let me explain how the calculation works. *(She explains the concepts of deductible and reasonable and customary charges.)* Now, does that make sense, Mr. Quintano? Do you have any questions?

Notice that Ms. Bradley again uses a research *question to ensure that she understands the customer's needs.*

Customer: *(voice hesitant)* Well, yes, I suppose it's right.

Ms. Bradley: Are you sure? I get the feeling that you still have some questions.

At this point, Ms. Bradley senses the nonverbal message. The customer's words indicate that he understands, but his hesitant tone indicates otherwise.

Customer: Well, I guess I am still a little uncertain. It sounds like you are saying that my doctor is overcharging me. You don't think he tried to cheat me, do you?

Ms. Bradley: I'm sure he's an excellent doctor, Mr. Quintano. Your insurance policy limits the amount that can be paid for that procedure, but your doctor has the right to charge whatever he feels is appropriate. Maybe the next time you plan to have a procedure done, you could check with me to find out what the reasonable and customary charges are in your area. Then, you could discuss the costs with your doctor before the procedure is done.

Customer: Okay, I think I will do that. Thank you.

even if it means interrupting. Also, you might need to interrupt a customer to ask for or confirm important facts—such as a name, account number, or specific date or dollar amount—before the customer continues talking about her problem or concern. Similarly, if you don't understand a customer, courteously interrupt her to clarify what she is saying rather than allow her to continue speaking at length about something you don't understand. Most customers will appreciate your efforts to understand them at the beginning of a conversation more than they will if you wait until the end of a long explanation to say, "I'm sorry, but I'm not following you."

You might also need to interrupt a customer who begins to dominate the conversation either by simply talking too much or by ranting about a problem he has with you, your company, or with larger issues such as the economy or government regulations. Although it's important to acknowledge an angry customer's emotions (as we will discuss later in this chapter), it is also important not to let one customer monopolize your time with unproductive chatter or tirades that keep you from doing your job helping other customers. When a customer starts to dominate the conversation in an unproductive way, you can interrupt and steer him back to the original purpose of his call, which is to resolve a problem. As always when interacting with customers, remember to acknowledge the customer's feelings and be friendly and courteous.

> Although it's important to acknowledge an angry customer's emotions...it is also important not to let one customer monopolize your time with unproductive chatter or tirades.

Ultimately, keep in mind that interruptions should not be used simply to make your job easier—they should be used only to help you better understand and meet your customers' needs.

DON'T TAKE NEGATIVE COMMENTS PERSONALLY

Customers who are upset or frustrated sometimes make negative or hurtful comments to service providers. Try not to take those comments personally, because doing so will interfere with your ability to actively listen. Remember that these customers typically are upset with the company or with the situation, and you just happen to be the person to whom they vent their frustration. Try to ignore negative comments and instead concentrate fully on the customer's message—remember, the sooner you can meet the customer's needs, the sooner the negative comments will end. We will further discuss how to effectively handle upset customers in Chapter 9.

LISTEN TO THE WHOLE MESSAGE

Messages often have more than one level of meaning. When you interact with a customer, listen to the entire content of the message, both verbal and nonverbal. Be careful not to tune out or ignore topics that don't interest you or that you think you already understand. Don't draw any conclusions or formulate solutions until the speaker has finished and you're sure you have heard and understood the total message.

For instance, suppose Blustery Bank customer Bei Liu has been having a 30-minute telephone discussion with customer service representative Edna Nix, insisting that his February account statement contained an error. Ms. Nix, who was tired and had dealt with many unhappy customers that day, listened only casually to Mr. Liu and accessed his most recent account statement, which did not contain the error he was describing, as she repeatedly told him. Eventually, Mr. Liu became so frustrated that he asked to speak to Ms. Nix's supervisor. When the supervisor spoke with Mr. Liu, she verified the date of the account statement in question and discovered that Ms. Nix had been looking at Mr. Liu's March statement instead of his February statement. The supervisor accessed the correct statement and determined that Mr. Liu had correctly identified an error in his statement. If Ms. Nix had listened carefully to Mr. Liu's entire message, she could have quickly identified the problem and avoided a lengthy and unpleasant conversation that undoubtedly left the customer feeling frustrated and questioning the reliability of Blustery Bank.

LISTEN CRITICALLY

Listening critically means that you evaluate the message when you hear it. Is the message accurate? Is it honest? Is it logical? Is it reliable? If something in a customer's message seems unclear or inconsistent, ask questions to gather more information. Use your judgment to determine whether a customer has supplied all the facts necessary for you to answer her question or fulfill her request. Customers, like the rest of us, sometimes make mistakes. Being an active listener includes evaluating the information provided and tactfully helping the speaker realize when she has made an error.

If something in a customer's message seems unclear or inconsistent, ask questions to gather more information.

For example, suppose Jacques Pradel, a CSR at Worldwide Bank, answers a call from customer Ronetta Maxwell, who is upset because she has not yet received notice of whether the loan she applied for has been approved. By listening critically, Mr. Pradel realizes that Ms. Maxwell has given him two different dates on which she applied for the loan. To tactfully clarify the facts, Mr. Pradel says, "Ms. Maxwell, I can certainly understand your frustration in not yet receiving notice of whether your loan has been approved. As we have been talking, I am jotting down notes, and I noticed that I have both May 1 and May 10 as the date you applied for the loan. Would you please clarify the date, as this will help me research your transaction?" Mr. Pradel's response demonstrates that he is listening carefully to Ms. Maxwell and allows him to point out the conflicting information without directly accusing Ms. Maxwell of making a mistake.

By correctly following these guidelines and the six steps presented in the CARESS model, you will become an active listener. Active listening tells customers that you are interested in them and in fulfilling their needs and wants, and makes possible the delivery of outstanding customer service.

Techniques to Improve Understanding

In Chapter 5 we discussed the need for financial services companies to understand their customers' expectations and perceptions. In this section, we look more closely at the need to understand what customers are saying.

Two commonly used and effective techniques for better understanding a customer's message are paraphrasing and questioning.

Even when you actively listen to a customer, you must make sure that what you heard is what the customer meant. As you listen, think about the message the customer is sending, including both the verbal and non-verbal parts of the message. Financial services products and services are often complex, and customers do not always communicate clearly, so sometimes you must probe further to determine exactly what a customer needs. Two commonly used and effective techniques for better understanding a customer's message are paraphrasing and questioning.

Paraphrasing

Paraphrasing is the process of stating, in your own words, your understanding of another person's position, proposition, or request. By restating what you think another person has said, you give the speaker an opportunity to verify that you correctly understand the message. If you assume that you understand what a customer is talking about without verifying your assumptions, communication problems can occur easily.

Service providers can paraphrase a customer's message in many ways, including paraphrasing only a part of it or summarizing the entire message. The following guidelines can help you understand how to paraphrase:

- Give a brief summary of the entire message in your own words. Summarize a long or complex message to show that you understand how the entire message fits together.

- Don't add any information that the customer did not include.

- Be positive and nonthreatening. Make sure your voice does not sound sarcastic or arrogant.

- Tactfully point out any contradictory parts of the message.

- Repeat important information such as telephone numbers or the spelling of a name.

Repeating some of a customer's words is called content reflection.

- Use clarifying sentences such as "Did I understand you to say that..." and then repeat some of the customer's message. Repeating some of a customer's words is called **content reflection**. You can use this kind of paraphrasing to show you are interested in hearing more about a specific part of a customer's message, to verify that you heard the words correctly, or to encourage the customer to continue speaking by showing that you are listening.

- Summarize the emotional content of the message by acknowledging that you understand the customer is upset or angry. For example, you could say, "I'm sure it's very frustrating to have several forms to fill out." Acknowledging a customer's feelings can help you establish a rapport with her and give her the opportunity to see her feelings objectively, which can be very helpful in tense situations. The process of paraphrasing someone's emotions is called a **reflection of feelings.**

The process of paraphrasing someone's emotions is called a reflection of feelings.

- Make your paraphrase tentative, and ask the customer whether you have understood correctly. This lets the customer know that you're interpreting the message as well as you can, and you realize you could be mistaken. You can make a paraphrase tentative by using a questioning tone of voice or by using a phrase like "As I understand you," or "Is that correct?" Making your paraphrase tentative makes it more likely that the customer will feel comfortable correcting any errors in the paraphrase.

Figure 8-4 provides examples of various ways to paraphrase a customer's message.

Questioning

In the context of listening and understanding, **questioning** is the practice of asking a speaker questions designed to initiate or direct a conversation, clarify information, or probe for details. Like paraphrasing, questioning

FIGURE 8-4. How to Paraphrase a Customer's Message.

The following situation is an example of how a service provider might paraphrase a customer's message.

Customer: "Hello, my name is Ronald Tanner, and my account number is 33199-03. I hope you can help me. I mailed my loan payment about two weeks ago, and now I've received a notice from your company that my payment hasn't been received and that I'm going to be charged additional interest and a late-payment fee. I think it is unfair to charge me a late fee when I mailed my payment on time".

Possible Paraphrases:

"Let me be sure I understand what you've said. You mailed your payment on November 15, and now, two weeks later, you've received a notice of nonpayment?"

"So, you mailed your payment on November 15, and today received a notice of nonpayment. Is that correct?"

Notice that, in both paraphrases, the service provider summarizes the facts of the message briefly, in his own words, and makes the paraphrase tentative by using phrases that invite the customer to correct or clarify inaccurate information. At this point, the customer can respond to the service provider's paraphrase with clarifying statements, such as

"Well, actually I think it was more like November 20 when I mailed the check."

Notice that the service provider has tactfully led the customer to provide information that is more precise and accurate than his initial statement. The additional information gathered from paraphrasing will help him provide the customer with faster and more efficient service.

helps service providers verify their understanding of a customer's message. And, as we discussed earlier in this chapter, asking appropriate questions can elicit information that helps a service provider identify—and therefore satisfy—his customers' real needs.

OPEN AND CLOSED QUESTIONS

There are basically two types of questions: closed questions and open questions. A **closed question** is a specific inquiry that can usually be answered with "yes," "no," or a short factual statement. Because closed questions limit the range of possible answers, they are appropriate when you want

Closed questions keep a conversation brief and are easy for your customers to understand.

specific information from a customer. Closed questions keep a conversation brief and are easy for your customers to understand. Examples of closed questions include

"What is your account number?"

"When did you transfer the funds?"

"How much money would you like to borrow?"

"Have you been pleased with the performance of your account?"

"Did you cancel your previous policy?"

An **open question** is a broad and general inquiry that cannot be answered appropriately in one or just a few words. Open questions often ask for opinions, thoughts, or feelings. Open questions allow the respondent a great deal of flexibility in choosing what to say, so they are appropriate when you want a customer to elaborate on or express his feelings about a particular topic. Examples of open questions include

Open questions allow the respondent a great deal of flexibility in choosing what to say.

"What has your financial planner told you about this product?"

"Why did you choose to invest with us instead of with another company?"

"How did you hear about our new product?"

"How do you feel about the service you have received in the past?"

"What else can I do for you today?"

Exercise 8-2 tests how well you can identify open and closed questions.

QUESTION SEQUENCES

Effective questioning requires asking the appropriate type of question at the appropriate time. Therefore, before you begin asking questions, you need to know what information you want to obtain and the best way to obtain it. Often, the customer's personality, wants, and needs determine which types of questions you should use and in what order. For example:

- When speaking with a very talkative customer, you might need to focus the conversation by asking only closed questions.

- A quiet, withdrawn customer might respond better at first to closed questions that ask for specific, narrow responses. After using closed questions to begin the conversation, you could shift to open questions to find out more about what the customer needs.

Exercise 8-2. Identifying Open and Closed Questions.

Section A. First, determine whether each of the following two questions is an open question or a closed question. Then, choose the question that would be most appropriate for determining a customer's opinion about using electronic funds transfer (EFT).

1. Would you like to use electronic funds transfer to pay your bill?

2. How do you feel about using electronic funds transfer to pay your bill?

Section B. Identify which of the following questions are examples of an open question and which are examples of a closed question.

1. _____ Can we interest you in any of our other products?

2. _____ What is your phone number?

3. _____ What do you think about the new commission payment schedule?

4. _____ What would you change about the service we provide?

5. _____ On what date did you submit the form?

6. _____ Why do you want to close your account?

Answers:

Section A.

1. Closed question

2. Open question. This question would be most appropriate for finding out what a customer thinks about electronic funds transfer because it allows you to check the customer's understanding of EFT and gives you an opportunity to clear up any misconceptions the customer may have about that form of payment.

Section B.

1. Closed

2. Closed

3. Open

4. Open

5. Closed

6. Open

■ An upset or dissatisfied customer might respond best to general, open questions at first. Then, after the customer has expressed her feelings and calmed down, you could use more closed questions to narrow your search for answers to the problem.

Two basic questioning strategies are (1) the funnel technique and (2) the inverted funnel technique. The *funnel technique* is a questioning strategy in which the person asking questions moves from general to specific questions, beginning with broad, open questions and progressing to narrow, closed questions. The broad questions help build the customer's trust. Such questions often begin with "Tell me about…" or "How do you feel…" Then, the service provider asks increasingly narrow questions to help customers focus concerns and reach a resolution. Figure 8-5 illustrates how to use the funnel technique.

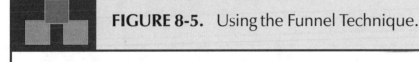

FIGURE 8-5. Using the Funnel Technique.

"What happened to make you unhappy with our product?"
(Very open question. Lengthy answer is probably expected.)

"What happened when you called our company and reported the problem?"
(Open question. More specific answer expected, but answer still likely to be fairly broad.)

"Did you think that your problem was being taken care of at that point?"
(More narrow open question. Even more specific answer expected; customer could respond in as little as one sentence.)

"Has your problem been resolved?"
(Closed question. Yes or no answer is expected.)

The ***inverted funnel technique*** is a questioning strategy in which the person asking questions moves from specific to general questions, starting with closed questions and progressing to open questions. A service provider can use the inverted funnel technique, which reverses the order of the funnel technique, to help a customer move from a specific problem to a much broader one. This questioning sequence helps the customer gradually become more comfortable sharing information. Figure 8-6 illustrates the inverted funnel technique.

NEUTRAL AND LEADING QUESTIONS

As a service provider, your job requires you to gather accurate, objective information that you can use to appropriately help customers. You can obtain such information by asking neutral questions. A ***neutral question*** is an inquiry that has no bias and does not imply a correct answer. Instead, a neutral question encourages the respondent to give whatever

FIGURE 8-6. Using the Inverted Funnel Technique.

"Are you having difficulty understanding the provisions of your contract?"
(Closed question. A yes or no answer is expected.)

"Which sections of your contract seem to be the most confusing?"
(Closed question. Very specific, factual information is expected.)

"What about these sections makes them confusing?"
(Open question. Less specific answer is expected, but the response could be fairly broad.)

"How could we change our contracts so that they were less confusing?"
(Very open question. Broad, extensive answer is probably expected.)

answer is most accurate. For example, the following questions are neutral questions that ask for objective information:

"Have you ever applied for a loan with us before?"

"How would you like us to contact you in the future?"

In contrast, leading questions generally do *not* help service providers obtain objective information and therefore should be used sparingly in a customer service situation. A **leading question** is an inquiry that is phrased in a way that encourages the respondent to give a particular answer. Leading questions are designed to provide the person asking the question with the answer that will support his position, whatever that position may be. For instance, the following questions are examples of leading questions:

"You haven't ever applied for a loan with us before, have you?"

"Wouldn't you prefer for us to contact you by e-mail?"

Although most customer service situations require a service provider to ask neutral questions, asking leading questions is appropriate in some situations. For instance, leading questions can sometimes help service providers quickly assess a customer's situation. After reviewing a customer's records, for example, a service provider might ask questions such as, "You don't normally send payments through the mail, do you?" or "You have never accessed your account on our Web site, have you?" to verify that the service provider correctly understands the customer's situation.

Although asking leading questions is sometimes helpful when talking with customers, service providers generally should strive to ask neutral questions, which elicit the kind of objective, factual information that is most helpful in determining customers' needs and wants and determining the best possible way to satisfy them.

As we have seen, listening to customers and understanding their real messages requires skill and effort. Most of us can improve our ability to listen and understand by studying the guidelines and practicing the techniques presented in this chapter. Of course, listening and understanding are only part of a service provider's role when interacting with customers—the next step is learning how to respond effectively to customers, which we will discuss in the next chapter.

To practice and review the skills and information you learned in this chapter, see the interactive CD, *Practicing Your Customer Service Skills*, included with this book.

Key Terms

perceptual error   content reflection
selective perception   reflection of feelings
attribution   questioning
attributional bias   closed question
fundamental attribution error   open question
projection   funnel technique
stereotyping   inverted funnel technique
active listening   neutral question
paraphrasing   leading question

Endnote

1. "Customer Dialogue," *Executive Excellence* (February 1996): 5.

Interacting with Customers

After studying this chapter, you should be able to

- Discuss the guidelines you can use to provide effective explanation

- Discuss the importance of credibility and logical reasoning in using persuasion

- Identify and describe the steps in the negotiation process

- Use explanation, persuasion, and negotiation in your customer service activities

- Understand why customers become upset

- Describe the steps service providers can take when working with upset customers

I n the last chapter, you learned how to use active listening, paraphrasing, and questioning to understand a customer's request or situation. The next step in providing customer service is responding to the customer. Simple requests—such as changes of address—require simple, straightforward responses. When the customer's request is more complicated, however, the response may be more involved. If a customer calls to complain about a service problem, you must address the customer's concerns. Moreover, if the customer is upset, you must work to calm the customer and instill confidence in you and your company. Before responding, you might ask yourself, "What is the overall goal of this interaction? What do the customer and I hope to achieve?" Then, as you proceed, keep this goal in mind.

In this chapter, we will discuss explanation, persuasion, and negotiation in customer service. We also will consider why customers become upset, and we will describe conflict and conflict management. Finally, we will present some guidelines to help you deal with upset customers.

Responding to Customers

When a customer asks a question or makes a request that cannot be addressed with a simple answer or action, then a service provider's response often involves some form or combination of explanation, persuasion, or negotiation.

Explanation

An *explanation* is a factual description of how things work or why certain actions are taken. An explanation presents facts without any attempt by the speaker to influence the listener. For example, explaining a loan application review procedure is not an attempt to sell a customer on the appropriateness of the company's processes, but simply to describe how the procedure works.

HOW TO USE EXPLANATION EFFECTIVELY

Explanations are more effective if you follow the guidelines shown in Figure 9-1 and described in the following paragraphs.

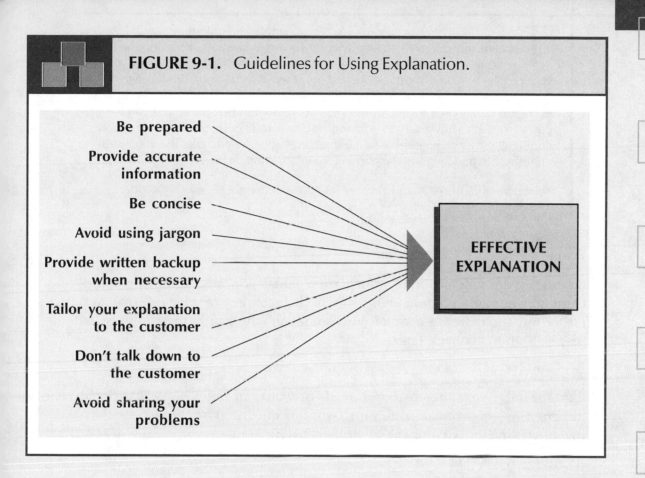

FIGURE 9-1. Guidelines for Using Explanation.

Be prepared

Provide accurate information

Be concise

Avoid using jargon

Provide written backup when necessary

Tailor your explanation to the customer

Don't talk down to the customer

Avoid sharing your problems

EFFECTIVE EXPLANATION

Be Prepared

When customers contact your company, they expect to deal with someone who is knowledgeable about financial services in general and about your company's products and services in particular. Several of the suggestions discussed in earlier chapters will improve your explanations. For example, you can take advantage of training and education opportunities at your company; you can gather information about topics that customers frequently ask questions about; you can have reference material available; and you can become proficient at using computer-based information sharing tools. Exercise 9-1 describes one way to gather and use information to assist you and your coworkers in providing answers to frequently asked questions (FAQs).

Exercise 9-1.   Preparing for Frequently Asked Questions.

Take responsibility for keeping your Frequently Asked Questions (FAQ) file updated. You can even involve your coworkers in this task by asking them to write down questions posed by customers—in the customers' own words. Periodically compile all the questions and send them to your coworkers through your company e-mail system, asking everyone to submit answers. You'll help strengthen everyone's ability to provide answers to these common questions, and you'll discover clues as to how everyone can improve their level of personal service. If your company uses a computer-based information sharing system, take the initiative to contribute to updating and maintaining the information on file.

Source: JoAnna F. Brandi, *Building Customer Loyalty: The 21 Essential Elements…IN ACTION* (Dallas: Walk the Talk Company, 2001), 23.

Provide Accurate Information

Be sure to provide accurate information when you are explaining something to a customer. If you aren't sure of the accuracy of your information, either put the caller in contact with someone who can help or offer to do research and call back later.

Be Concise

Explain only what the customer needs or wants to know. Any additional information might raise irrelevant issues or questions without contributing to the overall goal of the customer interaction.

Avoid Using Jargon

Unless you are certain that the person you are talking to understands the jargon used in your department or business, avoid using jargon. Keep your language simple. Use everyday, conversational words.

Provide Written Back-Up

If an explanation is complex, the spoken word may not be the best medium. Offer to send the customer a detailed explanation by mail, e-mail, or fax.

Tailor Your Explanation to the Customer

As noted in Exercise 9-1, service providers often receive similar questions from many customers. Although standard explanations provide an efficient way to deal with such requests, you should be careful not to let these explanations become so automatic that you forget about the customer. All customers are not alike. While a standard explanation may work in many cases, it may not work for everyone. Be aware of each customer's situation and needs.

Don't Talk Down to the Customer

Not all customers have an in-depth understanding of financial services products, and they are not likely to be familiar with the procedures your company follows. Just as you might need help understanding what is wrong with your car or your personal computer, your customers often rely on your expertise and communication skills to help them understand financial services products and procedures. They do not appreciate being lectured to, belittled, or talked down to, so keep your explanations simple, friendly, and objective.

Avoid Sharing Your Problems

Avoid sharing your problems or the company's problems with customers. For instance, it would be unprofessional to say something like, "You'll have to call back tomorrow, because our resident expert is out today, and nobody else knows how to handle your request." Also, avoid expressing negative opinions about company systems or practices. For example, don't say, "I'm sorry, but I can't get you that information because our system is down again. Can you believe it? This is the third time in less than a month." Responses like these give customers a poor impression of your company's ability to provide customer service. Instead, you should apologize for the inconvenience without explaining the reasons.

Persuasion

Service providers sometimes must use persuasion when interacting with customers. **Persuasion** is an intentional verbal attempt to influence the attitude or behavior of others. For example, suppose you are a CSR at a financial services company and a customer calls and demands that you change the beneficiary designation on his pension plan. Rather than complete and mail the necessary form, he wants to handle the transaction over the telephone—a practice your company does not allow. In this situation, instead of insisting that the form be completed, you will need to explain to the customer the reasons behind your company's position on beneficiary changes and persuade him to follow the applicable procedure.

In addition, service providers sometimes rely on persuasion when interacting with coworkers. Suppose, for example, that you receive a telephone call from a customer who intended to withdraw $1,000 from her

While a standard explanation may work in many cases, it may not work for everyone. Be aware of each customer's situation and needs.

individual retirement account, but received a check for only $100, and she needs the money as soon as possible. Although your company's typical processing time for fund disbursements is three to five business days, you must persuade the disbursement unit to process this transaction immediately, so that the check can be sent to the customer via overnight mail.

A customer service representative who is not a licensed sales agent should not attempt to advise or persuade customers.

When using persuasion, you must be aware of regulatory requirements or prohibitions that apply to customer interactions. For instance, in the United States, only licensed representatives are permitted to provide financial advice to customers. Therefore, a customer service representative who is not a licensed sales agent should not attempt to advise or persuade customers. A statement such as, "I suggest you convert your term insurance to a permanent life policy" could result in legal or regulatory problems if the customer follows the advice and is unhappy with the outcome. Instead, a CSR can discuss in general terms the advantages and disadvantages of each type of insurance and then provide the customer with the name and telephone number of a licensed agent.

Some people react negatively to the word *persuasion*, perhaps because they incorrectly associate it with coercion. **Coercion** is an attempt to convince others to do something they really don't want to do. However, persuasion is not coercion; it is merely a way of encouraging others to think in a certain direction. Your ability to persuade others will improve if you have personal credibility and you use logical reasoning to support your position.

PERSONAL CREDIBILITY

Credibility exists when what a person says or does can be believed. If you have personal credibility, your customers will trust you and have confidence in your words and actions.

Most customers want to believe what you say. Customers like to think they are dealing with people and companies they can trust. However, if you appear unreliable to a customer just one time, you risk damaging your own credibility and the company's credibility with that customer. As Figure 9-2 illustrates, personal credibility comes from competence, intention, personal impression, character, and association.

Competence

Competence is a person's knowledge and ability. If you have a thorough knowledge of financial services, completely understand your company's

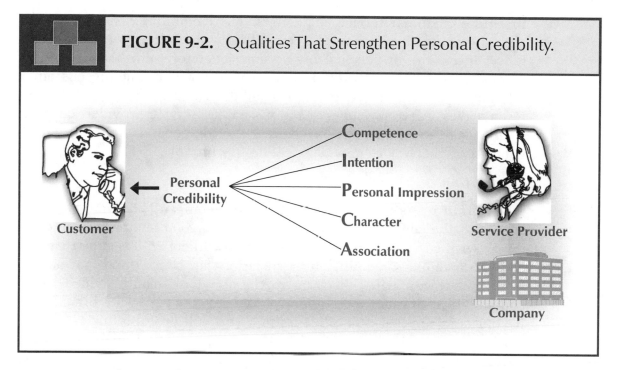

FIGURE 9-2. Qualities That Strengthen Personal Credibility.

products and services, and know how to work through your company's administrative systems quickly and effectively, you will be perceived as being competent, and thus more credible.

Intention

Intention is a person's apparent motive. If you demonstrate to customers that you are doing your job with their needs in mind and that your motives are in their best interests, they will tend to appreciate your effort, and be more likely to trust you.

Personal Impression

Personal impression is the image a person presents to others. Personal impression is determined in part by appearance: your personal grooming and clothing, and your office environment. Over the telephone, your attitude, tone of voice, and degree of organization also contribute to the personal impression you create. By presenting yourself as organized, pleasant, concerned, and helpful, you create a positive, professional impression, and thus are more credible to your customers.

Character

Character refers to a person's integrity and principles. Such traits are complex and difficult to judge, so they may not be apparent during brief or

By presenting yourself as organized, pleasant, concerned, and helpful, you create a positive, professional impression, and are more credible to your customers.

first-time customer service encounters. The credibility that comes with character takes more time to achieve than credibility through competence, intention, or personal impression. Therefore, character often becomes important for service providers who develop ongoing customer relationships, such as intermediaries and dedicated customer service representatives. After several interactions with a service provider, customers may start to form an opinion about the person's character. If the opinion is positive, the service provider's credibility improves.

Association

Association refers to the reputation of your company and your relationship with the company. If your company has a good reputation and credibility with customers, those customers most likely will assume that you also are credible. Credibility by association can be an important advantage—but if you fail to perform to the standards established by your company's reputation, you could lose that advantage. On the other hand, if your company has a poor reputation, you will probably have to work harder on the other qualities that strengthen personal credibility with customers. Regardless of your company's current reputation, your actions play an important part in shaping that reputation. Customers base their opinions of a company largely on their interactions with employees. To the customer, employees are the company. How you treat the customer can either reinforce or damage the image that your company strives to develop and maintain.

Customers base their opinions of a company largely on their interactions with employees.

LOGICAL REASONING

In addition to personal credibility, you can persuade customers by using logical reasoning. You use logical reasoning when you present justification for a suggested plan or action, demonstrating or proving why it is in the customer's best interest to do something or agree to something. To be effective, logical reasoning must come from the customer's point of view. Begin by asking yourself, "What benefit will the customer obtain or what harm will the customer avoid by agreeing with me?" The answer to this question will be the basis for your logical reasoning. Logical reasoning should be valid and supportable, and it should make an impact.

A *valid argument* is one in which the reasons given are true, and the conclusion is a logical extension of those reasons. For example, suppose you are a CSR at an insurance company and a customer, Eli Crocker, informs you that he wants to cancel his individual health insurance policy and purchase a less expensive policy from a company with which you are familiar. You want to convince Mr. Crocker that keeping his current policy is in his best interest. To persuade him, you could explain how the other company sometimes offers a low rate for the first year of coverage and then increases the rate sharply the second year. You also could stress the excellent customer service your company provides and the long-term nature of your company's relationship with Mr. Crocker.

To strengthen a valid argument, you should provide evidence to support it. For instance, in the previous example, you could offer to send Mr. Crocker independent data to illustrate how the rates of your competitor's policies have increased substantially in the second year. Or, you could offer to send him a copy of a magazine article about a customer service award your company recently won. This information provides the supporting evidence that might persuade the customer to agree with your position.

Finally, your reasons should have an impact on the person you are trying to persuade. Suppose that to keep Mr. Crocker's business, you point out that the policy he owns is your company's best-selling product. This information probably means little to him. Your attempt at persuasion would work better if you explain that the policy is your company's best-selling product because it offers customers more benefits for the price than comparable policies. When using logical reasoning, always consider the impact, because it makes you think about the customer's needs and requires you to look at the situation from the customer's point of view.

Negotiation

Through *negotiation*, you try to find a solution that is acceptable to both parties.

Negotiation is the process of reaching a mutually acceptable solution in the event of a disagreement or a conflict of interest. Although closely related to persuasion, negotiation goes a step further. Through *persuasion*, you try to convince someone to accept a certain position; through *negotiation*, you try to find a solution that is acceptable to both parties. When negotiating, you might use persuasion to convince a customer of your position, but you engage in negotiation because you have concluded that the other party is not going to accept your position completely.

In negotiation, you are usually willing to give up something to get something in return. The ultimate aim of negotiation in customer service is a *win/win outcome*—that is, both parties feel that they have gained something worthwhile from the negotiation, as Figure 9-3 illustrates.

FIGURE 9-3. A Win-Win Negotiation.

Consider the following exchange between an intermediary and a customer service representative.

Intermediary ▶ I need that commission accounting report right away.

CSR ▶ I understand that you need this information, but the commission accounting reports will not be ready for another week.

Intermediary ▶ I can't wait another week. I'm going on a cruise in two days, and I won't be back for a month.

CSR ▶ Would it be OK if we just get you the numbers but not the quarterly report?

Intermediary ▶ What do you mean?

CSR ▶ The quarterly commission accounting report won't be available until next week, but I might be able to obtain the information another way. I could call accounting and see if they could pull your numbers for me. Then I could give you the numbers over the telephone or send them to you via e-mail. Does that sound acceptable?

Intermediary ▶ Sure. That would work. Just as long as I get the information I need.

In this negotiation, the customer is willing to accept information over the telephone or in an e-mail message rather than in a formal quarterly report, while the CSR is willing to attempt to bypass regular procedures to help the intermediary get the information he wants. The CSR then might have to use persuasion to convince a coworker in accounting to provide the necessary information to satisfy this intermediary who is an important customer.

Sometimes, negotiation takes on adversarial qualities, and you may feel that you have to "win" the argument. If you come out of a negotiation feeling that you "beat" the customer, then, in the long run, you and your company have probably lost, because the customer will be less likely to continue doing business with your company, and probably will tell others about the incident. As the saying goes, "You can't win an argument with a customer."

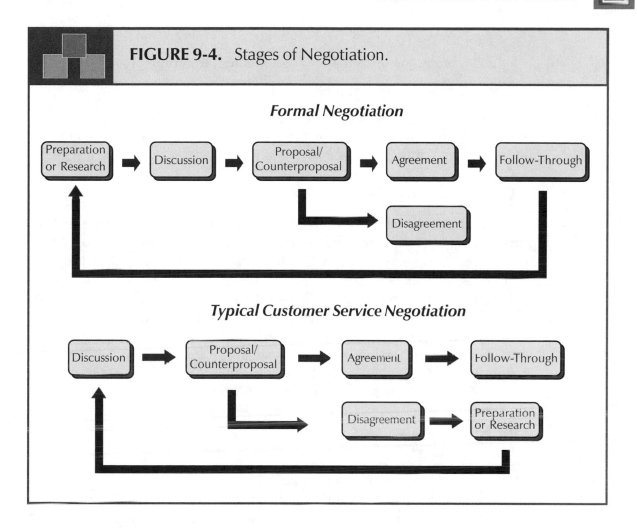

FIGURE 9-4. Stages of Negotiation.

In many business situations, formal negotiation consists of five stages: preparation or research, discussion, proposal/counterproposal, agreement/ disagreement, and follow-through. Ideally, both parties have time to gather information and prepare for the negotiation; however, in customer service, negotiations often develop spontaneously, and the service provider has no time to prepare. Consequently, negotiations in customer service often begin at the discussion stage. For this reason, we will describe preparation and research at a later stage in the negotiation process. Figure 9-4 depicts the stages of negotiation.

DISCUSSION

The discussion stage is the fact-finding portion of negotiation. You and the customer discuss the facts and the customer's feelings about the situation. Discussion allows each person to see the situation from the other person's point of view. It gives each of you the opportunity to state your position, including information such as

- Needs

- Limitations that might make agreement to certain proposals difficult

- Grievances regarding the situation

Try to keep the discussion as objective as possible. As the service provider, you are responsible for setting the tone of the interaction so that the negotiation begins and proceeds with a good chance of success.

PROPOSAL/COUNTERPROPOSAL

After each person has had a chance to state his point of view, the next stage of negotiation is proposal/counterproposal. One person proposes how to resolve the situation, and the other person responds with a proposal stating his preference. These proposals and counterproposals can go back and forth, usually modified slightly each time through give and take, or tradeoff, until a proposal is offered that both parties can agree to—or until both parties decide they cannot agree (see Agreement/Disagreement). During the proposal/counterproposal stage, you try to address the customer's **underlying needs**—the needs on which a person's stated needs are based—and ideally, the customer tries to understand the reasons for your company's position. You and the customer also might explain any constraints you are facing.

During the proposal/counter-proposal stage, you try to address the customer's **underlying needs**—the needs on which a person's stated needs are based.

AGREEMENT/DISAGREEMENT

The next stage in negotiation is agreement/disagreement. The negotiation in Figure 9-3 ended in agreement when the intermediary accepted the CSR's counterproposal. Unfortunately, not all negotiations end in resolution. Sometimes the negotiators need to go back to the discussion stage. Maybe something in the stated positions, such as an underlying need or a constraint, was not mentioned or clearly stated in the discussion. The parties may even need to go to the preparation stage (see Preparation or Research). Suppose, for example, that you receive a telephone request that requires negotiation. You don't have time to prepare, and you soon realize that the negotiation is failing to produce a win-win outcome. You might say to the customer, "If you don't mind, I'd like to research this problem and call you back tomorrow. Maybe I can find a solution that we haven't thought of."

Because service providers sometimes have to reconcile customer requests with company policy or regulatory requirements, they must recognize when compromise is or is not appropriate. Sometimes, after examining all possible solutions, you may have no choice but to say something the customer does not want to hear. However, before you say no to a customer, you should make sure the answer really is no. If it is, then you must tactfully decline the customer's request.

Some people find it easier to say no to a customer if they think of their response as providing information the customer needs. Make sure you understand and are able to explain the reasons behind your position. Be prepared to listen to the customer's feedback and to respond tactfully.

Also, when saying no, try to present alternatives or offer to assist the customer in any way possible. Suppose you are a CSR at a bank and a customer, Sam Hamilton, asks you to remove a late fee that appears on his monthly mortgage statement because he forgot to mail his payment on time. You might respond by saying, "I'm very sorry, Mr. Hamilton, but because your payment arrived 19 days late, I cannot remove the late charge. However, I'd be happy to work with you to prevent something like this from happening in the future. Would you like to look into our online or pay-by-phone options? Or would you be interested in having your mortgage payments automatically drawn from your checking account?"

PREPARATION OR RESEARCH

The preparation or research stage is normally the first stage in formal negotiation. However, because of the spontaneous nature of many customer service situations, you don't always have the opportunity to prepare first. Research sometimes comes later in customer service negotiations, after the discussion, proposal/counterproposal, and agreement/disagreement stages. The preparation stage gives you time to look for possible solutions. This might mean looking through databases, contracts, or procedural manuals; it might mean talking with a supervisor or a subject expert; or it might mean brainstorming with other team members. When you have gathered relevant information and decided on an approach, you can call the customer back and resume the negotiation.

FOLLOW-THROUGH

Never commit to something that you know you cannot deliver.

Follow-through means taking the action you agreed to take during the negotiation or, in some cases, making sure that another person or area takes the agreed upon action. While follow-through is not technically a part of negotiation, you need to keep follow-through in mind during the negotiation process. *Never commit to something that you know you cannot deliver.* Avoid committing to something that you may have trouble accomplishing. Some people say that in negotiation, you should always

If you think you can have something for a customer by the end of the day, but you're sure you can have it by noon tomorrow, commit to noon tomorrow. Then, if you're able to have it by the end of the day, your customer will be ecstatic that you performed even better than promised.

— Mark Sanborn[1]

"under-promise" and "over-deliver." If you do what you agreed to do—and more—you are likely to gain your customer's trust.

ADDITIONAL GUIDELINES FOR NEGOTIATING

Following are some additional guidelines to keep in mind when you negotiate with a customer:

- **Identify common goals.** Find goals that are common to you and your customer, and build your negotiation around these goals.

- **Be open and honest.** Present your position as clearly and completely as possible.

- **Control your emotions.** No matter how frustrating the negotiation may be, remain calm. If your customer becomes emotional, focus the discussion on the goals of the negotiation and their importance.

Working with Upset Customers

Suppose you pick up the telephone and hear, "You people can't do anything right!" or "I've tried three times, and I still can't get an answer to a simple question!" It happens sometimes. Working with upset customers is one of the greatest challenges you face as a service provider. However, when handled properly, these situations also give you opportunities to retain and develop loyal, satisfied customers.

Customers get upset for a variety of reasons. Sometimes, the reasons have nothing to do with you or your company—for instance, a customer may be having personal problems or a bad day at work. Other times, a customer may be distressed by financial woes or by the illness or death of a family member. In fact, because you work in the financial services industry, the chances are that you will interact at times with customers who are upset by situational factors like these.

On the other hand, a customer may be unhappy with your company in general or angry about something you or another employee said, did, or neglected to do. Maybe the caller has been holding for 20 minutes after first being transferred to the wrong department and then being disconnected—and the reason he called was that your company made an error!

"I'm in a bit of a hurry, so I'd like to skip the explanation, persuasion, and negotiation, and go straight to the part where I get upset, if that's okay with you."

Often, customers are upset because of unmet expectations. Recall from Chapter 5 that customers come to you with certain expectations about the quality of your company's products and services based on personal needs and experience. Customers may be upset because they are unhappy with a product or because they received service that was slow, inaccurate, indifferent, or discourteous.

Regardless of the reasons behind the customer's unhappiness, you can address the situation by taking the following four steps:

1. Recognize the customer's feelings

2. Empathize and apologize for the inconvenience

3. Determine the facts of the situation

4. Find an appropriate solution

Recognize the Customer's Feelings

Whatever the reasons for a customer's unsettled emotional state, you and the customer need to deal with the emotions before you can conduct business effectively. Sometimes, when confronted by an angry customer, service providers react emotionally or become angry with the company for putting them in an unpleasant situation. Always remember that you are a professional, and you should try to maintain a professional attitude. In most situations, the customer does not know you, is not angry with you personally, and is upset about something else. One way to improve your ability to remain composed during difficult customer interactions is to study your behavior in these kinds of situations, as suggested in Exercise 9-2.

Exercise 9-2.   Learning to Keep Your Composure.

Try keeping a log of customer interactions that make you upset or angry. Write down what the customer said and how it made you feel. Write down how you responded and how that made you feel. Try to determine why you had difficulty with the interaction. Review your log and determine how you could have handled the situation better and prevented an emotional reaction. Ask a supervisor or coworker who is effective in dealing with these types of situations for input and advice on keeping your composure with difficult customers.

Source: Adapted from LOMA, *ASR On-the-Job Activities* (Atlanta: LOMA, © 1993), 5. Used with permission; all rights reserved.

When a customer is upset, in addition to calming yourself, you should try to calm the customer before attempting to proceed. Use the "feelings first, facts second" model, introduced in Chapter 5, to allow the customer to express his feelings. Sometimes a customer just needs time to vent, and your best option is to be quiet and listen. Never say, "You need to calm down." Even if the customer *does* need to calm down, your telling him to do so could make matters worse. And in many cases, the customer may need to express his frustration before being able to proceed with the conversation.

You can't foster an objective atmosphere for logical problem solving until your customer is calm. Therefore, as you learned in Chapter 8, avoid interrupting the customer without reason—even if you've heard a similar complaint many times before or you know you can resolve the customer's problem quickly. Resist the temptation to explain, defend, or debate. Remember, the customer may not always be right, but always has the right to complain and the right to be wrong with dignity. This does not mean, however, that you must tolerate rude or abusive language or behavior. Later in this chapter, we will discuss working with difficult customers.

Empathize and Apologize

Empathy, as you saw in Chapter 3, is the process of understanding another person's emotional state and imagining how you would feel in a similar situation. Empathizing with customers lets them know that you care about their needs. It involves *listening* to their concerns and *responding* in ways that show you recognize their feelings. To foster

When dealing with people, remember you are not dealing with creatures of logic, but creatures of emotion.

— Dale Carnegie[2]

empathy, some companies hold periodic training sessions, using role-playing exercises. In these exercises, one person plays the role of the service provider and another plays the role of the customer. In some scenarios, the service provider shows empathy, and in other scenarios, the service provider does not. The person playing the role of the customer is then able to experience the difference that empathy can make in a customer service interaction.

The following guidelines might help you listen and respond with empathy.

- Listen carefully to the words that the customer uses so you can understand the verbal message.

- Listen carefully to the customer's tone of voice and compare that tone to the verbal message. Listen for clues that might indicate the customer's emotional state. Does the tone of voice confirm or contradict the verbal message?

- Think about the situation that the customer is in, then think back on your own experience. If you have been in a similar situation, use your experience to help you appreciate the customer's situation. If you haven't been in a similar situation, imagine how you would respond if you were in the customer's situation.

- Show your empathy. For example, you can say something like, "I can imagine how you feel," or "I appreciate the situation you are in." Try to make your tone of voice convey warmth and interest in the customer.

Your response should include an apology for the difficulty the customer is having. Even if you and the company are in no way responsible for the customer's problem, the customer is still upset. You can always honestly say, "I'm sorry that you are so upset." If the company is in some way responsible, apologize, but resist the tendency to blame company systems or processes or other departments or employees. Simply apologize and move on. Figure 9-5 presents a hypothetical telephone call from an upset customer and shows how a service provider might use empathy to listen and respond.

Do not identify so strongly with your customer's feelings that you lose sight of your role as a service provider.

Determine the Facts

Although empathizing with customers is important, remember that empathy also has to be objective, so you must continue thinking clearly to analyze the situation. Do not identify so strongly with your customer's feelings

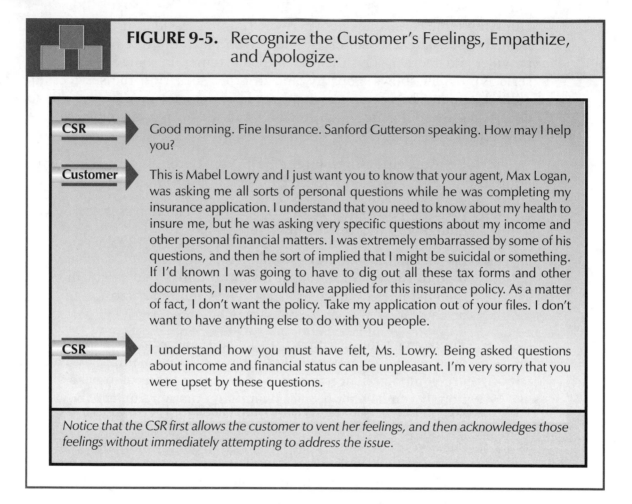

FIGURE 9-5. Recognize the Customer's Feelings, Empathize, and Apologize.

CSR   Good morning. Fine Insurance. Sanford Gutterson speaking. How may I help you?

Customer   This is Mabel Lowry and I just want you to know that your agent, Max Logan, was asking me all sorts of personal questions while he was completing my insurance application. I understand that you need to know about my health to insure me, but he was asking very specific questions about my income and other personal financial matters. I was extremely embarrassed by some of his questions, and then he sort of implied that I might be suicidal or something. If I'd known I was going to have to dig out all these tax forms and other documents, I never would have applied for this insurance policy. As a matter of fact, I don't want the policy. Take my application out of your files. I don't want to have anything else to do with you people.

CSR   I understand how you must have felt, Ms. Lowry. Being asked questions about income and financial status can be unpleasant. I'm very sorry that you were upset by these questions.

Notice that the CSR first allows the customer to vent her feelings, and then acknowledges those feelings without immediately attempting to address the issue.

that you lose sight of your role as a service provider. Avoid relating stories about similar experiences that you have had. Empathize, but remain objective, because after dealing with the customer's feelings, you need to determine the facts. One of the most effective ways to determine facts is by using the paraphrasing and questioning techniques presented in Chapter 8. Figure 9-6 continues the scenario introduced in Figure 9-5 and shows how the service provider might proceed to make sure he understands all the facts of the situation by paraphrasing and questioning.

Find an Appropriate Solution

Once you have confirmed your understanding of the facts, you can thank the customer for providing the information. For instance, you might say, "Thank you for pointing this out to me." Then you should address the

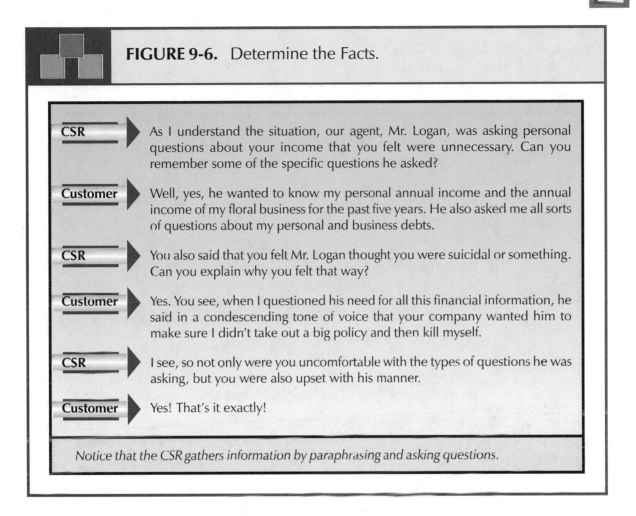

FIGURE 9-6. Determine the Facts.

CSR → As I understand the situation, our agent, Mr. Logan, was asking personal questions about your income that you felt were unnecessary. Can you remember some of the specific questions he asked?

Customer → Well, yes, he wanted to know my personal annual income and the annual income of my floral business for the past five years. He also asked me all sorts of questions about my personal and business debts.

CSR → You also said that you felt Mr. Logan thought you were suicidal or something. Can you explain why you felt that way?

Customer → Yes. You see, when I questioned his need for all this financial information, he said in a condescending tone of voice that your company wanted him to make sure I didn't take out a big policy and then kill myself.

CSR → I see, so not only were you uncomfortable with the types of questions he was asking, but you were also upset with his manner.

Customer → Yes! That's it exactly!

Notice that the CSR gathers information by paraphrasing and asking questions.

customer's problem and provide the appropriate service. Many times, the response is apparent or is documented in a procedural manual; other times, the problem will be unique. You must be prepared to think creatively about such problems and to provide solutions that are not necessarily addressed by standard procedures.

Sometimes, customers feel they have no control over the situation. As a service provider, you can help by saying or doing things that give your customers more of a sense of control, offering options and choices. You might say, "Here are some things I can do for you... Which do you prefer?" Or, "Are either of these two options OK with you? We can..."

Figure 9-7 continues the conversation from the previous Figures, showing how the CSR might suggest an appropriate solution.

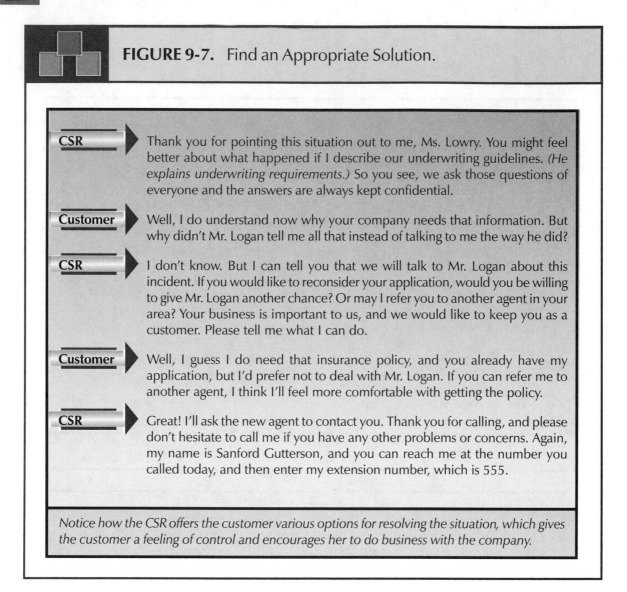

FIGURE 9-7. Find an Appropriate Solution.

CSR Thank you for pointing this situation out to me, Ms. Lowry. You might feel better about what happened if I describe our underwriting guidelines. *(He explains underwriting requirements.)* So you see, we ask those questions of everyone and the answers are always kept confidential.

Customer Well, I do understand now why your company needs that information. But why didn't Mr. Logan tell me all that instead of talking to me the way he did?

CSR I don't know. But I can tell you that we will talk to Mr. Logan about this incident. If you would like to reconsider your application, would you be willing to give Mr. Logan another chance? Or may I refer you to another agent in your area? Your business is important to us, and we would like to keep you as a customer. Please tell me what I can do.

Customer Well, I guess I do need that insurance policy, and you already have my application, but I'd prefer not to deal with Mr. Logan. If you can refer me to another agent, I think I'll feel more comfortable with getting the policy.

CSR Great! I'll ask the new agent to contact you. Thank you for calling, and please don't hesitate to call me if you have any other problems or concerns. Again, my name is Sanford Gutterson, and you can reach me at the number you called today, and then enter my extension number, which is 555.

Notice how the CSR offers the customer various options for resolving the situation, which gives the customer a feeling of control and encourages her to do business with the company.

Conflict and Conflict Management

An understanding of conflict and conflict management can be helpful for people who work with upset customers. *Conflict* is the clash of opposing attitudes, desires, interests, ideas, behaviors, goals, or needs. Often, an upset customer is someone who is in conflict with your company.

The various ways that people approach or handle conflict can be grouped into four categories: cooperation, avoidance, surrender, and coercion. Usually, the best way for a service provider to manage conflict is through cooperation. However, many conflicts are managed (or mismanaged) through the other three conflict patterns, so you should understand and avoid using inappropriate approaches.

COOPERATION

Cooperation is a conflict management approach in which the parties involved in a conflict discuss the conflict openly and honestly and look for a resolution. Defusing an emotional situation is critical to the success of cooperation. Cooperation frequently involves using the techniques of effective negotiation. Also, the four steps presented earlier in this chapter for working with upset customers provide a cooperative approach to managing conflict.

AVOIDANCE

Avoidance is a conflict management approach that entails physically or psychologically removing oneself from a conflict situation. Avoidance tends to be an ineffective way of dealing with conflict because it does not solve the problem causing the conflict. With service providers, avoidance often takes the form of not calling back or otherwise not contacting an upset customer. Avoidance typically compounds rather than solves a problem. However, when conflict becomes emotionally charged and resolution of the problem seems unlikely, temporary avoidance can be useful. By temporarily avoiding an emotionally charged conflict, both parties have an opportunity to calm down and collect their thoughts. A cooling-off period can foster more effective conflict management later.

Avoidance typically compounds rather than solves a problem.

SURRENDER

Surrender is a conflict management approach that involves one person giving in to end the conflict. Surrender is not an effective way of dealing with conflict because the conflict is not resolved based on logical reasoning, and neither party is likely to feel that the conflict has come to any real resolution.

Sometimes during a telephone conversation, a customer might suddenly agree with you, even though you sense that the customer still has a difference of opinion with you or your company. If you allow a customer to surrender this way, no meaningful resolution occurs. Instead, the customer might resent the outcome and take his business elsewhere.

COERCION

As we noted earlier in this chapter, coercion is an attempt by one person to talk others into doing something they really don't want to do. A coercive person uses aggression to resolve a conflict, and aggression is an emotional rather than a reasoned reaction to conflict. The use of coercion by a service provider is never appropriate and can even expose companies to legal or regulatory liabilities.

Often, approaches to conflict are closely related to personality. For example, a customer who has an aggressive personality will tend to handle conflict in a coercive manner. Therefore, getting this person to deal with conflict cooperatively might be a challenge. However, by persistently using assertive behavior, as discussed in Chapter 5, and by employing effective negotiating skills, you can improve your chances of helping a coercive customer use a more cooperative approach.

Dealing with Difficult Customers

As we noted earlier, a customer always has the right to complain, but never has the right to be rude or abusive or to use profanity or offensive language. If a customer makes an inappropriate remark, you can politely but firmly direct the conversation back to the issue at hand by saying something like, "I understand your frustration. Now let's see if there's something we can do about this situation." Don't let the customer make you forget that you are a professional. Don't let the customer draw you into an argument or get you angry. If a customer says something like, "Every time I deal with you people, you get it all wrong," you can reply by saying, "I'm very sorry that you have had some bad experiences with us in the past, but I'll do everything I can to help you with this problem."

> Don't let the customer make you forget that you are a professional. Don't let the customer draw you into an argument or get you angry.

If a customer becomes verbally abusive, you should act quickly to stop the inappropriate behavior. Insight 9-1 describes some techniques for you to consider. Before using any of these techniques, however, you should be sure that they do not conflict with company policy where you work. Also, because some of these techniques have the potential to further antagonize a customer, always use good judgment before deciding to use them.

General Guidelines for Interacting with Customers

Although we have discussed many of the following guidelines in previous chapters, they are worth repeating here as a reminder for interacting with customers:

- Use the "feelings first, facts second" model for conversation.

- Listen attentively using the CARESS model (**C**oncentrate; **A**cknowledge; **R**esearch; **E**xercise emotional control; **S**ense the non-verbal message; **S**tructure) and other guidelines for active listening.

INSIGHT 9-1. Managing Abusive Situations.

If a customer becomes rude or abusive, you might try one of the following techniques to stop the negative behavior:

- Never allow yourself to get drawn into an angry exchange; remain polite, firm, and professional.

- Ask a question. Sometimes asking questions is a good way to slow down customers and give them a chance to compose themselves.

- Call for a break by suggesting that the communication be continued another time.

- State calmly that if the customer does not stop the abusive language, you will hang up. You might say, "I can understand your frustration and I really want to help, but I can't help if you continue using abusive language. Please stop using this type of language or I will have to hang up."

- If the customer persists, you might say, "Due to the abusive nature of your language, I will not be able to assist you." Then hang up and document the file.

- In a non-threatening way, remind the customer that the call is being recorded, if it is. You might say something like, "Excuse me, but before we continue our conversation, I wanted to remind you that some of our calls are recorded."

- Ask a manager or coworker to intercede.

- Use a pleasant tone of voice; never use a sarcastic tone.

- Don't use technical jargon.

- Don't take anything that a customer says personally, and don't be afraid to give yourself a few seconds to breathe deeply and compose yourself when necessary.

- If you do react in a way that you regret, try to recover by saying something like, "I'm sorry about our misunderstanding and the part I played in it."

- At the conclusion of the conversation, summarize the actions that you and the customer agreed to take. Make sure the customer understands and accepts these actions. If appropriate, send a written acknowledgment. Then make sure you do what you say you are going to do. When necessary, take appropriate steps to correct problems or to prevent them from occurring again.

A company and its service providers should approach every customer interaction with the same determination to satisfy the customer, regardless of how routine or challenging the interaction may be. A poorly handled interaction, whether or not it is with an upset customer, can result in lost business. A company's less difficult customers are often the most profitable and loyal. They are also more likely to quietly take their business elsewhere if they do not receive the level of service they expect. Your challenge is to conduct every customer interaction with the appropriate communication and interpersonal skills. With practice, you can learn how to interact effectively with customers in all types of situations.

In this chapter, you have learned about conflict management and interacting with customers, as well as how to use explanation, persuasion, and negotiation in customer service. In the next chapter, we will shift our focus from customer interaction at the individual level to customer service at the organizational level.

 To practice and review the skills and information you learned in this chapter, see the interactive CD, *Practicing Your Customer Service Skills*, included with this book.

Key Terms and Concepts

explanation	valid argument
persuasion	negotiation
coercion	underlying needs
competence	follow-through
intention	conflict
personal impression	cooperation
character	avoidance
association	surrender

Endnotes

1. Mark Sanborn, "The Ten Practices of Exceptional Service," *Best Practices in Customer Service*, ed. Ron Zemke and John A. Woods (New York: HRD Press, 1998), 207.

2. JoAnna F. Brandi, *Building Company Loyalty: The 21 Essential Elements...IN ACTION* (Dallas: Walk the Talk Company, 2001), 16.

The Customer-Centric Organization

After studying this chapter, you should be able to

- Describe corporate culture and explain its importance in providing exceptional customer service

- Identify some of the major factors affecting corporate culture

- Identify the steps involved in implementing change in an organization

- Describe the steps involved in corporate strategic planning and customer service strategic planning

- Explain how service objectives, service strategies, and tactical plans work together to help ensure effective customer service

- Give examples of how work groups and employees in financial services companies cooperate to provide customer service

Five years ago, a new CEO joined Innovative Life and Casualty and announced that the company was changing its business philosophy from product-centric to customer-centric. This organization-wide, customer-based initiative continues today. Throughout the organization—from the boardroom to the mailroom, from strategic planning to claim processing—virtually all Innovative employees focus on the customer.

Recently, Margaret Robinson, an experienced customer service representative, joined Innovative Life and Casualty. Ms. Robinson previously worked at Archaic Life, where she always tried hard to provide exceptional customer service. However, many of her coworkers did not place the same emphasis on customer service that Ms. Robinson did. Customers who received substandard service sometimes became irritable, making Ms. Robinson's job difficult and stressful. Meanwhile—down the street from Archaic Life—Innovative Life and Casualty was developing a reputation as a customer-focused organization, and when increased business led to additional openings in the customer contact center, Ms. Robinson left Archaic and went to work at Innovative.

Some employees think of concepts like business philosophy, corporate culture, and strategic planning as management activities that have little to do with their day-to-day responsibilities. However, as Ms. Robinson's experience shows, these concepts can greatly affect employees and the customers they support. Furthermore, the nonmanagerial employees who process transactions and interact with customers on a daily basis can directly influence customer perceptions. Consequently, for a financial services company to be successful, all employees must understand and apply the organization's overall goals and be committed to providing superior customer service.

In this chapter, we will discuss corporate culture—what it means to a company and its employees and how it is established, especially as it relates to customer service. We also will describe how and why companies develop a customer service strategic plan. Finally, we will examine customer service as a company-wide function.

Customer Service and Corporate Culture

Corporate culture determines what your company deems important and how your company believes work should be done.

As you saw in Chapter 7, corporate culture refers to the beliefs, attitudes, experiences, practices, and behaviors that are learned and shared by the employees of an organization. Your company's corporate culture is, in effect, its personality. Corporate culture determines what your company deems important and how your company believes work should be done. Corporate culture gives you and your coworkers a sense of what is expected of you and how you should approach your jobs. Furthermore, customers get a sense of your company's corporate culture through their interactions with you and your fellow employees and through various signs your company displays, both figuratively and literally, as Insight 10-1 illustrates.

Types of Corporate Culture

Every organization has a distinct culture. In some cases, a company may have a *dominant culture*, which is the culture that is

---

INSIGHT 10-1.   A Sign of Change.

At one financial services company, the corporate culture was changing. A culture that had been inwardly focused on processes rather than customers was becoming more outwardly focused on customers rather than processes. For years, the sign above a service counter where customers could pick up checks had read "Check *Dispensation*," to indicate that this was where employees distributed checks to customers. One day, customers saw a new sign: "Check *Collection*," to emphasize that this was where customers came to pick up checks. This simple, one-word change reflected an important change in the company's corporate culture, viewing service from the customers' rather than the company's perspective.

most prominent throughout the organization, and one or more *subcultures*, which are cultures unique to particular units within an organization. Subcultures may be similar to or totally different from the dominant culture. Often, subcultures are shaped by the nature of the work employees perform. In Chapter 1, you saw how some employees, especially when they are not directly involved with external customers on a regular basis, may develop a manufacturing mentality. These employees concentrate so much on their job functions that they forget about the customer. In some companies, a manufacturing mentality is shared by most of the employees in one or more departments, and it becomes a main characteristic of a subculture within the organization.

Corporate cultures can be weak or strong. In a *strong corporate culture* employees clearly understand and consistently apply the company's business philosophy, goals, priorities, and practices. A strong corporate culture can produce either positive or negative results, depending on the nature of the behavior it encourages. A strong corporate culture that focuses exclusively on individual and departmental goals, without encouraging customer-oriented cooperation, might hinder customer service, while a culture that values cooperation and teamwork to support customers is more likely to satisfy its customers.

In a *weak corporate culture* employees do not understand clearly or apply consistently the company's business philosophy, goals, priorities, and practices. Consequently, one or more subcultures might thrive, leading to conflicts between departments. Furthermore, employees might lack direction or they might encounter conflicting priorities. As you saw in Margaret Robinson's experience at Archaic Life, a weak corporate culture is likely to undermine customer service efforts or to encourage the development of subcultures that work at cross-purposes with company goals.

Employees who identify with their company's culture are inclined to support it. Employees who do not like the culture might ignore it, form opposing subcultures, try to change it, or leave the company to work for a company with a culture more compatible with their own views.

Factors That Affect Corporate Culture

A company's corporate culture can be influenced by the broader culture of the society in which the company operates and in which its employees

---

In a *strong corporate culture* employees clearly understand and consistently apply the company's business philosophy, goals, priorities, and practices.

Factors that affect a company's corporate culture are its organizational characteristics, its senior managers, and its work groups.

reside. For example, a company located in a small town or rural environment might have a corporate culture that values hospitality and relationship building in customer interactions. On the other hand, a company that operates in an urban environment might have a corporate culture that values a more formal approach to customer interactions. Cultural norms affect the way people approach their work.

Similarly, the nature of the industry in which a company operates often influences corporate culture. For example, the corporate culture in an insurance company is likely to be different from the corporate culture in a telecommunications company or a high-volume retail chain. Other factors that affect a company's corporate culture are its organizational characteristics, its senior managers, and its work groups.

ORGANIZATIONAL CHARACTERISTICS

Organizational characteristics include a company's size, corporate structure, history, and products and services. A large, decentralized company might have a weak corporate culture and strong subcultures, while a small, centralized company with a highly visible CEO might have a strong corporate culture that closely reflects the CEO's business philosophy.

Corporate restructuring typically has a major impact on corporate culture. If two companies merge, the employees face many challenges in adjusting to the new corporate culture that eventually takes shape. Employees might ask themselves: "Will the new culture be similar to the culture I'm used to working in? Will it be a combination of both cultures? Will I be able to thrive or even survive in this new culture?" Although managers are responsible for proactively addressing these kinds of questions on an organization-wide basis, individual employees are also responsible for understanding their roles in the newly formed corporate structure.

In addition, because *customers* become accustomed to the practices and attitudes that arise from a company's corporate culture, they often are concerned about and affected by corporate restructuring. Consequently, front-line employees play an important role in communicating to customers what they can expect as a result of major organizational changes.

MANAGERS

Everyone in an organization, regardless of job title or responsibilities, helps shape corporate culture. However, senior managers are in a position to exert the most influence, especially in terms of how employees within the organization perform the day-to-day activities of their jobs. If senior managers clearly communicate and demonstrate exceptional customer service, then other employees—from middle managers to supervisors to nonmanagerial employees—are likely to focus on customer service in their daily activities.

Managers can show their commitment to customer service by interacting regularly with customers and staff—perhaps by sitting in on the front lines—and by challenging employees to consider the effect that their attitudes and actions can have on customers. Insight 10-2 describes the efforts of one CEO to foster a customer-centric culture.

WORK GROUPS

A **work group** consists of two or more people who work together on a regular basis and coordinate their activities to accomplish common goals. The way you and your coworkers respond to each other and view your jobs helps shape your company's corporate culture. You are likely to have a positive impact on your organization's corporate culture if

- The goals of your work group and your individual goals are clear and well aligned, and you accept them

- You are committed to your work

- You support your coworkers

- Your morale is high

- You feel your work is important and that you are valuable to the organization

- You feel you are appropriately rewarded for your contributions

If members of a work group feel isolated and disgruntled, they are likely to have a negative impact on the organization's culture.

Some of the above factors are within each employee's control, while others depend to varying degrees on the support provided by supervisors and managers. If members of a work group feel isolated and disgruntled, they are likely to have a negative impact on the organization's culture.

As you have seen, work groups sometimes develop separate subcultures. The members of such groups might work well together, but at cross-purposes to the company's goals. In situations like this, customer service usually suffers. Later in this chapter, we will discuss how various work groups coordinate their activities to support each other in providing exceptional customer service.

INSIGHT 10-2. A CEO's Role in Creating a Customer-Centric Culture.

Jan Jobe, president and CEO of Pan American Life, spoke at a LOMA Customer Service Conference to spotlight the role of a CEO in creating a customer-oriented culture. "As a CEO, what do I have to do [in helping to create customer satisfaction]? First I have to believe, then I have to communicate, and then I have to act," he said. "And those are the fundamentals.

"What do we believe, in terms of our mission? First, we believe in focusing on the organization. We will choose our customers carefully and deliberately, because to attempt to serve everyone is to serve no one well. Second, we will listen to our customers; only they will tell us what they really want, what they really need, and how they want it. And we also follow that through with our service; we will have the tools, the skills, and the desire to serve our customers. And we focus on convenience, value, and building the relationship."

In addition to making sure the work done in the call center and other departments is customer-focused, the CEO must perform specific tasks in creating this culture, Jobe said. "I have to set a clear expectation, in terms of the attitudes, systems, processes, training, recruiting, and overall performance that we want to achieve in the organization. I am constantly asking our senior management people, 'What are you doing in the way of talking to your employees, to all of our management team, about the importance of customer service, about sharing new customer service ideas with them, and getting their feedback on ways that we can service our customers better?'

"As a CEO, I must give good service to the people inside and outside of an organization. I view the employees of Pan American as a customer of mine; I view our outside customers as customers of mine, and I try to take actions that will make sure this is understood."

One of the ways Jobe has done this is by literally driving home the company's vision statement: *We will do what we say we will do. We will.* "I

actually have 'WE WILL' on my license plate," he said. This message is reinforced by Pan American employees wearing 'WE WILL' clothing whenever they volunteer and serve in the community (an activity the company strongly encourages), as well as through toll-free "We will" telephone numbers, e-mail addresses containing "wewill4u," and optional "We will" screen savers. "We try to make it something that's in front of people every day," Jobe concluded.

Another example that shows how Pan-American makes customer service an important part of every employee's job is through a program that Jobe developed called "Service Over-Performance." The objective of this program is to improve customer service by having employees clearly define and focus on their customers. Each employee creates a "roadmap to the customer," a diagram that connects her job to the people she supports within the organization. Every diagram ends with an external customer. For example, consider an administrative employee whose primary responsibility is to locate files and forward requested information to customer service representatives. On the diagram, this administrative employee would connect with the CSR who in turn would connect with the external customer.

After the employee draws the roadmap, she thinks about how she can change her attitudes or her approach to her job so that she can provide better service to the first person on the roadmap, the person she serves. To commit to making a change, the employee

1. Interviews the internal customer, the first person on the roadmap
2. Writes down the specific changes that she is going to make in terms of attitude and approach
3. Tells the internal customer what she is committing to, so that person knows what to expect
4. Repeats steps 1 through 3 for each of her routes to the external customer

Source: Adapted from Stephen Hall, "Conference Explores CRM's Role in Getting to Know Customers Better," *Resource* (August 2001): 8–9, and information provided by Pan American Life Insurance Company.

Changing to a Customer-Centric Culture

In response to a constantly changing environment and increasing customer expectations, some companies seek to cultivate a corporate culture that effectively adapts to change and recognizes the critical importance of its customers. In a customer-centric culture, employees are empowered to take quick action, within certain parameters, to do whatever is necessary to meet and exceed customer expectations. Customer-centric companies anticipate customer questions and concerns to provide proactive customer service.

Transforming an organization's corporate culture from product-centric to customer-centric is a huge task. Yet, some companies have been able to successfully reshape their corporate cultures to adapt to change and to encourage greater flexibility and dedication to customer service. In most organizations, a major culture change takes at least four years to implement.

In most organizations, a major culture change takes at least four years to implement.

Generally, a successful organizational transformation follows a series of activities, called a **change sequence**, which consists of (1) recognizing the need for change, (2) assessing the organization's readiness for change, (3) identifying appropriate changes and the methods for implementing the changes, and (4) implementation.

RECOGNIZING THE NEED FOR CHANGE

A company can identify the need for changing its culture by observing factors such as activities of its competitors, new demands from customers, a decline in employee productivity or morale, a decline in the quality of its products and services, fewer customers, and declining profits. Typically, these warning signs develop because a company's mode of operation is not well suited to the current business environment or because the

www.grantland.net

company's industry is going through a major transformation. In some cases, a company must change to accommodate the growth of the company or because of corporate restructuring.

ASSESSING THE ORGANIZATION'S READINESS FOR CHANGE

One way senior managers can take stock of employee readiness for change is to conduct an employee opinion survey.

Culture change cannot be imposed on an organization. Although a company's senior managers may be convinced of the need for change, they rely on the support of company employees to make change happen. One way senior managers can take stock of employee readiness for change is to conduct an employee opinion survey. Such a survey can help identify the values employees embrace as well as their level of commitment to moving towards a customer-centric culture.[1]

IDENTIFYING APPROPRIATE CHANGES AND THE METHODS FOR IMPLEMENTING THE CHANGES

After assessing the organization's readiness for change, the company determines what changes to make and how to implement the changes. Methods that are used to determine and implement change include

- Conducting surveys or focus group interviews with customers to find out what customers think about the company and how the company should change

- Holding "town hall meetings" or open forums with employees to obtain input; when employees participate in the planning process, they are more likely to embrace change and have a personal stake in its successful implementation

- Hiring business consultants to help develop new operating methods and to help train employees in these methods

- Offering or arranging training seminars in sensitivity, diversity, and team building to provide employees with the skills needed to work together more effectively

- Forming task forces to determine the best ways to implement change

Although no approach guarantees success, most companies strive to include employees as an integral part of the change process. Because frontline and administrative employees are closest to the customers and procedures, they can provide valuable input as to what may need to be changed. When a company seeks input from employees and asks them to help make the change become a reality, employees are more likely to buy into change and contribute to its successful implementation.

IMPLEMENTATION

Employees must make sure they understand how the company's vision, goals, and strategies affect their jobs.

Implementing and maintaining a customer-centric culture requires the long-term commitment and constant attention of everyone in the organization. Managers must "walk the talk;" their actions must be consistent with the company's vision, goals, and strategies for change. Employees must make sure they understand how the company's vision, goals, and strategies affect their jobs. Throughout the change process, the company conducts follow-up studies and continuous training to make sure the change is progressing as planned and that customer service skills and attitudes are being developed and maintained.

But no matter how carefully a company plans and implements change, individual employees or entire organizational units are likely to resist. Change is difficult; it creates uncertainty and fear. Some employees feel that change threatens their status in the company. Others, who may have helped develop the old way of doing things, might view change as a personal affront to their previous hard work. Many people find a certain comfort level in the way things are done, and they are afraid that they won't understand the new way of doing things. Other people might fear losing their jobs. Often, change increases the influence of some organizational units and reduces the influence of others. In such cases, employees who work in areas that are losing influence might resist the change even if they know it is better for the company and its customers.

To counteract the natural resistance to change, companies take steps to reassure and encourage employees throughout the process, providing timely and appropriate information, as well as opportunities and techniques to help implement the change. They also reward employees for their efforts in supporting the change.

As you can see, developing a customer-centric culture is a challenge that requires commitment throughout an organization. A company cannot just install a new culture and then have everyone return to their "regular" job duties. Most organizations transform or reinforce their corporate culture through ongoing strategic planning.

Companies that reengineer to face the customer, to serve the customer, and to make life easier for the customer will flourish. Those that don't will perish.

— Michael Hammer[2]

Customer Service Strategic Planning

To compete successfully in increasingly competitive markets, many financial services firms develop a customer service strategic plan or pursue a corporate-wide, customer-oriented initiative known as customer relationship management. Customer-based strategies and initiatives like these, which we describe later in this section, are typically included in an overall corporate strategic planning process.

Developing a Corporate Strategic Plan

As you saw in Chapter 2, strategic planning is the process of determining an organization's long-term corporate objectives and deciding the overall course of action the company will take to achieve those objectives. It often involves four activities: (1) conducting a situation analysis, (2) defining the organization's mission, (3) establishing corporate objectives, and (4) developing corporate strategies.

CONDUCTING A SITUATION ANALYSIS

A *situation analysis* provides many of the assumptions upon which the strategic plan is based. It consists of gathering information about events and relationships in the external environment, and then forecasting the major trends that will affect business activities within a specified period. A situation analysis also includes examining the organization's current activities and its ability to respond to potential threats and opportunities in the environment.

DEFINING THE ORGANIZATION'S MISSION

By addressing customers in its mission statement, a company helps assure that customer service will be emphasized.

The function of a *mission statement*, which describes an organization's fundamental purpose and the scope of its business activities, is to establish the right focus, as well as continuity and consistency, throughout the organization. By addressing customers in its mission statement, a company helps assure that customer service will be emphasized in its corporate objectives, corporate strategies, and day-to-day operations. Typically, a company's mission statement remains constant. Occasionally, however, a situation analysis might uncover the need to reexamine and modify the company mission to adapt to significant changes in the environment.

ESTABLISHING CORPORATE OBJECTIVES

Corporate objectives are realistic, specific, and measurable statements that describe the long-term results an organization intends to achieve. To be meaningful, a company's corporate objectives should be tied to its mission. The following examples of corporate objectives are related to customer service:

- Increase the overall customer satisfaction level to 95 percent within the next three years

- Reduce the lapse rate of first-year insurance policies by 25 percent within the next four years

- Increase sales leads produced by the customer contact center by 10 percent in each of the next three years

DEVELOPING CORPORATE STRATEGIES

Corporate strategies establish the long-term methods by which an organization intends to achieve its corporate objectives. For example, to increase sales leads produced by the customer contact center by 10 percent in each of the next three years, a company might develop the following strategies:

- Train all CSRs to inquire about and recognize customers' additional financial needs

- Establish an incentive system to reward CSRs who identify leads that generate sales

- Establish a system to improve communications between CSRs and intermediaries

Developing and Implementing a Customer Service Strategic Plan

A customer service strategic plan provides consistent customer service goals and direction throughout an organization. In addition, a customer service strategic plan indicates that senior management has embraced and intends to support customer service. Although individual departments and employees often find ways to provide exceptional customer service, the overall level of a company's customer service rises significantly when executives budget the necessary funds, authorize the hiring and training of the right personnel, and establish customer-focused systems and procedures through a formal customer service strategic plan.

Depending on the corporate culture or subcultures within the organization, service providers and other nonmanagerial employees play varying

A customer service strategic plan indicates that senior management has embraced and intends to support customer service.

All employees are responsible for understanding and incorporating the customer service mission and objectives into their daily activities.

roles in developing and implementing their company's customer service strategic plans. In some financial services firms, employees are invited to participate directly in the planning process. In others, employees provide input through opinion surveys, meetings, and focus groups. However, regardless of their role in developing the plan, all employees are responsible for understanding and incorporating the customer service mission and objectives into their daily activities.

As Figure 10-1 illustrates, the customer service strategic plan takes its direction from the corporate strategic plan, and typically includes similar steps: conducting a customer service situation analysis, developing a customer service mission statement, establishing service objectives, and devising customer service strategies and tactical plans. These planning activities are then followed by implementation and monitoring.

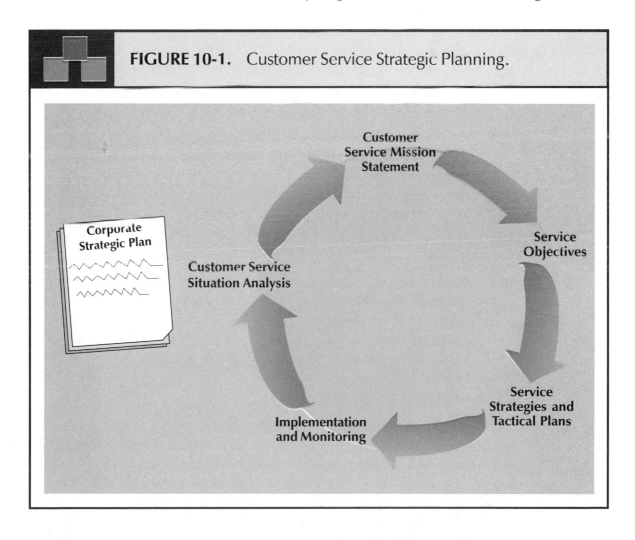

FIGURE 10-1. Customer Service Strategic Planning.

CUSTOMER SERVICE SITUATION ANALYSIS

The situation analysis for a customer service strategic plan focuses on evaluating customer expectations regarding service and on examining the company's current performance in meeting those expectations. In Chapter 5, you read about research techniques that financial services firms can use to determine customer expectations and perceptions; and in Chapter 12, you will see how companies measure the performance of their customer service systems and processes. Here, you will learn about some of the sources of information that companies use to evaluate customer service. The four primary sources are (1) customers, (2) employees, (3) competitors, and (4) acknowledged leaders in customer service.

■ **Customers.** Because customers are the most important source of information about customer service, customer-centric companies try to stay close to their customers and learn from them. These companies obtain feedback from surveys, focus groups, and advisory panels to find out how customers feel about the service they are receiving and what products and services they would like to have.

■ **Employees.** Companies can ask their employees to identify areas in which customer service is lacking and to specify the activities and resources needed to provide better customer service. Because many employees interact directly with customers, they are an excellent source of information about what customers want and how customers perceive the company's products and services.

■ **Competitors.** In the interest of better serving the public, some companies are willing to share a certain amount of information about their customer service activities. Such information is provided by individual companies or through networking activities arranged by industry, trade, and professional associations. This type of information is available in published reports, Web sites, seminars, and conferences.

■ **Acknowledged leaders in customer service.** Most customers expect a certain level of customer service, whether doing business with a company that provides financial services, air travel, appliances, or any other type of product or service. The type of service that customers receive from *any* company helps determine the type of service that they expect to receive from *all* companies. For this reason, financial services companies seeking to learn more about customer service often look beyond their own

The type of service that customers receive from any company helps determine the type of service that they expect to receive from all companies.

INSIGHT 10-3. Acknowledged Leaders in Customer Service.

The University of Chicago Hospitals (UCH), as part of an effort to enhance the patient experience, spent several years comparing its practices to many notable service-based organizations, including the Walt Disney World Resort. On the surface, academic medicine and theme park entertainment might seem worlds apart. But these two organizations had much in common, such as a commitment to service excellence and customer satisfaction, as well as a diversity of customers with high expectations.

Though the Walt Disney World Resort is excellent technically at providing world-class attractions and entertainment, and UCH is excellent clinically, many visitors can't easily evaluate either expertise. But they can remember how well they were treated at either place. Most employees want to be part of a positive "show." Unfortunately, in many organizations employees are inadvertently set up as service failures, with no support systems. But the Walt Disney World Resort and UCH go to great lengths to set up their employees as "service heroes." As part of that pursuit, selected team representatives from UCH attend programming on an annual basis at Walt Disney World Resort's external training organization, Disney Institute, in Lake Buena Vista, Florida. They have several learning objectives:

- Learn new non-healthcare-focused methods of customer service from a recognized customer service leader.

- Understand how an organization as large as Disney applies customer service principles so effectively.

- Learn how to keep a balance between providing customer service excellence and having fun on the job.

Source: Judy Schueler, "Customer Service Through Leadership: The Disney Way," *Training & Development* (October 2000): 28. © October 2000, <u>Training & Development</u>, American Society for Training & Development. Adapted with permission. All rights reserved.

---

industry to those companies that are acknowledged leaders in customer service, as Insight 10-3 describes.

CUSTOMER SERVICE MISSION STATEMENT

Taking its lead from the customer service component of the corporate mission statement, the *customer service mission statement* tells why a company provides customer service and expresses the company's overall customer service goals. Figure 10-2 provides an example of a customer service mission statement.

SERVICE OBJECTIVES

Service objectives define the specific goals that a company must meet to fulfill its customer service mission. Service objectives help transform the general purpose and direction of the mission into meaningful and measurable targets. For example, suppose the company develops a customer service mission statement that stresses the importance of prompt,

FIGURE 10-2. A Customer Service Mission Statement.

Our mission is to work proactively and as a team to provide superior customer service—service that is prompt, seamless, responsive, accurate, consistent, courteous, and convenient to our customers.

accurate, and courteous service. The company then sets out to fulfill this mission by developing service objectives based on its mission, such as

- For the next calendar year, complete 90 percent of inbound customer contacts upon initial contact [prompt service]

- For the next calendar year, complete 98 percent of customer service transactions with no errors [accurate service]

- For the next calendar year, reduce customer service-related complaints to less than 1 percent of total customer service transactions [prompt, accurate, and courteous service]

SERVICE STRATEGIES AND TACTICAL PLANS

Although service objectives clarify goals, they do not provide methods for reaching those goals. This direction comes from service strategies and tactical plans. *Service strategies* are the general plans companies develop and follow to achieve their service objectives. Whenever possible, service objectives, service strategies, and tactical plans are stated in quantifiable terms with a time frame for completion or review. In this way, a company and its employees can accurately plan to accomplish goals and monitor results. Figure 10-3 provides examples that show how service strategies are linked to a service objective. This figure assumes that the company's current accuracy rate is 97 percent.

While service strategies establish the general plans for achieving service objectives, more detailed plans must be developed to effectively implement the strategies. These detailed business plans, which outline the specific tasks the company will undertake to implement a strategy, are called **tactical plans** (or *operational plans*). For example, in Figure 10-3 the service objective is to complete 98 percent of customer service transactions with no errors, and one of the service strategies is to establish quality teams to identify problems and develop solutions. To specify the activities needed to implement this service strategy and meet the service objective, a department's tactical plan might resemble the plan shown in Figure 10-4.

IMPLEMENTATION AND MONITORING

Some companies distribute copies of the customer service strategic plan to all employees; others conduct meetings to discuss and reinforce the strategic plan so that everyone in the organization is aware of the company's mission, objectives, and strategies.

Ideally, service providers link their individual objectives and their day-to-day activities to the larger objectives and plans for their work group and for the entire organization. In many companies, employees align their

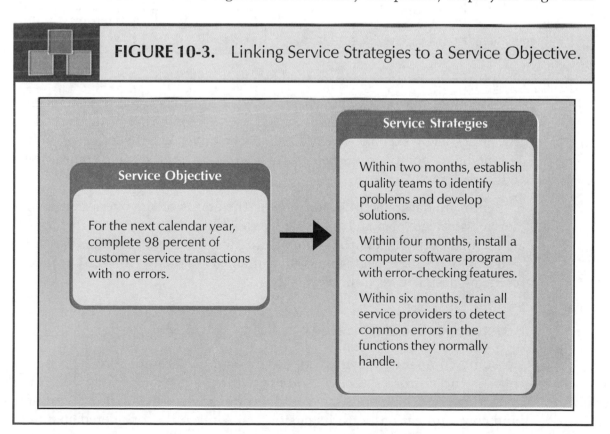

FIGURE 10-3. Linking Service Strategies to a Service Objective.

Service Objective

For the next calendar year, complete 98 percent of customer service transactions with no errors.

Service Strategies

Within two months, establish quality teams to identify problems and develop solutions.

Within four months, install a computer software program with error-checking features.

Within six months, train all service providers to detect common errors in the functions they normally handle.

FIGURE 10-4. An Example of a Tactical Plan.

Tactical plan for implementing service strategy to establish a quality team that will identify problems and develop solutions:

What	Who	By when
1. Announce Quality Team initiative to department; select Quality Team Leader	Manager	January 3
2. Send e-mail to department asking for staff volunteers to serve on Quality Team	Quality Team Leader	January 4
3. Conduct first meeting of Quality Team to establish operating procedures and to schedule meeting dates	Quality Team Leader and Quality Team	January 17
4. Develop and send survey to staff to help identify problems and solutions	To be determined	January 24
5. Review survey results and identify (1) significant problems and (2) problems that can be solved with "quick fixes"	Quality Team	February 7
6. Expand tactical plan to assign tasks and completion dates based on #5 above	Quality Team Leader	February 14

individual objectives and activities with organizational objectives and strategies through the performance evaluation process described in Chapter 4. For example, an individual objective for all service providers might be to complete 98 percent of their customer service transactions with no errors.

Senior managers periodically review the status of the overall customer service strategic plan and applicable performance results. Similarly, department managers review the status of tactical plans and results. If results are not meeting expectations, then managers work with staff to make changes designed to improve results.

Customer Access Strategy

In some companies, an important part of the customer service strategic plan is the *customer access strategy*, which is a strategy focused on the selection, development, and coordination of an organization's contacts and communications with its customers. A carefully considered customer access strategy supports customers in ways that are easy and convenient for customers. For example, many financial services firms establish several communication options, such as telephone, in-person visits, fax, e-mail, and Internet access. The primary goals of a customer access strategy are to

- Provide choice, convenience, and ease of use for customers

- Enable customers to use the communication channels that most effectively deliver the requested information or service

- Encourage customers to use the least costly communication channel(s)

- Maintain a basic level of quality and consistency in all customer contacts, regardless of who the customer is or what communication channel the customer uses[3]

Customer Relationship Management

Customer relationship management (CRM) is a business initiative that allows an organization to manage all aspects of its interactions with current and potential customers. Although CRM goes beyond customer service to include a variety of other functions—such as marketing and sales—customer service is at the heart of every CRM initiative. The purpose of CRM is to enable a company to build customer loyalty by (1) learning from every interaction with a customer and (2) using what has been learned to anticipate the customer's needs and offer customized products and services. CRM integrates an organization's people, processes, and technology to maximize the value of the relationship for the customers' benefit and for the company's profit. In short, CRM strives to make relationships beneficial for customers as well as the company.[4]

Although CRM goes beyond customer service to include a variety of other functions—such as marketing and sales—customer service is at the heart of every CRM initiative.

Customer Service: An Enterprise-Wide Function

As we noted earlier, some organizational units have subcultures that focus almost exclusively on their own agendas and isolate themselves from other parts of the organization. When a group strongly identifies itself as a unit, it might consider other groups or individuals as outsiders or rivals, a concept known as a *tribal mentality*. Occasionally, such a subculture even views customers as outsiders who interfere with the department's routine operation. To establish a customer-centric corporate culture, an organization must constantly stress the importance of cooperation and customer service, and it must eliminate tribal mentalities.

A company with a strong customer service culture develops strategic and tactical plans that focus on the customer; it implements systems and processes designed with the customer in mind; and it fosters an environment in which each employee makes customer service a top priority. At both the organizational and individual levels, the goal is to pool resources to meet the expectations and needs of customers. The interdependent nature of customer service is often evident in the interactions between customer service departments and intermediaries. As you saw in Chapter 2, exceptional customer service often depends on mutual support between the home office and the field.

Some companies have a saying: "Customer service is not a department; it's an attitude." People who subscribe to this notion view "caring for the customer" as everyone's business and not just the job of employees who work in departments that have the word "customer" in their name. All employees, including people who seldom interact with customers, make valuable contributions to customer service by conducting transactions "behind the scenes" or by providing internal customer service to front-line employees. Only when employees and departments throughout an organization are communicating and cooperating can a company provide exceptional customer service. We conclude this chapter by examining a few of the many ways interdepartmental cooperation enhances customer service in the financial services industry.

Only when employees and departments throughout an organization are communicating and cooperating can a company provide exceptional customer service.

How Customer Service Affects and Supports Other Activities

As we saw in Chapter 1, most financial services firms try to provide intermediaries with the highest possible level of customer service. When customers come to an intermediary with questions or service requests, the intermediary often turns to customer service and transaction-processing areas for support. Timely and competent service reflects well on the company and the intermediary. Unresponsive service risks alienating both the external customer and the intermediary.

In some financial services companies, service providers relay customer-specific information to field offices to inform intermediaries about customer preferences and to pass along sales leads. In other financial services companies, the role of service providers has been expanded to include sales-related functions. For example, during the course of a telephone call, a CSR might inform the customer of additional products or services available for purchase. Through an activity called *cross-telling*, the CSR informs the customer of the product, but does not attempt to make a sale. Instead, the CSR may transfer the customer to a sales representative, arrange for a sales representative to contact the customer, or send the customer additional information.

In some companies, CSRs transact sales through an activity called ***cross-selling***, in which customers are invited to purchase a product other than the product they already own. Similarly, some CSRs transact sales through ***up-selling***, in which customers are invited to purchase additional amounts or features of a product they already own or are considering purchasing. An example of cross-selling is when a CSR offers a medical policy to a customer who owns a life insurance policy. An example of up-selling is when a CSR offers additional coverage amounts to a customer who owns a life insurance policy. CSRs who cross-sell or up-sell must be appropriately trained and licensed for such activities. When CSRs cross-tell, cross-sell, or up-sell, they can minimize misunderstandings and confusion by informing intermediaries of any sales-related activities they have performed.

Customer contacts are an excellent source of information about the products customers want, the prices they are willing to pay, and the type of service customers value.

Customer contacts are an excellent source of information about the products customers want, the prices they are willing to pay, and the type of service customers value. By sharing this type of information, customer service departments and employees can add value to a variety of organizational activities such as product development, advertising, pricing, and transaction processing. For example, if a handful of customers begin complaining to CSRs about a problem with their monthly account statements, then CSRs can alert the area that generates these statements to correct the problem quickly before it becomes widespread. On the other hand, if customers express satisfaction with a recently implemented procedure, then CSRs can pass this valuable feedback on to the appropriate department.

Compliance and legal departments also benefit from information gathered by customer service and transaction-processing staff. For example, insurance companies are required by law to keep accurate records of customer complaints. CSRs and employees in functional areas, such as the claim department, obtain much of this information and create the records that the compliance department submits to regulatory agencies. If a complaint arrives in an insurer's compliance department by way of the state Insurance Department, the compliance coordinator often relies on service providers to gather all necessary information and provide an opinion as to the company's position on the issue. In addition, a company's legal staff sometimes calls upon service providers to furnish documentation and records of disputed transactions.

How Other Activities Affect and Support Customer Service

Just as various areas in an organization depend on service providers for support, service providers rely on other areas for essential information and valuable assistance. In group insurance, for example, if sales representatives do not accurately convey plan details to the appropriate operational areas of the company, then problems usually arise. Suppose the short-term disability benefit for employees of the XYZ Company is limited to 75 percent (instead of the standard 66 2/3 percent) of an employee's regular income. If the sales representative fails to note this non-standard feature in the plan details, claim representatives will apply the standard limit of 66 2/3 percent, prompting complaints from employees whose disability payments are incorrect.

To provide exceptional customer service, CSRs often rely on prompt, reliable internal customer service. For example, suppose a customer calls to cancel his automobile insurance policy because the premium is too high. Looking for ways to lower the premium, the CSR discovers that this customer's policy appears to be rated for an accident that occurred just over three years ago. According to the company's underwriting guidelines, accidents should be dropped from an insured's record after three years, so the CSR obtains the customer's permission to put him on hold, and then quickly calls an underwriter who checks and confirms that the policy has in fact been rated too high. The underwriter recalculates the rate and the CSR delivers the good news to the customer, who decides to keep the policy.

Service providers rely on a variety of employees and departments to perform their jobs.

Service providers rely on a variety of employees and departments to perform their jobs. For instance, a company's compliance staff might review transaction-processing procedures to ensure compliance with applicable regulations; legal staff might review telephone scripts to reduce the risk of customer challenges or lawsuits; and information technology staff might install and maintain a number of different information systems and communications technologies to support customer service activities.

Ultimately, however, the key question is not which department supports the other, but how various departments and employees work together to support the customer. Suppose, for example, that a bank develops a new credit card that allows customers to earn monthly cash-back awards that are automatically deposited into an educational savings fund for a child designated by the cardholder. When the first batch of monthly statements is mailed, the call center receives a number of calls from customers asking why their cash-back award amounts are not shown on their statements. To make matters worse, the call center's computer system is not linked to the accounting system that tracks the cash-back awards, so

CSRs are unable to tell customers the amounts their purchases have earned. After numerous complaints from frustrated customers (and equally frustrated CSRs), the call center manager arranges an emergency meeting with the marketing, accounting, and information technology departments to try to resolve these serious customer service problems.

As the preceding examples illustrate, customer service often depends on cooperation across organizational boundaries. In this chapter, you have seen how corporate culture, strategic planning, and interdepartmental cooperation affect a company's ability to provide exceptional customer service. In Chapter 11, we will continue our exploration of organizational issues by examining how financial services companies use organization and teamwork to enhance customer service.

To practice and review the skills and information you learned in this chapter, see the interactive CD, *Practicing Your Customer Service Skills*, included with this book.

Key Terms and Concepts

dominant culture
subcultures
strong corporate culture
weak corporate culture
work group
change sequence
situation analysis
mission statement
corporate objectives
corporate strategies
customer service mission
    statement

service objectives
service strategies
tactical plans
customer access strategy
customer relationship
    management (CRM)
tribal mentality
cross-telling
cross-selling
up-selling

Endnotes

1. Bill Brendler and Sharon Vonk, "Creating a Customer-Centric Culture Through Organizational Assessment," *CRMguru.com*, 9 May 2002, http://www.crmguru.com/features/2002b/0509bb.html (16 May 2002).

2. Daniel H. Pink, "Who Has the Next Big Idea?" *Fast Company* (September 2001): 114.

3. Mark Adel, *Customer Contacts: Strategies and Operations* (Atlanta: LOMA, 2002), 58.

4. Gene Stone, *Customer Relationship Management* (Atlanta: LOMA, 2002), 4.

CHAPTER 11

Organization and Teamwork in Customer Service

After studying this chapter, you should be able to

- Describe how a company's organizational structure can affect customer service

- Identify four types of management systems

- Name and describe various types of work groups and teams

- Explain the difference between a full-service customer contact center, a gatekeeper customer contact center, and a service center

- Discuss the advantages and challenges of special organizational arrangements, such as outsourcing and virtual work teams

- Describe how a team mission statement, team compact, and code of conduct can improve customer service

- Name and describe the stages of team development

- Discuss the attitude, knowledge, and skills that effective team leaders and team members must possess

Imagine you work for a financial services company called Finster's Financial—and you are Finster. You own and operate the entire business; you develop, modify, advertise, sell, and administer every product, and you handle every customer request. It's hard to imagine, isn't it? Other than certain types of intermediaries, the people who work in the financial services industry are employed by organizations that consolidate the time, effort, knowledge, and skills of many people. However, bringing these people together is just the beginning. To function well, companies rely on a framework of organizational structure achieved through division of labor, a hierarchy of authority, and coordination of effort.

Organizational structure refers to the assignment of task responsibilities and authority relationships within a business entity. *Division of labor* refers to how an organization breaks down a large, complex undertaking into manageable parts to enable work groups and individual employees to become proficient at specific tasks. A *hierarchy of authority* is a system that determines which people in an organization make certain types of decisions and direct the actions of others. To complement division of labor and a hierarchy of authority, organizations rely on *coordination of effort* to synchronize the various activities conducted throughout the company. These concepts are illustrated in Figure 11-1.

As a service provider, you have to be familiar with your company's products, services, procedures, resources, and technology. In addition, you have to be familiar with your company's organizational structure, and you must use your interpersonal skills to function effectively as a member of your work group. At the end of Chapter 10, you saw how various organizational units coordinate their efforts to provide customer service. In this chapter, we will describe how companies are structured and organized. We also will examine various types of work groups and how they function. We will consider some special organizational arrangements, and we will discuss several attributes and activities that contribute to the success of customer service work groups.

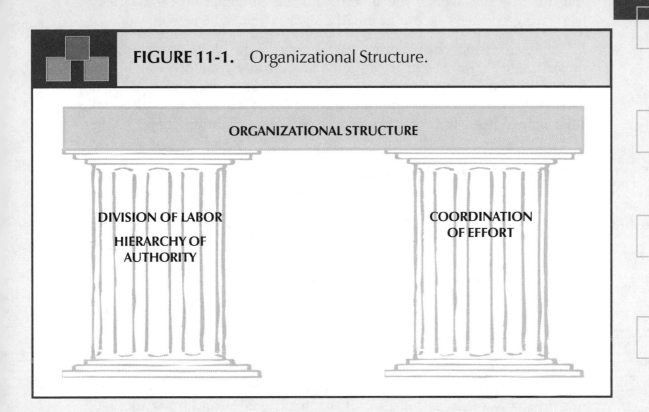

FIGURE 11-1. Organizational Structure.

ORGANIZATIONAL STRUCTURE

DIVISION OF LABOR

HIERARCHY OF
AUTHORITY

COORDINATION
OF EFFORT

Organizational Structure

An **organization
chart** is a visual
display of the
functional areas,
job positions, and
formal lines of
authority in an
organization.

Most firms use organization charts to depict their organizational structure. An **organization chart** is a visual display of the functional areas, job positions, and formal lines of authority in an organization.

Being familiar with the way your company is organized can help you better meet the needs of your customers. Suppose you are a CSR at a mutual fund company and you receive a telephone call from a customer who is trying to obtain information about his investment account. Unfortunately, another division of your company handles that account. With this knowledge, you can quickly direct the customer to the appropriate area. Without this knowledge, you might have to put the customer on hold while you try to find out where to transfer the call. Worse, you might send the customer off on a series of frustrating transfers before he finally reaches the right person.

An organization chart can provide a broad view of all of a company's major functional areas, or it can provide a narrow view of a single work team within an organization. The two basic types of organizational structure—tall organizational structure and flat organizational structure—take their names from the way they appear on an organization chart.

Tall Organizational Structure

Some organization charts resemble a pyramid. One person, the CEO or president, occupies the top spot, a few senior vice presidents are positioned at the next level, and many additional layers of directors, managers, associate managers, supervisors, and assistant supervisors occupy the space between top management and nonmanagerial employees. This type of corporate structure is called a **tall organizational structure**, or *tall organizational pyramid*, and is illustrated in Figure 11-2.

Often, in a company with a tall organizational structure, job responsibilities are relatively narrow in scope and closely supervised, so customer service employees conduct activities in a consistent and productive manner. In many organizations, a tall organizational structure works well. However, a tall organizational structure also can lead to a rather mechanized attitude toward tasks and a rigid conformity to procedures. Policy makers and decision makers might be many layers removed from customers, so they might not always be in touch with customer wants and needs. Also, when an unusual situation arises, a layered hierarchy of authority can lead to slow decision making because employees have to obtain approvals before they can act.

Flat Organizational Structure

Some financial services firms have flattened the organizational pyramid. A **flat organizational structure** (or *flattened organizational pyramid*), as illustrated in Figure 11-3, is a corporate structure that has relatively few layers of supervision between top management and nonmanagerial employees. This organizational structure places decision making closer to the level where service is provided.

The two basic types of organizational structure—tall organizational structure and flat organizational structure—take their names from the way they appear on an organization chart.

FIGURE 11-2. Tall Organizational Structure.

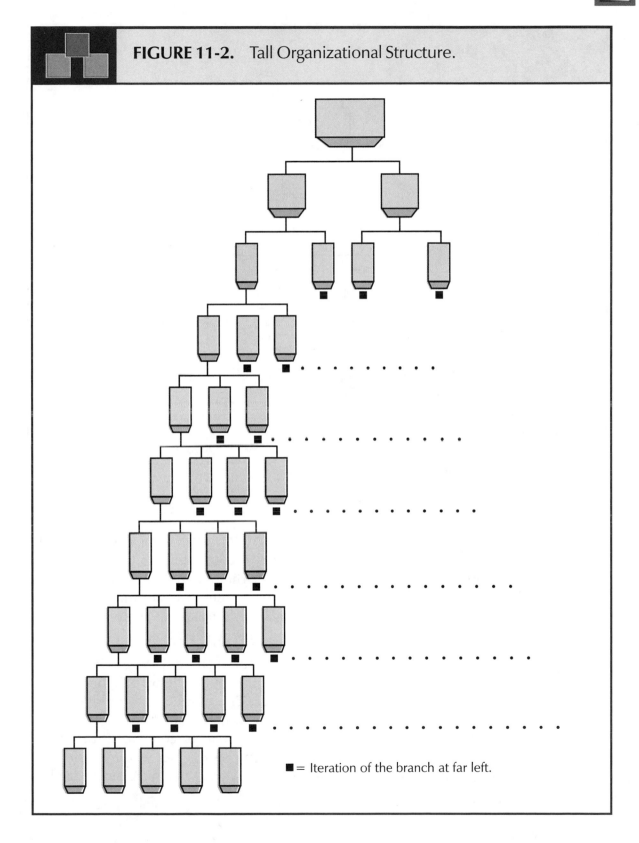

■ = Iteration of the branch at far left.

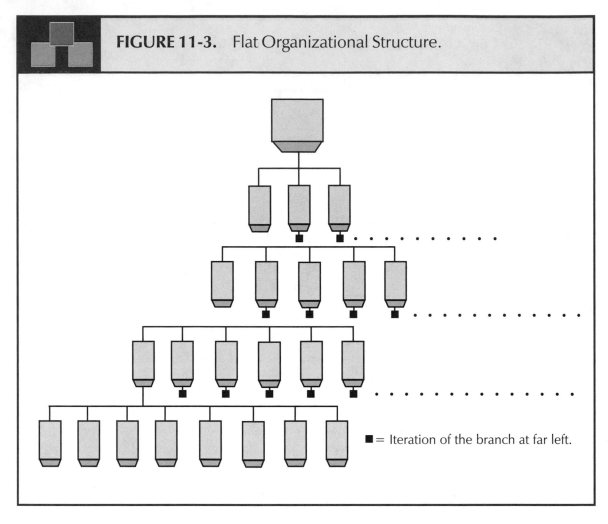

FIGURE 11-3.   Flat Organizational Structure.

■ = Iteration of the branch at far left.

With a flatter organizational structure, companies hope to (1) operate more efficiently by decreasing the time to communicate and implement plans, instructions, and ideas throughout the organization; (2) strengthen relationships among employees and departments by facilitating communication up, down, and across the organization; and (3) reduce operating expenses by eliminating certain management positions.

Managers in a flat organizational structure usually have a wide span of control. **Span of control** refers to the number of people who report directly to a manager, supervisor, or team leader. The number of employees that one person can supervise effectively is limited, but every situation is unique, and no formula can state an ideal span of control. With a wide span of control, a manager has less time to oversee each employee's activities. Although a wide span of control does not necessarily lead to inconsistent customer service, it typically requires effective internal communications, sophisticated information management resources, and well-trained and capable supervisors and staff to help ensure consistency.

Neither a tall nor a flat organizational structure is inherently superior to the other. The most appropriate organizational structure depends on a variety of factors such as the experience and skills of the company's managers and employees, the complexity of the products and services the company provides, and so on. To determine the best organizational structure for delivering customer service, a company must balance the need for consistent customer service with the need for independent, customer-focused initiative.

Types of Management Systems

An important characteristic of a company's organizational structure is its management system. Although no company fits neatly into any one category, most companies have a management system that falls somewhere along a continuum from an exploitative autocratic system to a participative team system, as Figure 11-4 illustrates.[1]

A company's management system is influenced by its corporate culture, and vice versa. Generally, *autocratic* systems focus on strict methods for completing tasks, while *consultative* and *participative* systems emphasize the people who perform tasks. Like tall and flat organizational structures, each type of management system has certain advantages and disadvantages.

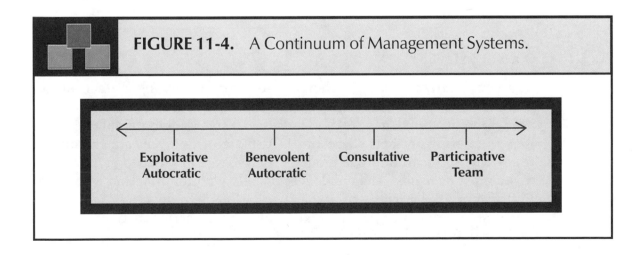

FIGURE 11-4. A Continuum of Management Systems.

Exploitative Autocratic — Benevolent Autocratic — Consultative — Participative Team

EXPLOITATIVE AUTOCRATIC SYSTEM

In an *exploitative autocratic system*, authority and decision making are centralized with managers, especially senior executives, who often maintain secrecy about the company's intentions, place little confidence in the workforce, and rarely delegate responsibility. Managers give orders; employees take orders. Strict, inflexible procedures control most activities, often resulting in uniform customer service. However, an exploitative autocratic system tends to hinder service providers' ability to take necessary action when presented with situations not addressed by company guidelines. Also, because an exploitative system does not value employees, morale is often low, which can lead to poor service.

BENEVOLENT AUTOCRATIC SYSTEM

In a *benevolent autocratic system*, authority and decision making are centralized with managers, especially senior executives, but the relationship between management and the workforce is fairly cordial. Senior executives take a paternalistic interest in the company's employees, as if saying, "Just do your job the way we tell you to, and we'll take good care of you." When procedures are closely aligned with customer expectations, a benevolent autocratic system can lead to efficient customer service. Because benevolent autocratic systems foster uniformity, they work well in companies where there is a high volume of pre-defined tasks. However, in benevolent autocratic systems, employees are seldom encouraged to offer their unique insights and suggestions for improving customer service. Moreover, because autocratic systems require close adherence to policies and procedures, the chain of command takes precedence over individual initiative, so employees are less inclined to pursue independent action when helping customers.

CONSULTATIVE SYSTEM

In a *consultative system*, authority and decision making are centralized with managers, but the relationship with employees is cordial, and managers exhibit confidence in the workforce, often seeking employee opinions and acting on their suggestions. Although employees are encouraged to provide input to improve products, services, and procedures, managers make most decisions, and employees usually wait for direction when serving customers, especially in atypical situations. Employees in a consultative system are not as likely to take independent action as they would be in a participative team system.

PARTICIPATIVE TEAM SYSTEM

In a ***participative team system***, employees at all levels of the organization are involved in making decisions. Managers see themselves as coaches, counselors, and helpers as well as directors. In many cases, employees are given the responsibility and authority to make decisions independently, along with the accountability for the consequences of those decisions, a concept known as empowerment, which we introduced in Chapter 2.

When employees know they can fail on occasion without being punished, they are likely to be more creative, productive, and motivated.

One aspect of empowerment in a participative team system involves allowing employees to take risks and to make mistakes. When employees know they can fail on occasion without being punished, they are likely to be more creative, productive, and motivated. However, not all employees are comfortable working in this type of environment; some employees prefer more structure and may struggle in a participative team system. Without capable and motivated employees, a participative team system can lead to poor customer service. In a participative team system, the company must spend a great deal of time and money training its employees and providing them with opportunities to increase their skills and knowledge.

Exercise 11-1 encourages you to think about the management system and culture at your company and how you might approach your job within that environment.

Exercise 11-1.   What Type of Management System Does Your Company Have?

Now that you are familiar with the continuum of management systems, consider the management system where you work.

- What characteristics does your company's management system have?

- Where would you place your company's management system on the continuum shown in Figure 11-4?

- In what ways does your company's management system affect your job?

- How should you conduct your job activities to complement your company's management system?

How Work Groups Are Organized and Operated

As you saw in Chapter 10, a work group consists of two or more people who work together on a regular basis and coordinate their activities to accomplish common goals. If you work for a financial services company, you are probably a member of at least one work group. A work group can be as small as two bank tellers who share customer service responsibilities in a branch office, or as large as a call center staffed by 30 CSRs who handle telephone requests from around the world.

A work group can be as small as two bank tellers in a branch office, or as large as a call center staffed by 30 CSRs.

Typically, for the reasons mentioned in our discussion of span of control, if a department has a large number of employees, it is broken down into smaller, more manageable work groups. For example, a billing department of 36 service providers could be divided into three work groups, each supporting customers from a different geographical region, and each consisting of 10 to 13 employees and a supervisor reporting to the department manager. On the other hand, a billing department of 10 employees might be the sole work group in that department, and would be considered both a department and a work group.

Although a work group is an organizational unit, it is more than just a collection of names and job titles on an organization chart. Ideally, a work group fosters a sense of belonging and provides clear goals and direction for its members—in other words, every work group has a team identity. Some people use the term *work team* or *team* to refer to a specific type of work group in which members play an active role in managing the team. Other people use the terms *work group* and *work team* interchangeably, as we do in this text, because any work group, regardless of how it is managed, needs to operate as a team.

Team Autonomy

Degree of autonomy refers to the extent to which team members, rather than a supervisor, direct team activities. In this section, we will discuss the degree of autonomy in traditional, semi-autonomous, and self-directed work teams. Similar to management systems, few work groups fit neatly into any one category. In terms of degree of autonomy, work teams fall somewhere along a continuum from traditional to self-directed, as we describe next.

Without a goal, there is no team.

— United States Office of Personnel Management[2]

TRADITIONAL TEAMS

On a **traditional team**, the manager or supervisor performs most or all of the management tasks, such as organizing, planning, monitoring, and controlling the work, as well as the human resource activities described in Chapters 3 and 4. Other team members concentrate solely on doing the work—performing the business functions for which the team is responsible.

SEMI-AUTONOMOUS TEAMS

On a **semi-autonomous team**, the manager or supervisor manages the team, while the other team members, in addition to doing their "regular" work, provide input into planning, organizing, and monitoring the work. Team members have the clearly defined freedom to resolve problems and can make certain decisions without asking permission from the supervisor. However, they report directly to the supervisor who has overall accountability for the team's activities. Team members provide feedback to the supervisor about a variety of issues, such as the type of customer inquiries being received, response times, and patterns of customer complaints. Although team members recommend solutions, the supervisor typically makes the final decisions.

SELF-DIRECTED TEAMS

On a **self-directed team** (sometimes called a *self-managed team*), team members handle many traditional management responsibilities, such as planning and monitoring work. The members of a self-directed team have the authority to make decisions and perform activities necessary to achieve objectives by reviewing incoming work, monitoring workload, directing workflow, developing schedules, reassigning work in the event of absences, preparing reports, and so on. Also, team members on well-established teams may be involved in the hiring, training, evaluation, and dismissal of other team members.

Because management employees remain ultimately accountable for the team's performance, the supervisor (often called a team leader) on a self-directed team almost certainly will provide direction and oversight. However, on a self-directed team, the team leader might have a wide span of control, or might be free to take on special projects in addition to day-to-day management responsibilities. The team leader operates as a *coach* helping the team to achieve its best performance, rather than as a *boss* giving orders and expecting employees to do exactly as they are instructed.

What Work Groups Do

Most work groups are formed to solve problems and identify opportunities for improvement or to conduct ongoing business activities. Many financial services firms recognize the benefits of involving employees in improving work processes and customer service activities. To this end, they sometimes encourage and formalize employee work groups such as quality circles and problem-solving teams, while continuing to rely on functional work teams to perform day-to-day business activities. In this section, we examine (1) quality circles, problem-solving teams, and cross-functional teams, (2) functional work teams in general, and (3) customer service work teams in particular.

Quality Circles, Problem-Solving Teams, and Cross-Functional Teams

A **quality circle**, sometimes called a *work improvement team*, is a group of employees that meets on an ongoing basis to find ways to improve work processes. Sometimes quality circles begin voluntarily and then gain recognition as formal work teams. More often, quality circles are sponsored, formed, and supported by company management from the outset. Quality circles may consist of employees from a single work group or may draw upon employees from two or more work groups or departments.

Problem-solving teams operate under a variety of names, such as *task force* or *ad hoc committee*.

A **problem-solving team** is a work group that typically consists of employees who, because of their knowledge and expertise, are assigned to participate in a project that has a specific, limited objective. Problem-solving teams operate under a variety of names, such as *task force* or *ad hoc committee*. For example, a company might establish a problem-solving team (or task force) to produce, print, and distribute pension fund statements for clients at the end of each year. Throughout the year, these team members are assigned to their regular work groups, but they join the "Year-End Statement Team" on a temporary basis to lend their expertise to assemble data, provide customer-friendly text, ensure regulatory compliance, and print and mail the year-end statements to customers. Like quality circles, problem-solving teams may consist of employees from a single work group or, as the previous example illustrates, they may consist of employees from two or more work groups or departments.

Typically, the members of quality circles and problem-solving teams participate on a part-time or temporary basis, while they retain their regular job duties. The degree of autonomy of a quality circle or problem-solving team varies, depending on the company, its corporate culture, and its management system. For example, one company might establish several problem-solving teams as traditional work teams, each led by a supervisor or manager, while another company might address similar issues by establishing self-directed work teams.

Typically, the members of quality circles and problem-solving teams participate on a part-time or temporary basis, while they retain their regular job duties.

While quality circles often operate indefinitely, problem-solving teams are usually disbanded when they achieve their specific objectives. For example, an insurer might create a problem-solving team to determine why the company's average claim processing turnaround time compares unfavorably with industry standards. Team members work together to examine the problem, identify the causes, and recommend solutions, perhaps in the form of a memorandum to management. Once the recommendations are considered and, if applicable, implemented, the assignment ends and the team disbands. To better understand the responsibilities of a member of a problem-solving team, see Exercise 11-2.

As you saw at the end of Chapter 10, establishing lines of communication and cooperation among departments and work groups is important for an organization. While work groups may operate effectively within their own boundaries, the overall work of the company will suffer if the company's organizational units are isolated. To address this challenge,

---

Exercise 11-2. Preparing for an Assignment on a Problem-Solving Team.

Suppose you are assigned to a problem-solving team in your organization. Think of a specific process or procedure that could benefit from closer examination, or, if you prefer, consider one of the following issues:

- How can we improve internal communication within our work group?

- How can we decrease telephone hold times for our customers, while continuing to provide quality customer service and without adding to staff or increasing expenses?

- How can we improve the menu of options for customers who call our automated telephone answering system?

After you select an issue, think about what ideas you would bring to the initial team meeting and how you would present these ideas to your fellow team members.

some companies establish cross-functional teams. A ***cross-functional team***, which consists of representatives from two or more work groups that perform related business activities, is a team dedicated to improving processes and procedures that cross organizational boundaries. A cross-functional team establishes common standards and procedures, and its members communicate regularly to make sure that each organizational unit is aware of the other's activities. Cross-functional teams can be formed as quality circles operating on an ongoing basis or as problem-solving teams to address specific issues that arise. Figure 11-5 provides some examples of cross-functional teams.

Functional Work Teams and How They Are Organized

Quality circles, problem-solving teams, and cross-functional teams play an important role in many financial services companies. However, most of the day-to-day work that a company's customers depend on is the responsibility of ***functional work teams***, which are permanent organizational units that perform one or more ongoing business activities.

Financial services firms can be organized into as many functional work teams as they have business functions. The method of organization can be based on one or more factors, such as

FIGURE 11-5. Examples of Cross-Functional Teams.

At ABC Financial, a cross-functional "internal communication" team includes a management and a nonmanagerial employee from each administrative department. The management employees are permanent members of the team; the nonmanagerial employees rotate membership. The purpose of this internal communication team is to improve customer service by sharing information and resolving conflicts between and among work groups.

At XYZ Financial, a cross-functional team reviews ideas generated by the company's employee suggestion program to determine which ideas have merit and can be implemented. This cross-functional team is also responsible for responding to each employee who makes a suggestion and for implementing or overseeing implementation of the ideas that are selected.

At Alphabet Life, a cross-functional problem-solving team was established to review the correspondence sent by all of the company's business units to external customers. This team's goal was to improve the quality of communication across the organization. As a result, many form letters were revised to bring about greater consistency and to improve both the format and the content of the company's correspondence with its customers.

- business function, e.g., underwriting, billing, loan processing

- product, e.g., insurance, banking, investments

- customer, e.g., intermediaries, individuals, employer groups

- geographic region, e.g., east, west, central

- priority of request, e.g., fast track or regular processing

- method of communication, e.g., telephone, Web site, walk-in

Note that for the purposes of this discussion, we use the term *functional work team* broadly enough to refer to any organizational unit that performs an ongoing business activity. In this context, a functional work team could be a two-person commission payment unit as well as a 65-person claim department made up of several work teams. In terms of managing and operating these organizational units, the differences are substantial. In this discussion, however, we focus on the activities a team performs and how the team is organized.

SINGLE-FUNCTION AND MULTIPLE-FUNCTION WORK TEAMS

Generally, functional work teams can be categorized as either single function or multiple-function. A **single-function work team** is an organizational unit that primarily performs one specific function—such as billing, claim processing, or loan processing. Team members specialize in handling this one type of transaction, while other teams or departments handle other functions. For example, in an insurance company, the service providers on a policy issue team would produce insurance policies, relying on the underwriting team to supply them with specific information to be included in each policy. Typically, single-function work teams are composed of specialists. A **specialist** is a team member who performs primarily one type of transaction, such as billing or claim processing.

Because of the complexity of handling a broad array of functions, multiple-function work teams sometimes support a limited number of products or customers.

A **multiple-function work team** is an organizational unit that combines various business functions to provide a "one-stop" service department. For example, rather than have separate departments for underwriting, policy issue, policyowner service, and customer service, an insurer could establish a multiple-function work team that performs all of these functions. Because of the complexity of handling a broad array of functions, multiple-function work teams sometimes support a limited number of products or customers. For instance, the work team just described might support only life insurance products (rather than life, disability, and medical products) or it might support only customers from a specific geographical region.

If specialists staff a multiple-function work team, then team members perform different tasks and they work together to complete transactions. Specialists on multiple-function work teams often spend a considerable amount of time coordinating decision making and other activities.

Some multiple-function work teams consist mostly of generalists. A *generalist* is a team member who is cross-trained to handle most or all of a team's functions. A multiple-function work team staffed by generalists is sometimes called a *cross-trained work team*. On a cross-trained work team, each team member is able to complete a variety of transactions. Tasks are often completed quickly and efficiently because each team member can perform most of the tasks associated with a request. Generalists usually require extensive training to acquire the necessary skills and knowledge to complete the variety of requests they are responsible for handling. Therefore, teams composed of generalists typically require more of an investment in training than do teams staffed by specialists.

Insight 11-1 describes how one company changed its organizational structure from single-function work teams to geographically based, multiple-function work teams.

Customer Service Work Teams

When establishing an organizational structure for customer service, financial services companies must consider two basic types of activities: (1) interacting with customers and (2) processing transactions. The challenge lies in determining where to draw the line—through organizational structure and workflow processes—between communicating with customers and performing specific services for customers. Although each company develops its own approach, and some companies use different names to refer to these approaches, a company is likely to provide customer service by way of a full-service customer contact center, a gatekeeper customer contact center, and/or one or more service centers.

FULL-SERVICE CUSTOMER CONTACT CENTER

A *full-service customer contact center* is a department or work group that handles a relatively high percentage of customer contacts, while transferring relatively few requests to administrative and transaction-processing units for handling. A full-service customer contact center allows administrative and transaction processing units to concentrate primarily on performing "back office" functions instead of interacting directly with customers. Typically, team members in the administrative departments have an in-depth knowledge of transaction processing, but do not receive extensive training in customer communication. On the other hand, members of the full-service customer contact center are expected to have strong interpersonal skills and a working knowledge of a variety of transaction-processing activities, although they do not have the depth of knowledge and experience of service providers who work in the transaction-processing units. Insight 11-2 describes a full-service customer contact center that not only handles remote customer contacts, but also provides service to walk-in customers.

GATEKEEPER CUSTOMER CONTACT CENTER

A **gatekeeper customer contact center** is a department or work group that serves as a clearinghouse or "triage unit" for inbound customer contacts. The CSRs handle whatever inquiries and requests they can, and they quickly forward all other customer contacts to the appropriate administrative or

---

INSIGHT 11-1. Organizing Customer Service Work Teams.

In the past, Hypothetical Financial used a function-based approach to organizing its customer service activities. Each work team specialized in furnishing a specific type of function for customers. However, if customers needed more than one type of service, they had to contact more than one work group. For instance, a customer who wanted to check account values and make deposits and withdrawals from different accounts had to place multiple telephone calls or ask to be transferred to several areas to obtain the desired services.

Recently, Hypothetical began using a region-based approach to organizing its customer service activities. Now, when customers call the centralized toll-free telephone number, their calls are automatically routed to the appropriate service team: East, Central, or West. The service providers on all three teams are trained to help customers with a variety of inquiries and transactions, such as:

- Requests for account values

- Fund transfers

- Disbursements

- Monthly bank deductions

- Name, address, and telephone number changes

Working on these region-based work teams, service providers are more familiar with their customers and are able to deliver more consistent customer service. Furthermore, the cross-trained team members seldom have to transfer customers to other work teams; they can provide one-stop customer service in most instances.

INSIGHT 11-2. A Full-Service Customer Contact Center.

At The Great Eastern Company in Singapore, a full-service customer contact center staffed with twenty-five customer service representatives handles telephone calls from 600,000 policyholders, 2,500 insurance agents, and 500 bank assurance personal financial consultants. Also, customers can contact Great Eastern using touchpoints like e-mail, fax, or transactions on its Web site. The state-of-the-art customer contact center is located on the ground floor of Great Eastern Centre inside the Centre Business District, where customers are also welcome to walk into the reception area to obtain information and seek personal assistance. Because Great Eastern's CSRs rotate between the customer contact center and the reception area, they must develop skills in written, telephone, and face-to-face communication, as well as the knowledge to handle a variety of transactions for the customers they support.

Great Eastern Customer Service

---

transaction-processing unit for handling. Team members in a gatekeeper customer contact center are expected to have strong interpersonal skills and to be familiar with the activities that various areas in the organization perform, but they are not trained to handle specific transaction processing activities or to provide in-depth answers to customer inquiries.

SERVICE CENTERS

In some companies, administrative and transaction-processing departments handle customer contacts, working in conjunction with or in place of a customer contact center. This type of department—called a *service center* or *working customer contact center*—is an administrative or transaction-processing unit that is also responsible for handling customer contacts related to the functions it performs. A service center has a dual role, operating as both a transaction-processing area and a customer contact center. For instance, customers might contact the billing department service center for billing inquiries, the claim department service center for claim inquiries, and a full-service customer contact center for all other requests. Typically, members of a service center have an in-depth knowledge of transaction-processing functions, and they receive additional training in communication skills.

Figure 11-6 depicts the full-service, gatekeeper, and service center models of customer service.

FIGURE 11-6.   Types of Customer Service Work Teams.

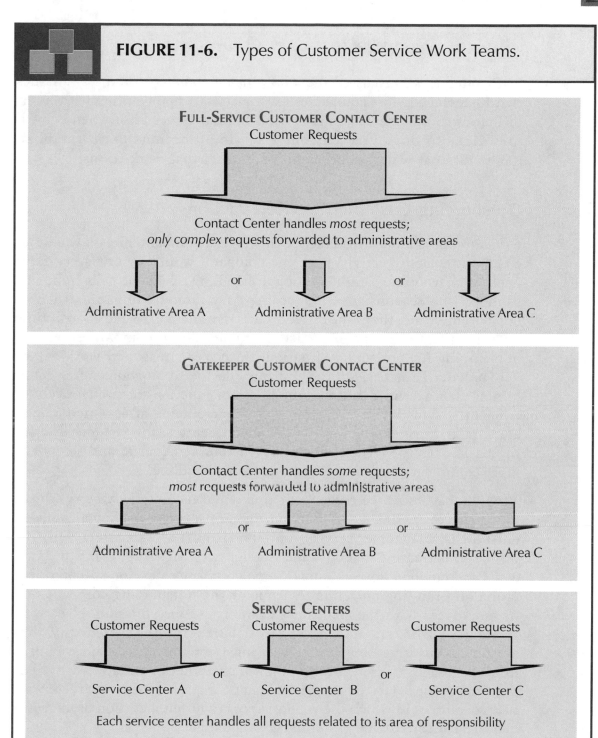

FULL-SERVICE CUSTOMER CONTACT CENTER

Customer Requests

Contact Center handles *most* requests;
only complex requests forwarded to administrative areas

Administrative Area A   or   Administrative Area B   or   Administrative Area C

GATEKEEPER CUSTOMER CONTACT CENTER

Customer Requests

Contact Center handles *some* requests;
most requests forwarded to administrative areas

Administrative Area A   or   Administrative Area B   or   Administrative Area C

SERVICE CENTERS

Customer Requests   Customer Requests   Customer Requests

Service Center A   or   Service Center B   or   Service Center C

Each service center handles all requests related to its area of responsibility

Special Organizational Arrangements

In Chapter 2, we discussed the *who's-the-customer-syndrome* and issues that financial services companies must address when working with intermediaries to provide customer service. Similar issues arise when companies elect to outsource customer service functions or to establish non-traditional work arrangements such as virtual work teams.

Outsourcing Customer Service Functions

Some companies rely on outsourcing for temporary situations such as increases in workload or new product launches.

Outsourcing is a business practice in which a company hires a vendor to conduct a specific activity that the company would otherwise perform itself, such as billing administration or handling telephone calls from customers. The reasons for outsourcing vary. Some companies turn to outsourcing when they take on a new activity and don't have enough time to build the necessary expertise in-house. Some companies rely on outsourcing for temporary situations such as increases in workload or new product launches. Other companies decide to outsource after determining that a vendor can perform a certain function more effectively or efficiently than the company can. Some outsourcing arrangements operate similar to gatekeeper customer contact centers: the vendor performs the basic activities, such as routine customer requests, and refers the more complicated tasks to the company for handling.

As we have stressed throughout this text, customer service is critical to the success of financial services firms. Consequently, when a company outsources a customer service function it must work closely with the vendor to determine that customer service activities meet company standards and customer expectations. Some companies develop special orientation and training programs to acquaint the outsourcing company and its employees with the company's customer service mission, objectives, strategies, products, and procedures. Furthermore, a company that outsources customer service activities must obtain contractual assurances from the vendor to protect the privacy of customer information as well as the firm's proprietary information. Many companies also obtain contractual guarantees in which the vendor agrees to forfeit a portion of its fees if it fails to meet specific performance standards.

Virtual Work Teams

A *virtual work team* electronically links geographically separate business sites to form a single work group for purposes of managing, scheduling, monitoring, and conducting business activities.

Advances in technology and changes in corporate culture have led to organizational arrangements, called virtual work teams, which are used to perform a variety of business functions, including customer service. A **virtual work team** electronically links geographically separate business sites to form a single work group for purposes of managing, scheduling, monitoring, and conducting business activities. Virtual work teams are called *virtual* because their members do not all work at the same location. The term also refers to an arrangement in which service providers work from their homes, or telecommute, as you saw in Chapter 4.

Some companies link separate customer contact centers electronically to draw upon a large pool of qualified employees to provide customer service. The separate work sites can support one another across time zones and during periods of overflow volume or emergencies. If one location is experiencing an unusually heavy volume of work, the manager can ask another site to take on some of the work. Similarly, if a request requires a particular type of expertise, the company can draw upon service providers from throughout the organization, regardless of location, to handle the transaction.

However, the benefits of virtual work teams do not come easily. Besides the complexity and costs of obtaining and operating the necessary technologies, virtual work teams present communication and team-building challenges. Because all the members of a virtual team seldom, if ever, meet in person, the greatest challenge for the team is to foster a sense of team identity. For example, telecommuting employees—who spend most of their working hours alone—may have difficulty thinking of themselves as part of a team. They don't have access to the kind of information that often is exchanged informally—in hallways or at lunch tables—and they may not be able to participate in morale-boosting activities.

To help address some of these challenges, companies use team compacts and codes of conduct (discussed later in this chapter) to clearly document the expectations and responsibilities of virtual team members. Companies also rely on electronic communications to facilitate the flow of information. For example, a company can arrange to have teleconferences instead of in-person team meetings. Another option is to have **net meetings**, which combine audio, video, and data communication over the Internet, enabling participants to log on to an Internet site at a scheduled time to "meet" and share information.

Making Work Teams Work

Any group that strives to achieve common goals must have skilled and motivated team members who understand what they are expected to do and how they are expected to interact. Teamwork contributes greatly to the success of most work groups and organizations, and it is often a specific performance objective in employee performance evaluations. In this section, we examine how work groups establish guidelines to operate more effectively, and how employees contribute to the success of their work groups.

Team Mission Statement

A *team mission statement*, which is derived from the corporate and/or customer service mission statement, defines the team's purpose and goals, and serves as an overall guide for the team's activities. Often, the work group shares its mission statement with senior management to ensure that the statement is compatible with the corporate mission. Individual team members regularly review the team mission statement to make sure their attitudes and activities align with the team's mission. Typically, a team mission statement focuses on the importance of teamwork, and it serves as the basis for work group and individual objectives. An example of a team mission statement is shown in Figure 11-7.

FIGURE 11-7. A Customer Service Team Mission Statement.

Together we strive to provide excellent customer service, to encourage sales of our products and services, and to enhance retention by supporting our customers quickly, competently, and courteously.

Some work groups operate with very few written guidelines. New team members learn what is expected of them through orientation and training and by observing, interacting, and communicating with experienced team members. To provide an overall framework for team activities, these work groups might develop a team mission statement, but provide little else in the way of formalized guidelines. Other work groups take a more structured approach to communicating expectations. They might begin with a team mission statement, but also develop (1) a team compact, (2) an overview of roles and responsibilities, and/or (3) a code of conduct.

Team Compact, Roles and Responsibilities, and Code of Conduct

A **team compact**—often used by highly autonomous teams—is an agreement between the company and the team's members indicating that (1) the company will grant certain rights, responsibilities, and resources to team members and (2) the team will achieve specified performance goals. A team compact describes what the company and the team can expect of each other. For example, a team compact might distinguish between decisions reserved for management and decisions the team can make on its own; or it might indicate the level and type of information that management communicates to the team, and vice versa.

A team compact describes what the company and the team can expect of each other.

In semi-autonomous and self-directed work teams, the supervisor shares management responsibilities with team members. In traditional work teams, the supervisor performs most or all of the managerial functions, while team members concentrate on activities that support customers. Each team ultimately develops its own relationships and dynamics that further define the *roles and responsibilities* of team members. Some teams put these guidelines in writing; other teams take a less formal approach. However, if arguments arise around statements such as, "That's not my job," then a work group needs to pay closer attention to clarifying the roles and responsibilities of team members.

A **code of conduct**, also called *guiding principles*, is a document that provides guidelines for how employees are expected to approach their jobs. It identifies the attitudes, behaviors, and goals that a work group or organization deems most important. Ideally, a code of conduct becomes a part of the team culture and influences the way team members interact with each other and with customers. For example, in a call center, where unscheduled absences negatively affect service results, most team members are very much aware of the importance of beginning their workday on time. If a team member consistently comes to work late, her coworkers might remind her of the importance of punctuality.

Some companies develop a code of conduct or guiding principles for the entire organization, not just specific work teams. Often, these guidelines emphasize qualities such as professionalism, communication, and teamwork. In the area of professionalism, for instance, the code of conduct might call upon employees to protect the confidentiality of customer information as well as proprietary company information. In the area of communication, the code of conduct might call upon employees to understand their role in sharing information and handing off and receiving work assignments. Companies also develop guidelines for common activities, such as meetings. Figure 11-8 shows a code of conduct for an entire organization, for a customer service work team, and for meetings.

Stages of Team Development

Suppose you have been assigned to a newly formed cross-functional team. Or perhaps your current work group is merging with another work group. Or maybe you are a member of a new work team created to support a new product. Typically, in situations like these, you will find that the work group needs time to develop and reach a high level of performance. Supervisors and team members must understand and address the dynamics of newly formed or restructured work teams, and they must exhibit patience and perseverance as they learn to work in new ways and with a variety of people.

Newly formed work groups usually go through several developmental stages on their way to becoming high-performing groups. Psychologist Bruce W. Tuckman identified four stages of team development: forming, storming, norming, and performing.[3] By recognizing and taking steps to facilitate these stages, as discussed in Figure 11-9, you can improve your team's chances for success.

Effective Customer Service Team Leaders

Regardless of their degree of autonomy, all work groups depend on effective leadership. One of the most important traits of an effective team leader is the ability to work well with many different people. Team leaders must be able to motivate team members and help employees through

FIGURE 11-8. Codes of Conduct.

CODE OF CONDUCT FOR AN ORGANIZATION

- Expect change, embrace it, and grow.
- Help us achieve our financial goals each year.
- Success relies on achieving a balance of value, timeliness, and customer perception; we call this our Performance Triangle.
- Focus on the customer in everything you do.
- Follow the Platinum Rule: Do unto others what they would like to have done.
- We're all on the same team; we must work together to succeed.
- Set goals, ask for the support you need, and take action.
- Learn from your successes and failures; be ethical; keep a positive attitude; have fun.
- Take advantage of the opportunities we provide for the continued professional growth of our employees.
- Think, listen, then think again.

CODE OF CONDUCT FOR A CUSTOMER SERVICE WORK TEAM

We interact with customers in a positive way, we confidently communicate information, and we make our customers feel better about their day with each call. Our goal is total customer satisfaction.

We contribute to a productive work environment, one that is positive, team-oriented, and supportive of individual achievement.

We support one another, which allows us to operate efficiently and maximize the care we give each customer.

We support the organization as a whole, which means providing assistance to other departments, when needed, for the benefit of our customers.

We are knowledgeable and compassionate when dealing with customers. We maintain an excellent knowledge of the products and we accurately communicate information. We show our respect for customers by utilizing their time effectively and by responding in a timely manner.

Customers expect speed, simplicity, and excellent customer care, and we strive to deliver these.

We ask questions and engage in active listening to understand customer expectations and needs, so we may meet them. Listening and asking questions is the foundation of our success in communicating with customers.

We treat all of our colleagues and coworkers with the same respect and courtesy we afford customers.

We recognize that integrity is the basis of all customer communication and must be the basis of everything we do.

continued on next page

Figure 11-8.   Codes of Conduct (*continued*).

GUIDELINES FOR MEETINGS

- Start and end on time
- Follow the agenda
- Listen actively and paraphrase or ask questions if you don't understand
- Don't dismiss an idea before it is considered
- Focus on the message, not the person
- Participate openly, but don't interrupt
- Don't have side meetings, i.e., don't have conversations with people around you when someone else is speaking
- Headline ideas, i.e., express the main point but don't go into too much detail (otherwise, the meeting will not end on time)

difficult times. They must foster an environment in which each team member feels that she is contributing to the success of the team. Effective team leaders find ways to recognize and reward exceptional customer service, and they provide support and coaching to team members during stressful periods. Team leaders also must encourage and reward performance that supports team and organizational goals, rather than behaviors that focus exclusively on individual achievements. In addition, through words and actions, effective team leaders must demonstrate the importance of customer service.

Another important skill for team leaders is the ability to delegate. ***Delegation*** is the process of transferring a task or activity along with appropriate decision-making authority to another person. Effective delegation entails knowing which activities to delegate (and which to retain), communicating expectations, and providing necessary resources.

Team leaders also must encourage and reward performance that supports team and organizational goals.

Although all successful team leaders have certain skills in common, supervisory styles do vary, depending on the person and the situation. The most versatile supervisors can modify their leadership styles based on the characteristics of the work team they are leading.[4] For example, if a supervisor is assigned to a traditional work team or a work team with a large number of inexperienced employees, a supervisory leadership style works well. ***Supervisory leadership*** is a leadership style in which the supervisor performs most of the planning, makes most of the decisions, and handles most of the problems that arise. Supervisory leadership is not appropriate for semi-autonomous or self-directed teams.

FIGURE 11-9. Stages of Team Development.

FORMING

When team members first get together, they typically do not yet have a clear picture of what is expected of them. The initial stage of team development, or **forming**, involves developing operating guidelines that serve as a template for how the team members interact. A mixture of excitement, anxiety, and insecurity is usually present at the beginning of a new team endeavor. During the forming stage, you can facilitate team development by (1) getting to know and being sensitive to other team members and (2) helping create a positive work climate.

STORMING

The **storming** stage occurs as team members look for their common ground and work through their differences. Frustration and anger may emerge as team members begin trying to work together to determine what the team is to accomplish and how. Then, as team members clarify their roles and responsibilities and learn to work together, the storm subsides. Research reveals that this stage is essential to the development of an effective team. Without a storming stage, team members do not learn how to resolve differences, and teams tend to be less creative and may develop subgroups that hinder overall performance. You can facilitate the storming stage of team development by (1) understanding that conflict is normal, (2) remaining positive and open, (3) looking for common ground, and (4) helping to define and clarify roles.

NORMING

As the team finds its footing and develops standard operating procedures, it enters the norming stage. **Norming** is characterized by greater harmony among team members, who begin to trust each other and communicate more openly. Although achieving balance helps the team to operate smoothly, this stage may result in some team members holding back good ideas to avoid conflict. During the norming stage, you can facilitate team development by (1) helping other team members, (2) remaining open and honest, (3) clarifying your role, if necessary, and (4) seeking further development and training.

PERFORMING

In the **performing** stage, the team has discovered how to achieve a balance between its members' common goals and their differences, thereby achieving smooth, productive operation without sacrificing the talents and creativity of the individual members. Members of a team in the performing stage have developed the mutual trust and respect that allow them to value individual opinions, while acting as a team to achieve common goals. You can facilitate the performing stage of team development by (1) taking initiative, (2) concentrating on tasks, (3) dealing with conflict, and (4) demonstrating commitment to the work group.

After a team reaches the performing stage, it might at some point revert to an earlier stage. New challenges or problems that provoke strong differences of opinion may return the team to the storming stage. A change in the composition of the team may even send the group back to the forming stage as it assimilates new members or adjusts to the loss of valuable members, reevaluating the team's basic method of operation to compensate for the change.

Participative leadership is a leadership style in which the supervisor acts as a coordinator, planning team activities and making decisions affecting the team after obtaining input from team members. Participative leadership works well for semi-autonomous work teams. A manager or supervisor who exhibits a participative leadership style sets high goals for achievement and output, while encouraging and supporting employee autonomy and teamwork.

Team leadership is a leadership style in which the supervisor shares responsibility for the team's operation with the team members and spends more time on larger organizational issues that affect team performance. In some cases, the team leader is not actually involved in the day-to-day operations of the team but is available to meet the needs identified by team members. Team leadership is appropriate for mature, self-directed teams.

Effective Customer Service Team Members

As one employee among many, you might wonder what impact you could have on your company's operations and results. But if you look at your role as a member of a smaller work group, you will see that you certainly can have an impact on your coworkers and your team. A member of a customer service work group has two main responsibilities. One responsibility is to effectively perform the activities of your job by understanding what tasks you are supposed to perform and the expected level of performance. However, your value to your work group is not confined to the quantity and quality of your work. Your other main responsibility involves how you interact with your coworkers and how you contribute to the success of your team and the organization.

In previous chapters, you saw how service providers rely heavily on interpersonal skills to deliver customer service to internal and external customers. In addition, to provide exceptional customer service, you must form cooperative relationships with the other members of your work group. You must possess or be willing to develop certain skills and knowledge to function effectively as a member of a team. For instance, you should

To provide exceptional customer service, you must form cooperative relationships with the other members of your work group.

- Make sure you understand your work group's mission and goals, and what you can do to help achieve those goals

- Maintain a pleasant, professional demeanor, treat coworkers with courtesy and respect, and act in a trustworthy manner

- Provide and receive constructive feedback; support and encourage other team members

- Avoid inappropriate, sarcastic, or condescending comments; avoid fostering ill will or holding grudges against fellow employees

- Avoid spreading rumors and constantly complaining; direct your concerns to someone who can help; strive to support all organizational goals and decisions, even if you disagree

- Communicate and cooperate with your coworkers

- Take ownership of your responsibilities; act in a proactive manner to meet team and individual goals and to support internal and external customers; avoid dwelling on mistakes (yours or your coworkers'); learn from mistakes and move on, always striving for a high level of performance

In this chapter, you have seen how financial services firms and their employees use organizational structure to assign customer service responsibilities and authority, to help coordinate activities, and to provide superior customer service through teamwork. As you will see in Chapter 12, another way that companies and their employees accomplish these important goals is by developing and following processes and procedures that enhance customer service.

To practice and review the skills and information you learned in this chapter, see the interactive CD, *Practicing Your Customer Service Skills*, included with this book.

Key Terms and Concepts

organizational structure	participative team system
division of labor	degree of autonomy
hierarchy of authority	traditional team
coordination of effort	semi-autonomous team
organization chart	self-directed team
tall organizational structure	quality circle
flat organizational structure	problem-solving team
span of control	cross-functional team
exploitative autocratic system	functional work teams
benevolent autocratic system	single-function work team
consultative system	specialist

Key Terms and Concepts (*continued*).

multiple-function work team
generalist
full-service customer contact
  center
gatekeeper customer contact
  center
service center
outsourcing
virtual work team
net meetings
team mission statement

team compact
roles and responsibilities
code of conduct
forming
storming
norming
performing
delegation
supervisory leadership
participative leadership
team leadership

Endnotes

1. Based on Rensis Likert's four systems of management in *The Human Organization* (New York: McGraw-Hill, 1967).

2. Office of Personnel Management, "Building a Collaborative Team Environment," *Workforce Performance Newsletter Report*, August 1997, http://www.opm.gov/perform/articles/072.htm (19 April 2002).

3. John H. Zenger et al., *Leading Teams: Mastering the New Role* (Homewood, IL: Business One Irwin, 1994), 85.

4. Ibid., 17.

CHAPTER 12

Customer Service Workflow and Measurement

After studying this chapter, you should be able to

- Discuss several kinds of customer service processes and work practices

- Explain the difference between efficiency and effectiveness

- Describe process management and workflow analysis

- Identify several attributes of effective performance measurement

- Describe the uses of qualitative and quantitative performance measurement and the differences between them

- Describe the advantages and disadvantages of using internal standards, industry standards, and universal standards for benchmarking

- Discuss various performance measurement techniques that are effective in evaluating customer service

Gloria Sabino has decided to start saving for retirement, so she contacts Bill Bosley, a broker with TBT Associates, and they discuss several strategies to help Ms. Sabino achieve her goal. Mr. Bosley then calls Archaic Life Insurance Company, Straight-Ahead Financial Services, and Juniper Financial Group, asking each to provide information about investment products, rules, costs, and historical rates of return. When Mr. Bosley contacts these financial services firms, he initiates customer service processes that generate the information he and Ms. Sabino requested.

After Ms. Sabino reviews the information with Mr. Bosley, she decides that Juniper Financial offers an annuity product that best meets her needs. She completes an application, and indicates that she would like to have her monthly premiums automatically drafted from her checking account. Mr. Bosley mails the application to Juniper's new business unit, which approves the application and sends an annuity contract to Mr. Bosley. When Ms. Sabino receives the contract, she gives Mr. Bosley a check for the first monthly payment, which he sends to Juniper. The accounting department establishes an account for Ms. Sabino and approves a commission check for Mr. Bosley.

So far, the customer service processes have worked smoothly and Ms. Sabino and Mr. Bosley are satisfied customers. However, when the first premium payment is withdrawn from Ms. Sabino's checking account, she notices that Juniper has taken $20 too much. Her telephone call to Mr. Bosley starts another customer service process. Mr. Bosley calls Juniper's customer contact center to explain the problem. Then an employee from the billing department calls Ms. Sabino to acknowledge the error and explain how Juniper intends to correct the problem.

As this example illustrates, processes play a vital role in the delivery of customer service. In this chapter, we will discuss customer service processes and the actions companies and their employees take to ensure the integrity of these processes. We will also examine how financial services firms evaluate their customer service systems and processes through performance measurement.

Customer Service Processes

In Chapter 2, you learned that a process is a series of steps involved in performing a recurring activity designed to produce a specific outcome. Service providers follow processes (also called *workflows*, *work practices*, or *procedures*) to perform a variety of customer service activities such as explaining product features, reviewing applications, calculating benefits, and producing monthly account statements. In most cases, well-designed processes enable service providers to perform their jobs more quickly, accurately, and consistently, and with fewer frustrations than would be possible without such processes. In this section, we discuss typical customer service processes in the financial services industry.

In most cases, well-designed processes enable service providers to perform their jobs more quickly, accurately, and consistently, and with fewer frustrations than would be possible without such processes.

Although different companies have different methods for delivering customer service, many processes fall into general categories, such as receiving and routing requests from customers, fulfilling requests, handling complaints, and documenting and sharing information within the organization.

Receiving and Routing Requests

One of the keys to delivering exceptional customer service is linking the customer with the person or work group most capable of handling the customer's request. In a perfect world, a company's communication system would direct each customer to the appropriate person on the first try. As you will see in Chapter 13, companies use various technologies to enhance customer contact routing. In reality, however, service providers sometimes receive customer requests that they have to transfer to other people in the organization. Most companies expect their employees to accomplish this transfer by using a conference transfer, as discussed in Chapter 7.

Another important step in receiving customer requests is to verify customer identity—that is, to confirm that people really are who they claim to be. Because financial services companies maintain confidential customer information, service providers and self-service systems such as Web sites and automated telephone systems must protect the privacy of customers by ensuring that confidential information is not released to unauthorized individuals.

Service providers verify customer identity in a number of ways. For example, they can request that the customer provide information such as home address, telephone number, social security number, or mother's maiden name. Some companies assign each customer a personal identification number (PIN) or customer identification number (CIN), which the customer must provide to proceed with a request.

To further ensure privacy, many financial services firms establish guidelines that help employees determine what information they can release and to whom. These guidelines are particularly important for inexperienced service providers who might not realize the significance of maintaining confidentiality. Suppose the husband of a policyowner/insured calls to find out how many life insurance policies his wife owns, the face amounts of those policies, and the names of the beneficiaries. Francisco Ayala, the service provider who receives the call, apologizes and explains that he cannot provide the information requested because the caller is not the policyowner. Although the caller angrily expresses his displeasure and threatens to complain to the company president, Mr. Ayala politely but firmly explains the company's position on the release of confidential information.

To Mr. Ayala, who is a new employee, the request seems harmless enough and the procedure appears needlessly strict. Later, however, he learns that the caller and the policyowner are in the middle of a bitter divorce proceeding, and the husband was attempting to obtain information without his wife's knowledge. By following company guidelines regarding confidentiality of customer information, Mr. Ayala may have avoided a serious problem.

Fulfilling Requests

Because no two employees have the same knowledge and skills, the potential for unintended service variation is always present. Therefore, most companies maintain documented procedures to provide consistent customer service. Service providers learn and follow these procedures through training and by referring to resources such as manuals, memos, and computer-based information systems.

Because no two employees have the same knowledge and skills, the potential for unintended service variation is always present.

Clearly defined and communicated processes help service providers complete customer requests as quickly and accurately as possible. Sometimes, however, follow-up work is necessary. ***Follow-up work*** refers to any type of activity a service provider and/or a customer decide cannot be completed during or soon after the initial customer contact. Typically, follow-up work involves additional research. In some cases, the service provider completes the follow-up work. In other cases, the service provider initiates a ***service request***, which is a requisition for another person or area to complete the work that was initiated by the customer's request.

To foster customer loyalty, some financial services firms establish guidelines for making exceptions to standard procedures, an activity known as ***exception processing***. For example, a financial services firm might do business with intermediaries who have relationships with several companies, and these intermediaries might have little tolerance for processes that are substantially different from the processes used by other companies. So, under certain circumstances, the company might authorize service providers to take steps not included in the standard procedures. Most exception processing guidelines specify which procedures are open to exception and the criteria for making exceptions, as well as which procedures are non-negotiable. For instance, the guidelines might point out situations in which service providers can initiate compensation advances for intermediaries up to specified dollar amounts.

> To foster customer loyalty, some financial services firms establish guidelines for making exceptions to standard procedures, an activity known as ***exception processing***.

When standard procedures and exception processing fail to meet customer expectations, escalation is sometimes an alternative. An ***escalation process*** is a procedure that specifies how and to whom a particular type of request should be addressed and directed when the service provider is not able or authorized to resolve the issue. In companies with autocratic management systems, discussed in Chapter 11, escalation processes might be prevalent because service providers are required to adhere closely to established procedures. In participative team systems, also discussed in Chapter 11, service providers are more likely to be empowered to resolve issues on their own. However, regardless of a company's management system, there will be times when escalation is necessary.

> Arguably, nothing is more telling about an organization's commitment to customer service delivery than how that organization solves customer service problems.
>
> —R. Eric Reidenbach, Gordon W. McClung, and Reginald W. Goeke[1]

An escalation process can be as simple and informal as transferring a call to a manager on duty. However, since escalation often involves dissatisfied customers, many companies establish formal procedures. A formal escalation process is an acknowledgment to service providers that despite their best efforts, not all customer requests can be resolved to the customer's satisfaction, and the organization recognizes that procedures must be in place to handle these situations. In addition, by analyzing the types of situations that trigger escalation, a company might be able to identify shortcomings in its standard procedures and thus improve its processes.

Handling Complaints

Most financial services firms have procedures for handling customer complaints. These procedures are designed to comply with regulatory requirements, minimize the risk of lawsuits, and/or improve customer service. Complaint handling procedures vary by company and product. In some companies, for instance, complaints are logged into a shared database by the CSR who receives the complaint. CSRs input their name, the customer's name, the date and time of the complaint, the nature of the complaint, and any special comments. They forward this information along with any supporting documentation to the appropriate work group or person for handling. Then the recipient resolves the issue and updates the database. In other companies, complaints arriving anywhere in the organization are immediately forwarded to a complaint team. A member of the complaint team logs the complaint into a database and either attempts to resolve the issue or forwards it to the appropriate area for handling.

An important part of any complaint-handling process is to carefully document all relevant information. Insight 12-1 describes the complaint handling procedures used by managed health care companies in the United States.

Information gathered through customer contacts can be used to improve future customer contacts and to assist in many other areas.

Documenting and Sharing Information

Most companies have procedures for documenting and sharing information related to routine customer requests, as well as complaints. Service providers record data such as the customer's name and account number, the nature of the request, and the information or service requested or provided. Information gathered through customer contacts can be used to improve future customer contacts and to assist in many other areas—such as marketing, sales, compliance, legal, and transaction-processing departments, as you saw in Chapter 10.

INSIGHT 12-1. Managed Health Care Complaint Resolution Procedures.

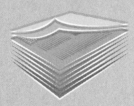

In the United States, managed care organizations (MCOs) establish specific complaint resolution procedures (CRPs) to handle complaints from plan members and medical providers. These CRPs address both informal complaints and formal appeals. Informal complaints are the member's or provider's initial attempt to address a problem. Formal appeals become necessary when an informal complaint is not resolved to a member's or provider's satisfaction.

Under a formal appeal, a dispute is reviewed and resolved by a party other than the employee who made the initial decision or performed the service that led to the complaint. The appeal process follows established procedures and typically includes at least two levels of appeal.

In a Level One appeal, a medical director or other officer of the company reviews the original decision and any additional supporting information submitted by the complaining member, and either upholds or overturns the initial decision. Generally, decisions on appeals are communicated in writing to all involved parties. If the Level One appeal upholds the original decision, the company informs the member in writing of his right to appeal to the next level.

A Level Two appeal is often handled by an MCO appeals committee, which might consist of representatives from various areas within the company. If the appeal involves a medical issue, the committee includes a physician. Some appeals committees also include plan members from the community.

An MCO's complaint resolution procedures specify maximum time frames for conducting each level of appeal. MCOs also have procedures for expediting appeals to address a situation in which the standard time limits for appeals might be harmful to the member's health.

Many states have laws regarding CRPs. Although specific CRP requirements vary by state, they often require MCOs to inform all members about CRPs, track and report complaints, comply with specific time frames when responding to complaints, and provide an option for independent external review of complaints when internal appeals are exhausted.

Source: Adapted from Academy for Healthcare Management, *Managed Healthcare, An Introduction*, 3rd ed. (Washington, D.C.: Academy for Healthcare Management, © 2001), 10-35–10-36. Used with permission; all rights reserved.

Some companies use information-sharing systems to route and monitor customer requests. For example, if a customer calls to change her insurance premium payment method from check to electronic funds transfer, the CSR can enter the request in the system and forward it to the billing department for handling. The CSR can also check the system several days later to view the status of the request and make sure it has been completed. We will discuss these types of workflow systems in more detail in Chapter 13.

Compliance and Liability Issues

As you saw earlier in this chapter, financial services companies typically verify the identity of customers before providing confidential information. Protecting the privacy of customers, in addition to being a good customer service practice, is often required by law. Although prevalent in many countries, privacy laws vary widely. In the European Union, for instance, privacy is regulated on a comprehensive basis across all industries, whereas in the United States privacy is regulated on an industry-by-industry basis with different requirements for different financial services products.

In addition to privacy requirements, service providers must be aware of the impact of many other types of laws and regulations. Because work practices often vary due to the regulatory requirements of various jurisdictions, employees must be knowledgeable of or have access to information about all applicable regulations. Among other things, failure to comply with laws and regulations can result in fines, lawsuits, and negative publicity for a company.

Service providers must be knowledgeable of work practices designed to reduce the risk of costly errors, lawsuits, unintended liability, and fraud.

Furthermore, service providers must be knowledgeable of work practices designed to reduce the risk of costly errors, lawsuits, unintended liability, and fraud. At one company, for instance, when service providers suspect fraud, they enter the incident into a company-wide tracking system. Then they give all applicable information and documents to their supervisor, who reviews the facts and decides whether or not to forward the incident to the company's compliance department for further investigation.

All financial services companies have procedures for disbursing funds. Typically, these procedures are designed to address issues such as acceptable communication channels (e.g., telephone, fax, or e-mail) and methods of verifying customer identity. For instance, some companies accept telephone requests for fund disbursements, but only for amounts under specified amounts. Before accepting such requests by telephone, service providers might have to verify personal information, such as the caller's Social Security number or personal identification number. For amounts in excess of the specified amounts, the procedures might require the customer to mail a signed form, so the signature can be compared to the signature on file. In addition, the procedures for handling disbursement requests might stipulate that checks be mailed only to the address specified

According to one survey, almost 68 percent of individual life insurers require the policyowner's original signature before the company will complete a cash surrender.
Source: LOMA[2]

in the company's records. At some firms, if a request for a disbursement is accompanied by an address change, the service provider calls the customer to make sure the address is valid.

Successful Customer Service Processes

So far in this chapter, we have examined several uses of customer service processes and how these processes work. In this section, we briefly describe the characteristics of the best customer service processes.

SEAMLESS PROCESSES

The ultimate purpose of any customer service process is to encourage customers to continue doing business with the company.

A **seamless process** (also referred to as an *invisible system*) is a process that is designed so a customer is not inconvenienced by—or even aware of—the steps involved in fulfilling the request. The ultimate purpose of any customer service process is to encourage customers to continue doing business with the company. The company's work practices and procedures, as well as the resources that support the processes, should be flexible enough so customers never hear statements like, *I'm sorry, but... the system won't allow me to do that;* or *we can only do it this way;* or *you'll have to call the _____ department for that.*

Ideally, all of a company's processes are designed to deliver convenient customer service. However, not all processes meet this objective and sometimes problems arise even with the best of processes. In these situations,

"I'd be delighted to help with that request ma'am. It's my favorite process. First, I verify your identity by asking you to tell me your date of birth or your mother's maiden name. I love that part. Then I ask you what type of change you would like to make. Next, I ask you to wait just a moment while the computer retrieves the appropriate information. It's amazing what these new computer systems can do. After that..."

"Cindy must have missed the training session on seamless processes and invisible systems."

the service provider's role is to keep the process as seamless as possible from the customer's perspective. Suppose you receive a telephone call from a customer who is looking for information usually provided by another department. Your first choice would be to obtain this information from an electronic database and quickly relay it to the customer. However, if this option is not available, you could offer to have someone from the other department call the customer back, or you could offer to gather the information yourself and call the customer. Similarly, if an intermediary calls because he is having trouble obtaining information from your company's Web site, you could offer to obtain the information for him, or to work with him and an information technology employee to try to resolve the problem.

EFFICIENT AND EFFECTIVE PROCESSES

An effective customer service process is one that provides customers with the service they expect.

To provide the greatest value to customers and the company, business processes must combine efficiency (doing things right) and effectiveness (doing the right things). Management consultant Peter Drucker[3] defines *efficiency* as the ability to achieve objectives with a minimum of waste and with few errors or delays. *Effectiveness*, on the other hand, is the ability to establish and achieve appropriate objectives. An effective customer service process is one that provides customers with the service they expect.

Consider the Straight-Ahead Financial Services Company, which has been losing customers at an alarming rate, although its departments are meeting or exceeding all objectives and its employees are consistently following established work practices. Recently, Straight-Ahead completed an extensive customer satisfaction survey and learned that external customers were unimpressed with the service they were receiving, intermediaries were overwhelmingly dissatisfied, and employees were critical of internal customer service.

Apparently, Straight-Ahead was doing things right (meeting objectives), but was not doing the right things (satisfying customers). In other words, this company's business systems and processes were efficient but not effective. According to Drucker, "Effectiveness is the foundation of success—efficiency is a minimum condition for survival after success has been achieved."[4] Drucker also states, "The pertinent question is not how to do things right, but how to find the right things to do, and to concentrate resources and efforts on doing them."[5]

To find and correct the root cause of its problems, Straight-Ahead Financial Services Company needs to evaluate its customer service systems and processes. One activity that many companies pursue to accomplish this goal is process management.

Process Management

Process management is a formal method of defining, documenting, evaluating, and modifying the resources and workflow involved in processes so that the processes better achieve the tasks they were designed to accomplish. Process management can help ensure that a company's customer service system—its employees, resources, and processes—work together to effectively and efficiently provide the services its customers expect.

Who Is Involved in Process Management?

A **process improvement team** is a type of problem-solving team that includes employees from different areas or specialties within an organization who analyze processes and make recommendations for improvement.

As we noted in Chapter 10, financial services companies sometimes hire business consultants to help implement change. Companies can also turn to their internal auditing departments or they can establish process improvement teams to help streamline processes and reduce expenses. An **internal auditing department** is a work group whose primary responsibility is the independent appraisal of the departments, processes, and systems within an organization. A **process improvement team** is a type of problem-solving team that includes employees from different areas or specialties within an organization who analyze processes and make recommendations for improvement.

Often, employees who work directly with the processes being analyzed are invited to participate in process management efforts. These employees have an opportunity to analyze and improve their own jobs, examine their work from the perspective of their managers and customers, and improve customer service systems and processes. A few of the many ways that employees can contribute to process management include collecting data, analyzing workflow, identifying common process problems, raising issues and concerns expressed by customers, and providing support and backup for team members who are serving on a process improvement team.

In the following pages, we will discuss how process improvement teams conduct process management. We assume that the company has already conducted the planning activities discussed in Chapter 10 to determine its mission, objectives, and strategies; knows what services it should be providing; and is now ready to concentrate on developing the best resources and processes to provide these services.

Resource Analysis

In the context of process management, **resource analysis** is an examination of how a company's human resources, technology, and financial and physical resources are used to support specific processes. When performing resource analysis, a process improvement team typically answers questions such as

- Do we have enough resources to meet or exceed our objectives? Are there enough employees to do the work? Have we budgeted enough money and equipment to make sure processes operate efficiently and effectively?

- Are we using too many resources and spending too much money to achieve our objectives?

- Are resources being used properly? Is the staff well trained? Are they doing the work they were trained to do? Do employees have the right equipment and technology to do their work?

Workflow Analysis

Workflow analysis examines all the steps or tasks involved in a particular process to ensure the greatest efficiency and effectiveness.

In addition to reviewing its resources, a company examines its processes and the reasons for using them. Process improvement teams accomplish this task by performing a thorough analysis of the workflow throughout the customer service system. **Workflow analysis** examines all the steps or tasks involved in a particular process to ensure the greatest efficiency and effectiveness. The goals of workflow analysis are to align processes with customer expectations and company performance standards, overcome organizational barriers, eliminate unnecessary or redundant procedures, reduce processing time, and control costs. Generally, workflow analysis consists of three components:

1. Identifying the processes required to perform functions and ranking them in order of importance

2. Analyzing and evaluating the steps involved in each process

3. Reranking and modifying the processes so that they serve the needs of customers more logically, effectively, and efficiently

IDENTIFYING AND RANKING

Before analyzing each process, the process improvement team identifies and ranks processes in terms of importance to the company and its customers. When ranking customer service processes, the team considers factors such as

■ **Impact of the process on company objectives.** A major indicator of the importance of a process is the impact it has on the company's ability to achieve objectives.

■ **Revenues from and expenses created by the process.** The importance of a process is often determined by the amount of money it generates or saves.

■ **Customer perceptions and expectations.** One of the most useful factors for ranking processes is the effect that a process has on customers, because this encourages employees to think about how a process affects customers. Sometimes, when ranking internal processes, companies turn their attention inward, basing rankings on what is most important to or easiest for the people performing the tasks, and they forget to look "from the outside in" to gain the customers' perspective.

ANALYZING AND EVALUATING

After identifying and ranking the applicable processes, the process improvement team analyzes and evaluates each process. This stage of workflow analysis involves determining what each process is intended to accomplish, how it is initiated, the sequence of steps required to complete the transaction or fulfill the request, the resources required, the expected time needed to complete each step, and the outcomes currently produced.

Because service providers are very familiar with customer service processes, they can often provide valuable information during the analysis and evaluation phase of process management.

To simplify this task, process improvement teams often develop flow charts. Some companies prominently display these flow charts and invite all employees to comment on the processes. Because service providers are very familiar with customer service processes, they can often provide valuable information during the analysis and evaluation phase of process management.

Figure 12-1 shows the process flow chart for a request for information on an annuity. Note that this illustration is based on a manual process. In many companies, some or all of the steps depicted in a flow chart are automated. One of the considerations in analyzing processes is to determine which steps can be automated to improve processes.

When analyzing a process, the team determines whether the process is currently meeting its established goals in terms of

■ Support and improvement of customer relationships

FIGURE 12-1. Process Flow Chart.

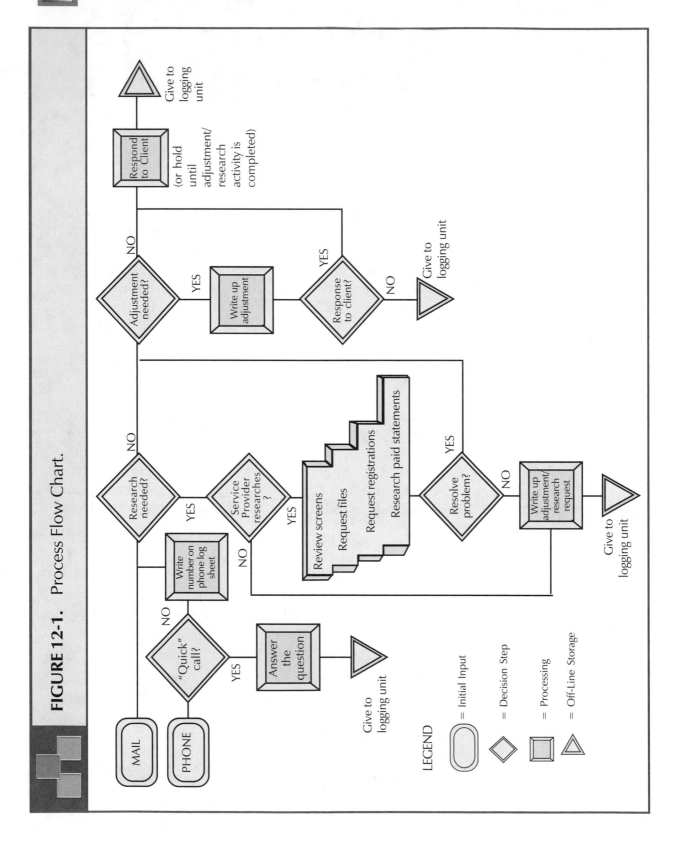

- Time and cost efficiency

- Compliance with applicable regulations and company risk management procedures

- Support of and interaction with other processes

RERANKING AND MODIFYING

Using the information gained through analysis and evaluation, the process improvement team might decide that the order in which it had originally ranked the processes does not accurately reflect the importance of some processes. In addition, the team might determine that certain processes are not as customer-oriented, efficient, or effective as they should be.

For example, in the course of conducting workflow analysis, a process improvement team in an insurance company might discover that a process developed several years ago requires employees to prepare and distribute a monthly claim report. Upon further investigation, the team learns that by the time this report reaches the company's intermediaries, the information is outdated. Consequently, the intermediaries ignore the report and call the claim department whenever they need the most current claim information. Because of workflow analysis, the process improvement team decides that this report should be replaced by an online inquiry system.

Through workflow analysis, a company can better determine the appropriate time and resources to devote to each process, concentrating on high-ranking processes, cutting back on low-ranking processes, and implementing improvements, as Insight 12-2 illustrates.

Performance Measurement

As you saw in Chapter 10, an important part of the strategic planning process is to establish objectives that indicate the results a company or work group plans to achieve. Consequently, a company must determine ways to measure results so it can compare actual performance to the standards set by its objectives. Just as a company uses performance evaluations to help assess and improve the performance of employees, it uses performance measurement to help assess and improve the performance of work teams, departments, customer service systems, and the company as a whole.

INSIGHT 12-2. Process Improvements Strengthen a Bank's Customer Service.

Customer service representatives (CSRs) in Bank of America's telephone banking centers and financial services contact centers have participated in a company-wide initiative in which they help redesign their jobs. Although the primary goal of this initiative is to attract and retain employees, the program also has produced many process improvements. For example, employees have identified the following customer service issues and solutions:

Issue: The service operations unit (administrative support) was returning "maintenance on account" requests to CSRs because the request forms had minor errors. This delayed the process by two to three days, negatively impacting customer service.

Solution: Whenever possible, the service operations unit completes the request immediately, whether or not the form has minor errors. The unit also tracks quality trends in the request forms and shares the results with CSRs for improvement, as needed.

Issue: Support unit turnaround times varied because service level agreements varied by state. For example, turnaround time for a copy of a check was three to five days in one state and five to seven days in another. Inconsistencies like these created a negative experience for customers and extra work for employees who had to look up turnaround times prior to responding to customers.

Solution: Establish the same service level agreements and turnaround times for all support units.

Issue: Employees were receiving too many internal e-mails and updates, making it difficult for them to determine which were most important to their jobs.

Solution: Create a communication specialist (gatekeeper) in each center whose role is to prioritize internal communications based on customer impact. Other less critical information is communicated in a condensed format.

Example of a recommendation NOT implemented: Provide photocopying service 24 hours a day. When the late-evening and third-shift volume was evaluated and the costs were considered, the advisory team suggested not implementing this recommendation, because the low volume did not warrant the additional expense. Customer service was not affected, because customer-related items for photocopying had always been given first priority each morning.

Source: COPYRIGHT NOTICE:
Reprinted with permission from *Customer Interface* Vol. 14, Number 2 (February 2001): 26. Copyright © 2002 Advanstar Communications Inc. Advanstar Communications Inc. retains all rights to this material.

Through ***performance measurement***, a company decides which activities to measure, how to measure performance in those activities, and what levels of performance, or performance standards, it hopes to achieve, and then the company gathers the information and communicates the results. A ***performance standard*** is an established level of performance to which a company or an individual compares actual performance. Using the information obtained by comparing results to objectives and performance standards, an organization revises its strategies and modifies its customer service systems and processes. The feedback provided through performance measurement enables a company to spot problems, take corrective action, and identify opportunities for continuous improvement.

Performance measurement starts at the corporate level and moves down to the department and work group levels where it is incorporated into the employee performance evaluation process. Ultimately, a company's performance is the sum of each employee's performance. Measuring performance at the corporate, department, work group, and individual levels helps align efforts throughout the organization, making them consistent with the company's overall objectives and strategies.

Attributes of Effective Performance Measurement

Performance measures should not focus too much on short-term results at the expense of long-term success factors.

To obtain the greatest benefit from performance measurement, most companies follow some basic guidelines. For instance, companies measure performance regularly and study results promptly to identify relevant issues and opportunities for improvement. In addition, companies strive to maintain performance measurement systems that do not disrupt the activities they are designed to measure and that are flexible enough to allow for changes due to shifting customer expectations and modifications in business strategy. Furthermore, companies must be aware of certain performance measurement pitfalls. For example, ease of measurement should never be the sole factor used to select a performance measure. Also, performance measures should not focus too much on short-term results at the expense of long-term success factors. Finally, companies must make sure the performance standards they establish are meaningful, valid, realistic, understandable, and accepted, as shown in Figure 12-2.

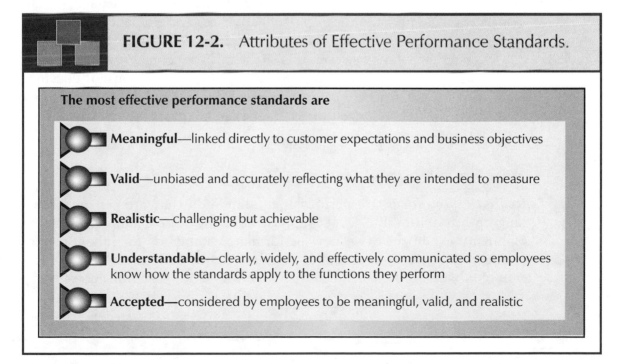

FIGURE 12-2. Attributes of Effective Performance Standards.

The most effective performance standards are

Meaningful—linked directly to customer expectations and business objectives

Valid—unbiased and accurately reflecting what they are intended to measure

Realistic—challenging but achievable

Understandable—clearly, widely, and effectively communicated so employees know how the standards apply to the functions they perform

Accepted—considered by employees to be meaningful, valid, and realistic

MEANINGFUL STANDARDS

Meaningful standards are performance standards that can be linked directly to customer expectations and business objectives. In other words, meaningful standards measure activities that truly matter to customers and the company, and they establish a level of performance that meets or exceeds expectations and objectives.

If a company fails to set performance standards for a service that is important to customers or if it sets standards lower than what customers expect, then the company risks losing business. On the other hand, a company is wasting valuable resources if it sets performance standards for an activity that has little value to customers.

In addition, performance standards must be linked to activities that can be modified. Sometimes companies need to know about certain activities that cannot or will not be changed, but focusing extensive efforts on measuring these kinds of activities is of limited value, because the information cannot be used to improve performance. Similarly, meaningful standards facilitate timely measurement and analysis, so the results can be examined and changes can be made quickly enough to address problems and improve performance.

> A company is wasting valuable resources if it sets performance standards for an activity that has little value to customers.

VALID STANDARDS

Valid standards are performance standards that are unbiased and accurately reflect what they are intended to measure. For example, suppose an insurer wants to measure the overall effectiveness and efficiency of its claim operations. As a performance standard, it specifies the number of claims to be processed each day. However, this single measure of claim volume is not a valid standard for overall effectiveness and efficiency because it does not take into account whether claims are processed accurately, whether they are processed within budget, or whether they are processed to customers' satisfaction.

REALISTIC STANDARDS

Realistic standards are performance standards that are set at a challenging but achievable level. Suppose that the XYZ Financial Services Company establishes two new performance standards for inbound telephone calls. The first, a quality standard, requires that at least 90 percent of inbound calls be handled without errors. The second, an accessibility standard, requires that all calls be answered within 10 seconds of the first ring.

At XYZ Financial, neither of these performance standards is realistic. Employees know they can achieve a 95 percent accuracy rate without much effort, so the 90 percent standard accomplishes nothing. In effect, this performance standard encourages employees to perform below their capabilities. On the other hand, because the number of inbound calls at XYZ far exceeds the number of CSRs available to answer them, the 10-second accessibility standard is impossible to achieve. A company that sets performance standards unreasonably high is likely to discourage employees.

UNDERSTANDABLE STANDARDS

All of a company's employees should be familiar with the company's over-all customer service standards and the performance standards for their jobs. **Understandable standards** are performance standards that are clearly, widely, and effectively communicated so service providers know how the standards apply to the functions they perform. For performance standards to be understandable, they must be stated in a way that can be measured. In other words, employees must know what to aim for in order to hit the target.

ACCEPTED STANDARDS

In addition to knowing *what* the performance standards are, employees need to know *why* the standards are important. **Accepted standards** are performance standards that employees understand and believe are mean-ingful, valid, and realistic. If the people who provide customer service do not accept and believe in the performance standards for their jobs, then the standards will have little influence on how employees provide cus-tomer service. Also, to be accepted, performance standards must fit into and not disrupt normal workflow.

One of the best ways to make sure service providers accept performance standards is to ask them to help set the standards. The employees who actually do the work are familiar with the practical necessities of the processes. They know the obstacles they must deal with and how to achieve specific goals. By establishing standards through a collaborative effort, a company and its employees can develop accepted standards that the com-pany believes will help it achieve its business objectives and that employ-ees are willing to attain.

If the people who provide customer service do not accept and believe in the performance standards for their jobs, then the standards will have little influence on how employees provide customer service.

Qualitative and Quantitative Performance Measurement

Most financial services companies evaluate their customer service systems and processes by using qualitative and quantitative performance measurement, although usually with a greater emphasis on quantitative measurement. At the employee level, however, performance measurement often provides more of a balance between qualitative and quantitative measures.

QUALITATIVE PERFORMANCE MEASUREMENT

Qualitative performance measurement (also called *behavioral performance measurement*) focuses on behaviors, attitudes, or opinions to determine how efficiently and effectively processes and transactions are completed. For example, qualitative performance measurement can be used to evaluate employee interactions with customers. In evaluating a customer service transaction, an observer could assess the accuracy of the information provided, the level of courtesy displayed, the clarity of communication, and so on.

Note that the term qualitative performance measurement does not necessarily refer to the quality or accuracy of work. The terms qualitative and quantitative performance measurement relate to *how* something is measured, rather than what is measured. Qualitative performance measures focus on behaviors, attitudes, or opinions to assess various aspects of performance, such as responsiveness, timeliness, courtesy, and quality.

When applying qualitative measures, an evaluator makes subjective judgments. Consequently, qualitative performance measurement, especially on a large scale, is more difficult to administer and interpret than quantitative measurement. To obtain the most value from qualitative measures a company must (1) develop specific, well-constructed standards and measures and (2) provide evaluators with thorough and consistent training in how to apply these measures.

QUANTITATIVE PERFORMANCE MEASUREMENT

Quantitative performance measurement relies on numerical methods to track and report results to determine how quickly, how often, how accurately, and how profitably processes and transactions are completed. Quantitative measures might indicate the number of inquiries handled per day, the percentage of telephone calls answered within 20 seconds, the average length of time spent assisting each customer, the percentage of transactions processed without errors, or the number of customer complaints and compliments.

Just as qualitative performance measurement does not refer solely to quality of work, quantitative performance measurement does not refer

Qualitative performance measurement (also called *behavioral performance measurement*) focuses on behaviors, attitudes, or opinions to determine how efficiently and effectively processes and transactions are completed.

Quantitative performance measurement relies on numerical methods to track and report results to determine how quickly, how often, how accurately, and how profitably processes and transactions are completed.

solely to quantity of work. Quantitative performance measures use numerical methods to assess various aspects of performance, such as responsiveness, timeliness, productivity, cost, and quality. To be measured quantitatively, a performance dimension must be quantifiable.

Compared to qualitative performance measures, quantitative measures are easier to gather and communicate, and they provide more objective information. Some of the quantitative measures that financial services companies use to measure customer service are described in the following sections.

Service Level

Service level is the percentage of inbound customer contacts answered within a specified time frame—for example, 80 percent within 20 seconds. In this context, answered does not mean that the customer's request was handled, but simply that someone answered the telephone. Reports on service level help a company determine how accessible the company is to its customers. In addition to service level, companies have developed a number of other accessibility measures for inbound customer contacts, as Figure 12-3 shows. Note that these measures focus on only one aspect of customer service—how accessible a company is to its customers—and do

---

FIGURE 12-3. Accessibility Measures for Inbound Customer Contacts.

Financial services companies use a variety of performance measures to evaluate how accessible they are to customers, including

Number of blocked calls	which indicates the number of telephone calls that encounter a busy signal and cannot get through to the customer contact center
Average speed of answer	which is the amount of time, on average, that telephone callers are on hold before being connected with a service provider
Abandonment rate	which is the percentage of inbound telephone calls that are automatically placed on hold and then terminated by the caller before the call is answered by a service provider
Misdirected calls	which indicates the number or percentage of inbound telephone calls that are transferred to the wrong department

According to one survey, the average service time for completing address changes for fixed annuity customers was 2.4 days.

Source: LOMA[6]

not address other performance dimensions such as quality, productivity, or cost.

Timeliness

One type of timeliness measure used in customer contact centers is called *response time*, which is the time that transpires from receipt of a customer contact to resolution of the request.

Timeliness (also called *turnaround time* or *average handling time*) indicates the time it takes to complete a customer-initiated request or transaction, such as answering a question, underwriting an application, adjudicating a claim, issuing a commission check, or processing a withdrawal or an account transfer. One type of timeliness measure used in customer contact centers is called *response time*, which is the time that transpires from receipt of a customer contact—such as correspondence or e-mail—to resolution of the request. Generally, timeliness shows how responsive a customer service system or process is to the customers who rely on it. The most meaningful timeliness measures begin at the point the customer initiates the request and end when the customer receives the requested information or service. An increasingly popular timeliness measure for inbound customer contacts is *first contact resolution*, which measures the percentage of inbound customer contacts that are successfully completed at the initial point of contact—that is, without being transferred and without the need for follow-up work.

Quality Rate

Quality rate measures the accuracy of a particular type of transaction. It is often expressed as a percentage of the total number of transactions handled or processed, such as 99.5 percent of account transactions having no reported errors. Similar to a quality rate is an *error rate*, which indicates the percentage of transactions that resulted in errors, such as 0.5 percent of account transactions having reported errors.

Processes Completed

The number of *processes completed* measures how many transactions are handled within a specified period of time, such as the number of telephone calls received, applications processed, claims adjudicated, checks released, or withdrawals and transfers processed in a month. This measurement indicates how quickly and efficiently a customer service system or process is working. Processes completed can also be expressed as *average processing time*.

Customer Loyalty and Retention

Other quantitative measures reflect customer loyalty and retention. For example, insurers track the number of policies lapsed and replaced. They also track the number of up-sales and cross-sales. Although these types of measures often indicate how customers feel about customer service, they also can reflect how customers feel about a variety of other factors such as availability and selection of products, quality of products, and pricing.

Communicating and Using Performance Measurement Results

Most companies share performance results with employees to communicate how the company, department, or work group is performing. For example, in customer contact centers, "real time" results are typically posted on large display boards or on each CSR's computer monitor so everyone can see the number of customers on hold, the current service level, and so on. CSRs use this information to help meet or exceed performance standards. During peak periods, for instance, CSRs might decide to defer taking breaks or they might postpone paperwork or special projects to help meet accessibility standards.

In some companies, employees receive bonuses based on team performance results. In other companies, individual performance standards are identical to team standards. For instance, if the work group has a quality objective of 99 percent, then employees are expected to maintain or exceed a 99 percent quality rate for their individual workload.

Although quantitative measures often provide valuable performance-related information, companies must be careful when interpreting results. For instance, suppose a call center handled an average of 150 calls per day last year and is handling only 130 calls per day this year. Senior managers might interpret these results to mean that the department is working less efficiently. But remember the difference between efficiency and effectiveness—between doing things right and doing the right things. It could be that CSRs are now providing callers with more complete and accurate information. Or, this year the call center could be supporting products that are more complex. To obtain the greatest value from performance measurement, a company must look at each performance measure in context and, often, in association with other measures, including qualitative measures.

Internal Standards, Industry Standards, and Universal Standards

Many companies establish benchmarks for their performance. **Benchmarks** are performance standards, often based on standards achieved by leading companies, that represent a company's goals for performance.

If the work group has a quality objective of 99 percent, then employees are expected to maintain or exceed a 99 percent quality rate for their individual workload.

Benchmarking—comparing actual performance results with benchmarks—encourages continuous improvement by enabling a company to determine how well it is performing in relation to a standard it aspires to achieve. The performance standards that financial services companies use for benchmarking can come from inside the company or from other companies both inside and outside the financial services industry.

INTERNAL STANDARDS

An *internal standard* is a performance standard that is developed inside a company, based on the company's own historic performance levels. Companies use internal standards because these standards (1) are fairly easy to establish, (2) reflect actual processes followed in the companies that have developed them, and (3) allow the companies to compare their current performance to past performance.

Internal standards, however, tend to provide a fairly narrow and introverted perspective on a company's customer service performance. If a company looks only at its own past performance to set customer service standards, it risks ignoring customer expectations that are influenced by the service provided by other companies. Therefore, many companies also look outward to help determine the benchmarks they must establish to meet or exceed customer expectations.

Internal standards tend to provide a fairly narrow and introverted perspective on a company's customer service performance.

INDUSTRY STANDARDS

Most financial services firms observe how their competitors handle customer service. An *industry standard* is a performance standard based on the performance results for a specific process or activity achieved by companies within the company's own industry. A company can stay informed by studying industry standards for basic customer service processes. Then the company compares its own results to the industry standards.

UNIVERSAL STANDARDS

Customers seldom differentiate between the service they receive from financial services firms and the service they receive from other types of companies. By looking beyond its own industry at universal standards, a financial services firm can determine best practices. A *universal standard* is a performance standard based on the performance results for a specific process or activity achieved by other companies both within and outside a company's own industry. A **best practice** is a business practice that represents the ultimate criterion for performing a specific type of process.

Despite the value of benchmarking, companies must remember to look at benchmarks in light of what their own customers expect and desire. The customer research methods that we discussed in Chapter 5 can help a company determine which benchmarks are most useful in meeting or exceeding customer expectations.

Performance Measurement Techniques

Financial services firms can choose from a variety of methods to gather performance-related information. Often, as you will see in Chapter 13, performance-related information is gathered through information management and telecommunication systems. In this section, you will learn about the role that sampling plays in gathering relevant performance information and how companies gather performance information using customer satisfaction surveys, observation, monitoring, mystery shoppers, and complaint monitoring.

SAMPLING

One way to keep performance measurement from becoming too time-consuming is to use sampling techniques.

Organizations with an overabundance of performance standards sometimes find that they spend too much time gathering performance data and too little time using the data to support customers. One way to keep performance measurement from becoming too time-consuming is to use sampling techniques. As you saw in Chapter 5, sampling allows researchers to examine a portion of a given population to make conclusions about the entire population. Using sampling, a company measures a representative number of transactions rather than every single transaction.

Suppose Elixir Life Insurance Company's policyowner service department decides to start measuring its quality rate for processing policy loans. The department does not have the time or staff to check the accuracy of every policy loan transaction. Therefore, it samples a portion of these transactions to obtain a representative picture of the quality of the entire population. Another example of sampling is the random selection and evaluation of a portion of customer service telephone calls and correspondence.

CUSTOMER SATISFACTION SURVEYS

In Chapter 5, you saw how companies use customer surveys to learn about customer expectations and perceptions. Companies also use surveys to

If you want to know what is happening, go to the people to whom it's happening. We do not assume we know how others feel and think.

— Alan D. Wolfson[7]

measure performance. ***Customer satisfaction surveys*** are surveys designed to help a company determine whether its products, prices, and services are meeting customer expectations. Surveys are used to measure overall customer satisfaction and customer loyalty, as well as customer service systems and processes. Generally, customer satisfaction surveys are not used to provide feedback on the performance of individual service providers.

Customer satisfaction surveys should be conducted regularly to provide an ongoing view of customers' perceptions of company performance. Ideally, customer feedback indicates how well the company's customer service system is performing and provides the company with the information it needs to make any necessary adjustments. Some financial services firms send a short general survey to randomly selected customers every three months and distribute a longer survey once a year. Other companies send a short survey to obtain feedback on each transaction or a sampling of transactions.

The main benefit of customer surveys is that the people the customer service system is supposed to serve, the customers, are given the opportunity to evaluate the service. The main drawback is that designing, developing, administering, and reviewing surveys can be a difficult and time-consuming task. If not used properly, surveys can provide a company with useless or misleading information.

Some financial services firms send a short general survey to randomly selected customers every three months and distribute a longer survey once a year.

OBSERVATION AND MONITORING

Observation is a data-collection method in which a person or process is observed and evaluated. Observation can be as general as walking around a department to get a feel for how customer service interactions are being handled or as specific as monitoring a telephone call. As you saw in Chapter 4, monitoring is a process used to review and evaluate the quality of customer service interactions either as they happen or after the fact. Managers and service providers often use monitoring as a performance evaluation tool and as a way to improve individual performance. In addition, many companies use monitoring to measure the performance of customer service systems and processes. For example, if a company observes significant or frequently recurring problems during monitoring, it might decide to modify a process, provide additional resources for service providers, or revise its training program.

MYSTERY SHOPPERS

Another means of conducting qualitative performance measurement is through mystery shoppers. A ***mystery shopper*** is a trained evaluator who approaches or calls customer service employees and pretends to be a customer. Mystery shoppers may be company employees who are not known to the service providers, or they may be employed by an outside company. The mystery shopper conducts a transaction with the employee and then evaluates the employee's handling of the transaction. Mystery shoppers provide greater flexibility than monitoring "real" customer interactions because mystery shoppers can manipulate the circumstances to see how employees respond to various scenarios.

COMPLAINT MONITORING

Studying complaint letters, e-mails, and telephone calls can be a valuable performance measurement technique. Typically, isolated complaints are not a reliable measure of a customer service system's overall performance, but a study of the source, number, frequency, and nature of complaints can indicate customer service problems or trends. Companies must be careful, however, not to assume that a lack of complaints means customer service systems and processes are performing well, because many dissatisfied customers don't bother to complain; they simply take their business elsewhere.

Finally, a company and its service providers must be careful not to lose sight of the reason for having performance measures in the first place. When customers make a request, they don't care if you are meeting your individual performance objectives or if the company is meeting its corporate goals. The customers' concern is how well you and your company handle their requests—and this should be your concern as well.

As you have seen in this chapter, financial service companies can choose from numerous performance measurement techniques and standards to evaluate customer service processes. Advances in technology have led to increasingly sophisticated methods for tracking and reporting these results. In the next chapter, you will see how companies use technology to enhance performance measurement as well as a variety of other customer service activities.

To practice and review the skills and information you learned in this chapter, see the interactive CD, *Practicing Your Customer Service Skills*, included with this book.

Key Terms and Concepts

follow-up work
service request
exception processing
escalation process
seamless process
efficiency
effectiveness
process management
internal auditing department
process improvement team
resource analysis
workflow analysis
performance measurement
performance standard
meaningful standards
valid standards
realistic standards
understandable standards
accepted standards
qualitative performance
  measurement

quantitative performance
  measurement
service level
number of blocked calls
average speed of answer
abandonment rate
misdirected calls
timeliness
response time
first contact resolution
quality rate
processes completed
benchmarks
benchmarking
internal standard
industry standard
universal standard
best practice
customer satisfaction surveys
observation
mystery shopper

Endnotes

1. R. Eric Reidenbach, Gordon W. McClung, and Reginald W. Goeke, "How to Let Customer Value Drive Customer Problem Solving," *Best Practices in Customer Service*, ed. Ron Zemke and John A. Woods (New York: HRD Press, 1998), 137.

2. Neil Milstein, *Individual Life Insurance Service Turnaround Time Survey: 2001 Report* (Atlanta: LOMA, 2001), 10.

3. Peter F. Drucker, *Management: Tasks, Responsibilities, Practices* (New York: Harper & Row, 1973), 45–46.

4. Ibid., 45.

5. Peter F. Drucker, *Managing for Results* (New York: Harper & Row, 1964), 6.

6. James R. Huffman, *Individual Annuity Service Turnaround Times Survey: 2001 Report* (Atlanta: LOMA, 2001), 5.

7. Alan D. Wolfson, "The People Strategies and Practices of the Most Admired Companies That Drive Customer Satisfaction and Retention," LOMA's Customer Service Conference, The Walt Disney World Resort, Orlando, Florida, 25 February 2002.

Better Customer Service Through Technology

After studying this chapter, you should be able to

▣ Describe how financial services companies can enhance customer service by using technologies such as workforce management systems, intelligent call routing, automatic call distributors, interactive voice response systems, computer telephony integration, knowledge management systems, document management systems, and automated workflow systems

▣ Discuss how financial services companies address privacy and security challenges associated with using technology to support customer service

▣ Discuss the impact technology has on customer service employees and the importance of internal customer service when technology is used to support external customer service activities

Technology improves customer service in many ways. With the right technology, a CEO can announce a new company wide customer service initiative to employees across the globe. Supervisors can check the status of customer requests without leaving their desks. Service providers and customers can have conversations from thousands of miles apart. And customers can select and view a variety of product brochures in the comfort of their own homes. In these examples, the management and delivery of customer service remain the same—a CEO communicates with employees, supervisors monitor work, service providers interact with customers, and customers obtain product information. However, technology makes these activities more convenient, efficient, and effective.

Broadly speaking, the term *technology* refers to the practical, scientific tools used to accomplish tasks; and *customer service technology* refers to various communication and information systems used by organizations to support customers or to enable customers to help themselves. Many different technologies are associated with customer service, providing everything from strategic support at the highest levels of an organization to tactical support of day-to-day business activities. In this chapter, we will discuss the role technology plays in managing and delivering customer service in financial services companies. We also will describe several challenges of using technology in a customer service environment. To begin, try testing your knowledge of customer service technology by taking the quiz in Exercise 13-1.

Using Technology to Manage Customer Service

Information technology is an integral part of strategic initiatives like customer relationship management (CRM) and customer access strategies. In addition, technology plays a prominent role at the department and work group levels where it is used to plan, route, monitor, and measure customer service communications, transactions, and activities.

Planning

Typically, customer service areas in financial services companies have to manage high volumes of customer inquiries and requests that require prompt if not immediate attention. A tool that many customer service areas use to help plan for and manage this demand is a **workforce management system**, which is a computer program that projects staffing and scheduling needs by analyzing

Exercise 13-1.   Test Your Technology Knowledge.

Determine whether each statement is True or False:

1. *Web chat* is a technology that enables text-based conversations over the Internet in real-time.

2. *Voice over Internet protocol (VoIP)* is a technology that transmits voice over an Internet connection.

3. A *workforce management system* is a computer program that projects staffing and scheduling needs by analyzing the past volume of customer contacts and predicting the future volume.

4. The term *intelligent call routing (ICR)* refers generally to any automated process of analyzing and routing inbound telephone calls.

5. An *automatic call distributor (ACD)* is a device that, at the most basic level, answers telephone calls and directs them to the appropriate employee or work group.

6. An *interactive voice response (IVR)* system is a computer-based technology that answers telephone calls, greets callers with a recorded or digitized message, and prompts them to enter information or make requests by voice or telephone keypad.

7. *Computer telephony integration (CTI)* refers to the hardware, software, and programming that integrate computers and communication technology, particularly telephones, to enhance customer contacts and the information they provide.

8. A *document management system* is a technology that stores, organizes, and retrieves documents that have been created electronically and converted to digital images or created on paper and converted to digital images.

Answers: 1–True; 2–True; 3–True; 4–True; 5–True; 6–True; 7–True; 8–True the past volume of customer contacts and predicting the future volume. Some managers and supervisors rely on workforce management systems to determine how many service providers to hire and how many to schedule to work at specific intervals throughout each day. Workforce management systems enable companies to have the right number of people in the right place at the right time to keep customer wait times within established targets, balancing customer expectations with the cost of providing service.

Routing Customer Communications

The term ***intelligent call routing (ICR)*** refers to any automated process of analyzing and directing inbound telephone calls. Intelligent call routing uses information about the caller, the call, and/or employees to determine which employees or work groups will receive which calls and when. Managers can specify in advance the people or work groups to whom calls will be routed or the order in which calls will be answered. For years, routing technologies have been used to route telephone calls, but they also can be used to route other types of communication.

E-mail management systems automatically analyze, route, and, in some cases, reply to inbound e-mail messages. These systems recognize one or more keywords in a message and route the e-mail accordingly. With an e-mail management system a customer service area can route e-mails to the appropriate service provider based on workload, customer priority, employee experience, type of request, and other factors.

With an e-mail management system a customer service area can route e-mails to the appropriate service provider based on workload, customer priority, employee experience, type of request, and other factors.

Some e-mail management systems can identify specific properties of the text of incoming e-mail messages, such as the nature of the request, the product involved, the type of customer, or even the attitude reflected in the message. Based on this analysis, the system then classifies the message and, if possible, generates a response. For certain types of requests, the system can be programmed to send the response automatically. For more complex requests, the system might generate a draft response to be routed to a service provider to use as a template.

Companies that support a variety of remote customer contacts can use a universal queue for routing. A ***queue*** is a series of telephone calls or other types of communication awaiting handling. A ***universal queue*** is a routing system that handles all customer contacts together, regardless of the type of communication. Instead of having separate queues for telephone calls, e-mails, Web chats, and faxes, a universal queue provides a complete view of all customer contacts together. Universal queue technology allows managers to specify different routing criteria for different types of communications. For example, telephone calls and Web chats could be routed immediately, while e-mails and faxes might be delayed.

Universal queue technology also supports **automatic transaction distribution**, a type of routing that directs customer contacts to service providers based on the person's proficiency with a particular communication channel. For example, some service providers might receive only telephone calls, others might receive e-mails and Web chats, and others might receive telephone calls, e-mails, and Web chats.

In many companies, automatic call distributors are used to route inbound customer contacts. An **automatic call distributor (ACD)** is a device that, at the most basic level, answers telephone calls and directs them to the appropriate employee or work group. For example, an ACD can be programmed to route calls using the longest idle agent method or the uniform call distribution method. Using the **longest idle agent (LIA)** method, each inbound telephone call is routed to the available CSR who has gone the longest time without receiving a call. Using **uniform call distribution (UCD)**, inbound calls are distributed in a predetermined order among available CSRs so that each person receives approximately the same number of calls. When no one is available to take a particular call, the ACD places the call in a queue, where it remains until a CSR answers the call or the caller hangs up.

In addition to routing, ACDs can perform a variety of other functions. They can facilitate workforce management, link multiple service centers, and integrate telephones with other communication and information technology (such as e-mail, fax, a Web site, or an information database).

An **automatic call distributor (ACD)** is a device that, at the most basic level, answers telephone calls and directs them to the appropriate employee or work group.

Monitoring and Measuring

ACDs provide a wealth of information about work group performance for use in both real-time monitoring and regular performance measurement reports. Many call centers use readerboards to display key information captured from the ACD. A **readerboard**, also called a *suspended monitor* or *electronic display* (see Figure 13-1), is a screen mounted in a customer contact center that displays real-time statistics and recent performance results for a particular work group. Similar data can be provided on desktop computers.

FIGURE 13-1. A Readerboard and a PC-Based Electronic Display.

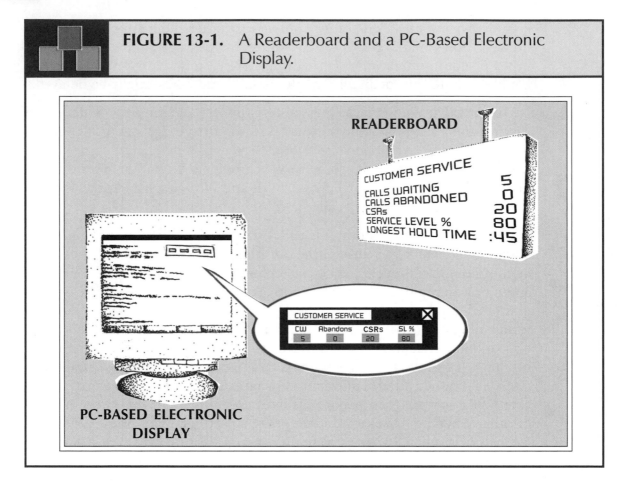

Managers and CSRs check readerboards to obtain workload information such as the number of callers on hold, the longest current hold time, and the percentage of calls being answered within a specified number of seconds. Using this information, they can take appropriate action to maintain desired service levels. For example, if the number of callers on hold and the average hold times are increasing, the manager might temporarily assign supervisors and trainers to handle inbound calls.

Technology also is used to generate performance measurement reports, which provide information on accessibility, timeliness of service, quality of service, productivity, and cost. Managers examine performance results to assist in planning and to decide on changes necessary to improve performance. For example, by observing service level, peak utilization periods, and abandonment rates, call center managers are able to determine staffing and scheduling needs more accurately.

Technology can play an important role in obtaining feedback through customer surveys. Telephone systems can be programmed to randomly

Today, the Internet is enabling customers to provide feedback more easily, quickly, cheaply, and accurately than ever before.

— John Chisholm[1]

select inbound callers and invite them to participate in brief automated surveys at the end of calls. Web sites can be set up to randomly display messages that solicit and capture information from Web site visitors. Some companies send e-mails to customers, inviting them to participate in Web-based customer service surveys; the recipients click on a link embedded in the e-mail message, which takes them to the Web site where they can complete the survey. Figure 13-2 describes one technology-based approach that goes beyond the typical survey to establish an ongoing dialogue to obtain in-depth feedback from customers.

FIGURE 13-2. Continuous Customer Service Surveys.

To help improve service, some companies use technology to conduct continuous research by establishing ongoing dialogues with customers. First, the company sends an e-mail asking its customers' permission to contact them periodically to learn what the company is doing well and what the company needs to improve upon.

If a customer agrees to participate, then the next time the customer receives any type of service, the company sends an e-mail to find out if the customer was satisfied with the way the transaction was handled. When the customer's response is favorable, the company might ask the customer to act as a reference.

When the response indicates that the service was poor or only fair, then the company thanks the customer for the honest feedback, and requests permission to ask specific questions related to the transaction. If the customer agrees, then the e-mail is forwarded to the department that handled the transaction, and this area investigates and follows up with the customer.

In addition, the company gathers data related to all customer dialogues and develops reports that show overall customer satisfaction levels for a variety of functions, thus providing a customer-based view of the quality of service throughout the organization and indicating where improvements need to be made.

Source: Jack Shaw, "Hire Your Customers: Using Digital Technology to Make Your Customers Part of Your Business," LOMA's Customer Service Conference, The Walt Disney World Resort, Orlando, Florida, 26 February 2002.

Using Technology to Deliver Customer Service

Generally, technology affects customer service processes through *automation* of certain activities or by providing *self-service* or *direct service* options to customers. Automation allows service providers to help customers in ways that are more efficient and effective; for example, instead of looking for product information in paper reference manuals, service providers can obtain the same information more quickly and easily from a computer database. Self-service takes automation a step further and allows customers to help themselves.

A technology that combines both self-service and automation is the interactive voice response system. An ***interactive voice response (IVR)*** system, also called *voice response unit (VRU)*, is a computer-based technology that answers telephone calls, greets callers with a recorded or digitized message, and prompts them to enter information or make requests by voice or telephone keypad. In many financial services firms, IVRs and ACDs are linked to allow callers to either (1) obtain information or services from a menu of prerecorded options or (2) transfer to the appropriate person or department for assistance.

Typically, IVR systems prompt the caller to enter a unique identifier such as a policy or account number by pressing the numbers on the telephone keypad or by saying the numbers. Then the IVR system refines the routing of the call by asking the caller to choose from a menu of options—such as billing inquiries or recent transactions—by again pressing or saying the applicable number. After the information is processed, an ACD routes the call to the specified self-service option or to a service provider.

Customers can use IVR systems to perform many activities. They can change account information, check account balances, transfer funds, request brochures, select a primary care physician, check the status of a claim, or talk to a CSR for assistance. With these options, many customers have a feeling of control, because they can obtain the information and services they need quickly, easily, and on their own terms. Service providers also benefit by spending less time handling routine and repetitive customer requests.

Technologies like IVR are sometimes called computer telephony integration. The term ***computer telephony integration (CTI)*** refers to the hardware, software, and programming that integrate computers and communication technology, particularly telephones, to enhance customer

> An ***interactive voice response (IVR)*** system...is a computer-based technology that answers telephone calls, greets callers with a recorded or digitized message, and prompts them to enter information or make requests.

contacts and the information they provide. Figure 13-3 illustrates how several types of CTI can be used to enhance customer service provided over the telephone.

CTI can be used to enhance many types of communication. Suppose Nancy Snead, who is researching products on the Singer Financial Company's Web site, initiates a click-to-call. Recall from Chapter 7 that click-to-call is a communication device that allows Web site visitors to initiate a conversation with a company representative by clicking on an icon, which then automatically places a call over the computer to a company representative. When Ms. Snead's click-to-call is received by Yuling Ji, a CSR at Singer, it is accompanied by information sent to his desktop computer. This information indicates which products Ms. Snead has been researching at the Web site and what areas of the Web site she has visited. With this information, Mr. Ji is better able to assist Ms. Snead with her request.

FIGURE 13-3. An Example of How Technology Supports Telephone Customer Service.

n some companies, the customer service process begins with **automatic number identification (ANI)**, which is a technology that identifies an inbound telephone call by the number from which the call is placed. For example, when Andy Demeter calls Capitol Insurance Company, ANI technology compares Mr. Demeter's telephone number to the numbers stored in a customer database.

If Mr. Demeter's number matches a number in the database, then computer telephony integration (CTI) technology locates information about Mr. Demeter in the customer database. Otherwise, the interactive voice response (IVR) system prompts Mr. Demeter to provide identifying information.

The IVR system invites Mr. Demeter to obtain assistance from a menu of automated services. If Mr. Demeter declines self-service, then through a type of CTI called *screen pop*, the customer-specific information (obtained from the customer database or entered by Mr. Demeter via IVR) is sent to the CSR's desktop computer, while the ACD routes the call to the CSR's telephone.

If information is provided from the customer database, the CSR can see what products Mr. Demeter has purchased, what transactions he has conducted, and so on. Using this information, some technologies can prompt the CSR to ask the customer a specific question, such as, "I see that you recently added your daughter to your automobile insurance policy, Mr. Demeter. This might be a good time to consider adding roadside assistance coverage. Would you like to hear more about this option?"

Automated Customer Service Functions

Financial services companies have long used technology to make customer service more efficient and effective. For example, insurers have relied on operational systems to support underwriting, policy issue, billing, and claim functions. In addition, as we saw in Figure 13-3, technology plays an important role in furnishing people throughout an organization with information that improves the speed and accuracy of customer interactions. Increasingly, the foundation for information sharing in financial services companies is the computer network.

COMPUTER NETWORKS

An internal network can help employees in a branch office obtain access to information in home office electronic files to provide more timely service to customers.

A **computer network** is two or more computers linked together to provide a platform for electronic communication and information sharing. Two types of computer networks are internal networks and external networks. An **internal network** is a computer network that a company creates to link its people and equipment to each other. An **external network** is a computer network that links a company to people and computers outside the company.

An internal network can be as modest as two desktop computers linked to a printer in a small office or as ambitious as 20,000 desktop computers linked to numerous servers and mainframe computers operated by a global financial services firm. Internal networks allow employees to share resources. For example, an internal network can help employees in a branch office obtain access to information in home office electronic files to provide more timely service to customers.

When all the equipment that makes up an internal network is situated in one location, the network is called a **local area network (LAN)**. When the equipment that makes up a network is geographically dispersed, the network is called a **wide area network (WAN)**. WANs can cover just a few miles or thousands of miles, and they can be internal or external. An example of an internal WAN is a network, accessible only to company employees and representatives, that links a company's branch offices and home office. An example of an external WAN is the Internet.

The **Internet** (or the *Net*), the world's largest computer network, consists of thousands of interconnected networks, all freely exchanging information and connecting millions of computers around the world. Users can "plug into" the Internet to access services such as e-mail, music file exchanges, and the World Wide Web.

The **World Wide Web** (or the *Web*), one of many services available on the Internet, is a network of links to hypermedia documents (text, graphics, video, and sound). It consists of thousands of independently owned Web servers working together. The computer that holds the documents on the site and makes them available for remote browsers is known as a **Web server**. Visitors access Web sites by using a **browser**, which is a software program that allows a user to navigate the Internet. Users are able to jump from one Web server to another, creating the illusion of using one big computer. Because of its multimedia capabilities, the Web has emerged as the most popular means of accessing information on the Internet.

Some companies share news, information, and company publications via an internal network called an **intranet**, which looks and functions much like the Internet, but is designed to be accessible only to company employees.

Electronic data interchange (EDI) is the computer-to-computer exchange of standardized business transaction data between two or more organizations.

Financial services companies sometimes establish links with external WANs to gather information from different sources, exchange documents with other parties, and communicate with a variety of customers and potential customers. One of the most important benefits of joining an external WAN is the ability to conduct business using electronic data interchange. **Electronic data interchange (EDI)** is the computer-to-computer exchange of standardized business transaction data between two or more organizations. Companies that want to participate in an EDI network must agree to use the same standardized document formats. Documents exchanged in this fashion then are transmitted directly from one computer system to another.

Through EDI, companies can eliminate much of the paperwork and delay usually associated with certain transactions. A primary use of EDI for insurance companies is the electronic submission of medical insurance claims. Medical providers such as hospitals, laboratories, and doctors' offices can transmit claim information electronically to an insurance company. EDI eliminates the time-consuming and costly process of printing and mailing paper claims that must then be input by a data entry operator into the insurer's computer system. Customers and medical providers receive claim responses, including payments, much more quickly with EDI than with paper claims.

KNOWLEDGE MANAGEMENT SYSTEMS

Knowledge management is a term used to describe the overall strategies, resources, and processes that organizations use to apply knowledge to business activities. Strictly speaking, a knowledge management system can operate entirely with people and paper resources; however, technology is an important tool in most knowledge management systems today. Using technology, a company can take information about products and procedures—which once may have been hidden in volumes of procedural manuals—and make this information accessible electronically throughout a department or the entire organization. Similarly, a company can provide information about customers—which once may have been limited to the people who worked directly with those customers—to all employees who need this information to perform their jobs.

Employees use expert systems software as a starting point upon which to base their decisions or recommendations.

One way to apply knowledge management is through **expert systems software**—an application that performs many of the functions and makes many of the decisions that once required the attention of trained professionals, such as underwriters, loan officers, claim processors, or investment advisors. Often, employees use expert systems software as a starting point upon which to base their decisions or recommendations. For example, if a service provider is using expert systems software to conduct an underwriting interview with a life insurance applicant who indicates he has diabetes, then the system can prompt the service provider with the appropriate questions to ask.

Another valuable technology resource is a **retrieval tool**, also called a *search tool*, which is a computer application designed to provide users with the specific information they seek. For example, suppose you work for a group medical insurer and you receive a telephone call from a covered employee asking about the third-party liability provision in his contract. You can enter the phrase "third-party liability" in a search field on

"Apparently, their automated phone system called our automated phone system and they both consulted with their expert systems and decided to merge."

your computer and obtain an explanation of how this contractual provision operates. Retrieval tools also can provide scripts or talking points for specific products or topics, as discussed in Chapter 7.

DATABASES

The information supplied by retrieval tools comes from databases. Some databases are maintained separately for specific functions. For example, a call center might maintain its own database by requiring CSRs to input information into a customer contact system after each transaction. A **customer contact system** is a customer database and work tracking tool that combines a variety of features—such as data entry and retrieval, history of previous customer contacts, document management, scripted presentations, and follow-up tools—to provide a framework for handling and documenting customer contacts.

Many companies are moving away from a compartmentalized approach to information management by building data warehouses to be used on an enterprise-wide basis. A **data warehouse** is an information system that stores, consolidates, retrieves, and manages large amounts of data from across an organization, bringing together all relevant information to support company operations as well as management decision making. The data in a data warehouse is extracted from various operational systems (such as a customer contact system) throughout the organization and also may be acquired from sources outside the company. The operational and external data are consolidated and standardized to remove inconsistencies and then integrated to create a new information database.

A **data warehouse** is an information system that stores, consolidates, retrieves, and manages large amounts of data from across an organization.

Typically, data warehouses are used for management analysis and reporting, rather than day-to-day transactions. One such use is **data mining**, which is the process of selecting and exploring large amounts of data to uncover previously unknown patterns for business advantage. For example, a financial services company might use the information obtained from data mining to develop sales and customer service strategies designed to attract, retain, or phase out specific types of customers.

Regardless of how the information from a data warehouse is used, service providers play an important role in maintaining the quality of that information. Every customer interaction provides an opportunity to gather and update data. Service providers continually collect new customer information and verify the accuracy of existing data. Without current, accurate information, knowledge management systems and databases quickly lose their effectiveness.

DOCUMENT MANAGEMENT SYSTEMS AND AUTOMATED WORKFLOW SYSTEMS

Suppose an intermediary asks you to send him a copy of every document on file for one of your company's most valuable customers. The intermediary needs the information for a meeting with the customer tomorrow. How would you respond? If your company uses a paper filing system, you might have to negotiate with the intermediary to limit the request and obtain only the most important documents from the files. On the other hand, if your company uses an electronic document management system, you might be able to locate every document and send them all to the intermediary via e-mail attachment.[2]

Imaging, or *scanning*, is a process of converting printed characters or graphics into digital images on a computer.

A ***document management system*** is a technology that stores, organizes, and retrieves documents that have been created electronically and converted to digital images or created on paper and converted to digital images via imaging. ***Imaging***, or *scanning*, is a process of converting printed characters or graphics into digital images on a computer. Once documents are entered into a document management system, employees can use a computer to search for, view, print, and share the documents.

Document management systems provide service providers with computer access to a variety of company-specific forms, such as completed applications, explanations of benefits, account statements, and signature cards. In addition, these systems can provide computer access to correspondence and other documents—such as medical, financial, or real estate records—from outside the company.

Using a document management system, a service provider can obtain quick and easy access to important information. Suppose Molly Usher, a service provider at Lutz Bank, receives a telephone call from George Callison, a customer who wants to know if there is a prepayment penalty on his automobile loan. Rather than walk to the file room, pull the file, return to her desk, and call Mr. Callison with the answer, Ms. Usher can simply view the document on her desktop computer and respond.

Document management systems also reduce the frustration, delays, and wasted time that result from lost and misfiled documents. In addition, these systems facilitate document sharing. Suppose Ms. Usher goes to the file room and discovers that another employee is using the loan agreement she is looking for. She then has to contact that employee to obtain the information she needs. However, with a document management system, several employees can retrieve a document at the same time. Furthermore, document management systems reduce the costs associated with storing and moving paper documents.

Increasingly, document management systems play an important role in automated workflow systems. An ***automated workflow system***, also called *automated workflow distribution (AWD)*, is a technology used to create computer-based records pertaining to the status and processing of specific transactions. One way to think of an automated workflow system is to envision a tracking sheet that accompanies a transaction through the entire workflow process from initial receipt through completion and filing. The automated workflow system shows the type of transaction, the person to whom it was assigned, when it was received, questions that arose, actions taken, documents created, completion dates and times, and so on. Rather than include this information in a paper file, however, an automated workflow system stores it electronically, creating a "paperless" environment.

One way to think of an automated workflow system is to envision a tracking sheet that accompanies a transaction through the entire workflow process from initial receipt through completion and filing.

For example, if Mr. Callison calls Lutz Bank to apply for another loan, Ms. Usher can use the automated workflow system to launch the application process from her desktop computer. The application can be updated at each point in the process. Any supporting documents, such as a copy of Mr. Callison's most recent paycheck, can be scanned into the system to accompany the initial work order. If a loan processor has a question, she can record the question and the outcome in the system. At the end of the process, the application, loan agreement, and all supporting documents are filed electronically for future reference. If Lutz Bank uses a quality review process, then the system can be programmed to randomly select a specified percentage of applications and send the files to a quality reviewer. Also, if Lutz Bank has customer service operations in more than one location, then the automated workflow system, if it is networked, allows service providers in these separate locations to view the same document at the same time.

Figure 13-4 illustrates how document management and automated workflow systems can streamline a paper-based process.

Self-Service Options

Advances in technology have led to a variety of self-service options for customers and intermediaries. We have seen how IVR allows callers to choose from a menu of self-service options. Another self-service technology, which many of us now take for granted, is the automated teller machine (ATM), which enables customers to perform a variety of banking functions such as withdrawals, cash advances, deposits, fund transfers, and account inquiries. Other self-service functions are provided through fax-on-demand and the Internet.

FIGURE 13-4. Paper vs. Automated Workflow.

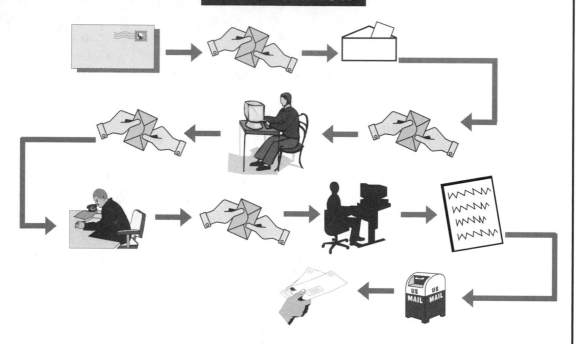

PAPER WORKFLOW

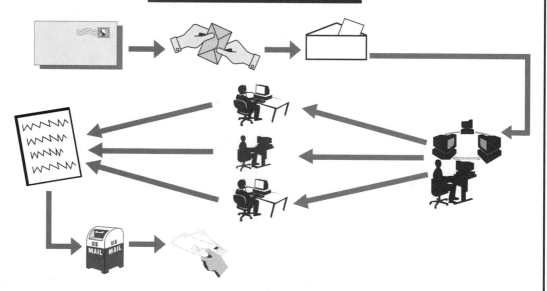

AUTOMATED WORKFLOW

Fax-on-demand is a technology that combines IVR with fax to enable customers to call a business at any time to have forms or other documents automatically faxed to them. For example, a managed care plan member could use fax-on-demand to order and receive a claim form or informational flyers on a variety of health-related topics.

Many companies now offer self-service options on their Web sites, prompting some observers to note that business systems are moving from the back office to the Internet. For Web-enabled self-service options to be of value to users, the content and design must provide accurate information and reliable service in an easy-to-use format.

> For Web-enabled self-service options to be of value to users, the content and design must provide accurate information and reliable service in an easy-to-use format.

A few of the many self-service options available to individual customers on financial services Web sites include

- Online insurance processes that allow customers to complete and submit paperless applications and claims, and to check on the status of these transactions

- Investment sites that allow customers to make stock and bond transactions, view account balances, and research the historical performance of mutual funds

- Banking sites that allow customers to move money between accounts, apply for loans, and view account balances

- Managed care sites that allow plan members to make address changes, add family members for coverage, locate participating providers, and file and check the status of claims

- Interactive programs, such as educational games or investment guides, that help customers determine their financial needs and invite them to seek assistance in implementing an appropriate strategy

Similarly, self-service options allows corporate customers to obtain information and conduct transactions over the Internet. For example, employees in the human resources (HR) department of a group policyholder can log on to the insurer's Web site to view monthly premium statements. If several employees recently left the company, the HR department can adjust the billing roster to show the dates that coverage for each of these employees ended, and

> One way to reduce the workload on customer service representatives while improving customer service is to implement a high-quality knowledge base for Internet customer service.
>
> — Doug Warner[3]

the employer's monthly premium will be automatically recalculated to reflect the changes. The HR department also can use the Web site to add or delete covered dependents, check the status of claims on behalf of its employees, and so on.

In addition, many financial services companies offer self-service options to intermediaries, who can visit a Web site to obtain information about products, plan design, fund performance, and underwriting requirements; print copies of marketing material; download interactive software that enables them to prepare sales presentations for customers; view information about sales commissions and the status of transactions they have submitted; and obtain information, complete forms, and submit changes on behalf of their customers.

While some customers view self-service as a convenience, others prefer to interact with service providers.

Although self-service technology allows customers to perform many types of transactions that once were handled by service providers, most companies continue to rely on employees to provide customer service. While some customers view self-service as a convenience, others prefer to interact with service providers. Consequently, most financial services companies offer customers a choice of self-service or human-assisted service. Also, as technology filters out most routine questions and transactions, the more complex and time-consuming work remains for service providers. Furthermore, as customers become increasingly proficient at self-service, they become more knowledgeable about their finances, and they ask questions and raise issues that are best handled by experienced employees.

Challenges of Technology

Technological developments like e-commerce create many opportunities and challenges for financial services companies. Broadly speaking, *e-commerce* means doing business electronically over computer networks. The phrase *doing business* covers a wide range of activities, from marketing, selling, and delivering products and services to processing transactions and providing customer service. With the wealth of information available over the Internet, customers are increasingly familiar with the products, prices, and services available in the marketplace, so if one company does not give them what they want, customers do not hesitate to take their business elsewhere. Customers who use the Internet to purchase products often expect to obtain customer service on the Internet as well. In the past, when customers contacted financial services companies by letter, they usually waited a week or more for a response. Today,

According to consumer attitude surveys conducted by the Independent Insurance Agents of America, about 80 percent of consumers want online access as one of their insurance service options.

Source: Rough Notes Co.[4]

when customers send an e-mail message using a company Web site, they might expect a response within 24 hours, if not sooner.

Because of pressures such as these, many financial services companies seek the greater efficiencies and competitive advantages that technology can provide. Used appropriately, technology brings greater value to customers and companies. However, most technologies are complex and expensive, and determining the best ways to use them can be difficult. The challenge for financial services companies is to transform the expectations and promise of technology into reality.

Privacy and Security

One of technology's greatest benefits—the ease with which it allows information gathering and sharing—is also one of its greatest liabilities. Businesses must ensure that their customers' personal information and the company's proprietary information are available only to parties with a legitimate need to know. Financial services firms, unlike most other businesses, maintain a great deal of sensitive financial, medical, and personal information about their customers. Therefore, they have an added responsibility to conduct their activities with discretion, skill, and diligence.

The term *security* refers to the physical, technical, and procedural steps a company takes to prevent the loss, wrongful disclosure (accidental or intentional), or theft of information.

To protect the privacy of personal and proprietary information, financial services companies establish security measures. In this sense, the term *security* refers to the physical, technical, and procedural steps a company takes to prevent the loss, wrongful disclosure (accidental or intentional), or theft of information.

Most companies establish password procedures to ensure that only authorized users are allowed access to certain types of records. For example, access to customer medical records in a managed care organization's document management system would be limited to employees—such as pre-authorization nurses or claim examiners—who need to examine the records to perform their jobs. These employees use special passwords that allow them to view confidential data. Many companies require employees to change their passwords periodically and to select passwords that do not include obvious personal information—such as their birthday, street address, or telephone number—to reduce the risk of unauthorized users obtaining access to confidential information.

> The greatest challenge facing our industry with regard to the use of technology is the ability to provide an environment that is flexible and responsive to changing business needs in a timely manner while maintaining data security and protecting customers' privacy.
>
> — James M. Middleton [5]

Many companies carefully separate the information in their systems so they can open their networks to the Internet, while protecting confidential information from unauthorized users. A common method of shielding information and protecting customer privacy is to install a firewall. A *firewall* is a type of hardware or software that sits between a firm's internal network and the outside Internet, which limits access into and out of the internal network, based on rules defined by the organization.

Another way companies restrict unauthorized access to confidential information is with *encryption* (the conversion of electronic data into a code) and *decryption* (the conversion of encrypted data back to its original form). For example, if a customer forgets his personal identification number and password to access his investment account on the Internet, the company sends this confidential information to him via encrypted e-mail. Similarly, if an intermediary registers with a financial services firm to obtain access to information through a self-service option on the company's Web site, the registration process uses encryption/decryption to protect the confidential information transmitted over the Internet.

Impact on Service Providers

As we have seen, technology provides many valuable tools for managers and service providers. However, technology also presents challenges at all levels of an organization. Managers, for instance, often participate in the selection and evaluation of the technologies that support customer service. As new technologies emerge, managers must decide how long to keep their existing systems and when to update or convert to new systems. They must determine if competitors are gaining an advantage with new technologies and if these technologies can truly provide value to customers and the company. The cost of purchasing and maintaining a system is substantial, so when a decision is made, the company lives with the consequences—positive or negative—for many years.

Like managers, service providers also face challenges related to technology. In the past, service providers needed extensive product and operations knowledge, effective interpersonal skills, and the ability to work with relatively simple technologies, such as the telephone or a copy machine. Today, service providers also must be familiar with a variety of computer-related technologies.

Consider the following two scenarios. In the first case, a CSR does not have access to a document management system. After speaking with a customer, the CSR writes a brief note asking a clerical support employee to locate a particular document, make a copy, and mail it to the customer. This process requires minimal technical expertise from the CSR, but is time-consuming and inefficient. In the second scenario, the CSR uses a document management system. During the telephone call with the customer, the CSR searches the electronic files, finds the form, attaches it to an e-mail, and sends the e-mail and attachment to the customer. This process is efficient, but it requires the CSR to use technology quickly and capably.

The term *crossing channels* refers to customer contacts that move from one communication channel to another.

As you have seen, service providers must develop the skills to support different types of communication. In the course of providing service, CSRs sometimes cross channels. The term *crossing channels* refers to customer contacts that move from one communication channel to another. For example, suppose you receive an ambiguous e-mail message from a customer. You might attempt to cross channels by sending a reply that asks the customer for permission to call her to discuss her request. Similarly, CSRs sometimes handle *multichannel customer contacts*, which are interactions that combine two or more communication channels simultaneously, such as Web collaboration and the telephone.

Legacy Systems

Other technology-related challenges come from older technologies, called legacy systems, used for certain functions. A *legacy system* is a relatively old computer system or application program that a company maintains because of the high cost of replacing or redesigning the system. Most legacy systems are large computer systems that run on mainframes, have been in use for many years, and contain a great deal of data. However, they often are not compatible with modern equivalent systems and are difficult to modify. Consequently, in some companies, service providers must be familiar with a variety of different legacy systems to gain access to the information they need to process service requests and complete service transactions.

Internal Customer Service

To make the most of technology, financial services firms depend on people who are capable of effectively selecting, maintaining, and using technology. Without these employees, a company is likely to spend large sums of money on technology that provides little benefit. By itself, technology is worthless; but with the right people, properly trained, technology is invaluable. Customer service areas rely heavily on support from information technology (IT) staff, referred to in some companies as information systems (IS) staff. This IT support can be classified as either strategic or tactical.

STRATEGIC SUPPORT (PLANNING TO MEET THE COMPANY'S NEEDS)

Although technology can have a significant impact on the success or failure of a financial services organization, few executives have the background and knowledge to make technology-related decisions on their own. Typically, they work closely with IT staff to choose and implement customer service technologies that most effectively meet business needs. Because IT staff are familiar with advances in technology, they often make recommendations to the business units.

TACTICAL SUPPORT (SUPPORTING DAY-TO-DAY OPERATIONS)

Customer service, like many other functions in a financial services firm, depends heavily on technology. If the phone system is not working, a call center is out of business. If the Web site is down, thousands of customers lose contact with the company. If the knowledge management system locks up, service providers lack the resources they need to support customers.

In most financial services companies, the accessibility and quality of customer service depend directly on IT systems. To keep customer service operations functioning smoothly, IT staff must be responsive to the immediate needs of customer service managers and service providers. In many cases, an internal help desk meets these needs. An *IT help desk* is a service provided by IT staff that enables technology users to obtain assistance, usually requested via telephone or e-mail. The help desk must quickly correct problems to keep telephones, the IVR, the Web site, and support systems available for customers and service providers. For example, if a CSR is denied access to a retrieval tool she needs to support customers, she calls the help desk to report the problem, and the help desk employee takes appropriate action or assigns the problem to another staff member to handle.

IT employees also add value to customer service operations by being responsive to suggestions from managers and employees. Some organizations conduct a **user needs analysis**, which is a series of activities designed to improve the effectiveness of a system by examining the interaction between the technology and the people who use it. Ideally, user needs analysis begins before a new technology is selected or designed and continues as the technology is implemented, maintained, and periodically reviewed. In addition, IT staff participate in making system changes needed to support ncw or modified products and services.

The Rapid Pace of Change

A major challenge for financial services companies is to keep up with technology's rapid pace of change. For example, wireless technology—such as cell phones, handheld computers, personal digital assistants, and wireless modems and networks for computers—are becoming increasingly popular. As wireless technology evolves, customers will have access to most of the functions of a personal computer and a telephone from virtually anywhere at any time.

> Advances in technology will lead to increased expectations, and customers will insist on receiving customer service whenever and wherever it is most convenient for them.

These types of technology provide financial services companies with additional opportunities to improve communication and customer service. For instance, regardless of where intermediaries or customers happen to be, a company can use text chat to send short messages notifying them of the approval of applications or loans. On the other hand, advances in technology will lead to increased expectations, and customers will insist on receiving customer service whenever and wherever it is most convenient for them.

As you have seen in this chapter, managers and service providers are constantly called upon to take advantage of technology to provide faster, better, and more personalized customer service. In the next chapter, you will see how service providers can meet the challenges presented by technology and other factors related to customer service in the 21st century. Although the future of customer service technology is difficult to predict, Insight 13-1 presents one possibility.

INSIGHT 13-1. Financial Services and the Internet.

To simplify her finances, Andrea Landrigan has decided to have her multiple insurance policies, credit cards, investments, and bank accounts aggregated on a single Web site. Using a wealth management application, she has begun working with a financial advisor, Ed Trenholm, for better management of her total finances. One day Ms. Landrigan receives an e-mail from Mr. Trenholm who has discovered that, on the basis of his review of her aggregated and wealth management data, she is over-insured. Worse, she has a number of old term life policies for which she is paying large premiums. He tells her she can exchange these policies for a policy that he recommends, saving money and obtaining better coverage.

If you view the Internet as just another delivery channel, you are about to miss the next big opportunity to hit the financial services industry. Financial services companies need to look to the Internet as a catalyst for enhancing customer relationships and cross-selling a broader array of financial products. The Internet can improve the speed, efficiency, and quality of the overall sales and buying cycle; it also can help financial services firms and intermediaries gather and share customer data across product and organizational boundaries to enhance sales and marketing, improve support processes, and deliver value-added customer service.

The key to success begins with personalization. Financial services companies and service providers must first recognize each customer's identity among the numerous "faceless" interactions each day. Then they must be able to leverage the information they have about each customer and about all lines of business—property and casualty insurance, life insurance, annuities, health insurance, banking, and securities. The goal is to enable effective collaboration through a common e-finance platform that integrates all financial services products into a seamless offering to each customer.

Source: Adapted from Gordon Sanders, "Aggregation + Wealth Management = Customer Service," *Resource* (September 2001): 26. Used with permission; all rights reserved.

To practice and review the skills and information you learned in this chapter, see the interactive CD, *Practicing Your Customer Service Skills*, included with this book.

Key Terms and Concepts

technology

customer service technology

workforce management system

intelligent call routing (ICR)

e-mail management systems

queue

universal queue

automatic transaction distribution

automatic call distributor (ACD)

longest idle agent (LIA)

uniform call distribution (UCD)

readerboard

interactive voice response (IVR) system

computer telephony integration (CTI)

automatic number identification (ANI)

computer network

internal network

external network

local area network (LAN)

wide area network (WAN)

Internet

World Wide Web

Web server

browser

intranet

electronic data interchange (EDI)

knowledge management

expert systems software

retrieval tool

customer contact system

data warehouse

data mining

document management system

imaging

automated workflow system

fax-on-demand

e-commerce

security

firewall

encryption

decryption

crossing channels

multichannel customer contacts

legacy system

IT help desk

user needs analysis

Endnotes

1. John Chisholm, "Using the Internet to Measure Customer Satisfaction and Loyalty," *Best Practices in Customer Service*, ed. Ron Zemke and John A. Woods (New York: HRD Press, 1998), 305.

2. Hedy Aref and Jereb Cheatham, "Workflow and Imaging for Customer Service," LOMA's Customer Service Conference, The Walt Disney World Resort, Orlando, Florida, 26 February 2002.

3. Doug Warner, "The Insider's Guide to Building an Effective Knowledge Base: Best Practices in Knowledge Acquisition, Management and Publishing," *RightNow Technologies*, 2000, http://www.rightnow.com/resource/whitepaper.html (15 October 2002).

4. John Ashenhurst, "Online Customer Self-Service," *Rough Notes* (1 July 2001).

5. Stephen Hall, "2002 Industry Outlook Positive Yet Cautious," *Resource* (January 2002): 14.

CHAPTER 14

Succeeding in Customer Service

After studying this chapter, you should be able to

- Discuss how service providers can align their work activities with their company's strategic plan
- Explain the benefits of personal planning
- Identify your own time-management personality profile
- Summarize the Time Management Matrix and its purpose
- Create an effective priority list and use it properly
- Define stress and distinguish between stressors and distressors
- Use the distress symptom scale to measure stress
- Describe three styles for coping with stress
- Explain the importance of taking initiative and being proactive in learning and development

By having read to this point in the book, you already have acquired much of the knowledge and many of the skills needed to become an outstanding customer service provider. The most successful service providers are committed to excellence. They find ways to do an exceptional job regardless of the circumstances and challenges—such as the increasing knowledge and demands of customers, changing corporate strategies and structures, complex products and workflow processes, and ever-changing communication and information technologies.

This chapter will provide you with tips on how to successfully deal with some of the greatest challenges of any customer-oriented job in a financial services organization. You will learn how to focus your planning and actions on what really matters. You will discover strategies that can help you better manage your time and cope with stress. And, last, but definitely not least, you will learn the importance of taking the initiative to develop the skills and knowledge you need to become an exceptional service provider.

Planning for Success

An important part of your job as a service provider is to align your activities with the mission and objectives in your company's strategic plan. Take time to learn about and understand your company's goals and then ensure that your work contributes to their achievement. Ask yourself, "How does my daily work help the company achieve its goals?" If you have difficulty answering this question, you might need to clarify your understanding of the company's objectives, your job activities, or both. Talk to your supervisor, manager, or another knowledgeable person within your organization to better grasp your role in helping the company carry out its strategic plans. If your company conducts performance evaluations (as discussed in Chapter 4), use them to evaluate your individual objectives and, together with your manager, make sure your objectives align with organizational goals. The more clearly you recognize and understand the link between your job performance and the company's success, the more likely you are to strive for excellence in your work and, as a result, succeed in your job.

> What lies behind us and what lies before us are tiny matters compared to what lies within us.
>
> — Oliver Wendell Holmes

Establish your personal objectives, then develop strategies to meet your objectives. On a regular basis, evaluate your progress and make adjustments, as needed, to improve the results.

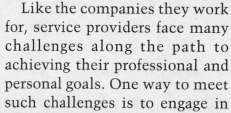

Like the companies they work for, service providers face many challenges along the path to achieving their professional and personal goals. One way to meet such challenges is to engage in personal planning. Many personal planning methods exist; the one shown in Insight 14-1 is based on the organizational planning process we discussed in Chapter 10. In this method, you begin by conducting a situation analysis and then developing a personal mission statement. Establish your personal objectives, then develop strategies to meet your objectives. On a regular basis, evaluate your progress and make adjustments, as needed, to improve the results.

In both their professional and personal lives, employees encounter obstacles and setbacks in their plans that require alternative strategies and revised goals. For example, a corporate reorganization, downturn in the economy, serious health problem, or other unexpected occurrence can interfere with a person's plans to achieve certain goals, such as advancing along a particular career path, purchasing a new home, or traveling to another country. Although we can't always avoid such occurrences, using personal planning can help minimize the effects of such events and help you stay focused on your ultimate goals.

Managing Your Time

We all sometimes feel that we have too little time to do everything we need to do. Many of us feel this way frequently, causing us to feel overwhelmed and harried. Since we can't add hours to the day, the best way to avoid these feelings is to manage our time more effectively.

Effective time management includes much more than simply making a list of things to do. As you'll learn in this section, identifying

INSIGHT 14-1. One Approach to Personal Planning.

STEP 1: CONDUCT A SITUATION ANALYSIS

A situation analysis helps you examine your career, your home life, your health habits, hobbies, and so on with the goal of gaining a better understanding of what is important to you, what steps you are taking or not taking to address these important matters, and how these activities relate to one another. For example, neglecting your personal health—perhaps by not exercising or eating properly—may affect your energy level and your ability to accomplish important tasks at work and at home. Situation analysis prepares you for developing your personal mission statement and for the rest of the personal planning process.

STEP 2: CREATE A PERSONAL MISSION STATEMENT

In their book *First Things First*, Stephen R. Covey, A. Roger Merrill, and Rebecca R. Merrill say that a personal mission statement captures "what you want to be and what you want to do in your life and the principles upon which being and doing are based. Clarity on these issues is critical because it affects everything else—the goals you set, the decisions you make, the paradigms you have, the way you spend your time."[1]

By writing and then regularly reviewing your personal mission statement you think carefully about what is most important to you, and then you are in a better position to align your actions with your beliefs. Your personal mission statement becomes the basis for planning and decision-making in your life; it guides you in setting and achieving meaningful goals.

STEP 3: SET INDIVIDUAL OBJECTIVES

After conducting a situation analysis and developing a personal mission statement, you are ready to set individual objectives. Like organizational objectives, your individual objectives should be realistic, specific, and measurable statements that describe the results you intend to achieve. Work-related objectives typically come from the performance evaluation process, and might include individual performance measurements (such as timeliness or quality results) as well as developmental goals (such as training or educational activities or advancement opportunities you are interested in pursuing).

Although your job may figure prominently in your individual objectives, it is important to remember that individual objectives should reflect a balance between your professional life and your personal life.

STEP 4: DEVELOP STRATEGIES

After you have established your individual objectives, you must decide the methods you will use to achieve them. For example, suppose one of your work-related objectives is to increase your skills in handling difficult customers, as measured through your department's call monitoring process. How would you go about accomplishing this objective? One strategy might be to keep a log of customer interactions that have upset or angered you, as discussed in Chapter 9, and to review this log with your supervisor to determine how you can better handle these situations. Similarly, if one of your objectives is to improve your health by exercising regularly, you could join a health club or start walking with a friend or relative.

STEP 5: EVALUATE RESULTS

As we saw in Chapter 12, a financial services organization must determine ways to measure results so it can compare actual performance to the standards set by its objectives. Similarly, you must evaluate your performance in meeting the individual objectives developed through personal planning. You and your supervisor will probably address most of your work-related objectives through the performance evaluation process or through employer-sponsored career development activities. You will have to make time on your own for evaluating other individual objectives. To obtain the most from a personal planning process, you should review your mission, objectives, and progress regularly, such as weekly, monthly, or yearly depending on your goals.

your time-management personality profile and using practical time-management techniques can help you better control your use of time.

Time-Management Styles

Each of us has a distinct style of managing time. Some people start projects immediately, always stay on schedule, and efficiently work on several tasks simultaneously. Some people wait until the last minute to begin a project and then work in a burst of creative energy. Others operate somewhere between those two extremes.

One way to identify your time-management style is to determine your tendency toward certain personality characteristics in five areas related to managing time: (1) attention to task, (2) type of focus, (3) approach to structure, (4) style of processing, and (5) strategy of action. In each of the following areas, most of us tend toward one personality or the other:[2]

People with **convergent personalities** like to stay on task until a project is finished.

- *Attention to task: divergent or convergent.* People with **divergent personalities** wander off the subject to whatever sounds interesting at the moment. People with **convergent personalities** like to stay on task until a project is finished. Convergent people draw energy from completing projects, whereas divergent people draw energy from starting new ones.

- *Type of focus: detail-oriented or globally oriented.* **Detail-oriented personalities** need facts and details about a situation to feel comfortable. **Globally oriented personalities** prefer to think about the possibilities of a situation rather than the facts of the current reality.

- *Approach to structure: Tightly structured or loosely structured.* People with **tightly structured personalities** need to have a system for accomplishing tasks; for example, they prefer meetings that start on time and follow a specified agenda. People with **loosely structured personalities** prefer to have flexibility in how they complete tasks; for example, they are comfortable with meetings that start late and proceed without an agenda.

- *Style of processing: parallel-processing or serial-processing.* People with **parallel-processing personalities** are comfortable performing more than one task at a time; people with **serial-processing personalities** prefer to focus on one task at a time.

■ *Strategy of action: reactive or proactive.* People with **reactive personalities** wait until the last possible moment to do a task and, as a result, spend a lot of time responding to crises or deadlines. People with **proactive personalities** like to make plans and then follow those plans; consequently, they rarely find themselves in crisis situations.

Each approach to time management has advantages and disadvantages. By identifying your own time-management personality profile in Exercise 14-1, you can recognize opportunities for improvement and build on your strengths. For example, are you a convergent, detailed person with a tightly structured approach to work tasks? Or, are you a divergent, global person with a loosely structured approach to work tasks? Although no one time-management personality profile is ideal, yours might have areas that could be improved. For instance, if your style of processing is very reactive, developing your planning skills might greatly improve your ability to manage time.

An *urgent* activity is one that is pressing and demands immediate attention, while an *important* activity is meaningful and has significant consequence in our lives.

Another way to evaluate your time-management style is to use the Time Management Matrix™, presented by management consultant and trainer Stephen R. Covey, A. Roger Merrill, and Rebecca R. Merrill in their book, *First Things First*, to analyze how you spend your time.[3] The Time Management Matrix, illustrated in Figure 14-1, categorizes activities into four quadrants: "Urgent and Important," "Important, but not Urgent," "Urgent, but not Important," and "Not Urgent and Not Important." An *urgent* activity is one that is pressing and demands immediate attention, while an *important* activity is meaningful and has significant consequence in our lives. The purpose of the Time Management Matrix is to help us understand how *important* and *urgent* activities affect the choices we make about how to spend our time. It allows us to see where we spend most of our time and why we spend it there, so we can adjust our behavior to better manage our time.

Quadrant I activities are both urgent and important—for example, dealing with an irate customer, meeting a deadline, repairing broken equipment, undergoing heart surgery, or helping a crying child who has been hurt. We need to spend time in Quadrant I because this is where we manage, produce, and use our experience and judgment to respond to many needs and challenges. But we also must realize that many *important* activities become *urgent* through procrastination, or because we don't do enough prevention planning.

> The bad news is time flies. The good news is you're the pilot.
>
> — Michael Althsuler [4]

Exercise 14-1.   Identifying Your Time-Management Personality Profile.

Answer each item according to how often that statement is true for you. Write your answer on the blank that precedes each item, using the following scale:

> **1 = Almost Never**
> **2 = Sometimes**
> **3 = Often**

1. _____ I have so many "to-do" lists that I don't know where to begin.

2. _____ I can make decisions about minor details without needing to know how the overall plan is coming together.

3. _____ I know where I have filed most of my important papers.

4. _____ A busy environment helps me work more efficiently.

5. _____ I find myself inundated with papers that I have to get to.

6. _____ I get distracted by the unimportant while I am in the middle of the important.

7. _____ If a party is being planned, I enjoy attending to the particulars more than I do planning the themes.

8. _____ I keep my "to-do" lists handy.

9. _____ I tend to take on several tasks at one time.

10. _____ I find myself losing sight of long-term goals when dealing with short-term crises.

11. _____ I find myself daydreaming during meetings or discussions.

12. _____ I am good at mapping out the steps needed to complete a project.

13. _____ Telephone and fax numbers for my business contacts are readily accessible.

14. _____ While working on one project, ideas about other projects come to my mind.

15. _____ I put off making decisions until a situation becomes urgent.

16. _____ My mind wanders when I'm working alone.

17. _____ In the midst of working on a project, attending to minor details as they come up helps me to keep on track.

18. _____ I am uncomfortable when my desk is overcrowded with papers.

19. _____ I am eager to start a new project before I even finish an existing project.

20. _____ I prepare for things at the last minute.

21. _____ Interruptions throughout the day affect the amount of work I am able to accomplish.

22. _____ I am very precise in how I handle projects.

23. _____ I keep track of all of my important deadlines.

24. _____ When I talk on the phone during a casual conversation, I also engage in other activities (e.g., cooking, grooming, cleaning, etc.)

25. _____ I avoid delegating work until it's absolutely necessary.

26. _____ I have scraps of paper scattered about with bits of information on them.

27. _____ I go home with my desk in order.

28. _____ I keep my legal and accounting records updated and in order.

29. _____ During a business conversation, I would rather look for a related file while talking than put the person on hold.

30. _____ I find it difficult to make time for the unexpected.

31. _____ I put off today what I can do tomorrow.

32. _____ It is important to capture specific details of business conversations and record them verbatim.

continued on next page

Exercise 14-1 Identifying Your Time-Management Personality Profile (*continued*).

33. _____ I object to meetings that start late.

34. _____ If I am trying to find a street address while driving, I would rather leave the radio on than turn it off.

35. _____ I find myself working long hours and never catching up.

36. _____ When I am in a meeting and someone brings up an interesting but unrelated topic, I join in the discussion about the new topic.

37. _____ I enjoy implementing the details of a project more than I do envisioning the end result.

38. _____ I think meetings that don't have an agenda are a waste of my time.

39. _____ If I am walking around a shopping center looking for a particular store, I am comfortable chatting with a friend as I look.

40. _____ I am disorganized because I do not have the time to get organized.

To obtain your scores for each section of this survey, write the appropriate number of points by each question number below. Then total your points for each section.

Section 1: Attention to Task	Section 2: Type of Focus	Section 3: Approach to Structure
1. _____	2. _____	3. _____
6. _____	7. _____	8. _____
11. _____	12. _____	13. _____
16. _____	17. _____	18. _____
21. _____	22. _____	23. _____
26. _____	27. _____	28. _____
31. _____	32. _____	33. _____
36. _____	37. _____	38. _____
Total _____	*Total* _____	*Total* _____

Section 4: Style of Processing	Section 5: Strategy of Action
4. _____	5. _____
9. _____	10. _____
14. _____	15. _____
19. _____	20. _____
24. _____	25. _____
29. _____	30. _____
34. _____	35. _____
39. _____	40. _____
Total _____	*Total* _____

Interpretation of Scores

Your total score in each category places you on a continuum ranging from 8 to 24 points for each category.

Section 1: Attention to Task. The higher your point total in this area, the more divergent your personality. The lower your point total, the more convergent your personality.

Section 2: Type of Focus. The higher your point total in this area, the more detailed your personality. The lower your point total, the more global your personality.

Section 3: Approach to Structure. A high point total in this area indicates you take a tight approach to structuring work tasks. A low point total indicates a loose approach to structuring work tasks.

Section 4: Style of Processing. A high point total in this area indicates a parallel processing style. A low point total indicates a serial processing style.

Section 5: Strategy of Action. A high point total in this area indicates a reactive strategy of action; a low point total indicates a more proactive strategy of action.

FIGURE 14-1. The Time Management Matrix™

	URGENT	NOT URGENT
IMPORTANT	**Quadrant I** ■ Crises ■ Pressing problems ■ Deadline-driven projects, meetings, preparations	**Quadrant II** ■ Preparation ■ Prevention ■ Values clarification ■ Planning ■ Relationship building ■ True re-creation ■ Empowerment
NOT IMPORTANT	**Quadrant III** ■ Interruptions, some phone calls ■ Some mail, some reports ■ Some meetings ■ Many proximate, pressing matters ■ Many popular activities	**Quadrant IV** ■ Trivia, busywork ■ Junk mail ■ Some phone calls ■ Time wasters ■ "Escape" activities

Source: Adapted from the *First Things First* book by Stephen R. Covey, A. Roger Merrill, and Rebecca R. Merrill. © 1994 FranklinCovey, www.franklincovey.com. The Time Management Matrix is a trademark of FranklinCovey. Used with permission. All rights reserved.

Quadrant II activities are important, but not urgent. Such activities include

- long-range planning
- anticipating and preventing problems
- empowering others
- broadening our minds and increasing our skills through reading and continuous professional development

- envisioning how we're going to help a struggling daughter or son

- preparing for important meetings and presentations

- investing in relationships through active listening

The more time we spend on Quadrant II activities, the more we increase our ability to accomplish tasks and reduce the number of activities in Quadrant I. On the other hand, ignoring the activities in Quadrant II increases the number of activities in Quadrant I, creating stress and deeper crises. One way to accomplish more Quadrant II activities is to spend some quiet time each day—perhaps early in the morning, during lunch, or in the evening—reviewing your tasks for the day or week and planning how you will do them. Taking even 15 minutes a day to focus on planning can give you an increased sense of direction and control in your life.

Quadrant III activities are urgent, but not important. These activities—such as many phone calls, meetings, and drop-in visitors—usually only *seem* important because of their urgent nature. But the actual activities, if they are important at all, are usually only important to someone else. Quadrant III includes many immediate, pressing matters (such as doing a favor for a coworker by reviewing his presentation for a committee meeting or reading and responding to e-mails as they arrive even though they may not be important) and many popular activities (such as attending one-time events like a large retail sale or the opening night of a movie or play). We spend a lot of time in Quadrant III meeting other people's priorities and expectations, thinking we're in Quadrant I.

Quadrant IV activities are neither urgent nor important. These activities are time-wasters and include, for example, reading addictive light novels, habitually watching mindless television shows, or gossiping in the office breakroom. Quadrant IV activities do *not* necessarily include recreational activities, because recreation in the true sense of re-creating energy and stamina is a valuable Quadrant II activity. We often use Quadrant IV activities to "escape" the stress of spending so much time on activities from Quadrants I and III. But Quadrant IV is not survival; it is deterioration.

Our goal should be to spend most of our time on *important* activities, rather than *urgent* ones.

We all face urgent tasks and important tasks in our daily lives, although usually one or the other tends to dominate. Our goal should be to spend most of our time on *important* activities, rather than *urgent* ones. When we focus on important activities, we spend most of our time in Quadrants I and II, and no time in Quadrants III and IV. And, as we dedicate more time to preparation, prevention, planning, and empowerment in Quadrant II, we spend less time dealing with crises in Quadrant I.

Using a Priority List

At one time or another, most of us have made a "to-do" list on which we write down—in no particular order—all the tasks that we need to complete. Then we begin to do the items on the list, either in the order in which they appear or according to which tasks we enjoy most, regardless of the importance of those tasks.

Although a "to-do" list can be helpful, it can be a much more effective time-management tool if you transform it into a priority list. A *priority list* is a listing of tasks that need to be completed and that are ranked according to their importance. To make a priority list, first write down all the tasks you face. Then review the list and rank the tasks, with the most important task being ranked No. 1, the second most important being ranked No. 2, and so on. As you can see from the example in Figure 14-2, the order in which the tasks were written down doesn't necessarily correspond to their importance.

FIGURE 14-2. Example of a Priority List.

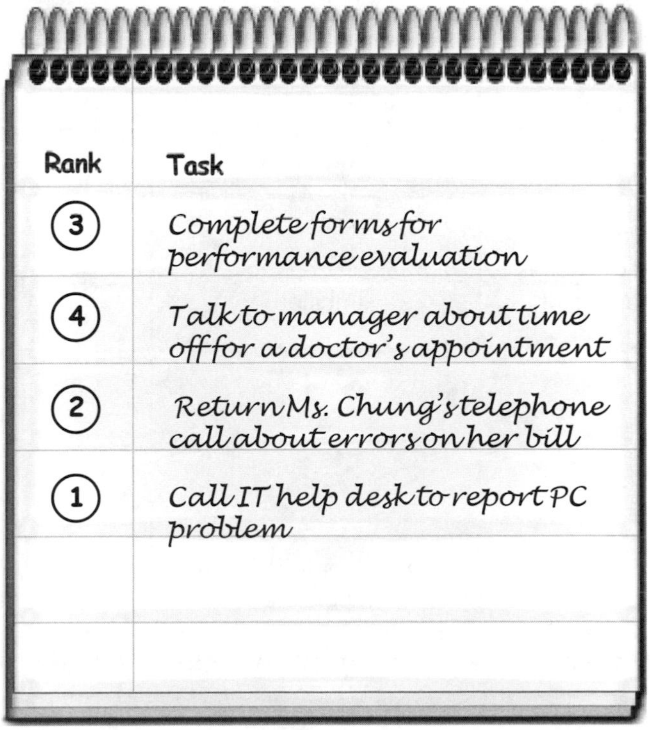

Rank	Task
3	Complete forms for performance evaluation
4	Talk to manager about time off for a doctor's appointment
2	Return Ms. Chung's telephone call about errors on her bill
1	Call IT help desk to report PC problem

CREATING AN EFFECTIVE PRIORITY LIST

To make an effective priority list, you must determine both the importance and the urgency of a task and rank each task accordingly. If you have difficulty deciding on priorities, ask your supervisor to help you; if possible, prepare a proposed priority list in advance to review with your supervisor and make changes, if needed. Several guidelines also can help you create an effective priority list. We summarize these guidelines in Figure 14-3 and discuss them in more detail in the following pages.

Make Sure Each Item Is Important or Urgent.

Before you include an item on your priority list, take a moment to ask yourself, "Is this task truly important or urgent? Does it contribute to my overall goals?" Don't get into the habit of cluttering your priority list with activities that are not really important or urgent, as explained in the previous discussion of the Time Management Matrix.

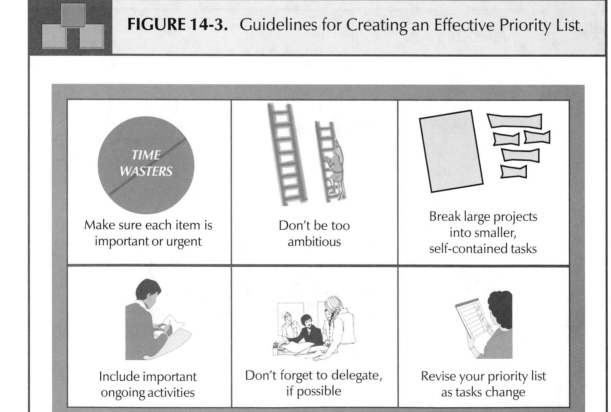

FIGURE 14-3. Guidelines for Creating an Effective Priority List.

TIME WASTERS Make sure each item is important or urgent	Don't be too ambitious	Break large projects into smaller, self-contained tasks
Include important ongoing activities	Don't forget to delegate, if possible	Revise your priority list as tasks change

Don't Be Too Ambitious

A daily priority list should include only one day's activities. Don't overestimate the amount of work you can reasonably expect to do in one day. If your list has more than 10 tasks, divide the tasks into priority groupings and rank each grouping of activities according to their importance. If you're not sure how much you can accomplish in a single day, keep track of your time for a week or a month, noting exactly how much time you spend on various activities, including breaks and interruptions. After tracking how you actually spend your time, you will be able to estimate more accurately the length of time you need to do certain things.

Break Long-Term Projects into Smaller, Self-contained Tasks

Long-term projects should not be excluded from your daily priority list just because they can't be completed in one day. Find logical project milestones to include on your priority list. For example, if you must conduct a telephone survey of customers in a certain region, determine how many customers you can reasonably contact in one day and put that number of telephone calls on your daily priority list. In that way, your priority list will show the progress you are making toward a project's completion.

Include Important Ongoing Activities

If you're not sure how much you can accomplish in a single day, keep track of your time for a week or a month, noting exactly how much time you spend on various activities, including breaks and interruptions.

If you are a customer service provider, the most important task you accomplish each day might be a continuous ongoing activity, such as responding to customer contacts. Even if this is your primary task, be sure to put it on your priority list. Although you won't forget to do this task even if it's not on your list, including it helps you realize that it is just as important as any other activities on your list. Also, at the end of the day you can note how much time you spent doing that primary task, which will help clarify your accomplishments for the day.

Don't Forget to Delegate

Exclude from your priority list any tasks that you can and should delegate to others. Whenever possible, use available resources—for example, a centralized processing center or your administrative support staff—so that you can focus your time and attention on more important tasks.

Revise Your Priority List as Tasks Change

A priority list, like any plan, should be flexible. You must revise your list as the day progresses, adding new tasks as you learn about them, reprioritizing existing tasks, and removing tasks that have been delegated to others. That way, at the end of the day, you will have a much more accurate picture of how you spent your time and exactly what you accomplished.

PUTTING YOUR PRIORITY LIST INTO ACTION

Creating a priority list is important to effective time management, but using the list appropriately is even more important. The following principles, which are summarized in Figure 14-4, can help you maximize the use of your priority list.

Protect Your Time from Outside Interruptions

Even a well-constructed priority list won't help you manage your time if you are constantly being interrupted. External interruptions can come from many sources, including coworkers and your manager. Remember, however, that responding to customer inquiries is part of every service provider's job responsibilities and, therefore, is not an interruption.

If it seems like coworkers constantly interrupt you, think about the reasons for their interruptions. If they just want to talk, you can explain that you're busy now, but you'd be willing to talk at lunch or during a break. When coworkers interrupt you to accomplish their own work goals,

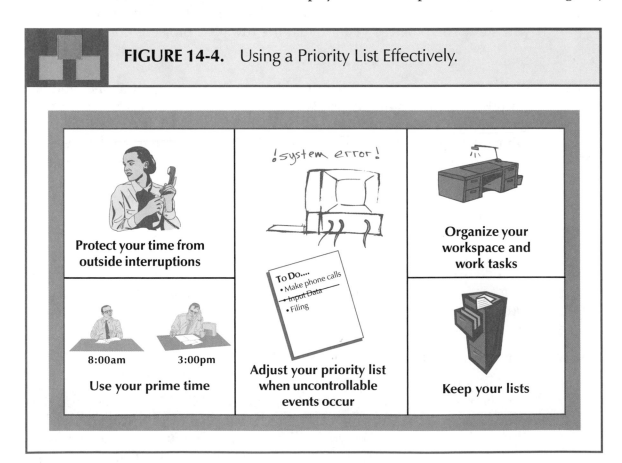

FIGURE 14-4. Using a Priority List Effectively.

Protect your time from outside interruptions

Use your prime time
8:00am   3:00pm

!system error!

To Do....
• Make phone calls
• ~~Input Data~~
• Filing

Adjust your priority list when uncontrollable events occur

Organize your workspace and work tasks

Keep your lists

If you're unsure about whether to delay or refuse a coworker's request for help, discuss the situation with your supervisor.

don't be afraid to say, "I can't do that for you right now." Just because an item is urgent for a coworker doesn't mean it is more important than your own work. Sometimes refusing a coworker's request causes that person to reevaluate her own objectives and priorities. If you're unsure about whether to delay or refuse a coworker's request for help, discuss the situation with your supervisor.

When your manager interrupts you to request that you do something immediately, then of course you have to revise your priority list. Keep in mind, however, that not every request from your manager must be done immediately. Be sure to ask for a deadline on additional work. If the task does not have to be done immediately, take the instructions, note the deadline, and add the task to another day's priority list. Then, continue with your original plan for the day. If the deadline is immediate, you might want to ask your manager for help in determining the most important tasks on your priority list. Your manager will see that one or more tasks will have to take a lower priority because of the additional work.

Adjust Your Priority List When Uncontrollable Events Occur

When you encounter unexpected events—such as when the person to whom you're making an urgent telephone call is unavailable or your computer system fails—you must adjust your priority list. For example, suppose your top priority is mailing a letter to a customer with an attached copy of the customer's contract. When you find that your department's photocopier is broken and there is a 30-minute wait to use the photocopier in another department, what should you do? Even if getting that letter in the mail is the most important task on your priority list, standing in line for 30 minutes is not a productive use of your time. Therefore, go to the next item on your priority list or work on another task that you know you can complete quickly before returning to the letter.

Organize Your Workspace and Work Tasks

Accomplishing the tasks on your priority list will be much easier if you put your workspace in order. For example, be sure you have everything you use in your work available and within easy reach. In addition, think about ways to sort and group your work tasks. For instance, some people set aside certain times of the day to read and respond to e-mail messages, perhaps mid-morning and mid-afternoon. You can use a similar approach for making telephone calls, opening mail, and handling administrative tasks.

Use Your "Prime Time"

Most people have a daily energy cycle. Some people have more energy in the morning; others are more alert in the afternoon. Because your energy cycle is part of your normal metabolism, you should learn to work with it rather than try to change it. Try to work on your highest priority tasks during the highest point in your energy cycle (your "prime time") and on your low-priority tasks during the low points in the cycle.

Keep Your Lists

Keep your list in plain sight to remind you of your priorities and so you can write notes about the status of various tasks throughout the day. For example, you can note the time you called a customer and left a detailed voicemail message for her. Such details will help you remember what you've done. In addition, keep your lists even after you have completed all of the tasks listed. By reviewing the lists at the end of the day or week, you can determine how much you did and what steps you can take in the future to manage your time more effectively. You also can use the information on the lists to help you recall your accomplishments, which can be helpful during performance evaluations. Some people keep track of their daily priority lists and follow-up activities by recording them in a daily calendar or diary for easy access and reference.

Some people keep track of their daily priority lists and follow-up activities by recording them in a daily calendar or diary for easy access and reference.

Understanding and Coping with Stress

Few jobs are free from stress. Most work brings responsibilities, deadlines, and pressures that can cause stress. As we discuss in this section, certain kinds of stress can be beneficial by driving us to achieve more than we would otherwise. But other types of stress are detrimental to our physical, psychological, and emotional health. In this section, we provide tips on how to cope with stress, first by explaining what stress is and then by presenting techniques for handling various types of stress.

What Is Stress?

Stress is the psychological and physical condition that people experience when they perceive a situation as harmful, threatening, or demanding. When stress occurs, your blood pressure, heart rate, breathing rate, and adrenaline levels increase. Many different factors can cause stress, including work, relationships with family and friends, and even daily hassles such as traffic jams and defective technology. Stress can be beneficial or harmful, depending on its intensity and duration.

Any activity, event, or occurrence that causes mild or short-term stress is called a **stressor**. Stressors usually do not result in harmful or lasting negative effects. On the contrary, many stressors often produce beneficial results by helping us grow and develop professionally, intellectually, emotionally, or physically. Examples of stressors include starting a new job, studying for an exam, buying a house, resolving a conflict with a friend or coworker, and competing in an athletic competition. Stressors are a part of daily life.

On the other hand, a **distressor** is an activity, event, or occurrence that causes intense or long-term stress. Distressors typically lead to physical, psychological, or emotional ailments. Examples of distressors can include the loss of a job, an unexpected financial hardship, a family breakup, or the death of a loved one. In the workplace, distressors can arise from the following situations:[5]

- Prolonged work pressure without relief

- A sense of powerlessness over demands being made

- A series of conflicting demands without easy resolution

- A continuous threat of violent or aggressive behavior with little or no defense

- A high degree of uncertainty about direction, purpose, or objectives in a job

Dealing with distressors keeps your body on a sort of permanent alert, causing both physical and psychological effects. Physical effects of stress can include an increased heart rate, headache, blurred vision, perspiration, dizziness, aching neck, clenched jaw, or skin rashes. Psychological effects of stress can include poor concentration, inability to sleep, and feelings of despair or depression. These physical and psychological effects contribute to many medical disorders and diseases including flu, arthritis, heart disease, high blood pressure, strokes, and certain types of cancer. Stress also can lead to detrimental changes in eating habits, alcoholism, drug addiction, tobacco addiction, and suicidal tendencies. Being aware of distress signals, such as those listed in Figure 14-5, can help you identify and cope with stress early to avoid more serious, long-term problems.

Although we have provided general examples of stressors and distressors, note that the difference between the two is often subjective. That is,

FIGURE 14-5. Distress Signals.

Although the following symptoms may indicate other health problems, they often are signs that you have high levels of stress, or distress, in your life:

- Insomnia
- Headaches
- Anxiety
- Upset stomach

- Lack of concentration
- Increase in colds
- Excessive fatigue

If you feel overwhelmed by stress, ask for advice. Talk to a friend or relative, or to your supervisor or manager. If stress is affecting your health, consult a medical doctor. Don't allow stress to eventually result in serious health problems such as a stroke or heart attack.

whether a person considers an event to be a stressor or a distressor depends largely on that person's background, motivation, experience, skills and knowledge, and support system (such as managers and coworkers or family and friends). Each of us copes with stressful events differently. For instance, adapting to a new supervisor might be a stressor for some employees (producing mild or short-lived stress) and a distressor for others (resulting in intense and prolonged stress). To measure the level of distress in your life, complete Exercise 14-2.

Coping with Stress

Like most jobs, working as a service provider can be stressful. Interacting with customers—whether internal or external—can lead to differences of opinion and conflicting needs, wants, and priorities. In addition, service providers in the financial services industry must contend with the many challenges we have discussed throughout this book, from more demanding customers and higher management expectations to technological innovations and corporate reorganization. One thing all of these challenges have in common is that they represent change—in people, expectations, products, processes, tools, and work environment. Figure 14-6 explains why change often causes stress.

Exercise 14-2.   How Distressed Are You?

Working under excessive stress for too long leads to *distress*, which includes symptoms such as anxiety, irritability, and insomnia. Complete the following inventory of distress signals to determine which signals you are experiencing in mind, body, and behavior. When you are finished, total your score.

Using the following scale, indicate which of the following things happened during the past two weeks:

> 0 = **Did not occur**
> 1 = **Occurred once or twice**
> 5 = **Occurred several times**
> 10 = **Occurred almost constantly**

_____ Irritability	_____ Trembling or nervous twitch
_____ Depressed feelings	
_____ Dryness of mouth or throat from tension	_____ Stuttering or stumbling in speech
_____ Impulsive, spur-of-the-moment actions	_____ Inability to concentrate
	_____ Difficulty organizing thoughts
_____ Emotional ups-and-downs	
_____ Strong urge to cry	_____ Difficulty sleeping through the night
_____ Strong urge to "run away from it all"	_____ More impatience than usual
_____ Grinding teeth	_____ Headache
_____ Difficulty sitting still	_____ Neck pain
_____ Nightmares	_____ Pain in back
_____ Diarrhea	_____ Loss of appetite
_____ Verbal attack on someone	_____ Decreased interest in sex
_____ Mental block	_____ Increased appetite
_____ Frequent need to urinate	_____ Forgetfulness
_____ Upset stomach	_____ Chest pain
_____ Strong urge to hurt someone	_____ Significant interpersonal conflict
_____ Fuzzy, foggy thinking	
_____ Talking faster than usual	_____ Struggling to get up to "face another day"
_____ General fatigue or heaviness	_____ Feeling things are "out of control"
_____ Feelings of being "overwhelmed by it all"	_____ Feelings of hopelessness
_____ Feelings of being emotionally unstable	_____ Difficulty staying with one activity very long
_____ Feelings of joylessness	_____ Short-tempered
_____ Feelings of anxiety	_____ Withdrawn
_____ Emotional tension	_____ Difficulty falling asleep
_____ Easily startled	_____ Slow recovery from a stressful event
_____ Hostility	
	_____ ***TOTAL***

continued on next page

Exercise 14-2. How Distressed Are You? (*continued*).

Find the category for your total score below.

High Distress Symptoms	**50 or higher**
Medium Distress Symptoms	**20–49**
Low Distress Symptoms	**0–19**

After determining your score, think about the following questions:

- Is your score higher than you would like?

- What do you see in your responses that is new or surprising?

- Underline the two or three items most troublesome to you during periods of overload.

- How do you suppose your mate, a close friend, or a working partner would rate you on the scale? Ask him or her.

Source: From STRESS MANAGEMENT FOR WELLNESS + 1st edition by SCHAFER. © 1987. Reprinted with permission of Wadsworth, a division of Thomson Learning: www.thomsonrights.com. Fax 800 730-2215.

Service providers must learn to accept stress as a part of their work lives and develop effective ways to deal with it. Researchers have identified three primary styles for coping with stress: emotion-focused, problem-focused, and relationship-focused.[6] Each style has advantages. For example, the emotion-focused coping style can help you better handle all kinds of stress. The problem-focused coping style can help you control or eliminate a specific problem that is causing you stress. And, the relationship-focused coping style will help you handle stress caused by other people.

EMOTION-FOCUSED COPING STYLE

The *emotion-focused coping style* is an approach to handling stress in which a person takes steps to improve his ability to cope with stress. This style encourages you to broaden your horizons, set realistic expectations, create a support system, condition yourself to withstand stress, enjoy your pleasures, and take a few minutes to relax.

Broaden Your Horizons

Research has shown that people who have a variety of interests are less likely to suffer stress reactions, particularly stress-related illness, than people who have few or no interests. Spending all or most of your time and energy on only one activity—such as work—can lead to stress. On the

FIGURE 14-6. Why Change Causes Stress.

For many of us, change is upsetting. We resist change for many reasons, including because

We don't want to learn a new way of doing things—even if it is a better way—because we find a certain comfort level in keeping the status quo.

We are afraid that we won't understand the new way of doing things and that we might not be able to perform well, so we might lose our jobs.

We feel that a change threatens our influence or even our social status.

We have an emotional investment in the old ways, and we view change as a personal affront to us and our previous hard work.

Fear and apprehension, then, are common and normal reactions to change. You can reduce the stress associated with change by remaining flexible and keeping an open mind about how a change will affect you. Holding onto the old ways of doing things in the midst of change will increase your frustration and your stress level.

other hand, having so many interests that your schedule is overloaded with activities also can cause stress. The goal is to achieve balance among a variety of activities that are important to you.

When your life is balanced, you are less likely to feel extreme distress when any one aspect of your life is causing distress. For example, if you focus most of your energy on your job, then job problems can cause much more intense stress reactions than they would if you had other interests to give you positive relief and diversion from your job.

Set Realistic Expectations

Don't put too much pressure on yourself to perform flawlessly all of the time. If you make a mistake, acknowledge that you need to do better next time, but recognize that no one is perfect. Errors can happen, especially during times of significant change. Giving yourself permission to make mistakes—and forgiving yourself when you do—will lower your stress levels.

Create a Support System

Discussing sources of stress with your coworkers, managers, friends, and family can help you relieve stress. For example, if your organization is undergoing restructuring, you could establish a rapport with someone who has more experience navigating workplace changes and who can help you develop better coping skills.

Condition Yourself to Withstand Stress

Healthy people are better able to withstand normal stress reactions. If your heart is strong, you can better handle the increased heart rate that accompanies stress. If you sleep enough and know how to relax, you won't feel as fatigued during and after stress reactions. If you eat properly, you'll have the necessary nutrients to fuel your body. Physically damaging activities—such as smoking, consuming excessive caffeine, abusing alcohol and drugs, and skipping meals and sleep—reduce your ability to withstand stress.

You can mentally condition yourself to withstand stress by accepting that a normal amount of stress is inevitable in any job. If you expect everything to remain stress-free and stable, you are setting yourself up for disappointment and frustration. Be realistic. Expect problems, expect change, and be ready to respond appropriately.

You can mentally condition yourself to withstand stress by accepting that a normal amount of stress is inevitable in any job.

Enjoy Your Pleasures

Take time to savor the moments that are particularly enjoyable to you. Celebrate your triumphs, even if the celebration is as simple as telling yourself, "I handled that perfectly." Take a moment to feel pleasure in your work while you are doing tasks that you particularly enjoy. While stressful events tend to force us to acknowledge them, quiet pleasures often are neglected, even though they make life richer and more relaxing.

Take a Few Minutes to Relax

When you feel yourself becoming tense, take a few minutes to calm down. Breathe deeply and remind yourself of what's important and what's not. Taking a moment to relax can help you avoid mistakes that occur when you rush from one stress-producing event to another or stay with a stress-producing event past the time that you need a break. For example, if you are in the middle of a contentious telephone conversation, find a valid reason to call back later. Then, relax and calm down before trying to find new solutions to the problem. You will be more creative and better able to handle the difficulty if you are not under severe stress. Figure 14-7 describes how changing your body language can help you relax.

FIGURE 14-7. Pay Attention to Your Body Language.

The next time you are in a tense situation, such as dealing with an upset customer or making a presentation, notice your posture and expressions. Notice your shoulder position, the way your jaw is held, where your legs are, and the way you are holding your hands. For example, many people tighten their shoulder muscles, grit their teeth, pick at their fingernails, or play with their hair when they are feeling stress.

Now, plan an alternative response. Slowly relax your position and release your tension. Drop your shoulders, consciously slow your breathing, and relax the muscles in your face. This technique can be especially effective when you are talking to an irate customer. When the discussion becomes too tense and you find yourself getting into your "upset" posture, make a conscious effort to alter your body language. The change that occurs in your tone of voice may influence the customer to change her tone as well.

One useful relaxation technique is **meta-imagery**, a process during which a person intentionally envisions himself in a stress-free environment. In other words, the person has a planned daydream. For instance, envision yourself in a serene place, doing something that you find enjoyable and relaxing. Immerse yourself fully into the daydream. By doing so, your body will release **syntoxins,** which are chemicals and hormones that are associated with good health. By contrast, when you feel angry or worried, your body releases **catatoxins**, which are chemicals and hormones that have been associated with disease.[7]

PROBLEM-FOCUSED COPING STYLE

The **problem-focused coping style** is an approach to handling stress in which a person focuses on the cause of the stress. Using this approach, you attempt to identify your options, avoid or eliminate distressors in your life, and reinterpret stressful events.

Identify Your Options

When you find a situation unpleasant or difficult to live with, consider alternative choices. For instance, if your newly hired manager is difficult to work with, can you discuss your concerns with him or with another manager? If that option is not available or is ineffective, can you work with the human resources department to request a transfer to another area in the company? Maybe your only choices are to work with that manager or quit your job. Identifying your options can help you determine possible solutions to a problem and reduce stress.

Avoid or Eliminate Distressors

Many times, you simply can choose to not be involved with activities or people that cause you distress. For instance, if the pleasure you derive from being with a friend is outweighed by the distress you feel because that friend constantly criticizes you, then avoid being with that friend. Don't continue to subject yourself to people you don't enjoy being around.

In addition, you can avoid distress by recognizing what you can and cannot change. For instance, complaining about a new telephone system that your company has already purchased and installed is useless. Instead, try to solve the problems you face. Be creative. Offer constructive suggestions. For example, you could organize a formal or informal discussion group to troubleshoot system problems and share user tips.

You also can eliminate a lot of stress in your life if you avoid procrastinating about things you must do.

You also can eliminate a lot of stress in your life if you avoid procrastinating about things you must do. For example, even if doing paperwork bores you, try to do it on a regular basis. Otherwise, it will accumulate until an overwhelming amount of paperwork must be completed in a short time. The sooner you complete an unenjoyable task, the less time you will spend worrying about it.

Reinterpret Stressful Events

How you view circumstances or events often makes a difference in how much stress you feel. One way to reinterpret a stressful situation or occurrence is to focus on its positive aspects rather than its negative ones. For example, would you consider new job responsibilities to be a positive step because they present an opportunity for growth and development, or a negative step because they are an additional burden that has been forced upon you? If you look for positives, you will usually find them. If you look for negatives you will find those, too, but in the process you also will cause yourself harm by increasing your stress level. Try to accept and make the most of the challenges you face.

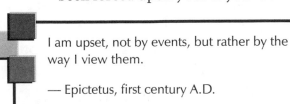

I am upset, not by events, but rather by the way I view them.

— Epictetus, first century A.D.

"I have a chocolate-focused coping style."

Another way to reinterpret a stressful event is to distinguish between things happening and things happening *to you*. Most of us, at one time or another, personalize events that are impersonal. For example, we might think the company isn't reorganizing, it's trying to get rid of our jobs. Or, a customer is not angry about a check being late, she's angry with us. In most situations, we are not the focus of an unpleasant event, and recognizing that fact can help us keep things in perspective. In addition, most events are not as earth-shattering as we think. To maintain the proper perspective the next time an event causes you stress, ask yourself, "Will this really matter next month or next year or in five years? Will I even remember it?"

In most situations, we are not the focus of an unpleasant event, and recognizing that fact can help us keep things in perspective.

RELATIONSHIP-FOCUSED COPING STYLE.

The *relationship-focused coping style* is an approach to handling stress in which a person discusses a stressful situation with those people involved in the situation. Sometimes, a person might not even realize that he is causing you distress. For example, a coworker who continually offers suggestions on how you can improve your interactions with customers might think that you appreciate the helpful advice. If her comments upset you, telling her how you feel could lead to an open and honest discussion that changes her future behavior. When using this coping style, however, remember that changing other people's behavior can be difficult, no matter what you say.

Taking the Initiative

In this chapter, we have presented strategies that can help you plan for success, manage your time, and cope with stress. By using these approaches to meet the challenges of your job, you can increase your chances of career success. But don't stop here. When you have completed this course, look for other sources of information that can help you continue developing your job skills, product and industry knowledge, and personal management techniques.

As we discussed in Chapter 3, service providers need continuous training throughout their careers. Although many financial services companies encourage continuous learning, don't wait for your supervisor or manager to suggest additional training and education experiences—seek them out on your own. Take responsibility for ensuring your own success

Exercise 14-3. Be Proactive®

Being proactive means that we take responsibility for our lives. Instead of blaming circumstances, conditions, or chance for our behavior, we choose our own responses and make our own decisions. The following questions can help you begin to be more proactive in your life:

- What is one improvement I could make in my professional life?

- What is one improvement I could make in my personal life?

- What activity can I plan that will help me make one of these improvements? (It may just be one step toward making the change. Set a date and time for the activity you chose, and mark it on your calendar.)

Try these other tips for being more proactive in your life:

- Decide to be proactive for a day. Turn around a difficult situation or take the initiative to make improvements. If you are assigned to work on a project that has been poorly defined, don't complain about it. Analyze the project, outline the information you need, find someone with answers, and enjoy the positive energy of accomplishment.

- One of the keys to successful living is being able to keep commitments and promises. Remember to take time to plan activities that will help you keep your commitments. For instance, if you promise to go to a movie with a friend, schedule time the day before to finish up work or deal with anything else that could interfere with your outing.

Source: Adapted from the "Be Proactive" FranklinCovey planning page. © 2000 Franklin Covey, www.franklincovey.com. Be Proactive is a registered trademark of FranklinCovey. Used with permission. All rights reserved.

> People are always blaming their circumstances for what they are. I don't believe in circumstances. The people who get on in this world are the people who get up and look for the circumstances they want, and, if they can't find them, make them.
>
> — George Bernard Shaw

by looking for and taking advantage of opportunities to grow and develop professionally and personally. Exercise 14-3 can help you start taking the initiative and being more proactive in your life.

Enhancing your skills and knowledge can be as informal as picking up a book from the library about a topic that interests you or as formal as enrolling in a structured educational course or program through an educational institution or an independent organization, such as LOMA. Many financial services companies offer in-house training for employees on topics ranging from specific work activities to technology to personal growth and development. Also, many industry organizations and professional associations, as well as companies that specialize in business training, offer self-study courses and programs, seminars, and conferences that can boost your professional and personal development. In addition, the increasing availability of information and training resources available through the Internet allows you to access materials conveniently and according to your own schedule. Regardless of the resources and support provided by your company, the ability to learn is available to anyone who has the determination and drive to do so.

Taking initiative is more important than ever for service providers in the financial services industry. As we have discussed throughout this book, financial services companies want and need service providers who not only can perform their job duties well, but who also are capable and willing to continually learn more about their work, their customers, their organizations, and their industry. Financial services companies also value employees who continually look for ways to improve how the company can provide exceptional service to its customers. As these companies increasingly rely on customer service efforts to attract, keep, and delight customers, they rely on people who have the power to greatly influence those customers: service providers.

Successful service providers understand the meaning of "exceptional" customer service, know their customers and how best to communicate with them, and recognize the important role of customer service—and service providers—in a financial services organization. By embracing the concepts and practicing the skills presented in this book, you can become one of these service providers and help make a difference in people's everyday lives and help ensure your company's financial success.

To practice and review the skills and information you learned in this chapter, see the interactive CD, *Practicing Your Customer Service Skills*, included with this book.

Key Terms

divergent personalities
convergent personalities
detail-oriented
    personalities
globally oriented
    personalities
tightly structured
    personalities
loosely structured
    personalities
parallel-processing
    personalities
serial-processing personalities
reactive personalities

proactive personalities
priority list
stress
stressor
distressor
emotion-focused coping style
meta-imagery
syntoxins
catatoxins
problem-focused coping style
relationship-focused coping
    style

Endnotes

1. Stephen R. Covey, A. Roger Merrill, and Rebecca R. Merrill, *First Things First* (New York: Simon & Schuster, 1994), 79.

2. Adapted from Seid and Piker, "Time-Management Personality Profile," *The 1995 Annual, Vol. 2*. Copyright © 1995 Pfeiffer/Jossey-Bass Inc., Publishers. This material is used by permission of John Wiley & Sons, Inc.

3. Adapted from the *First Things First* book by Stephen R. Covey, A. Roger Merrill, and Rebecca R. Merrill. © 1994 FranklinCovey, www.franklincovey.com. The Time Management Matrix is a trademark of FranklinCovey. Used with permission. All rights reserved.

4. "Famous Quotes and Famous Sayings Network," http://www.att.net/~quotations/time.html (17 June 2002).

5. "A Guide to Work-Related Stress," WorkSafe Western Australia Publications, Saftek.com, http://www.saftek.com/worksafe/stress2.htm.

6. "Coping Styles," *Clinical Tools' Health Center*, 1998, http://www.health-center.com.

7. Hans Selye, *The Stress of Life*, rev. ed. (New York: McGraw-Hill, 1976), 408, as cited in George Manning and Kent Curtis, *Stress Without Distress* (Cincinnati: South-Western Publishing, 1988), 83.

GLOSSARY

360-degree feedback. A performance evaluation method in which feedback about the employee's performance is solicited from many sources, including the employee's superiors and peers, any people the employee supervises, and the internal and external customers the employee serves. [4]

abandonment rate. A performance measure that indicates the percentage of inbound telephone calls that are automatically placed on hold and then terminated by the caller before the call is answered by a service provider. [12]

accepted standards. Performance standards that employees understand and believe are meaningful, valid, and realistic. [12]

ACD. See automatic call distributor.

active listening. The process of concentrating entirely on a speaker's verbal and nonverbal communication. [8]

adaptors. Unconscious motions that release some form of tension or emotion. [6]

adult ego state. A behavior pattern in which a person objectively analyzes data and makes decisions based on this analysis. [5]

advisory panel. A standing group that meets on a regular basis to provide a company with qualitative information about the company's services and to suggest ways to improve those services. [5]

advocates. People who are so convinced of a company's merit that they share their strong feelings with family, friends, and acquaintances. [2]

affect displays. The facial expressions that people use to show emotion. [6]

aggressive behavior. The opposite of passive behavior, a behavior pattern that occurs when a person lashes out at others with little regard for their feelings. [5]

ANI. *See* **automatic number identification**.

assertive behavior. A behavior pattern that occurs when a person states his positions clearly and firmly, but in a constructive rather than destructive manner. [5]

asset and wealth accumulation. The gathering of a substantial amount of money over time. [1]

association. The reputation of an employee's company and the employee's relationship with the company. [9]

assurance. A service dimension that refers to the competence and credibility of service providers, their ability to convey trust and confidence, and the courtesy and respect they show to customers. [5]

attribution. The perceptual process of assigning reasons for a person's behavior in order to explain his actions. [8]

attributional bias. A perceptual error that occurs when we assign generalized, poorly thought-out reasons for the behavior of others. [8]

auto-greeting. A telephone technology used to record someone's "best" greeting, and then automatically play that greeting each time a call arrives. [7]

automated workflow system. A technology used to create computer-based records pertaining to the status and processing of specific transactions. Also called automated workflow distribution (AWD). [13]

automatic call distributor (ACD). A device that, at the most basic level, answers telephone calls and directs them to the appropriate employee or work group. [13]

automatic number identification (ANI). A technology that identifies an inbound telephone call by the number from which the call is placed. [13]

automatic transaction distribution. A type of routing that directs customer contacts to service providers based on the person's proficiency with a particular communication channel. [13]

auto-signature. An e-mail option that automatically includes the user's complimentary close at the end of each e-mail message the user sends. [7]

average speed of answer. A performance measure that indicates the amount of time, on average, that telephone callers are on hold before being connected with a service provider. [12]

avoidance. A conflict management approach that entails physically or psychologically removing oneself from a conflict situation. [9]

behavioral tendencies test. A type of pre-employment screening test that attempts to discover the candidate's typical job behaviors, such as whether the person is a team player, is honest, follows rules and procedures, and remains calm under pressure. Also known as a personality test. [3]

benchmark. A performance standard, often based on standards achieved by leading companies, that represents a company's goal for performance. [12]

benchmarking. The process of comparing actual performance results with benchmarks; it encourages continuous improvement by enabling a company to determine how well it is performing in relation to a standard it aspires to achieve. [12]

benevolent autocratic system. A type of management system in which authority and decision making are centralized with managers, especially senior executives, but the relationship between management and the workforce is fairly cordial. [11]

best practice. A business practice that represents the ultimate criterion for performing a specific type of process. [12]

blind transfer. When one employee transfers a call to another employee without introducing the caller or explaining the nature of the call. Also called a cold transfer. [7]

body language. The way people use their bodies to communicate. Also known as kinesics. [6]

body of a letter. The part of a business letter that follows the opening and provides the information that accomplishes the letter's purpose. [7]

bonus. A lump sum amount awarded to an employee to recognize achievement by either the employee or a work group. [4]

browser. A software program that allows a user to navigate the Internet. [13]

business etiquette. The rules that govern appropriate behavior in business situations. [7]

business partner. In the context of customers, an organization that helps a company develop, distribute, or service its products. [1]

business system. A set of processes and other elements designed to work together to meet a company's performance requirements. [2]

call center. In customer service, an organizational unit that receives and/ or places telephone calls to customers. [1]

career path. An outline of the types of advancement available to an employee within a particular department and within the company; providing a logical progression through positions that offer increasing responsibility and pay. [3]

cash management. The process of using readily available funds for everyday living expenses, as well as for savings and investment purposes. [1]

catatoxins. Chemicals and hormones that are released by the body when a person feels angry or worried and that have been associated with disease. [14]

CBT. *See* **computer-based training**.

change sequence. A series of activities that typically occurs in successful organizational transformation; it consists of (1) recognizing the need for change, (2) assessing the organization's readiness for change, (3) identifying appropriate changes and the methods for implementing the changes, and (4) implementation. [10]

channel. In the commmunication process, the medium used to transmit or deliver a message. Also called communication channel. [6]

character. A person's integrity and principles. [9]

child ego state. A behavior pattern in which a person responds to others in the helpless, complaining tone of an unhappy child. [5]

chronemics. The nonverbal messages conveyed by the way people use time. [6]

classroom training. A training method in which an instructor typically lectures to the group, leads the group in discussion, or directs the group as they do various exercises, such as role-playing. [3]

click-to-call. A communication mechanism that enables Web site visitors to initiate a conversation with a company representative by clicking on an icon, which then automatically places a call, using voice over Internet protocol, to a company representative. [7]

closed question. A specific inquiry that can usually be answered with "yes," "no," or a short factual statement. [8]

closing of a letter. The last paragraph or two of a business letter, which performs one or more of these functions: (1) summarizes all important points from the body of the letter, (2) indicates any steps the writer will be taking, (3) asks for any response needed from the reader, (4) gives specific information about how and when the reader's response should be communicated, and (5) concludes on a positive note. [7]

code of conduct. A document that provides guidelines for how employees are expected to approach their jobs. Also called guiding principles. [11]

coercion. An attempt to convince others to do something they really don't want to do. [9]

commission. An amount of money, usually a percentage of the sale amount, that is paid to an employee or intermediary for selling a product or service. [4]

communication. The process of transferring information and understanding from one person to another. [6]

company-specific orientation. A type of job-orientation training that introduces new employees to the company's organizational structure, shows how the employee's department fits into that structure, and explains how employees benefit from their employment with the company. [3]

competence. A person's knowledge and ability. [9]

complaint management system. A company's processes and procedures for recording, evaluating, and taking action on complaints. [5]

complimentary close. The formal wording used to end a business letter, followed by the writer's full name and title, if applicable. [7]

computer network. Two or more computers linked together to provide a platform for electronic communication and information sharing. [13]

computer telephony integration (CTI). The hardware, software, and programming that integrate computers and communication technology, particularly telephones, to enhance customer contacts and the information they provide. [13]

computer-based training (CBT). A training method that uses computer hardware, software, and, in some cases, networks, to deliver training. [3]

conference transfer. When the employee who transfers a call states the name of the caller and the nature of the inquiry or request before putting the call through, thus preparing the employee and saving the customer from having to repeat this information. Also called a warm transfer. [7]

conflict management training. A type of training that focuses on techniques that service providers can use to effectively handle customer complaints, especially in situations in which the customer is angry. [3]

conflict. The clash of opposing attitudes, desires, interests, ideas, behaviors, goals, or needs. [9]

connotative meaning. A word's suggested or implied meaning. [6]

consultative system. A type of management system in which authority and decision making are centralized with managers, but the relationship with employees is cordial, and managers exhibit confidence in the workforce, often seeking employee opinions and acting on their suggestions. [11]

content reflection. In paraphrasing, the practice of repeating some of a customer's words. [8]

convergent personalities. Personality types that like to stay on task until a project is finished. [14]

cooperation. A conflict management approach in which the parties involved in a conflict discuss the conflict openly and honestly and look for a resolution. [9]

coordination of effort. How an organization synchronizes the various activities it conducts; it complements division of labor and hierarchy of authority. [11]

core competency. An ability, skill, or characteristic that has been shown to cause or predict outstanding performance in a given job. [3]

corporate culture. The combination of beliefs, attitudes, experiences, practices, and behaviors that are learned and shared by the employees of an organization. Also called organizational culture. [7]

corporate objectives. Realistic, specific, and measurable statements that describe the long-term results an organization intends to achieve. [10]

corporate strategies. The long-term methods by which an organization intends to achieve its corporate objectives. [10]

cost-of-living pay raise. A type of salary increase that allows salaries to rise at a rate similar to the rate of inflation. [4]

credit. The ability to purchase now by giving a promise to pay in the future. [1]

critical incident appraisal. A performance evaluation method in which the supervisor records examples of an employee's accomplishments as well as any errors or problems that occurred during the evaluation period. [4]

CRM. *See* **customer relationship management**.

cross-functional team. A team that consists of representatives from two or more work groups that perform related business activities and is dedicated to improving processes and procedures that cross organizational boundaries. [11]

crossing channels. Customer contacts that move from one communication channel to another. [13]

cross-selling. A sales activity in which customers are invited to purchase a product other than the product they already own. [10]

cross-telling. A sales-related activity in which a person informs a customer of a product, but does not attempt to make a sale. [10]

CSR. *See* **customer service representative**.

CTI. *See* **computer-telephony integration**.

culture. The customary beliefs, attitudes, practices, and behaviors that are learned and shared by a group. [6]

customer. Any person or organization that interacts with a company. [1]

customer-centric philosophy. A business philosophy focused on the needs of customers and how to fill those needs. [2]

customer access strategy. A strategy focused on the selection, development, and coordination of an organization's contacts and communications with its customers. [10]

customer contact center. An organizational unit that provides customers with a variety of channels—such as telephone, fax, and e-mail—for communicating with a company. [1]

customer contact system. A customer database and work tracking tool that combines a variety of features—such as data entry and retrieval, history of previous customer contacts, document management, scripted presentations, and follow-up tools—to provide a framework for handling and documenting customer contacts. [13]

customer education. The activity of educating existing or potential customers about a company's products and the level of service it provides. [5]

customer loyalty. A customer's feeling of attachment to or preference for a company's people, products, or services. [2]

customer relationship management (CRM). A business initiative that allows an organization to manage all aspects of its interactions with current and potential customers. [10]

customer retention. The act of keeping the business of existing customers. [2]

customer satisfaction survey. A survey designed to help a company determine whether its products, prices, and services are meeting customer expectations. [12]

customer service. The broad range of activities that a company and its employees perform to keep customers satisfied so they will continue doing business with the company and speak positively about it to other potential customers. [1]

customer service mission statement. A statement that tells why a company provides customer service and expresses the company's overall customer service goals. [10]

customer service representative (CSR). A person whose primary job responsibility is to support external customers through face-to-face communications or through communications media, such as the telephone, fax, electronic mail (e-mail), or Internet chat sessions. Also known as a service representative, service associate, service agent, contact center agent, or call center representative. [1]

customer service strategic plan. A strategic plan that establishes corporate objectives specifically tied to customer service and determines an overall course of action the company and its employees will follow to achieve those objectives. [2]

customer service technology. Communication and information systems used by organizations to support customers or to enable customers to help themselves. [13]

data mining. The process of selecting and exploring large amounts of data to uncover previously unknown patterns for business advantage. [13]

data warehouse. An information system that stores, consolidates, retrieves, and manages large amounts of data from across an organization, bringing together all relevant information to support company operations as well as management decision making. [13]

decryption. The conversion of encrypted electronic data back to its original form as part of the process of restricting unauthorized access to confidential information. [13]

dedicated customer service representative. A service provider assigned to assist specific customers or groups of customers. Also known as an account manager. [1]

degree of autonomy. The extent to which team members, rather than a supervisor, direct team activities. [11]

delegation. The process of transferring a task or activity along with appropriate decision-making authority to another person. [11]

denotative meaning. The direct, literal meaning of a word. [6]

department-specific orientation. A type of job-orientation training that introduces new employees to the basic operations of the work group to which they are assigned and to the other employees in that work group. [3]

desktop faxing. A type of electronic communication that enables users to fax documents from applications available on their personal computers. [7]

detail-oriented personalities. Personality types that need facts and details about a situation to feel comfortable. [14]

detractors. People who have had one or more unpleasant experiences with a company and freely share their stories and disparaging remarks with others. [2]

direct customer service provider. A person who routinely communicates with his company's external customers and serves as their link to the information, products, or services that they need. [1]

distressor. An activity, event, or occurrence that causes intense or long-term stress. [14]

divergent personalities. Personality types that wander off the subject to whatever sounds interesting at the moment. [14]

diversity training. A type of training that focuses on first recognizing gaps caused by cultural or other differences and then developing the skills needed to bridge those gaps. Such gaps may exist with coworkers or with customers. [3]

division of labor. How an organization breaks down a large, complex undertaking into manageable parts to enable work groups and individual employees to become proficient at specific tasks. [11]

document management system. A technology that stores, organizes, and retrieves documents that have been created electronically and converted to digital images or created on paper and converted to digital images via imaging. [13]

dominant culture. The culture that is most prominent throughout an organization. [10]

e-commerce. Doing business "electronically" over computer networks. [13]

EDI. *See* **electronic data interchange**.

educational expense benefit. A type of financial reward that helps pay the cost of an employee's education. [4]

effectiveness. The ability to establish and achieve appropriate objectives. [12]

efficiency. The ability to achieve objectives with a minimum of waste and with few errors or delays. [12]

electronic communication. Communication made possible by the transmission of electronic signals to produce sounds, images, or text. Also called e-communication. [7]

electronic data interchange (EDI). The computer-to-computer exchange of standardized business transaction data between two or more organizations. [13]

e-mail. A form of electronic communication that enables a user to type a message into a computer and then send the message to other computers connected to a network. From the word electronic mail. [7]

e-mail management system. A program application that automatically analyzes, routes, and in some cases replies to inbound e-mail messages. [13]

emblem. A gesture that takes the place of a word such as stop, go, yes, no, or hello. [6]

emotion-focused coping style. An approach to handling stress in which a person takes steps to improve his ability to cope with stress. [14]

empathy. The process of understanding another person's emotional state and imagining how you would feel in a similar situation. [3]

employee suggestion program. A system that encourages employees to submit constructive suggestions, which are promptly and seriously reviewed and—when appropriate—implemented by the company. [4]

empowerment. A management approach that gives service providers the authority to make decisions on behalf of the company in the course of performing their regular job functions. [2]

encryption. The conversion of electronic data into a code to restrict unauthorized access to confidential information. [13]

enunciation. The articulation of sounds and the pronunciation of words. [6]

escalation process. A procedure that specifies how and to whom a particular type of request should be addressed and directed when the service provider is not able or authorized to resolve the issue. [12]

essay appraisal. A performance evaluation method in which, at the end of the evaluation period, the supervisor writes a description of an employee's performance during that period. [4]

etiquette. A code of both formal and informal conduct that defines the behavior considered appropriate in various situations. [7]

exception processing. Guidelines for making exceptions to standard procedures. [12]

executive summary. In some memos, a section that highlights the most important points; it appears after the heading and before the body of the memo. [7]

expectation. What a person believes is likely or certain to happen. [5]

expected service. The quality of the service that customers think they will receive. [5]

expert systems software. A knowledge management application that performs many of the functions and makes many of the decisions that once required the attention of trained professionals, such as underwriters, loan officers, claim processors, or investment advisors. [13]

explanation. A factual description of how things work or why certain actions are taken. [9]

exploitative autocratic system. A type of management system in which authority and decision making are centralized with managers, especially senior executives, who often maintain secrecy about the company's intentions, place little confidence in the workforce, and rarely delegate responsibility. [11]

external customer. Any person or organization in a position to buy or use a company's products; sometimes referred to as an end customer. [1]

external network. A computer network that links a company to people and computers outside the company. [13]

fact. A piece of objective information that can be proven to be true. [5]

fax. A paper document that contains text and/or images printed from signals electronically transmitted over a telephone line from one device to another. From the word facsimile. [7]

fax-on-demand. A technology that combines IVR with fax to enable customers to call a business at any time to have forms or other documents automatically faxed to them. [13]

feedback. In the communication process, a return message that a receiver sends in response to a sender's message; it can be either verbal or nonverbal. [6]

financial institution. A business that collects funds from the public and owns primarily financial assets, such as stocks and bonds, rather than fixed assets, such as equipment and raw materials. Also known as a financial services company. [1]

financial planning. A coordinated process for identifying, planning for, and meeting goals related to financial needs. [5]

financial protection. Insurance against the risk of financial loss. [1]

financial services industry. An industry consisting of financial institutions that offer products and services that help individuals, businesses, and governments save, borrow, invest, protect, and otherwise manage assets. [1]

firewall. A type of hardware or software that sits between a firm's internal network and the outside Internet, which limits access into and out of the internal network, based on rules defined by the organization. [13]

first contact resolution. A performance measure that indicates the percentage of inbound customer contacts that are successfully completed at the initial point of contact—that is, without being transferred and without the need for follow-up work. [12]

flat organizational structure. A type of corporate structure that has relatively few layers of supervision between top management and nonmanagerial employees. Also called a flattened organizational pyramid. [11]

focus group interview. An unstructured, informal session during which six to ten participants are asked to discuss their opinions about a certain topic. [5]

follow-through. Taking the action you agreed to take during negotiation or, in some cases, making sure that another person or area takes the agreed upon action. [9]

follow-up work. Any type of activity a service provider and/or customer decide cannot be completed during or soon after the initial customer contact. [12]

forming. The initial stage of team development, which involves developing operating guidelines that serve as a template for how the team members interact. [11]

full-service customer contact center. A department or work group that handles a relatively high percentage of customer contacts, while transferring relatively few requests to administrative and transaction processing units for handling. [11]

functional work team. A permanent organizational unit that performs one or more ongoing business activities. [11]

fundamental attribution error. The tendency to underestimate the influence of situational factors and to overestimate the influence of personal factors when we examine the behavior of other people. [8]

funnel technique. A questioning strategy in which the person asking questions moves from general to specific questions, beginning with broad, open questions and progressing to narrow, closed questions. [8]

gatekeeper customer contact center. A department or work team that serves as a clearinghouse or "triage unit" for inbound customer contacts. [11]

generalist. A team member who is cross-trained to handle most or all of a team's functions. [11]

globally oriented personalities. Personality types that prefer to think about the possibilities of a situation rather than the facts of the current reality. [14]

graphic rating scale appraisal. A performance evaluation method in which the supervisor grades an employee's work during the evaluation period based on a number of factors identified at the beginning of the period. [4]

hierarchy of authority. A system that determines which people in an organization make certain types of decisions and direct the actions of others. [11]

ICR. *See* **intelligent call routing.**

idiom. A phrase with a meaning that cannot be determined from the words in the phrase. [6]

illustrator. A gesture that complements words to enhance or clarify the verbal message. [6]

imaging. The process of converting printed characters or graphics into digitized images on a computer. Also called scanning. [13]

inbound telephone calls. Calls initiated by customers to request information, products, services, or transactions. [7]

in-depth interview. A loosely structured conversation during which a few respondents, usually customers, are interviewed individually and asked to provide detailed information on a specific topic. [5]

indirect customer service provider. A person who does not routinely interact with external customers, but who performs activities that facilitate customers' receipt of the information, products, and services that they need. [1]

individual customer. A person who buys or uses a product primarily for his own benefit or the benefit of his family. Also referred to as a consumer or household customer. [1]

industry standard. A performance standard based on the performance results for a specific process or activity achieved by companies within a company's own industry. [12]

inference. A conclusion based on facts as well as other information, such as our personal knowledge or past experiences. [5]

intellectual capital. The sum of all employee knowledge in a company that gives it a competitive edge in the marketplace. [3]

intelligent call routing (ICR). The general term for any automated process of analyzing and directing inbound telephone calls. [13]

intention. A person's apparent motive. [9]

interactive video training (IVT). A type of computer-based training that uses video to create a more interesting and realistic training situation. [3]

interactive voice response (IVR). A computer-based technology that answers telephone calls, greets callers with a recorded or digitized message, and prompts them to enter information or make requests by voice or telephone keypad. Also called a voice response unit (VRU). [13]

intermediary. A person who links buyers of financial products and services with the companies that sell those products and services. [1]

internal auditing department. A work group whose primary responsibility is the independent appraisal of the departments, processes, and systems within an organization. [12]

internal customer. A company employee or department that receives support from another employee or department within the organization. Sometimes referred to as a partner, a team member, or an associate. [1]

internal network. A computer network that a company creates to link its people and equipment to each other. [13]

internal standard. A performance standard that is developed inside a company, based on the company's own historic performance levels. [12]

Internet. The world's largest computer network, which consists of thousands of interconnected networks, all freely exchanging information and connecting millions of computers around the world. Also called the Net. [13]

interpersonal skills. The skills used to understand and interact with internal and external customers. Also called soft skills. [2]

intimate distance. In North American culture, a distance that people typically use when communicating with someone with whom they have a close relationship, such as a spouse, child, or parent; ranges from touching to about 18 inches. [6]

intranet. An internal network that looks and functions much like the Internet but is designed to be accessible only to company employees. [13]

inverted funnel technique. A questioning strategy in which the person asking questions moves from specific to general questions, starting with closed questions and progressing to open questions. [8]

IT help desk. A service provided by IT staff that enables technology users to obtain assistance, usually requested via telephone or e-mail. [13]

IVR. *See* **interactive voice response**.

IVT. *See* **interactive video training**.

jargon. A specialized language of technical terms and acronyms that only a small, specific group of people is familiar with and understands. [6]

job description. A document that identifies the duties, responsibilities, and accountabilities of a job. [3]

job enrichment. The process of increasing the authority and complexity of a job to make the job more rewarding to the employee. [3]

job orientation. A type of training program that introduces employees to the company they are joining and to the work they will perform. [3]

job rotation. A type of job-related training in which employees move periodically from one job to another, staying in each job just long enough to learn how the job is done and how it relates to other jobs in the company. [3]

knowledge management. The overall strategies, resources, and processes that organizations use to apply knowledge to business activities. [13]

LAN. *See* **local area network**.

lateral skill development. Growth within an employee's current job. [4]

leading question. An inquiry that is phrased in a way that encourages the respondent to give a particular answer; leading questions are designed to provide the person asking the question with the answer that will support his position, whatever that position may be. [8]

legacy system. A relatively old computer system or application program that a company maintains because of the high cost of replacing or redesigning the system. [13]

LIA. *See* **longest idle agent**.

local area network (LAN). An internal network that is made up of equipment situated in one location. [13]

longest idle agent (LIA). A type of routing that directs each inbound telephone call to the available CSR who has gone the longest time without receiving a call. [13]

loosely structured personalities. Personality types that prefer to have flexibility in how they complete tasks. [14]

management by objectives (MBO). A performance evaluation method in which the employee and his supervisor work together to set clear and attainable goals or objectives that the employee should achieve in the upcoming evaluation period and develop a plan for achieving the objectives. [4]

manufacturing mentality. A state of mind in which employees concentrate so much on the functions and procedures of their day-to-day responsibilities that they forget about the customer. [1]

MBO. *See* **management by objectives**.

meaningful standards. Performance standards that can be linked directly to customer expectations and business objectives. [12]

memo. A written communication that contains directions, guidelines, or information and is typically sent within an organization. From the word memorandum. [7]

mental abilities test. A type of pre-employment screening test that attempts to determine a candidate's general level of intelligence and reasoning ability by evaluating abilities such as remembering details, solving problems, and understanding and using words accurately. Also known as a cognitive abilities test or an aptitude test. [3]

mentoring. A type of job-related training in which a less experienced employee is assigned to work with a more experienced employee, or mentor, who answers questions, offers advice, and provides general guidance to the less experienced employee. [3]

merit pay raise. A type of salary increase used to reward an employee or a work team whose performance exceeds minimum performance standards. [4]

message. The information that is transmitted during communication. [6]

meta-imagery. A relaxation technique during which a person intentionally envisions himself in a stress-free environment. [14]

misdirected calls. A performance measure that indicates the number or percentage of inbound telephone calls transferred to the wrong department. [12]

mission statement. A statement that describes an organization's fundamental purpose and the scope of its business activities, and is intended to establish the right focus, as well as continuity and consistency, throughout the organization. [10]

moment of truth. An instant when a company has an opportunity to create a good or bad impression in the mind of a customer. [1]

monitoring. A process used to review and evaluate the quality of customer service interactions either as they happen or after the fact. [4]

multichannel customer contacts. Interactions that combine two or more communication channels simultaneously, such as Web collaboration and the telephone. [13]

multiple-function work team. An organizational unit that combines various business functions to provide a "one-stop" service department. [11]

mystery shopper. A trained evaluator who approaches or calls customer service employees and pretends to be a customer. [12]

need. A requirement to improve an unsatisfactory condition—for example, food to satisfy hunger, shelter to stay warm and dry, and transportation to travel to work. [5]

negotiation. The process of reaching a mutually acceptable solution in the event of a disagreement or conflict of interest. [9]

net meetings. The combining of audio, video, and data communication over the Internet to enable participants to log on to an Internet site at a scheduled time to "meet" and share information. [11]

neutral question. An inquiry that has no bias and does not imply a correct answer; a neutral question encourages the respondent to give whatever answer is most accurate. [8]

noise. Anything that interferes with communication. [6]

nonverbal communication. A type of communication that conveys messages in ways that do not rely on the meaning of words. [6]

norming. The third stage of team development, which is characterized by greater harmony among team members, who begin to trust each other and communicate more openly. [11]

number of blocked calls. A performance measure that indicates the number of telephone calls that encounter a busy signal and cannot get through to the customer contact center. [12]

observation. A data-collection method in which a person or process is observed and evaluated. [12]

on-the-job training. A type of training program in which an employee learns by performing real work in the actual work environment. [3]

open question. A broad and general inquiry that cannot be answered appropriately in one or just a few words; open questions often ask for opinions, thoughts, or feelings. [8]

opening of a letter. The first paragraph or two of a business letter; it attracts the reader's attention, establishes the tone of the message, and states the purpose of the letter. [7]

organization chart. A visual display of the functional areas, job positions, and formal lines of authority in an organization. [11]

organizational customer. A business or other organization (such as a government, educational institution, or charity) that buys a product or service for its benefit or the benefit of its employees or members. Also known as a business-to-business (B2B) customer or an institutional customer. [1]

organizational structure. The assignment of task responsibilities and authority relationships within a business entity. [11]

outbound telephone calls. Calls initiated by company representatives to customers. [7]

outsourcing. A business practice in which a company hires a vendor to conduct a specific activity that the company would otherwise perform itself, such as billing administration or handling telephone calls from customers. [11]

paralanguage. A term used to describe the information obtained from vocal quality, volume, rate of speech, pitch, enunciation, and pauses. [6]

parallel-processing personalities. Personality types that are comfortable performing more than one task at a time. [14]

paraphrasing. The process of stating, in your own words, your understanding of another person's position, proposition, or request. [8]

parent ego state. A behavior pattern in which a person responds to others as a parent might, as if he knows everything and wants to tell everyone else what to do. [5]

participative leadership. A leadership style in which the supervisor acts as a coordinator, planning team activities and making decisions affecting the team after obtaining input from team members. [11]

participative team system. A type of management system in which employees at all levels of the organization are involved in making decisions, and managers see themselves as coaches, counselors, and helpers as well as directors. [11]

passive behavior. A behavior pattern that occurs when a person does not try to influence the behavior of other people. [5]

passive-aggressive behavior. A behavior pattern that occurs when a person feels hostile about something but is afraid or unwilling to be openly aggressive and show hostility. [5]

perceived service. The quality of the service that customers believe they actually received. [5]

perception. The process by which a person selects, organizes, and interprets information to give it meaning. [5]

perceptual error. A mistake that occurs when a person bases his perception on limited information and/or incorrect assumptions, resulting in a flawed or limited view of reality. [8]

performance evaluation. A formal process of reviewing and documenting an employee's job performance with the primary goal of continually improving performance. Also known as a performance appraisal. [4]

performance measurement. A process through which a company decides which activities to measure, how to measure performance in those activities, and what levels of performance, or performance standards, it hopes to achieve, and then gathers the information and communicates the results. [12]

performance standard. An established level of performance to which a company or individual compares actual performance. [12]

performing. The fourth stage of team development, in which the team has discovered how to achieve a balance between its members' common goals and their differences, thereby achieving smooth, productive operation without sacrificing the talents and creativity of the individual members. [11]

personal distance. In North American culture, a distance that people typically use when talking with casual friends and business acquaintances; ranges from 18 inches to 4 feet. [6]

personal impression. The image a person presents to others. [9]

personality. A person's consistent, repeated patterns of behavior. [5]

persuasion. An intentional verbal attempt to influence the attitude or behavior of others. [9]

population. In sampling, the entire group about which conclusions are developed. [5]

prewriting. The part of the writing process that occurs before you produce a first draft, when you determine why and what you are writing, for whom the message is intended, and the best way to present it. [7]

primary data. Research information that has not been collected previously and that is observed and collected to provide information on a specific problem. [5]

priority list. A listing of tasks that need to be completed and that are ranked according to their importance. [14]

proactive personalities. Personality types that like to make plans and then follow those plans; consequently, they rarely find themselves in crisis situations. [14]

proactive service. A type of customer service that looks beyond what the customer asks in an effort to anticipate and fulfill the customer's unexpressed needs. [5]

problem-focused coping style. An approach to handling stress in which a person focuses on the cause of the stress. [14]

problem-solving team. A work group that typically consists of employees who, because of their knowledge and expertise, are assigned to participate in a project that has a specific, limited objective. Also called a task force or an ad hoc committee. [11]

process improvement team. A type of problem solving team that includes employees from different areas or specialties within an organization who analyze processes and make recommendations for improvement. [12]

process management. A formal method of defining, documenting, evaluating, and modifying the resources and workflow involved in processes so that the processes better achieve the tasks they were designed to accomplish. [12]

process. A series of steps involved in performing a recurring activity designed to produce a specific outcome. Also called a workflow, work practice, or procedure. [2]

processes completed. A performance measure that indicates how many transactions are handled within a specified period of time, such as the number of telephone calls received, applications processed, claims adjudicated, checks released, or withdrawals and transfers processed in a month. [12]

product-centric philosophy. A business philosophy focused on product features. [2]

profit-sharing plan. A system of financial rewards in which a company establishes a pool of money—based on some percentage of profits or the total compensation pool—and pays a lump sum bonus to each employee based on the employee's performance, his work group's performance, or a combination of the two. [4]

projection. A perceptual error that occurs when we attribute our own feelings to someone else, who may or may not have those same feelings. [8]

proofreading. The process of reading through and making corrections to a document. [7]

proxemics. The study of the way people use space while communicating. [6]

public distance. In North American culture, a distance that speakers use in a formal setting when addressing an audience; generally about 12 feet or more. [6]

qualitative performance measurement. A type of performance measurement that focuses on behaviors, attitudes, or opinions to determine how efficiently and effectively processes and transactions are completed. Also called behavioral performance measurement. [12]

qualitative research. Research that is designed to assess people's attitudes, opinions, and behaviors about or toward a particular subject. Often referred to as exploratory research. [5]

quality circle. A group of employees that meets on an ongoing basis to find ways to improve work processes. Also called work improvement team. [11]

quality rate. A performance measure that indicates the accuracy of a particular type of transaction. [12]

quantitative performance measurement. A type of performance measurement that relies on numerical methods to track and report results to determine how quickly, how often, how accurately, and how profitably processes and transactions are completed. [12]

quantitative research. Research designed to generate concrete information about a group's characteristics and behavior. [5]

questioning. In the context of listening and understanding, the practice of asking a speaker questions designed to initiate or direct a conversation, clarify information, or probe for details. [8]

queue. In customer service, a series of telephone calls or other types of communication awaiting handling. [13]

racial slurs. Derogatory words or statements pertaining to a person's race or, more broadly, to a person's ethnic or religious heritage. [6]

reactive personalities. Personality types that wait until the last possible moment to do a task and, as a result, spend a lot of time responding to crises or deadlines. [14]

reactive service. A type of customer service that responds only to a customer's specific request or problem—that is, answering the question or fulfilling a specific request, but no more. [5]

readerboard. A screen mounted in a customer contact center that displays real-time statistics and recent performance results for a particular work group. Also called a suspended monitor or an electronic display. [13]

realistic standards. Performance standards that are set at a challenging but achievable level. [12]

real-time monitoring. A monitoring process in which the evaluator observes and/or listens to a customer service interaction as it is taking place. Also known as live coaching. [4]

receiver. In the communication process, the person who obtains a message. [6]

recorded monitoring. A monitoring process in which customer service interactions, such as telephone calls, e-mails, Web chats, or videoconferences are recorded for later review. [4]

red-flag words. Words that carry strong emotional overtones and are likely to trigger negative feelings in listeners. [6]

reflection of feelings. The process of paraphrasing someone's emotions. [8]

regulators. Gestures people use to control the flow of conversation. [6]

relationship-focused coping style. An approach to handling stress in which a person discusses a stressful situation with those people involved in the situation. [14]

relative word. A word that implies some type of measurement, but can vary widely in meaning according to the interpretations of the sender and receiver. [6]

reliability. A service dimension that means performing the promised service consistently and accurately. [5]

resource analysis. In process management, an examination of how a company's human resources, technology, and financial and physical resources are used to support specific processes. [12]

response time. A performance measure that indicates the time that transpires from receipt of a customer contact—such as correspondence or e-mail—to resolution of the request. [12]

responsiveness. A service dimension that implies a willingness to help customers and an ability to provide them with prompt service. [5]

retrieval tool. A computer application designed to provide users with the specific information they seek. Also called a search tool. [13]

salutation. At the beginning of a business letter, a greeting that includes the name of the person who is to receive the letter. [7]

sample. In sampling, the portion, or subset, of the population that is studied to develop conclusions about the total population. [5]

sampling. A technique used in quantitative research in which a portion of a group is examined to develop conclusions about the entire group. [5]

script. A written dialogue or set of systematic instructions that employees usually follow word-for-word when handling certain types of customer inquiries or requests. [7]

seamless process. A process that is designed so a customer is not inconvenienced by—or even aware of—the steps involved in fulfilling a request. Also referred to as an invisible system. [12]

secondary data. Research information that has already been collected for some other purpose, either by the company doing the research or by some other organization. [5]

security. The physical, technical, and procedural steps a company takes to prevent the loss, wrongful disclosure (accidental or intentional), or theft of information. [13]

selective perception. The tendency to perceive only what we want or expect to perceive. [8]

self-directed team. A type of team in which the members handle many traditional management responsibilities, such as planning and monitoring work. Sometimes called a self-managed team. [11]

self-study training. A training method in which the trainee works independently to complete a training course or program. [3]

semi-autonomous team. A type of team in which the manager or supervisor manages the team, while the other team members, in addition to doing their "regular" work, provide input into planning, organizing, and monitoring the work. [11]

sender. In the communication process, the person who transmits a message. [6]

serial-processing personalities. Personality types that prefer to focus on one task at a time. [14]

service center. An administrative or transaction-processing unit that is also responsible for handling customer contacts related to the functions it performs. Also known as a working customer contact center. [11]

service dimensions. Criteria that customers typically use to judge the quality of service they receive and that influence customer perceptions of service. The five service dimensions are (1) reliability, (2) assurance, (3) empathy, (4) responsiveness, and (5) tangible factors. [5]

service gap. The condition that exists when the perceived quality of a company's service is lower than the customers' expectations regarding the service. [5]

service level. A performance measure that indicates the percentage of inbound customer contacts answered within a specified timeframe—for example, 80 percent within 20 seconds. [12]

service objectives. Statements that define the specific goals a company must meet to fulfill its customer service mission. [10]

service provider. A person whose primary focus is on meeting the needs of customers, regardless of the person's job responsibilities or position within a company. [1]

service recovery. The act of fully resolving to the customer's satisfaction a problem that initially caused customer dissatisfaction and might have resulted in a loss of business. [2]

service request. A requisition for another person or area to complete the work initiated by a customer's request. [12]

service strategies. The general plans companies develop and follow to achieve their service objectives. [10]

sexist language. Language that minimizes the value of someone because of his or her gender, usually implying a negative stereotype. [6]

simulation training. A training method that gives trainees an opportunity to experience a job's working conditions without the pressure of actually being on the job. [3]

simultaneous production and consumption. A process describing a commodity, such as customer service, which is consumed at the same time it is produced. [2]

single-function work team. An organizational unit that primarily performs one specific function—such as billing, claim processing, or loan processing. [11]

situation analysis. The first step in the strategic planning process, which provides many of the assumptions upon which the strategic plan is based. [10]

skills-based pay raise. A variation of a merit pay raise that rewards employees for developing and improving job skills. [4]

social distance. In North American culture, a distance that people typically maintain when conducting impersonal business; ranges from about 4 to 7 feet. [6]

span of control. The number of people who report directly to a manager, supervisor, or team leader. [11]

specialist. A team member who performs primarily one type of transaction, such as billing or claim processing. [11]

specific job skills test. A type of pre-employment screening test that attempts to evaluate how well the applicant has mastered specific skills needed to perform well in the position—for example, typing (keyboarding), using word processing or spreadsheet applications, and writing business letters. [3]

stereotyping. A perceptual error that occurs when we judge people solely on the basis of a group they belong to—for example, their age, sex, race, nationality, or profession. [8]

storming. The second stage of team development, which occurs as team members look for their common ground and work through their differences. [11]

strategic planning. The process of determining an organization's long-term corporate objectives and deciding the overall course of action the company will take to achieve those objectives. [2]

stress. The psychological and physical condition that people experience when they perceive a situation as harmful, threatening, or demanding. [14]

stressor. Any activity, event, or occurrence that causes mild or short-term stress. [14]

strong corporate culture. A corporate culture in which employees clearly understand and consistently apply the company's business philosophy, goals, priorities, and practices. [10]

subcultures. Cultures unique to particular units within an organization. [10]

supervisory leadership. A leadership style in which the supervisor performs most of the planning, makes most of the decisions, and handles most of the problems that arise. [11]

surrender. A conflict management approach that involves one person giving in to end the conflict. [9]

survey. A data-collection method that uses structured data-collection forms, such as questionnaires, to gather data directly from the group, or population, being studied. [5]

syntoxins. Chemicals and hormones that are released by the body when a person relaxes and that are associated with good health. [14]

tactical plan. A detailed business plan that outlines the specific tasks to be undertaken to implement a service strategy. Also called an operational plan. [10]

talking points. A list of important items that employees refer to using their own words when handling certain types of customer inquiries or requests. [7]

tall organizational structure. A type of corporate structure in which many layers of directors, managers, associate managers, supervisors, and assistant supervisors occupy the space between top management and nonmanagerial employees. Also called a tall organizational pyramid. [11]

tangible factors. A service dimension that refers to the physical aspects of a financial services company and its employees. [5]

team compact. An agreement between a company and a team's members indicating that (1) the company will grant certain rights, responsibilities, and resources to team members and (2) the team will achieve specified performance goals; often used by highly autonomous teams. [11]

team leadership. A leadership style in which the supervisor shares responsibility for the team's operation with the team members and spends more time on larger organizational issues that affect team performance. [11]

team mission statement. A statement, derived from the corporate and/or customer service mission statement, that defines a team's purpose and goals, and serves as an overall guide for the team's activities. [11]

technology. The practical, scientific tools used to accomplish tasks. [13]

templates. Sample documents that employees use as a model when writing specific types of correspondence. [7]

tightly structured personalities. Personality types that need to have a system for accomplishing tasks. [14]

timeliness. A performance measure that indicates the time it takes to complete a customer-initiated request or transaction, such as answering a question, underwriting an application, adjudicating a claim, issuing a commission check, or processing a withdrawal or an account transfer. Also called turnaround time or average handling time. [12]

traditional team. A type of team in which the manager or supervisor performs most or all of the management tasks, such as organizing, planning, monitoring, and controlling the work; other team members concentrate solely on doing the work—performing the business functions for which the team is responsible. [11]

transactional analysis. An approach to analyzing behavior patterns which suggests that, at any given moment, a person exhibits one of three behavior patterns or ego states: parent, adult, or child. [5]

tribal mentality. When a group strongly identifies itself as a unit and considers other groups or individuals as outsiders or rivals. [10]

UCD. *See* **uniform call distribution**.

underlying needs. The needs on which a person's stated needs are based. [9]

understandable standards. Performance standards that are clearly, widely, and effectively communicated so service providers know how the standards apply to the functions they perform. [12]

uniform call distribution (UCD). A type of routing that distributes inbound calls in a predetermined order among available CSRs so that each person receives approximately the same number of calls. [13]

universal queue. A routing system that handles all customer contacts together, regardless of the type of communication. [13]

up-selling. A sales activity in which customers are invited to purchase additional amounts or features of a product they already own or are considering purchasing. [10]

user needs analysis. A series of activities designed to improve the effectiveness of a system by examining the interaction between the technology and the people who use it. [13]

valid argument. An argument in which the reasons given are true, and the conclusion is a logical extension of those reasons. [9]

valid standards. Performance standards that are unbiased and accurately reflect what they are intended to measure. [12]

value-added customer service. Activities that provide customers with additional benefits that do not routinely come with the product or service they have purchased. [1]

variable compensation system. A method of paying employees in which a portion of an employee's annual salary is based on the profits the company earned during the preceding year. [4]

verbal communication. The use of language (spoken or written) to send and receive messages. [6]

videoconferencing. A method of electronic communication in which participants can see and hear one another. [7]

virtual work team. An organizational arrangement that electronically links geographically separate business sites to form a single work group for purposes of managing, scheduling, monitoring, and conducting business activities. [11]

voice over Internet protocol (VoIP). A technology that transmits voice over an Internet connection. [7]

voicemail. A computerized answering service that provides a personalized greeting and allows one person to leave a recorded message for another. [7]

VoIP. *See* **voice over Internet protocol**.

WAN. *See* **wide area network**.

want. A desire to have more than is absolutely necessary to improve an unsatisfactory condition—for example, gourmet food, a large house, or a sports car. [5]

weak corporate culture. A corporate culture in which employees do not understand clearly or apply consistently the company's business philosophy, goals, priorities, and practices. [10]

Web callback. A communication mechanism on a Web site that enables customers to request additional support by clicking on an icon and sending a request for a company representative to phone the customer. Sometimes referred to as call me back. [7]

Web chat. A technology that enables text-based conversations over the Internet. Also called text chat or instant messaging. [7]

Web collaboration. A technology that enables a customer and a service provider to meet on a Web site, synchronize their browsers, and explore the Web site together, communicating with each other in real-time. Also called collaborative browsing. [7]

Web server. A computer that holds documents on a Web site and makes them available for remote browsers. [13]

who's-the-customer syndrome. Uncertainty about whether the intermediary or the external customer is the actual customer. [2]

wide area network (WAN). A network, either internal or external, that is made up of equipment that is geographically dispersed. [13]

work group. Two or more people who work together on a regular basis and coordinate their activities to accomplish common goals. [10]

workflow analysis. An activity that examines all the steps or tasks involved in a particular process to ensure the greatest efficiency and effectiveness. [12]

workforce management system. A computer program that projects staffing and scheduling needs by analyzing the past volume of customer contacts and projecting the future volume. [13]

World Wide Web. A network of links to hypermedia documents (text, graphics, video, and sound); one of many services available over the Internet. Also known as the Web. [7]

INDEX

IMPORTANT—READ CAREFULLY BEFORE REMOVING THE INTERACTIVE CD FROM ITS JACKET. USE OF THE SOFTWARE PROGRAM ON THE ENCLOSED DISK IS SUBJECT TO THE TERMS OF THE LICENSE AGREEMENT PRINTED BELOW. BY REMOVING THE DISK FROM ITS JACKET, YOU INDICATE YOUR ACCEPTANCE OF THE FOLLOWING LOMA LICENSE AGREEMENT.

INTERACTIVE CD LICENSE AGREEMENT

This Interactive CD License Agreement (the "Agreement") is a legal agreement between You (either as an individual or a single entity) and LOMA (Life Office Management Association, Inc.) for the use of the Interactive CD software ("the Software") accompanying this Agreement. By removing the disk from its jacket, You are agreeing to be bound by the terms of this Agreement.

Definition of in "Use"

The Software is in "use" on a computer when it is loaded into temporary memory (RAM) or installed into permanent memory (hard disk, CD-ROM, or other storage device) of that computer.

Grant of License

Rights of an Individual. If You are an individual, LOMA grants to You a nonexclusive license to use one copy of the Software on your office computer and one copy on your home computer provided that You are the only individual using the Software.

Rights of an Entity. If You are an entity, LOMA grants to You a nonexclusive license to use the Software in only one of the following two ways, with the selection to be yours:

- You may designate one individual within your organization to have the sole right to use the Software in the manner provided above under "Rights of an Individual."
- Alternatively, You may install one copy of the Software on a single computer and allow multiple members of your organization to use the Software on that one computer. If You wish to use the Software on another computer, You must deinstall it from the computer it is on before installing it on another computer.

Copyright

The Software is owned by LOMA and is protected by U.S. copyright laws and international treaty provisions. Therefore, You must treat the Software like any other copyrighted material (e.g., a book or musical recording) EXCEPT that You may either make one copy of the Software solely for backup or archival purposes or transfer the Software to a single hard disk provided You keep the original solely for backup or archival purposes. You may not copy the written material accompanying the Software. The questions and instructions and instructional material (hereinafter "the Content") contained in the Software are also owned by LOMA and protected by U.S. copyright laws and international treaty provisions. It is illegal to make any copy whatsoever of the content; to install the Software on a network, intranet, or Web site; to download the content to another computer or device EXCEPT as expressly allowed under "Grant of License" above; to print screens or otherwise cause the content to be printed EXCEPT as expressly allowed on several screens; or to in any other way reproduce the content contained in the Software.

Other Restrictions

You may not rent or lease the Software. You may not reverse engineer, decompile, or disassemble the Software or in any way duplicate the contents of the code and other elements therein.

Disclaimer of Warranty

LOMA MAKES NO WARRANTY EXPRESS OR IMPLIED INCLUDING, WITHOUT LIMITATION, NO WARRANTY OF MERCHANTABILITY OR FITNESS OR SUITABILITY FOR A PARTICULAR PURPOSE. UNDER NO CIRCUMSTANCES SHALL LOMA BE LIABLE TO YOU OR ANY THIRD PARTY FOR ANY INCIDENTAL OR CONSEQUENTIAL DAMAGES WHATSOEVER.

Limitation of Liability

You agree to indemnify and hold harmless LOMA, its employees, its agents, and their successors and assigns against any loss, liability, cost or expense (including reasonable attorneys' fees) asserted against or suffered or incurred by LOMA as a consequence of, or in the defense of, any claim arising from or based upon any alleged negligence, act or failure to act whatsoever of You, its employees, their successors, agents, heirs, and/or assigns with respect to the aforementioned Software.